MAORI MUSIC

MAORI MUSIC

Mervyn McLean

AUCKLAND UNIVERSITY PRESS

First published 1996
Auckland University Press
University of Auckland
Private Bag 92019
Auckland

ISBN 1 86940 144 1

The Map of Tribal Distribution is reproduced with the
permission of the Department of Geography,
University of Auckland.

Cover design by Christine Hansen
Designed and typeset by Pages Literary Pursuits
Printed in Wellington by GP Print

Publication is assisted by the Lilburn Trust
and by Creative New Zealand

ARTS COUNCIL OF NEW ZEALAND TOI AOTEAROA

To
Arapeta Awatere (1910–1976)
and
Hoani Halbert (1890–1958)

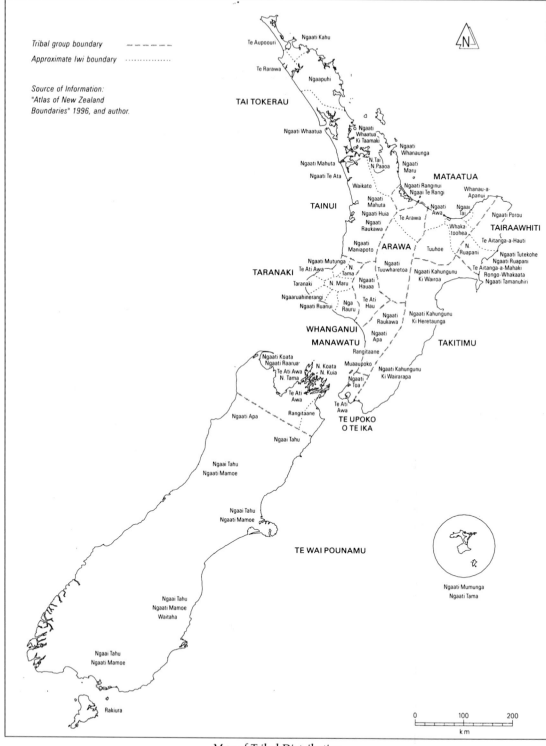

Source of Information:
"Atlas of New Zealand
Boundaries" 1996, and author.

Map of Tribal Distribution

CONTENTS

SECTION 2: MUSIC ETHNOGRAPHY

Chapter 5: Musical instruments

Chapter 6: Performance

Chapter 7: Composition

SECTION 3: MUSIC STRUCTURE

BOOK 2: THE IMPACT OF EUROPEAN MUSIC

Chapter 17: Types of influence and change

Chapter 18: Song loss

Chapter 19: Hymnody

Chapter 20: The modern genres

INTRODUCTION

In a 1983 article, Anne Salmond offers a critique of assumptions underlying the common distinction made between traditional and modern forms of Maori life. She makes the point that:

> judgements of what is 'traditional' have differed for each generation of scholars and bits and pieces of information from anywhere between 1769 and 1969 have been cobbled together in accounts of 'traditional' behaviour that included practices which never would have coexisted in any given Maori community at any given time.[1]

In Salmond's view, 'traditional' has been unduly equated with 'precontact', and Maori society has been falsely represented both as functioning in equilibrium until European contact and shattered beyond redemption after contact took place. Other criticisms of the standard accounts are that too little attention has been paid to regional diversity, chronological control has been lacking, and segmentation of Maori society into discrete topics such as economics, religion, art, music, warfare and marriage 'cuts across tribal ways of understanding the past'. Her solution to these perceived failings, now exemplified in her own award-winning book *Two Worlds* (1991), is to make use of written records in both English and Maori, together with oral accounts, to give a better understanding of how tribal life has changed in historic times.[2]

The present work takes a necessarily topical approach. One hopes, nevertheless, that Salmond's several points have been accommodated. The last of them was taken aboard by ethnomusicologists decades ago with the publication of Alan P. Merriam's book *The Anthropology of Music* (1964) and its then new concept of ethnomusicology as the study of music in culture. From Chapter 1 onwards, the present book treats music as integral with, rather than isolated from, Maori society. Also, in every section of the book the approach is both diachronic and synchronic to the extent that the data allow. Sources of information, both written and oral, are very diverse. The writer's own field work began in 1958 and continued for more than 20 years: some 1300 resulting recorded songs together with hundreds of pages of interviews with singers have provided a solid core for the study. From travel, missionary, historical and ethnographic literature have come numerous eyewitness statements and observations about music over a span of 200 years. Archaeological and other scientific evidence has been drawn upon as appropriate. Transcription and analysis of the recorded songs have provided further insights. There are gaps in the information, but a surprisingly coherent picture has emerged of Maori music as it is and was.

ABBREVIATIONS

A&M	*Hymns Ancient and Modern* (Baker 1861)
AMPM	Archive of Maori & Pacific Music, Anthropology Department, University of Auckland
Cyl	Numbers with this prefix refer to items in McLean & Curnow 1992b
DNZB	*Dictionary of New Zealand Biography* (v.1 W. Oliver et al. 1990; v.2 Orange et al. 1993)
McL	Numbers with this prefix refer to McLean collection, Archive of Maori & Pacific Music. For a catalogue see McLean & Curnow 1992a
McLean & Orbell	McLean & Orbell, *Traditional Songs of the Maori* (1975)
M&O	Song numbers in McLean & Orbell
MPFB	Maori Purposes Fund Board
NM	Song numbers in Ngata's *Nga Moteatea* (Ngata 1959, 1990; Ngata & Te Hurinui 1961, 1970)
NZNB	New Zealand National Bibliography (Bagnall 1969–85)
NZBS	New Zealand Broadcasting Service
RNZA	Radio New Zealand Archives
W	H. Williams, *A Bibliography of Printed Maori to 1900* (1924)
Williams	H. Williams, *A Dictionary of the Maori Language* (1975)

MUSICAL EXAMPLES

In the musical examples, conventional Western notation is used, with the following additional symbols:

[ ] = added

( ) = omitted

↑ = note to be sharpened by up to a quarter tone

↓ = note to be flattened by up to a quarter tone

↗ (on note stem) = gradual continuous ascent of pitch

↘ (on note stem) = gradual continuous descent of pitch

↷ (on note stem) = ascent of pitch followed by a fall

In recited compositions, where phrases are marked, there is usually a rise of pitch around the middle of a phrase followed by a fall at the end, whether or not this is shown by arrows.

♩̽ ♩̽ ♪̽ = spoken or of indeterminate pitch

♫ = portamento between notes

╱ = upward glissando

╲ = downward glissando

〜〜〜 = wavering note

𝄽 = short rest

┊ = dotted barline: structural subdivision, not necessarily followed by an accent as in Western music

♪ ♫ = grace notes: these take their time from the notes to which they are tied

A quirk of the computer software used for the music examples causes the phrase marks used in the music examples to be unclosed at the beginning. In all music examples, for ‾‾‾‾‾‾┐ read ┌‾‾‾‾‾‾┐ .

RECORDINGS

Nearly all of the musical examples are transcriptions from the writer's own field recordings. An accompanying CD of the examples was suggested by Auckland University Press as a useful supplement to the book; however, unfortunately this cannot be provided because of assurances given to singers that their songs would not be issued as recordings for sale. Bona fide researchers or Maori groups requiring specific recordings for learning purposes can obtain them by writing to the Archive of Maori and Pacific Music, University of Auckland.

VOCABULARY AND ORTHOGRAPHY

For Maori terminology relating to music the writer has relied primarily on information from singers, supplemented by reference to H.W. Williams's *A Dictionary of the Maori Language*, 7th edition (1975).[3] Additionally, Williams has been relied upon for checking vowel length in Maori words. In quotations from written sources, book titles, place names, twentieth-century personal names,[4] names of organisations and Maori words which have entered English, such as the word 'Maori' itself, vowel length has been left unmarked or unaltered. For all other Maori words, long vowels are marked in the present work by doubling; in Williams and most other publications they are indicated by macrons. In conformity with Auckland University Press house style, Maori words in the present work are not italicised, and -s is not added for plural forms, including words such as 'Maori' which are commonly used in English.

The Maori language is currently undergoing rapid change. Specialist vocabulary has entered Maori in two ways: the first and traditional way is either by modifying terms in the general vocabulary or by assigning new meanings to them; the other method is transliteration from English. For the past several years, a Maori language commission, using the first method by preference, has coined new terms for everything from Maori names for local bodies and government departments to Maori terms for use in commerce, broadcasting, the legal profession, libraries and school and university curricula. Whether most of these terms will catch on has yet to be seen. What is

3

reasonably certain is that there is no concept, however technical or however remote from earlier practice, that cannot be accommodated in this way. For all the writer knows, there are now Maori words for every musical term his informants told him had no equivalent in Maori; and if such words currently do not exist, they may do so in future.[5]

While the present book was being written, a new dictionary appeared by Hoani and Whai Ngata.[6] A valuable feature of the earlier dictionary by Williams is its use for some terms of quotations from literary sources such as Grey's *Nga Mahi a nga Tupuna* (1854) and *Nga Moteatea* (1851) of phrases exemplifying the word. The new dictionary greatly extends this practice, providing sample phrases for all words. On the face of it, this ought to have been a bonanza for the present writer. Unfortunately, however, none of the phrases in the new dictionary, unlike those in Williams, is sourced. It is impossible to tell whether any given word is in general use or is a neologism. Nor is there an indication of when the word might have entered the language. This being the case, nothing can be taken for granted without irretrievably muddying the waters if it is important to know whether a given meaning is old or new. Another problem is that many of the examples given may be specific to the compilers' own East Coast tribe of Ngaati Porou. Reluctantly, therefore, the present writer has accepted nothing from Ngata & Ngata unless it is confirmed by his own informants and/or Williams.

SONG TEXTS

Song texts associated with the musical examples in the book have been left untranslated for two reasons. First, the translation of Maori song texts is a specialist task, beyond the scope of the book, and the writer is not competent to offer them. Second, because the texts are in any case so typically dense and full of allusions, a line or two of translation would nearly always be meaningless except in the context of the entire song and even then only with the benefit of explanatory notes. Numerous Maori songs, including many of those in the present book, have been expertly translated and are available in publications such as those of Margaret Orbell[7] and in Ngata & Te Hurinui's classic volumes *Nga Moteatea* Pts 1–3.[8]

FIELD WORK

The writer's first 800 recordings were made while he was a student at the University of Otago, working first on an MA in 1958 and later on a PhD in 1962–64. The 1958 work was done in the Bay of Plenty area under the guidance of Arapeta Awatere and that of 1962–64 in successive solo field trips to Ngaati Tuuwharetoa, Waikato, Taranaki, and again to the Bay of Plenty (Tuuhoe, Te Arawa, Ngaaiterangi and other tribes). Up to this date, most songs were recorded not by request but as volunteered by singers.

The songs which form the basis of the present work are extremely precious not only intrinsically but also in terms of the effort required to collect them. Singers were recorded both at meetings and by visiting them in their own homes; this required 26,000 miles [42,000 km] of travel in 1962–64 alone.[9] Two and a half months were spent on initial field work in 1958 and more than a year in all during 1962–64. Even in 1958 few competent singers were left, and customary and other barriers made recording difficult. Often arrangements to record individuals and, especially, groups fell through when singers changed their minds or other events took precedence. Nevertheless, although the frustrations of the work at times seemed overwhelming, the results justified the attempt. Many hundreds of persons were interviewed and, ultimately, over 200 of them were recorded.

In the 1970s a systematic effort was begun to visit remaining tribal areas and to collect game songs, pao and other song types not thought important enough by earlier singers to record. Visits were made to the East Coast, Wanganui and Northland as well as return visits to tribes previously recorded. This salvage work was commented upon by Piri Mokena of Ngaapuhi tribe who said: 'You snapping up all the little worst things in the North!' But again the work proved worthwhile, and about 500 songs were added to the earlier total.

A halt was called in 1979 with the recording of a song which had been composed for the death of the writer's early benefactor and mentor Arapeta Awatere. By this time, more than 1300 songs had been collected, and all tribal areas had been given an opportunity to record their songs. By this time, also, the technology for recording was within reach of anyone who wanted it, and increasing numbers of Maori people were recording their own songs. The original recordings are housed in the Archive of Maori and Pacific Music at the University of Auckland,[10] along with other collections such as that of the Maori Purposes Fund Board recorded in 1952–57, the New Zealand Broadcasting Service in 1938–50, and an earlier Museum of New Zealand Te Papa Tongarewa collection of wax cylinders recorded in 1919–23 during a series of expeditions from the then Dominion Museum, and at Parliament Buildings during the 1930s by Sir Apirana Ngata.

Gaps in the writer's data have sometimes proved possible to fill by recourse to the other collections. Catalogues of the MPFB collection, Maori events from the NZBS collection, the McLean collection and the Museum of New Zealand collection have been compiled and published and are available from the Archive of Maori and Pacific Music, University of Auckland.[11]

ACKNOWLEDGEMENTS

Assistance is warmly acknowledged from librarians and curators over the years at numerous libraries and institutions, both in New Zealand and overseas, especially and most recently, Alexander Turnbull Library and National Library, Wellington; Auckland City Archives; Auckland Institute and Museum Te Papa Whakahiku Library; Auckland Public Library; Auckland University Library; H.B. Williams Memorial Library, Gisborne; Hawke's Bay Museum Archives, Napier; Hocken Library, Dunedin; Kinder Library, St John's Theological College, Auckland; Otago University Library; Don Stafford Collection, Rotorua Public Library; Rotorua Museum of Art & History Te Whare Taonga o Te Arawa; Takapuna Public Library; Taranaki Museum; and Victoria University Library.

Financial and other assistance towards the writer's early research came from sources acknowledged in publications resulting from the work.[12] Special thanks are due to the University of Auckland and the New Zealand University Grants Committee for their support during the 1970s.

Additionally the writer would like to thank: Bruce Biggs for his advice on tribal names; Michael King for his response to queries about Te Puea; Hamish Macdonald (Anthropology Department, University of Auckland) for photographing illustrations from books and journals; Kare Leathem for assistance with action song texts; Roger Neich for information about musical instruments at Auckland Institute & Museum; Sir Henare Ngata for information concerning Sir Apirana Ngata and his role in the development of action song; Margaret Orbell, for valuable comments on the MS and, with Sally McKean, for editing the texts of the musical examples; Kate Pinkham, Wanganui Regional Museum, for information about Henry Williams's barrel-organ; Hilary Pound for supply of recordings from the Archive of Maori and Pacific Music; and Jennifer Shennan for providing xeroxed extracts from *Te Kopara*.

In all tribal areas, songs were recorded only after much soul-searching by singers, and debate about recording often occupied many hours. On occasion, it stretched to days or weeks. Above all, thanks are due to the more than 200 persons who agreed to be recorded and/or interviewed during the course of field work in 1958, 1962–64 and intermittently throughout the 1970s. It is hoped that acknowledgements throughout the book will bear witness to the enduring debt owed by the writer to them and especially to Arapeta Awatere of Ngaati Porou and Ngaapuhi tribes, with whom extensive discussions were held in 1958, 1969, 1970 and for two hours every week over a period of 14 months during 1971 and 1973–74. Also deserving of special acknowledgement is the writer's old friend Kino Hughes of Tuuhoe tribe, who dedicated himself to recording over 100 songs, and with whom similar regular interviews were held over a period of six months in 1972. To Peta and Kino especially, but also to the many other elders who contributed their knowledge:

Haere raa oo koutou nui, oo koutou mana!

E kore e arumia i muri i oo koutou tua ei.

Mervyn McLean

BOOK 1

TRADITIONAL MUSIC
AND DANCE

SECTION 1

SONG AND DANCE STYLES

CHAPTER 1

SONG AND DANCE IN HISTORICAL AND SOCIAL CONTEXT

THE NEW ZEALAND MAORI[1]

POLYNESIAN ORIGINS

The Maori people are believed to have settled New Zealand from somewhere in Eastern Polynesia about 1000 years ago. Their immediate place of origin is still not known with the Society Islands, the Marquesas Islands and the Southern Cook Islands all as candidates. The ultimate origins of the Maori, in common with other Polynesian peoples, lie with remote Austronesian-speaking[2] ancestors who began their migrations between 5 and 10 millennia ago, most likely from somewhere in Southeast Asia.

ADAPTATION AND CHANGE

The shift from a tropical environment to a temperate one required numerous adjustments and adaptations. Two periods are distinguished by archaeologists. A so-called Archaic period lasted until about AD 1350 in the North Island of New Zealand and about 200 years longer in the northernmost part of the South Island. Settlements at this time seem to have been seasonally occupied and typically undefended; the economy was based on fishing, gathering and, especially in the South Island, the hunting of a large flightless bird called the moa. Although Europeans were responsible for the most thoroughgoing destruction of indigenous forest in New Zealand, there is evidence of considerable modification of the landscape by the Maori before European colonisation began. The burning of large tracts of forest in the South Island and its replacement by tussock and fern is thought to have reduced moa to the point where continued hunting exterminated them. In the North Island the same occurred after extensive firing of forests for agriculture and to increase supplies of fern-root.[3] It is possible that these changes contributed to the ushering in of the next phase of Maori culture. During the fourteenth century occurred an apparently abrupt transition to the Classic Maori phase as seen by Europeans two centuries later. By then, the moa was extinct, the climate was possibly less favourable, and the population, although low by European standards, had expanded to a point where there was fierce competition for resources. During this period warfare became endemic, as did customs associated with it. Archaeologically, the Classic phase is characterised by earthwork fortifications, increased use of storage pits for kuumara (sweet potato), and a greatly expanded inventory of artefacts. Amongst the latter were a standardised form of adze, new and improved fish-hooks, a variety of weapons and ornaments, and musical instruments such as flutes and shell trumpets.[4]

SUBSISTENCE

Compared with the tropical homeland, New Zealand must have seemed inhospitable in many ways but offered much also by way of compensation. Covering most of the country were forests teeming with edible bird life, and the coastal fishing resources were superb. The climate was colder but there was an apparently inexhaustible supply of wood for housing and for firewood, and the indigenous harakeke or flax plant (*Phormium tenax*) was available as a replacement for tropical barkcloth and pandanus to make clothing such as the rain-cape, dress cloaks, kilts and belts. Of the tropical food plants, coconut, breadfruit and bananas could not be grown in New Zealand, and taro and yams did not yield well in colder conditions. Their place was taken by fern-root which had the disadvantage of requiring pounding to be edible. It was also very hard on human teeth and during the Classic phase, when fern-root became an essential element of diet, most adults as a consequence lost teeth before they were 25 years old, eventually losing all or most by the age of 40, by which time a person was old.[5] The one familiar crop which remained a staple in New Zealand was the kuumara. But even this did not grow everywhere and a storage-pit technology had to be developed so that it could be kept between growing seasons without spoiling. As a treasured food, the kuumara assumed extraordinary significance in myth, legend and song, and elaborate rituals were observed during its cultivation. A famous oriori (song addressed to a child)[6] tells of its coming to New Zealand. In the opening lines the crying of a child motivates his father to return to the ancestral homeland Hawaiki to fetch the precious food:

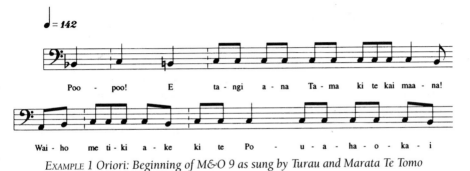

EXAMPLE 1 *Oriori: Beginning of M&O 9 as sung by Turau and Marata Te Tomo*

In New Zealand, although fish and forest birds were abundant, there were few other sources of protein. Pigs, a domestic animal everywhere else in Polynesia, were either not brought from the homeland or failed to survive. The moa was long gone by the time Europeans came. It must have been a bird which used its feet to defend itself, as one song (McL 832) has been recorded about a man who was kicked by a moa. The dog (kurii) and the rat (kiore) were both brought by the Maori to New Zealand and both were eaten. Additionally dog-skin was used for clothing. The introduction of the rat to New Zealand is credited in legend to the Horouta canoe, one of the ancestral canoes said to have returned to Hawaiki for the kuumara.[7] A different story is told by the singer of McL 1227, a karakia (incantation) which refers in its first line to the rat. The song is said to have been composed by Ruaanui, the captain of the Maamari canoe which landed at Hokianga and, like the Horouta, is credited with bringing rats to New Zealand. The karakia was for calling the rats back after Ruaanui had let them go. The rats are described as running round the window of the meeting house, Ohaki, at Ahipara. When he called them they came 'slipping and sliding down the banks'.

Other than the rat and the dog, the only source of animal protein for the Maori was human. Buck states that slaves or other persons were killed and eaten on special occasions such as the tattooing of a high chief's daughter, a chiefly marriage, or the funeral of a high chief.[8] And he points out that the frequent battles which took place in New Zealand provided a perennial supply of human flesh.[9] It should not be inferred, however, that human flesh was a primary, or even especially important, item of diet. The principle motive for cannibalism was revenge against enemies. A song type referring explicitly to it is the kaioraora (see later). Other songs also occasionally refer to it. According to the singers, McL 636, for example, is a lament for Terama Apakura, a cannibal who hunted for men and eventually ate his own niece. This crime was avenged by Tuuhourangi who killed Apakura and took his body to a place called Motutawa 'where they had a feast of him'.

LIFE SPAN

In a study of skeletal remains from archaeological sites, Houghton[10] provides objective evidence of Maori life span in pre-European times. The results by modern standards are startling. At Wairau Bar (the best-known Archaic site) the average adult age at death was 28 years for men and 29 for women; the oldest individual was only a little over 40. During the Classic period it would seem that life span was not much greater. Houghton estimates that agile old men commented upon by Cook would, in fact, have been in their forties.[11] As Davidson points out, such individuals would be respected elders, acknowledged as tribal experts, by the time they were about 35.[12] If, as this evidence suggests, the Maori population was predominantly young, its noteworthy vigour and spirited aggression at the time of European contact can be better understood.

MATERIAL CULTURE

Houses

The spectacular whare whakairo or carved meeting house present in such numbers today is a late development. Houses seen by Cook and others at the time of first contact were relatively small and used mostly for sleeping, though Banks saw one at Tolaga Bay which was 30 feet (9m) long.[13] Davidson points out that settlements in the eighteenth century were mostly too impermanent to warrant investment of labour in a fully carved house;[14] nor, it would seem, were meetings customarily held in such houses. The carved house of today, which is the focal point of marae (meeting place) ceremonies at which most musical activity takes place, is a nineteenth-century elaboration of the earlier chiefs' dwelling house.

Tools and implements

Bone was used for fish-hooks, harpoon-heads and spear-heads as well as a variety of needles, pickers, awls, chisels and other implements.[15] Chisels (whao) were mostly hafted and struck with wooden mallets. Cord drills (tuuwiri, porotiti) were used to drill holes in stone, bone and shell.[16] Ground was loosened for cultivation with the digging stick (koo) and the hafted stone adze was the all important tool for tree felling and carpentry. Hand nets and seine nets (kupenga) for fishing were made from flax.

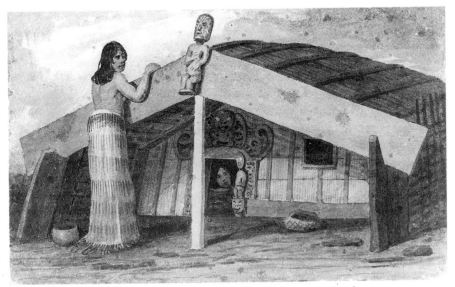

A chief's house of 1827. Watercolour by Augustus Earle.
PHOTO: *National Library of Australia*

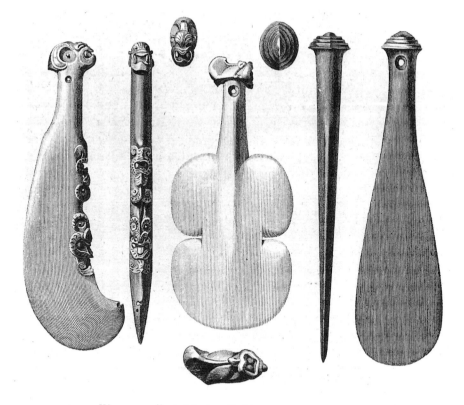

Weapons collected during Cook's visits to New Zealand

Weapons

All of the weapons used in Polynesia were present also in New Zealand except for the sling and the bow and arrow. The forms taken in New Zealand were, however, distinctive. Spears were not part of the Classic inventory but long stabbing spears (huata) and short throwing spears (tarerarera) are both said to have been used by the first settlers.[17] The general name for a short club in New Zealand was patu or, if made from greenstone, mere. The patu was used primarily for thrusting. It was reportedly well adapted to striking under the angle of the jaw or between the ribs, for smashing in a temple or splitting off the top of a skull. Long clubs or wooden staff forms of weapon, principally the taiaha, tewhatewha and pouwhenua, had in common a combination of a blade for striking and a proximal point for stabbing.[18] The operator could thrust with them as a spear and deliver a hefty blow with the butt in the fashion of a quarterstaff. The taiaha, with its elaborated carving, dog-hair and parrot-feather decoration and stylised out-thrust tongue expressive of defiance served also a ceremonial purpose as a status symbol for chiefs.[19] Besides being used in battle, weapons were an essential adjunct to several forms of war dance (see later).

Food utensils

The New Zealand Maori had no tradition of pottery and, because neither the coconut nor bamboo grew in New Zealand, was forced to do without these as materials for use as kitchen utensils. Moreover, the absence of such tropical staples as coconut cream and taro-pudding rendered unnecessary specialised utensils such as graters, strainers, pounders and pounding tables. Wooden beaters and perhaps a water-worn rock as an anvil served for beating fern-root; gourds were used as containers; bowls were laboriously hewn from blocks of wood;[20] and, according to Best, a few stone bowls were also fashioned.[21] Stones for use in the earth oven (umu) were also part of the kitchen equipment, as good stones were kept and reused. For the remainder, says Best: 'A flake of obsidian or other stone served as a knife; a shell served as a fish-scaler; while the ever present [flax] basket served as a dish and a plate.'[22] Food-bearing songs (hari kai or heriheri kai), performed while food was carried from its cooking place, are referred to later.

Canoes

In New Zealand, as in Polynesia at large, both rafts and canoes were used for transport. To cross lakes or for short journeys on safe inland waters, rafts were sometimes manufactured from raupoo bundles or from logs lashed together.[23] For most journeys, however, canoes were usual. The type used was the single dugout, without outrigger. Dispensing with the outrigger was possible in New Zealand because of the availability of large trees which provided hulls wide enough for the canoe not to capsize. Types of Maori canoe, classified by size, are described briefly in the section on paddling songs.

PERSONAL DECORATION

Many early descriptions of the Maori haka or posture dance include information about the appearance of the performers. The men are often reported as wearing face or body paint of red ochre (kookoowai), either dry or mixed with oil. But it was not confined to the war dance or even to men, as women appear also to have used it routinely as a facial decoration. Banks complained in his journal of the results after a salutation or 'kiss from one of these fair savages' as 'wrote in most legible Characters on our noses'.[24] Before conversion to Christianity, Maori men followed the Polynesian custom of wearing their hair long and tying it into a large topknot. Feathers were stuck into the topknot by their quills and a variety of wooden combs were also used for decoration.[25] Other ornaments used by the Maori were ear pendants, the most favoured of which were either sharks' teeth or made from greenstone; cloak pins made from ivory, bone and sometimes shell or greenstone; and breast ornaments or pendants. Whales' teeth and sharks' teeth were used as pendants by both Archaic and Classic Maori, and the characteristic heitiki

Warrior with dog-skin cloak and weapons.
Suspended from his neck is a nguru flute. Drawn by
Sydney Parkinson in 1769

(greenstone pendant) came into use in the latter period. Both Cook and Banks saw them worn, and many were made from obsolete greenstone adzes after the introduction of metal tools in the nineteenth century.[26] As will be seen, kooauau and nguru flutes were also customarily worn as a neck ornament.

VISUAL ART

In Polynesia, the principal forms of visual art were wood-carving, painting on tapa cloth and tattooing. New Zealand did not have tapa cloth, but in the Classic period painting was done on wood, mainly as rafter designs (koowhaiwhai). New Zealand also has a fine heritage of prehistoric rock drawings, found mostly in the limestone areas of Canterbury and North Otago in the South Island. The designs include dogs, birds (including moa), fish, human figures and mythical dragon-like creatures (taniwha).[27] They are thought to have been drawn on hunting trips before the disappearance of the moa from these areas around AD 1200 to 1500.[28]

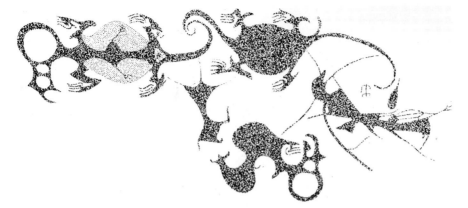

Taniwha rock drawing at Opihi, South Canterbury

Carved house slab (poupou) from Te Kaha at Auckland Museum showing a Whanau-a-Apanui ancestor, Tamatai Punoa, about to play on the puutoorino

A form of visual art without counterpart in Polynesia was a decorative style of upright lattice panel (tukutuku) used on the interior walls of meeting houses. Another local development was taaniko (finger weaving designs) on belts and the borders of clothing. Decorative designs were also worked into plaited baskets.

The pre-eminent Maori visual art in New Zealand was carving in wood on a huge variety of artefacts from canoes, ancestor figures and house structures to smaller objects such as ceremonial weapons, treasure boxes (waka huia) and flutes. An emphasis, unusual in Polynesia, on scroll and spiral ornamentation has led to speculation about connections between New Zealand and places as remote as China, South America and British Columbia.[29] However, as both Buck and McEwen have pointed out, there are closer correspondences in the Marquesas Islands and Niue.[30] Another perhaps more likely possibility is that the Maori emphasis on curvilinear patterns was a local development owing nothing to antecedents elsewhere.[31]

Tattooing

Tattooing was a practically universal form of decoration in Polynesia, varying in degree from place to place. It is generally acknowledged to have reached a peak of development in the Marquesas Islands and in New Zealand where it was an emblem of chieftainship. In New Zealand, men were tattooed mostly on the face, buttocks and thighs and women on the lips and chin. Maori tattooing (moko) used a distinctive and very painful technique of chiselling the flesh with straight-edged blades; the pigment was either applied to the blade or afterwards rubbed into the cut. To distract the patient, songs called 'whakawai taanga moko' are said to have been sung, but unfortunately no eye-witness account has been found of them. Best glosses the term as 'beguiling' songs,[32] and they are represented by Buddle and Colenso as sung by women.[33] However, the one recorded song identified as a tattooing song (McL 368) is a form of karakia or incantation. The use of karakia is also attested by Tiripou Haerewa of Tuuhoe tribe, who recorded a number of songs (McL 773–82) in 1964 and was later photographed by Hastings photographer Allan Baldwin. She recalled her tattoo being done by the riverside, with her father chanting a karakia as the work was carried out. She told Baldwin that the pain was almost unbearable at times but subsided with her father's chanting.[34]

In New Zealand the custom of tattooing men's faces led to the further custom of preserving the entire head of dead chiefs. Buck states that, because of the difficulty of transporting a whole body, chiefs who had died on campaign would have their heads brought home to be mourned over; conversely, the head of an enemy chief would be brought back so that he could be reviled in death by the widows and orphans he had created in life. Songs sung on these occasions would include kaioraora and tumoto (see later).[35]

Life mask cast in 1850 showing chisel tattoo of Taupua Te Whanoa, of Ngaati Whakaue. PHOTO: Augustus Hamilton. Museum of New Zealand Te Papa Tongarewa neg. no. C919

Although confined at first to chiefs, after 1815 the tattooing and drying of heads spread to commoner slaves who were tattooed and then killed by their Maori captors to take advantage of a European demand for dried heads as curios.[36] The traffic in dried Maori heads became so great a scandal that it was finally stopped by legislation in 1831.[37] Dried heads are referred to briefly in the section on puutoorino (see later).

SOCIAL ORGANISATION[38]

In social organisation, as much as in physique and appearance, the Maori people carried the legacy of their Polynesian origin. Kin units, family and household arrangements, settlement patterns, marriage and the system of rank and leadership are all plainly Polynesian in pattern.

Kinship grouping, in ascending order of group size, was by whaanau (extended family), hapuu (clan or subtribe), iwi (tribe) and waka (canoe). Descent was reckoned through both male and female lines to founding ancestors. Upon marriage, men generally continued to live with their parents' kin group and wives changed residence to the kin group of the husband. Social status depended principally upon seniority within the kin group, particularly through the male line, and three social classes were, in theory, recognised.

19

Those who could trace descent through senior lines were rangatira (chiefs); persons from junior lines or those whose ancestors had lost status were tuutuua (commoners); persons captured in war lost all status and became taurekareka (slaves).[39] In practice, as Firth points out, it can be argued that there was no commoner class as anyone except a slave could claim relationship to a chief.[40] Perhaps because of this, chiefs were not offered unqualified respect. Songs praising them were composed not in their lifetime but as laments to farewell them after death.[41] The only songs expressly linked to social status were oriori (see later) composed for children of high rank to educate them in matters appropriate to their descent. These have entered the common repertoire and are still remembered and sung. As will be seen later, karakia referring to the ancestral canoes are also still known and sung in most tribal areas.

In his book *The Pacific Islands*, Douglas Oliver characterises Polynesians as 'collectivists' rather than 'individualists'.[42] They formed groups to carry out most of their activities and their more valued possessions were corporately owned. To a degree this is true of the Maori and is seen to be so by writers such as Best[43] who claimed: 'In Maori society the individual could scarcely be termed a social unit, he was lost in the *whanau* or family group.' Nevertheless, as Firth points out, such a view is inconsistent with other, better founded observations by Best himself.[44] There was, in fact, much scope for males who could and did disagree with chiefs, might refuse to take part in group enterprises and were not debarred from accumulating personal property. Indeed there is a case for suggesting that the male individual in Maori society gained status by his ability to push at the boundaries of the rules and get away with it. As Salmond observes:

> It was such a society, based on hot pride and highly attuned to warfare, that was described by the earliest explorers. 'No people can have a quicker sense of injury done to them,' said Anderson in 1769, 'and none are more ready to resent it.' Every man except the slave, who by definition had no *mana* at all, was entered in this touchy contest for prestige.[45]

Women too, within the limits of their role, were quite capable of asserting themselves and did so in many cases brilliantly. A song type exemplary of this is the paatere, which was composed by aggrieved women who felt they had been slighted or who sought to redress wrongs.

MANA AND TAPU

In Polynesia, the social, political and religious systems were underpinned by twin concepts known as mana and tabu or (in New Zealand) tapu. Mana was supernatural power and also has connotations of prestige. Gods had it to a superlative degree, and chiefs, as descendants of the gods, also possessed it.[46] Tapu is generally translated as 'prohibited' either for sacred reasons or because of danger from mana. As Firth explains: 'Any person or thing which was regarded as *tapu* was only to be approached or handled with caution . . . Otherwise harm was believed to occur.'[47] In New Zealand, any person who was in a state of unusual tapu, as for example while being tattooed, could not touch any object without making it dangerous to others. Tapu likewise accumulated during activities such as carving a new meeting house, and had to be removed later with appropriate incantations and ceremony.

RELIGION

In pre-contact religion,[48] New Zealand again conformed closely to the overall Polynesian pattern. The first four gods in the New Zealand pantheon which follows appeared also in Polynesia, varying in powers and attributes according to area. In New Zealand, as summarised by Metge, there were eight principal deities, all offspring of the primeval parents Rangi and Papa. They were: Taane (god of the forests and father of man), Tuumatauenga (god of war and inventor of snares, nets and digging sticks), Rongo (god of peace and agriculture), Tangaroa (god of the sea), Taawhirimatea (the weather god), Haumia (god of uncultivated food), Ruaumoko (the earthquake god), and Whiro (the god of evil). Each tribe also had its own exclusive gods, mostly of war. And finally there were family gods and familiar spirits which originated from abortions, miscarriages and the ghosts of the dead.[49] The names of the gods appear frequently in karakia and also occasionally in haka and in songs such as oriori.

Throughout Polynesia, the means of communication with the gods was through priests. They gave oracles while in a state of trance and, as a rule, achieved office only after a long period of training. Membership of the priesthood tended to be hereditary and was strictly so in some areas. In New Zealand, according to Buck, the priesthood was not strictly hereditary though, as in other expert professions, a son usually followed in his father's footsteps. The priests of the departmental and tribal gods were educated men who occupied a responsible position in public life and were often of high birth. Priests of the family gods were usually self-taught and self-created.[50]

With the coming of the missionaries, the Maori embraced Christianity slowly at first but in increasing numbers until, by the 1840s, most were attending church services.[51] Even today, Maori meetings of an informal kind, more so than Pakeha ones, tend to begin conventionally with a prayer. In the nineteenth century and later, numerous exclusively Maori prophet movements emerged, most combining elements of Christianity with earlier religious practice.[52] Though most were short-lived, others were historically, socially and politically important. Pai Marire and Ringatu are referred to briefly in the section on karakia. The Te Whiti and Tohu religious movements are discussed in the section on poi. Additionally, the Ratana movement, which was founded in the Wanganui district by Tahupotiki Wiremu Ratana (1870–

1939) in the 1920s, although less influential than it once was, is a significant political force, having dominated the four Maori seats in Parliament for many years.[53]

UTU AND MURU

Underlying both warfare (see below) and domestic relations, were principles of reciprocity known in both cases as utu and in the latter as muru. Firth puts forward as a general principle in Maori exchange that 'for every gift another of at least equal value must be returned'.[54] The same applied to injury so that if a man were slain by someone from another tribe, the life of the offender or one of his relatives was demanded as utu.[55] Insults and slights also required the shedding of blood because to leave insults unavenged lowered both chiefly and tribal prestige. The result was a military 'seesaw' in which each tribe kept a tally of victories and defeats, making it a point of honour to avenge a defeat and so obtain payment (utu) while, better still, seeking to establish a credit balance with an extra victory.[56] In rare cases where blood revenge was not considered feasible, relief was obtained by indirect means. Firth notes the 'spinning of tops, the swinging from *moari* or giant strides, the rocking of a canoe towards the enemy's home, each to the accompaniment of an incisive chant . . .'[57] as alternative means, in such cases, of obtaining utu or equalising a death.

Muru operated within the group. It was a system of gaining utu by the destruction and seizure of property, not of the offender, but of the offender's immediate kinsfolk, who generally offered no resistance. Infringement of tapu, accidental wounding and adultery were all common causes.

> The *taua muru* or plundering party raided the village of the offender, made away with his movable property, ate up all his provisions — which were generally set out in readiness by the people invaded — and in graver cases burned his home and set one of their party to oppose him in a duel.[58]

The recipients of a muru party could comfort themselves with the thought that one day they might get their property back by taking part in a similar raid. Anthropologists, following Firth,[59] have tended on this account to interpret muru as a form of property exchange. Early missionaries who had become victims of it, often for what seemed to them the most trivial or even trumped up reasons, and without opportunity for redress, regarded it as theft and opposed it along with warfare as an unmitigated evil.

WARFARE[60]

Descriptions of song types such as the peruperu (war dance), kaioraora (cursing song) and tumoto (virulent song) would be incomprehensible without an understanding of the importance of warfare in Maori society. Bruce Biggs comments:

A war canoe drawn by Sydney Parkinson in 1769

The Māori were a fierce people, as the first arrivals from Europe found to their cost. Forty men were killed from the crews of Cook, the Dutch explorer Abel Tasman and the ill-fated French explorer Marion du Fresne.[61]

The first known Maori contact with Europeans was in 1642 when Abel Tasman sailed into what is now known as Golden Bay. At nightfall on 18 December, after Tasman had anchored his ship, two canoes came out to inspect it, paddled by men who shouted out in rough voices and blew many times upon an instrument[62] which Tasman said made a sound like a Moorish trumpet. Tasman had one of his sailors play trumpet blasts in reply and after several such exchanges and the firing of a cannon, the canoes paddled away.[63] The next day an attack occurred in which four of six men sent ashore by Tasman in a boat were beaten to death with long staffs. Tasman sailed away in disgust, calling the place 'Murderers' Bay', unaware that he had probably received and accepted a challenge to fight.

No further European contact is known to have taken place until the first visit of Captain James Cook to New Zealand, in 1769, in the *Endeavour*. Cook's ships made two further visits, in 1773–74 and in 1777 during his second and third voyages of Pacific discovery. His ethnographic and casual observations of the Maori people, along with those of his associates Joseph Banks, Johann Forster and others, were a model of their time and amongst the most valuable ever made. Amongst them were many on music and dance.

Cook circumnavigated New Zealand in 1769. Almost everywhere he was met by war canoes filled with large numbers of warriors who shouted threats, brandished weapons, performed war dances and in some cases attacked his ship by throwing spears or stones. In some instances they desisted and agreed to trade after being warned by Cook's Tahitian interpreter, Tupaia, that they would all be killed if they attacked. In others the same happened after they were fired upon. The Maori intention on these occasions may have been to determine the strength or weakness of the strangers and whether they could be defeated. In their journals both Cook and Banks gave clear statements as to their own perception of the Maori actions and the means found most effective in dealing with them. Cook remarked:

> Whenever we were Viseted by any number of them that had never Heard or seen any thing of us before they generaly came off in the largest Canoes they had, some of which will carry 60, 80 or 100 people, they always brought their best close along with them which they put on as soon as they came near the ship. In each Canoe were generaly an old man, in some two or three, these use'd always to direct the others, were better Clothed and generaly carried a halbard or battle ax in their hands or some such like thing that distinguished them from the others. As soon as they came within about a stone's throw from the ship they would there lay and call out 'Haromai hareuta a patoo age', that is come here, come ashore with us and we will kill you with our patoo patoo's, and at the same time would shake them at us, at times they would dance the war dance, and other times they would trade with and talk to us and answer such questions as were put to them with all the Calmness emaginable and then again begin the war-dance, shaking their paddles patoo patoo's &c and make strange contorsions at the same time, and as soon as they had worked them-selves up to a proper pitch they would begin to attack us with stones and darts and oblige us whether we would or no to fire upon them. Musquetary they never regarded unless they felt the effect but great guns they did because these could throw stones farther than they could comprehend.[64]

Banks's similar comment was:

> They always attackd us, tho seldom seeming to mean more than to provoke us to shew them what we were able to do in this case. By many trials we found that good usage and fair words would not avail the least with them, nor would they be convincd by the noise of our firearms alone that they were superior to theirs; but as soon as they had felt the smart of even a load of small shot and had had time allowd them to recollect themselves from the Effects of their artificial cour-age,[65] which commonly took up a day, they were sensible of our generosity in not taking the advantage of Our superiority and became at once our good freinds and upon all occasions placd the most unbounded confidence in us.[66]

Tasman's experience aside, it is hard to know whether these challenges were sometimes mere 'rituals of encounter' (see next), as they have lately been interpreted,[67] or were always in earnest. But, if the former were ever the case, the early explorers were obliged, effectively, to stake their lives on guessing right. Cook exercised common sense, took the threats offered to him seriously and survived,[68] in most cases apparently without ill will from the Maori. Marion du Fresne, who was killed three years later at the Bay of Islands, naively thought it would be enough always to be gentlemanly and kind, and went trustingly to his death, having divested himself of arms and ignored a warning. It appears he may unwittingly have violated a fishing tapu;[69] but other explanations have also been offered.[70]

An objective index of the state of war readiness in eighteenth-century New Zealand can be gained from a study of fortified sites known as paa. Most were built on easily defended positions such as hills, ridges or headlands or were protected by swamps or open water. Typically they were surrounded by palisades with or without ditches. A late development, by the sixteenth century and afterwards, according to Fox, was the addition of fighting stages from which missiles could be thrown.[71] Musical instruments associated with fighting stages were the pahuu (war gong) and puukaaea (war trumpet).

During his circumnavigation in 1769, Cook saw and described paa fortifications at Queen Charlotte Sound, Mercury Bay and the Bay of Islands. Crozet and Le Roux likewise provide good descriptions of them in the Bay of Islands in 1772. In a detailed description, Crozet characterised all of the villages there as 'situated on steep cliffs jutting out into the sea', surrounded by ditches and palisades and complete with fighting platforms.[72] Unobserved because of the rough seas along the west coast which prevented landfall were numerous paa fortifications in the Waikato and Taranaki, since documented by archaeologists.[73] Early nineteenth-century missionary and travellers' accounts of fortified settlements throughout the Bay of Islands, Hokianga, Thames, and the central areas of the North Island[74] show that from the eighteenth century onwards warfare had become endemic in New Zealand. Some territories such as the Auckland isthmus, which was a corridor between north and south, were fought over many times, with first one group and then another gaining ascendancy. Auckland is the site of numerous former volcanoes, all of which, according to Searle and Davidson, bear 'unmistakable evidence of man's activity'.[75] Terraces, some palisaded, were carved into the sides of the mountains both for defence and to provide living space. Immense effort was expended on creating these fortresses: the huge complex on One Tree Hill (Maungakiekie) was terraced on both inner and outer surfaces of the craters with implements no more sophisticated than the digging stick.

In a study of earthwork fortifications, Groube[76] has estimated that there are between 4000 and 6000 paa sites in New Zealand, mostly in the northern half of the North Island, a remarkable number for a population estimated to have been no more than 150,000 at the time of Cook's visit and to have declined (after the introduction of the musket and a devastating increase in the scale of tribal warfare) to only 80,000 or 90,000 by 1840.[77]

A fortification drawn by Sydney Parkinson at Mercury Bay in 1769

The paa at One Tree Hill (Maungakiekie) as it is today. PHOTO: *D.R. Simmons*

Song types used during warfare included karakia (incantations) both defensive and offensive, war songs of challenge and of triumph, kaioraora (cursing songs) and whakaaraara paa (watch songs) as well as some now obsolete such as piioi (head-brandishing songs).

RITUALS OF ENCOUNTER

Although Maori warfare ceased more than a century ago, reminders of it are built into the very structure of the formal Maori meeting or hui. The concept of the 'rituals of encounter' which take place at Maori meetings is explained fully in Chapter 5 of Anne Salmond's *Hui: A Study of Maori Ceremonial Gatherings* (1975).

The components of the ritual (optional elements in square brackets) are: [waerea 'protective incantation']; [wero 'challenge']; karanga 'call'; [poowhiri 'action chant of welcome'; tangi 'wailing']; whaikoorero 'oratory'; and hongi 'pressing noses'. Whaikoorero also follows a conventional pattern: of [whakaaraara 'warning call'; tau 'chant']; greet the dead; greet the living; take 'specific topic'; and waiata 'song'. All stages of the ritual involve song and/or the use of formal movement.

The ritual governs each stage of the reception of visiting groups (manuhiri) to the marae or meeting place by the local tribes (taangata whenua). At the beginning of the ceremony, the visitors are treated as potentially hostile, and they themselves are as wary of their hosts. The two groups stay spatially opposite each other throughout the ritual, and only at the end do they meet face to face in the hongi line.[78] Until the formalities are over, the visitors or manuhiri, as outsiders to the community, are known as waewae tapu (people with sacred feet). The object of the rituals is to decontaminate the visitors of their alien tapu.[79]

The waerea is delivered by the chief elder of a visiting group about to enter a strange marae. It is an incantation whose purpose is to waere or clear the path of supernatural obstacles.[80]

If performed, the wero or ritual challenge is delivered by one or more young local males. Its purpose is to find out whether the visitor comes in peace or in war. In former times, as explained by Salmond:

The encounter began with a firing-off of muskets on both sides, then the local warriors, stripped naked and armed, started up a wardance. The visitors followed with a *haka* of their own, and knelt down facing their hosts. A challenger came running out towards them, taunting them, leaping and making faces; he hurled a dart (*kookiri*) into their midst and raced back to his own people with one of the visiting warriors hard on his heels. On some occasions there might be three challenges together, or one after the other. The last challenger was chased by the visitors in a body, and as they approached the local people the sham fight began, 'a pell-mell sort of encounter in which numerous hard blows were given and received'. If the challenger was caught, he was especially roughly

Wero at Orakei marae, 1971. Photo: *Jeremy Salmond*

handled. The sham fight was a dangerous part of the ritual, because fighting could easily break out in earnest, but if it ended peacefully both sides joined in the *haka*, then pressed noses and wailed for the dead. After this the speechmaking began, followed by a feast, and the encounter had been successfully initiated.[81]

According to Salmond, the war dance (peruperu) is today performed only on rare occasions as part of the welcoming ritual. Instead haka and action songs may be performed later as entertainment after the visitors are seated on the marae.[82]

The wero is performed when an important visitor is about to enter the marae for the first time. For an especially distinguished visitor the procedure may be gone through three times. A young warrior runs out to meet the visitor, brandishing a taiaha (spear) with intricate weapon drill movements, 'leaping, grunting and grimacing'. When he gets near the visitor, who is standing awaiting his approach, he kneels and places a carved dart or stick (taki or 'challenge') at the visitor's feet. Then he rises and backs off,

*An old woman waits to karanga (call in) visitors as a
poowhiri group stands by at Turangawaewae marae,
1971. PHOTO: Jeremy Salmond*

still performing his weapon drill, while a male member of the visitor's party picks up the dart in token of peace.[83]

As soon as the hosts see that the visitors are ready, an old woman kai-karanga (caller), dressed in black, will karanga or call them in, beckoning as she does so with green branches. The visitors then move together in a group on to the marae while one of their women returns the call. The karanga texts are full of references to the dead, reminding both hosts and guests of persons who have died since the groups last met. The high-pitched karanga calls are redolent with emotion, 'providing the medium by which the living and the dead of the manuhiri may cross the physical space to unite with the living and dead of the tangata whenua'.[84]

By the time the callers have finished the dead are almost tangibly present on the marae. All the group, living and dead members alike, are brought together, making a long unbroken chain of kinsmen that stretches right back to Hawaiki and the Pō (Underworld).[85]

Next in the ritual is the poowhiri or poohiri, referred to by Salmond as the 'action chant of welcome'.[86] The chant almost invariably performed is a short haka 'Tooia mai te waka' in which the visitors are identified with the canoe in which the founders of their tribe are thought to have arrived from Hawaiki:

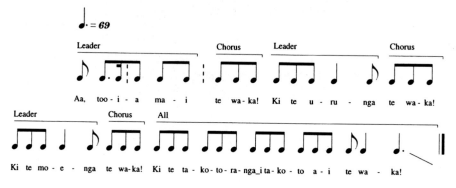

EXAMPLE 2 *Haka: M&O 1 as sung by Turanga Mauparaoa*

The leader begins the chant with the call 'Hei runga, hei raro' (raise, lower) as a signal for the welcoming group to move twigs or small branches of green leaves rhythmically up and down while hitting their thighs in unison in time to the chant. Any kind of greenery may be used but the preferred types are kawakawa, symbolising death, and mamaku (silver-backed fern), symbolising peace and welcome. At the end of the chant, the hands remain held for a while in the upright position, trembling, until the leader calls 'tukua iho' or 'ki raro'; then they are lowered. The chant, originally a too waka or canoe-hauling song, refers to dragging the canoe to its resting place, symbolically pulling the visitors safely on to the marae.[87]

Often, and nowadays indeed almost by convention, this chant is followed by the famous 'Ka mate' chant (see Example 9) performed, doubtless, because like 'Tooia mai' it is known by almost every Maori.

By this stage in the ritual, the element of challenge has begun to moderate. The poowhiri is performed in non-threatening fashion, predominantly by women, with gentle waving of greenery rather than the aggressive vigorous movements of the same items were they to be performed as war dances.[88]

Tangi or wailing,[89] expressive of loss and desolation, is especially audible and prolonged at funeral meetings (tangihanga) but may be performed at almost any meeting:

> The old women dress in black, the colour of mourning, and as they advance into the *marae* they begin a high uncanny wail, sometimes beating their breasts with a slow hopeless motion, or waving a handkerchief as they cry. The dead have been summoned to the *marae* by the callers, and this cry recognises their presence.[90]

Haka poowhiri at Turangawaewae marae, 1971. PHOTO: *Jeremy Salmond*

The visitors advance slowly on to the marae and, in memory of the dead, stand for a time with heads bowed and eyes lowered in front of the meeting house. If wailing is being performed, it now intensifies, rising to a crescendo.[91] Salmond describes some women as wailing:

> with a high, almost melodious keening, which rises and fades in a dying fall; others use a low-pitched moaning sound, falling off into the 'hum-wail'.[92] The wailing is stylised, and combines into a throbbing, harmonious chorus of grief.[93]

Some of the visiting women may now leave their group and join the wailing local women gathered in the porch of the meeting house. There they may engage in a practice designated by Salmond as 'tangi aatahu' or 'tangi koorero' (talking wail). 'Here a mourner tells a friend of her grief by breaking out into a spontaneous chant, talking through her tears.'[94] The terms given by Salmond for this practice may both be neologisms.[95] Arapeta Awatere, in an interview, said the correct term for it is 'tangi whakahuahua', and the same information was volunteered by Kino Hughes.[96] Awatere said a phrase applied to persons engaged in tangi whakahuahua was 'te puna o te aroha' (the spring of love). It is a sign of deepest grief and is generally done only by the next of kin, those closest to the deceased.[97]

In former times women mourners slashed their breasts with flakes of obsidian or with sea shells until the blood ran freely. Polack gives an eye-witness account of one such event at which:

A tangi or meeting of friends. From Angas The New Zealanders Illustrated

sharp mussel-shells were used to excoriate the body: and, in a short time, streams of blood trickled down the face, arms and every part of the body of each performer. . . . Their scanty garments were soon soaked through with tears, and some were almost saturated with the blood of themselves and their companions.[98]

Even on non-formal occasions the customary wailing when friends met could be prolonged. Potts mentions such ceremonies being kept up for half an hour or more.[99] Kerry-Nicholls writes of an occasion when the tangi wailing lasted an hour.[100] Nowadays the wailing may last for 10 or 15 minutes until an elder brings it to an end by calling out 'Kua ea' (It is requited), and on this signal the visitors move to benches which have been set out for them to await the speeches which will follow.[101]

Whaikoorero is the term applied to formal speech-making on the marae. An elaborate protocol governs who may speak, the order of speaking and the structure of speech-making itself. In most tribal areas, except in the East Coast, only men may speak. Two conventions govern the order of speaking: tribes from Wanganui, Taranaki and the East Coast have a system of bloc speaking (paaeke) in which local orators speak first, followed by an equal number of visitors. Most remaining tribes, predominantly from the Tainui and Te Arawa ancestral canoes, practise utuutu in which local and visiting speakers alternate. Practice in Northland evidently varies from place to place. Most speakers begin with a recitation known generally as a tauparapara, and each finishes with a waiata in which he is joined by his supporters.

At meetings, depending on the nature of the hui and its purpose, speeches may continue for many hours, new rounds beginning as successive groups are welcomed on to the marae. While the current group is welcomed the next awaits its turn outside the gates. When the speeches are over, the visitors are invited to hongi:

> The local people form a line across the front of the meeting house and the visitors begin to move along it, shaking hands with everyone in turn. . . . The *hongi* line is friendly and relaxed; all *tapu* [ceremonial restriction] has been lifted. . . . Most of the old people *hongi*, shaking hands and pressing noses two or three times . . . On most occasions . . . the *hongi* signals the end of the welcome. The visitors have been greeted with due ceremony, and now they are called to share the hospitality of the local people in a meal.[102]

The guests then move to an adjacent dining hall where food is awaiting them. As explained by Ranginui Walker:

> The decontamination process is completed when the guests sit down to partake of food. Food is noa (common or profane) the opposite of tapu (sacred). Once the guests have eaten they can then mingle freely with their hosts.[103]

At this point the manuhiri (visitors) become taangata whenua (home people or lit. 'people of the land') for the duration of their stay and are free to take part in the welcoming of other manuhiri.[104]

CHAPTER 2

RECITED SONG AND DANCE STYLES

Types of song as named by the Maori themselves are distinguished essentially in terms of song use. To sing without an object, as when travelling alone, was called 'koohau' and was regarded as a bad omen.[1] On musical grounds, the different song types can be grouped into just two categories, recited and sung. This turns out to be a useful division on textual and other grounds as well and is accordingly followed in ensuing chapters.

When sung by groups, both recited and sung genres of song are unison or monophonic, in contrast with European-derived action song and hymn-singing (see Book 2). Rhythmic unison is the rule for recited songs and both rhythmic and melodic unison for sung items. Reference to 'singing in parts' in some early reports probably refers to musical form; this certainly is the case with Nicholas who writes of singing in parts 'alternately'.[2] On the other hand, James Burney, who sailed with Cook and was qualified to judge, is specific: 'Sometimes they sing an underpart which is a third lower except the 2 last notes which are the same.'[3] Possibly this was an early example of rangi rua, now regarded as a singing fault. A fleeting appearance of parts in the form of heterophony sometimes results from the practice of 'riding in' to a note or through variant interpretations from some of the performers. However, the former is not regarded by singers as part of the song and the latter is again acknowledged as a singing fault. Further information on these topics can be found in Chapter 6.

Recited styles have no melody and no line organisation. Margaret Orbell characterises them as frequently performed when one social group confronted another, so there is often an element of social interaction and challenge.[4] Most are accompanied by dancing, gesture or action of some kind.

> In all recited songs, the verbal rhythms are relatively close to those of speech, though the language is very different in its imagery and concentrated energy from that of ordinary discourse. Songs accompanied only by gestures, such as pokeka and patere, tend to have long, flowing sentences, while haka, which are accompanied by vigorous posture dancing, have choppy rhythms and especially terse emphatic language, with much repetition.[5]

KARAKIA

Karakia are spells or incantations. They were used at every level of Maori society and entered into every Maori activity. Some were simple charms repeated by children over their toys; others were used by individuals in their everyday lives to cure minor ailments and to protect against danger; and a highly esoteric class was performed exclusively by priests.[6]

A perusal of Williams[7] reveals over 130 terms for different kinds of karakia and between 30 and 40 more for rites and ceremonies involving karakia. A selection of them appears in the following list given by Buck:[8]

aatahu: love charms.
hoa: to split stones, wither leaves, kill a bird.
hoa tapuae: to give speed to the feet and to retard an opponent.
hono: to unite fractures.
kaha: to gain success in fowling.
kawa: to remove the *tapu* from new houses.
kii tao: to give power to spears (weapons); also '*reo tao*'.
kii rakau: to give power to weapons.
ngau paepae: to avert sorcery against a war party.
pou: to fix, such as the memory during instruction.
raaoa: to expel the foreign body in choking.
rotu: to put people or the sea to sleep.
taa koopito: to cure abdominal troubles.
tohi: to sprinkle a child in the dedication or *tua* ceremony.
tohi taua: to sprinkle a war party proceeding to war.
tuuaa: to dedicate children after cutting the navel cord.
tuuaa paa: to ward off ill luck.
whai: to cure injuries, burns, choking.
whakanoa: to make common (*noa*) by removing *tapu*.

Most of the same terms, along with some 60 others, are also listed by Best who provides further information about many of them.[9] Details of numerous other named charms, spells and rites or ceremonies involving them can be found in the section on magic in Part 2 of Best's monograph *Maori Religion and Mythology*.[10]

Best and Buck both offer extended discussions of karakia, as used in ritual, and their relation to the concepts of mana and tapu.[11] Best insists that the efficacy of a karakia was recognised to depend upon the mana of the person uttering it. However, Buck points out that karakia of all kinds had to be repeated word perfect, and any slip of the tongue was thought to result not only in the karakia losing its power, but in the deity punishing the person who made the mistake.[12] This, says Buck, must have led some at least to believe that power also resided in the form of the words themselves. Firth takes a similarly balanced view:

The efficacy of the magic . . . was not wholly secured by the mere repetition of the spell. It was also contingent in Maori eyes upon the *mana,* the psychic power, of the person who recited it, and upon the method of his delivery. *Mana,* again, depended upon the state of a person and could be temporarily placed in abeyance or permanently lost by contamination in a variety of ways, such as contact with cooked food or other spiritually degrading objects. Hence to exercise magic properly and give force to the spell the practitioner was obliged to keep a number of regulations of *tapu.* The spell had also to be recited correctly not only as regards the form of words, but also with fluency and proper intonation.[13]

Best and Buck are agreed that karakia seldom involve appeal to higher powers or direct communication with a god and, for this reason, most should be called incantations rather than invocations.[14] A seemingly contrary view is advanced by Shirres in light of an analysis of karakia texts in nineteenth-century manuscript collections of Grey, White, Shortland and Taylor.[15] According to Shirres, karakia link the people of today not only with the ancestors and events of the past but also with the atua (gods).[16] All activities in the everyday world were seen as coming under the influence of the atua and ancestors and the effectiveness of a karakia depended on the faith of the people in the atua.[17] In support of this view, quotations are cited from manuscripts in Maori which explicitly associate failure of karakia with the adoption of Christianity 'so indirectly indicating that the effectiveness of the chants ceased when the people accepted the new faith, giving up their faith in the *atua*'.[18] On the other hand, although evidence is given by Shirres that the words of karakia were sometimes changed to accommodate new circumstances, a quotation in Maori from Te Rangikaheke[19] is definite that the words still had to be said correctly. The apparent conflict can be resolved if one takes the view that appeal to atua may often have been implicit rather than explicit in karakia. It may also be relevant that the texts cited by Shirres in support of the above view are exclusively ritual in nature and may not be typical of all karakia.

Shirres begins Chapter 3 of his thesis with a classification of karakia by Te Rangikaheke according to the atua invoked. They include karakia for the heavens, the sea, the forest, fern-root, kuumara, gourds, dogs and people, each the domain of a particular god. Shirres colourfully likens the gods to a kind of divine Cabinet: Taane as Minister for the forests and birds, Tangaroa as Minister of the sea and the fish, Haumia as Minister of Agriculture, Taawhiri, the god of the wind and storms, as Minister for the Environment and Tuumatauenga as Minister for Human Affairs. But many karakia are found not to invoke atua and some to invoke more than one. For this reason, and because so many karakia are found to belong within ritual complexes, Shirres prefers an alternative grouping by subject matter, also by Te Rangikaheke, and uses this as the basis of a classification of his own. Three groups are isolated. About half of the texts examined by Shirres fall into Group 1 in which are distinguished five major ritual complexes involving karakia: for children, canoes, kuumara, war parties and the dead. In Groups 2 and 3 are the karakia of minor rituals and those which do not form part of a ritual complex. Group 2 is subdivided into karakia concerning the weather, sickness, daily work, and daily living. Group 3 contains karakia maakutu (for curses and counter-curses). It would appear that atua are specifically invoked predominantly in karakia of the major ritual complexes. Common features of the rituals are the setting up of 'rods'[20] to act as pathways for the atua, the 'loosing' of atua seen as beneficial and the 'binding' of those re-garded as harmful ('pure'), and finally the ritual offering and eating of food to remove restrictions imposed during the performance.[21]

Karakia are performed usually in a rapid monotone punctuated by sus-tained notes and descending glides at the end of phrases. A prominent fea-ture is their extremely fast pace, exceeding at times, if the sustained notes are excluded, 300 syllables per minute. Another characteristic, which Firth explains, is that the flow of sound is meant to be unbroken:

> Some formulae of a highly ritualised nature had to be recited without a break, and to this end two or more persons were required. A slip or error in an incantation (*tapepa, tui whawhatirua, hewa*) was a serious matter, and in native belief spelt serious misfortune or even death to the reciter, by act of the gods. Magic was a double-edged tool, dangerous to the wielder if not prop-erly handled.[22]

Buck's view is that the latter sanction would have been instituted by priests 'as a safeguard to promote accurate memorising on the part of their neo-phytes and to prevent unauthorised persons from stealing their *karakia*'.[23] It may be surmised that the rapid delivery of karakia had the same objective of preventing appropriation of the magic.

Karakia of the ritual kind can still be heard today on occasions such as the kawa whare rite for opening a meeting house when tapu or ceremonial restriction placed on the house during its construction has to be removed. Many of the karakia relating to the ancestral canoes are also still remem-bered. One of them is the incantation which is said to have freed the Tainui canoe when it became fast on a legendary portage across the Tamaki isth-mus where Auckland now stands. The song was recorded in 1963 from Uehoka Tairakena of Ngaati Maahanga tribe of Waikato. It is recited in rapid speech rhythms with an underlying 2/8 metre (see Example 3).

The term karakia is now applied not only to pre-Christian incantations but also to religious utterances of later date. Adherents of the nineteenth-century religious movement known as Pai Marire had their own different forms of karakia, which are still performed in the Waikato area at King Move-ment ceremonies.[24] On the twelfth day of every month in the Tuuhoe and

♩ = 94

Too - i - a Tai - nu - i ta - po - tu ki te mo - a - na! Maa wai e too?

Maa te wha - ka - ro - ngo a - (ke)! Wha - ka - ro - ngo a - ke au

he ta - ra wai - nu - ku, he ta - ra wai - ra - ngi. Ti - ni - a

to - no - a, nau mai.

EXAMPLE 3 Karakia: McL 334 as sung by Uehoka Tairakena

Whakatoohea tribal areas, followers of the Ringatu religion, which was founded by Te Kooti, hold regular services, known as karakia, at which the tohunga leaders recite prayers (inoi) in karakia style.[25] And Christian prayers and services are also called karakia.

Te Kooti Rikirangi (d.1893), founder of the Ringatu religion and a prolific composer of waiata as well as liturgy. PHOTO: *Alexander Turnbull Library,* 90715¹/₂

TAUPARAPARA

Songs variously called tau marae (former Ngaati Porou usage), poohua tau (Arawa tribes), tauparapara (most other tribes), or occasionally simply tau are short compositions customarily recited on the marae by males before making a formal speech or whaikoorero. In the East Coast and in the Tuuhoe tribal area, the term paatere (elsewhere a different song type) is now often substituted. The name most commonly used, however, is tauparapara and this appears to be gaining ascendancy.

Many tauparapara are fragments of longer compositions, usually karakia. Williams, indeed, gives the term not as a recitation before speaking but as an incantation for moving a canoe, and examination of the texts of tauparapara shows many to be replete with canoe imagery. Although a ngeri (see later) or other recited composition may occasionally be pressed into service as a tauparapara, most are performed in the same manner as karakia with the identical rapid style of delivery characteristic of no other type of song.

In a study of Maori speech-making, Mahuta states:

> The *tau-parapara* is the introductory chant and is normally given from a standing position. There are different types of *tau-parapara* each being considered appropriate for a particular situation. Thus we find there are *tau-parapara* for welcoming visitors, farewelling the dead, removing *tapu*, soliciting support and establishing genealogical links. Depending on the nature of the occasion, the speaker will select from his repertoire the most appropriate *tau-parapara* for his *whaikoorero*.[26]

The example following is the beginning of a tauparapara performed in 1963 by Whati Tamati of Waikato tribe. It is a variant of a song which, according to another Waikato elder, Paraire Herewini, was originally a 'karakia taa moko' or tattooing incantation. It is recited in complex rapid speech rhythms with an underlying 2/8 metre which stabilises at the words 'He kura te winiwini'. A partial translation is offered by Mahuta who says most of the language is archaic and untranslatable.[27]

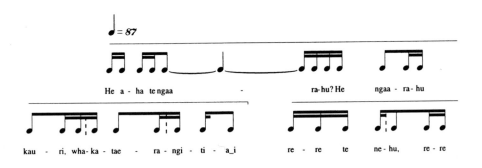

EXAMPLE 4 Tauparapara: Beginning of McL 368 as sung by Whati Tamati

WHAKAARAARA PAA

Sometimes, instead of a tauparapara, a speaker will perform a whakaaraara paa or watch song.[28] In its original context, the watch song was performed by sentries on duty at a fortified village or paa to warn of the approach of enemies or to signal that the paa was on the alert against attack. When performed as a preliminary to a speech, the song is intended to gain the attention of the audience. By performing what would otherwise be a 'call to arms' the speaker is figuratively saying 'Wake up everybody! Someone's here!'[29] Sometimes a speaker will begin his call while still seated in the audience; or he may perform it while moving forward to take his place in front of the gathering. On occasion a speaker may perform both a watch song and a tauparapara, and in this case will perform the watch song first.[30]

The following example is a complete watch song, often performed as a tauparapara. It was recorded in 1958 from Turanga Mauparaoa of Ngaati Manawa tribe. It can be found, with notes and a translation, as Song 2 in McLean & Orbell.[31]

EXAMPLE 5 *Whakaaraara paa: M&O 2 as sung by Turanga Mauparaoa*

PAATERE

Paatere are songs composed by women in reply to gossip or slander. The reply typically takes the form of a kind of social catalogue in which the woman names both her detractors and distinguished kinsmen who could be regarded as guarantors of her reputation. Chiefly forbears of relatives named in the song may be listed and places of residence or associated landmarks mentioned. Such a song becomes a kind of genealogical tour, 'at once a gazetteer and a Who's Who for the period of its composition'.[32] A

EXAMPLE 6 *Paatere: Beginning of M&O 4 as sung by Lucy Jacob*

famous example is 'Poia atu taku poi', a paatere composed by Erenora of Ngaati Raukawa tribe, in which an imaginary poi figuratively skims around New Zealand, touching down upon the places mentioned in the song. The song is transcribed and annotated in full as Song 4 in McLean & Orbell as sung by Lucy Jacob of Ngaati Raukawa. Example 6 shows the opening lines.

Although composed by or on behalf of an individual, the paatere, like most traditional Maori songs, is performed by groups of singers. The element of confrontation in the texts is given further expression by the use of defiant impromptu gesture and of facial grimaces (also used in haka) called puukana. Hand quivering and other haka actions may also be used, but the performers do not form into ranks as they would in a haka; instead 'each one of the company . . . gives free rein to his or her individual mood'.[33] The use of movements borrowed from haka is commented upon further by Kopu Erueti of Te Whaanau-a-Apanui tribe:

> [The *paatere*] was accompanied with appropriate hand movements, moving hips and turning heads; and at certain parts the eyes give the defiant or haughty stare, the chorus joins in and the singers seek to excel one another in the singing and generally to impart an air of exultation and elation to their performance. Almost, but not quite, the performance becomes a *haka* . . .[34]

On occasion, the use of movement in paatere approached that of pure theatre. Pei Te Hurinui gives a vivid account of another famous paatere, composed because of a sarcastic remark made at the marriage feast of Ngawaero, one of the younger wives of Potatau Te Wherowhero, the first Maori king. A chief called Kukutai had commented adversely on the absence of preserved birds at the feast, though the host tribes were famous for the delicacy. Ngawaero's people decided to take their revenge at an important meeting scheduled to be held in a few months' time. The time available was used to snare and preserve huge quantities of birds. A special wooden vessel was carved to contain them, so large that eight men were required to carry it. This, together with calabashes of preserved birds, would be presented at the meeting which the people knew would be attended by those who had complained at Ngawaero's wedding. The poets of Ngawaero's father's subtribe were consulted and with Ngawaero composed a paatere to be sung at the presentation. Finally the great day came:

> At high noon, under a cloudless sky, Ngawaero's party, after crossing the Waipa and resting some distance away from Whatiwhatihoe village, moved off on the last stage of the journey. When they reached the outer bounds of the village the party paused, as they had been seen, and the tribes gathered at Whatiwhatihoe were assembling and preparing to receive them with the time-honoured welcome of the Maori. After the last wailing sound of the

local women's welcoming chant had died away, Ngawaero and her party moved forward a distance as the women of their tribe responded with the chants of greeting. Then the great food vessel was lifted up on to brown shoulders, with the proud Ngawaero perched in front and sitting on a specially constructed seat. The party moved forward slowly on to the main courtyard of the village. Ngawaero, her eyes glistening, was the centre of attention as she sat up aloft with head slightly bent forward, her composure dignified and demure.

The appearance of this party betokened to all that a special presentation was to be made. An expectant hush settled on the assembled multitude. At a fitting moment, Ngawaero proudly raised her head and with eyes aglow, she began to sing the opening lines of her song in which later the specially selected party of singers and posture-dancers joined.[35]

EXAMPLE 7 *Paatere: Beginning of M&O 20 as led by Makarena Mariu*

The song appears in full as Song 20 in McLean & Orbell as sung by Makarena Mariu and others of Ngaati Tuuwharetoa tribe.

The musical style of paatere is single note or monotonic with prescribed continuous rises of pitch followed by a fall at the ends of stanzas. Singers sometimes also elevate the pitch for a short time when resuming the song after a pause for breath. Tempo is rapid and the rhythmic groupings seen in the above examples are characteristic. Performance is continuous with no breaks for breath. When performers are few, this is achieved with relays of singers as for karakia. Kopu Erueti explains:

> The tempo of an action song [paatere] is an even one, and is generally sung without any breaking off to mark the verses. The task is a heavy one for the song leader to keep up with the lines of the song; it is really too great a strain for the breathing of one man. That is why the singers take it in turns, to give the others a breathing spell; the relieving singer is well versed and by listening carefully he can sense when he should take up his part.[36]

Pomare and Cowan heard paatere continued without break in this way for more than half an hour.[37]

KAIORAORA

A kaioraora is a song performed in identical style to the paatere, but distinguishable by its especially virulent text. Williams calls it an 'abusive recriminatory song'. Best says it 'expresses savage and deadly hatred, a desire to slay cook and eat enemies against whom it is directed'. He adds that they were sometimes composed by widows of men slain in battle or by treachery.[38] Few are still sung and few have been recorded for fear of causing offence to the tribes against whom the songs were directed. Arapeta Awatere described the kaioraora as using 'the vilest language out' in which, for example, the ancestors of a murderer are eaten by the ancestors of the victim, cannibalism being the final act of desecration.[39] Karetu glosses the term as meaning literally 'to eat alive'.[40] According to Awatere, the kaioraora always takes the form of defamation of ancestors and in this respect is distinguished from an otherwise similar song type called hanihani which is a song of personal abuse defamatory of persons themselves rather than their ancestors.[41] It should also not be confused with the tumoto, which was a form of haka (see later).

The transcribed example is the beginning of a kaioraora recorded in 1958 from Turanga Mauparaoa of Ngaati Manawa tribe. The full text, a translation and an explanation of the words are given by Best who says the song was composed by Te Kiri-tapoa, one of the wives of Te Piki-huia, reviling the people who had slain her husband. The first few lines name the persons responsible and refer to roasting the heart of one of the enemy on a spit as a preliminary to eating the perpetrators.[42] The song is an excellent example of paatere style. The rhythm was obviously enjoyed by Arapeta Awatere and Ira Manihera who were both present when the recording was made and did actions during the item. When the song was finished, a woman listener remarked: 'That's vulgar', drawing a reply from Awatere: 'No that's not vulgar. That's true stuff!'

EXAMPLE 8 Kaioraora: Beginning of McL 32A as sung by Turanga Mauparaoa

HAKA

The haka is a posture dance with shouted accompaniment. Most New Zealanders would consider themselves familiar with it, if only because of its customary use by the All Blacks and other football teams as a preliminary to the game. The famous 'Ka mate' haka performed by the All Blacks is also amongst the most commonly performed at Maori meetings.[43] It is widely enough known, indeed, to be regarded almost as an emblem of New Zealand.

The transcribed version of the song was recorded in 1958 from Ira Manihera and others of Tuuhoe tribe. The accents represent foot stamping and body percussion.

EXAMPLE 9 *Haka: McL 25B as led by Ira Manihera*

Familiar as the haka may be, there are a number of mistaken ideas about it. It was not, as commonly supposed, exclusively a war dance. Nor was it performed only by men. According to Best, some haka were performed by males only, some by women only and some by both sexes, while children also had their simple haka.[44]

Best says that posture dancing was performed at any and all times as an amusement, but especially at night.[45] Angas notes that the haka was 'a favourite kind of song, frequently practised during the evening by young people, and accompanied with all manner of antics and gestures'.[46] A.S. Thomson confirms:

> Singing, or the Haka, was the amusement of village maidens and young lads on fine evenings. For this purpose they assembled with flowers and feathers in their hair, and red paint, charcoal, and petals of flowers on their faces. Most songs were accompanied with action. The singers first arranged themselves in a row, in a sitting attitude, on a conspicuous place; the best voices commenced and finished each verse, then all joined in the chorus, which consisted of a peculiar noise caused by repeated expirations and inspirations, slapping one hand on the breast, raising the other aloft and making it vibrate with great rapidity, and moving the body in indelicate attitudes.[47]

Such events were the equivalent of the later European small-town social dance or 'hop' and had similar associations in terms of courtship behaviour. Best states that young men or women who excelled in the haka were much admired, and so great pains were taken to acquire free, graceful and well regulated action.[48] Andersen quotes the legend of Te Ponga and Puhihuia who fell in love through admiration of each other's performance in the haka, and claims that such incidents happened frequently.[49]

Another use of the haka, today as much as in former times, is for welcoming guests at meetings. Buck observes: 'The *haka*, *poi* and to a lesser extent the *peruperu* war dance have been carried on for social reasons because they still constitute the heartiest form of welcome which a receiving tribe can give to its visitors on important occasions.'[50] The use of a war dance in the context of welcome may seem strange to non-Maori, but is part and parcel of the rituals of encounter still acted out, as Maning aptly puts it 'in honour . . . but quite as much in intimidation',[51] at almost every meeting on a marae. In early or pre-colonial times, visitors and hosts were sometimes seen even to engage in mock battle. Polack gives an account of sham fighting preceding a dance of welcome at the funeral of a Kawakawa chief. Using sticks, paddles, short spears and 'whatever lay in their reach', blows were exchanged 'some of which were no sinecure'.[52] Augustus Earle gives a graphic description of another such encounter between an armed Ngaapuhi group and his own visiting party in 1827:

> . . . they certainly formed one of the most beautiful and extraordinary pictures I had ever beheld. The fore ground was formed by a line of naked savages, each resting on one knee, with musket advanced; their gaze fixed on the opposite party; their fine broad muscular backs contrasting with the dark foliage in front, and catching the gleam of the rising sun. The strangers were clothed in the most grotesque manner imaginable; some armed, some naked, some with long beards, others were painted all over with red ochre: every part of each figure was quite still, except the rolling and glaring of their eyes on their opponents. The back ground was formed by the beach, and a number of their beautiful war canoes dancing on the waves; while, in the distance, the mountains on the opposite side of the bay were just tinged with the varied and beautiful colours of the sun, then rising in splendour from behind them.
>
> The stillness of this extraordinary scene did not last long. The Narpooes commenced a noisy and discordant song and dance, yelling, jumping, and making the most hideous faces. This was soon answered by a loud shout from our party, who endeavoured to outdo the Narpooes in making horrible distortions of their countenances: then succeeded another dance from our visiters; after which our friends made a rush, and in a sort of rough joke set them running. Then all joined in a pell-mell sort of encounter, in which numerous hard blows were given and received; then all the party fired their pieces in the air, and the ceremony of landing was thus deemed completed. They then approached each other, and began rubbing noses; and those who were particular friends cried and lamented over each other.[53]

War dance

Peruperu

The war dance proper has its own name, peruperu. In the Te Arawa canoe area, according to Awatere, an alternative name was puha, used when the war dance was performed as a call to arms.[54] A puha is transcribed in full as Song 46 in McLean & Orbell as sung by Kurauia Tahuriorangi of Ngaati Pikiao. The words are cryptic and the translation conjectural, but the intention of the song was clearly to insult the enemy. It begins as follows:

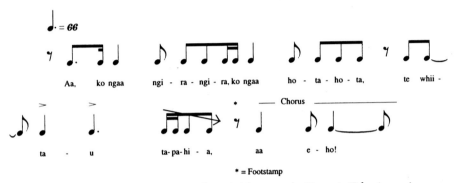

EXAMPLE 10 Puha: Beginning of M&O 46 as sung by Kurauia Tahuriorangi

The peruperu was performed both immediately before battle, at intervals during the battle and afterwards if the battle was successful. Best calls it 'a dance and song of defiance, and also an expression of the joy of the victors'.[55] As a battle performance, it can be regarded above all as a demonstration of rage. The name peruperu derives from the word 'peru', defined by Williams as 'fullness about the eyes and lips when a person is angry'. Many of the characteristics of the peruperu become explicable when this is understood. As Arapeta Awatere, himself a renowned exponent of haka, explains:

> The *peruperu* is the true war-dance and is performed with weapons when the warriors come face to face with the enemy in battle. Because it is the true war-dance, its purpose ought to be explained. Hard conditioning makes the warriors physically and mentally fit to perform this dance which has the psychological purpose of demoralising the enemy by gestures, by posture, by controlled chanting, by conditioning to look ugly, furious to roll the fiery eye, to glare the light of battle therein, to spew the defiant tongue, to control, to distort, to snort, to fart the thunder of the war-god upon the enemy, to stamp furiously, to yell raucous, hideous, blood-curdling sounds, to carry the anger, the *peru*, of Tuumatauenga, the ugly-faced war-god, throughout the heat of battle. *Peruperu* is the intensive form of *peru* 'anger' and this is how the war-dance got its name, and that is its psychological purpose which no other form of haka could match in the past, can match now nor ever will. The *peruperu* ever took pride of place in the warrior-armour of the *tamataane* of yore.[56]

Example 11 is a short peruperu recorded from Awatere in 1958. According to Armstrong it is often used as an introduction to longer peruperu.[57] As such it could also be referred to as a ngeri. The italicised lines are performed by the leader and the remainder by the chorus. Best gives a partial description: he states that on the word 'kuutia' the right arm is bent inwards until the weapon is brought in front of the body. At the word 'wherahia' the right arm is extended.[58]

EXAMPLE 11 *Peruperu: McL 73 as sung by Arapeta Awatere*

Buck gives different and fuller information about the movements:

The two solo lines refer to the action of the arms in the initial movements of the dance, the movement of closing-in signified by the word *kutia* being represented by crossing the arms in front of the body, the right arm carrying the vertical club to the left. The movement of *wherahia* (to open out) is made by uncrossing the arms with both arms extending outwards to their full length, the club being now to the right. Each movement is timed to the beat of the right foot, the left foot remaining stationary. The first solo line takes two beats on *kutia*, the introductory *kia* being clipped short. The first movement on the beat *ku* is open out, and the second on *tia* is closing in. The chorus *au, au* is two beats with a continuance of the sequence of opening out and closing in. Up to the end of the second *au, au*, the movements are measured and stately, but at the commencement of the fifth line, *kia rere*, the action becomes frenzied. The step and the action change and the words are yelled at the top of the voice. The performers leap into the air as one man and come down with both feet on the ground to mark the first beat. From then on, the beat is in two parts. In the first-part, the left foot makes a low hop while the right foot swings back and to the left off the ground. In the second part both feet are off the ground, then both come down with a thud to mark the end of the beat. The right arm swings in to the body in the first part of the beat and is thrust out vigorously to full arm length with the club vertical on the second part of the beat. The left hand is raised on the first half and smacks the left thigh on the end of the beat.[59]

A description of the same peruperu by Shortland, who calls it a 'ngeri', paints an arresting picture of it as seen in the middle of the nineteenth century:

The body of armed men being drawn up in column, four or five abreast, remain for some time in a squatting position, which posture corresponds to the *stand-at-ease* of our soldiers. Suddenly a signal is given by one of the chiefs, who, standing in front, shouts out a short sentence in a peculiar measured tone. On the instant he arrives at the last word, all start on their legs as one man; and the war-song and dance commence. Every right hand brandishes a weapon, while the left hands, being slapt violently against the naked thighs, in regular time, produce a wild sort of accompaniment to the song. At the words *kia rere*, the movements of the actors become furious. Leaping in the air and dancing with violent gestures — their features distorted with horrid grins, their tongues thrust out as far as possible, their eyes rolling upwards so as to show the white — they resemble what the idea may imagine demons to be, rather than human beings.[60]

Fifty accounts of haka in eighteenth- and nineteenth-century travel and missionary literature have been examined by the present writer. Most are identified as war dances and these will be considered first. They reveal numerous common features, several alluded to by Awatere in the passage above and some in the descriptions by Earle and Shortland. Some appear also in the following account of the war dance by J.S. Polack who lived in the Hokianga and the Bay of Islands between 1831 and 1837:

The prime impetus to the commencement of a fight is the practice of the war-dance, which inspires courage, and indomitable hatred towards the enemy, whose nerves in return are supposed to be contrarily affected. Each of the belligerents perform the dance previous to the battle, during every interval and at the close, by the victors. This wild movement is performed by the entire army, entirely naked, except a belt and cartridge-box well filled, firmly attached round the waist. During this mêlée, muskets are discharged in the air, the united yells of perhaps a thousand men, and at times treble that number, all of whom attempt to outvie each other, their voices being stretched to the topmost bent, and bodies keeping time in volitory movements uniform with each other. Some of them jump several feet from the ground, each trying in this also to emulate his neighbour. The feet falling with vehement force to the ground of so numerous a body, the yell in chorus, and the sound elicited by each man at the same moment clapping his left breast with his flattened hand, produces an astounding shock that may be heard in calm weather several miles distant. The valour of the combatants is principally shown in making sorties, there they present themselves (at a respectful distance from the musketry) before the enemy, making a variety of contortions of feature, and throw themselves into attitudes that would defy a European posture-master to copy. They almost roll their eye-balls out of their heads, distend their mouths to an extraordinary width, and show their contempt by darting their tongues in derision at the foe. Modesty is scouted in these exhibitions, the enemy is invited with vehement gestures and fitting language to take aim at the *sternest* portion of the human body as a natural target, and the fate that will eventually befall the besieged is elaborately recounted with all the truths of cannibal ferocity.[61]

Presenting the posterior to the enemy was characteristic of some rather than all war dances, but there is ample confirmation of the other elements of Polack's description and that of Awatere.

Diagnostic of the war dance is the use of weapons, absent in other forms of dancing. Cook's visits to New Zealand in 1769 and 1770 yield the earliest accounts of their use. Monkhouse describes a war dance in which lances carried by the dancers 'were . . . elevated a considerable height above their heads'.[62] Banks said that during the 'War Song and dance' they 'brandish their spears, hack the air with their patoo patoos and shake their darts as if they meant every moment to begin the attack'.[63] John Forster likewise refers to the 'brandishing of their battle-axes' during the war song.[64]

After the acquisition of European weapons, these too were used in the war dance, sometimes replacing the traditional weapons and sometimes in association with them. In one of his accounts of haka, Polack refers to male dancers brandishing muskets with much adroitness 'to display the burnished stocks'.[65] The missionary Henry Williams likewise writes in 1832 of each dancer 'jumping as high as his strength would allow him, tossing up at the same time the stock of his musket, to display the brass, which is kept perfectly bright'.[66] This use of muskets is illustrated to perfection in a well-known drawing first published as a frontispiece to A.S. Thomson's *The Story of New Zealand*.[67]

The shouted accompanying song, characteristic of all haka but especially rowdy in the war dance, is remarked upon by most observers. In some two-thirds of all accounts there are references to shouting, yelling, screeching or screaming. Bidwill described the sound as horrid and not a yell but 'far more dreadful'.[68] Canon Stack, who heard a performance around 1846, thought the yells and shouts were appalling.[69] Scherzer writes of 'loud discordant cries' and 'wild shrieks'.[70] Thomson refers to 'loud, savage whoops'.[71] Buller confirms the distance over which the shouting could be heard as miles in calm weather.[72]

Staring or rolling eyes are a highly visible characteristic of the war dance which impressed a similar number of witnesses. Staring eyes are variously described as 'fixed and starting',[73] 'glaring',[74] 'goggling',[75] and 'protruding'.[76] Samwell in 1769 writes of performers 'staring as if theyr eyes were ready to start out of their heads'.[77] Monkhouse writes of the same dancers staring wildly and 'most hideously'.[78] Cook confirms this as a wide-eyed, even frenzied stare by writing explicitly of 'the eye-lids so forcibly drawn up, that the white appears both above and below, as well as on each side of the lid, so as to form a circle round it'.[79] Banks similarly writes of 'the orbits of the eyes

The war dance, from a sketch by Lance-Sgt. J. Williams, 58th Regiment.
From Thomson 1859 (frontispiece)

enlargd so much that a circle of white is distinctly seen round the iris'.[80] Several writers attest to a still more startling and horrible effect of turning the eyes up until the pupils were hidden and only the whites were visible.[81] Maning evidently observed the same practice when he saw dancers 'showing the whites of their eyes' and 'the eyes all white'.[82]

Even more dramatic was the combination of the above methods with eye movement. Numerous writers affirm the use made in the war dance of distended rolling eyes or eyeballs.[83] In passages additional to the one already quoted, Polack writes of 'eyeballs rolling to and fro in their sockets' and 'rolling the eyeballs to and fro . . . that at times the ball becomes almost inverted'.[84]

Shared with other forms of haka, but again pre-eminent in the war dance or peruperu, was the use of facial contortions or grimacing (puukana). Similar grimacing was reported in the war dances of Tahiti at the time of first European contact, so this characteristic of Maori dancing may well date back to the departure of the Maori ancestors from Eastern Polynesia a thousand or more years ago.

Numerous reports of the war dance refer to the face or features as 'distorted'. Cruise[85] describes them as 'violently distorted' and Polack as 'dis-

51

Tahiti: 'The wry Mouth, or manner of defying their Enemies'. Pencil sketch by Sydney Parkinson, 1769

torted into every possible shape'.[86] Shortland,[87] as also Beechey,[88] writes of 'features distorted with horrid grins'. Mouths are referred to as 'gaping'[89] and nostrils as 'inflated'.[90] Polack characterised dancers as 'distending their mouths, like hammer-headed sharks, from ear to ear'.[91] Dix and Oliver, who saw a mock exhibition of the war dance on shipboard, were impressed with the 'hideous contortions and tiger-like ferocity' of the dancers' faces and 'the gnashing and grinding of their teeth'.[92]

Along with grimacing, again predominantly in the war dance, there are frequent reports of body contortions, though seldom specific as to their nature. From Cook's voyages, Banks,[93] Samwell,[94] and Cook himself[95] all refer to them. Nicholas, in 1817, writes generally of 'convulsive excesses'[96] and Bellingshausen six years later of 'extraordinary muscular contortions'.[97] Most later writers are no more enlightening. However, it would appear that convulsive movements were used involving most of the body. From about 1833 through to 1884, half a dozen writers independently speak of seeing every muscle in the dancers' bodies 'quivering'[98] or 'convulsed'.[99] Most graphic of all, Kerry-Nicholls states: 'the limbs trembled from the feet upwards, until every muscle in the body appeared to shake and twist, as if from the thrilling effects of a galvanic current'.[100]

The most extreme grimace used in the war dance was the out-thrust tongue. Nowadays it is sometimes used by Maori entertainers for comic effect. In the older accounts it appears to have been exclusive to the war

'The manner in which the New Zealand Warriors defy their Enemies.'
Drawn by Sydney Parkinson in 1769

dance. Descriptions of the war dance from Captain Cook onwards refer to tongues extended, extruded, hanging out, lolling, lolling out, out-hanging, protruding, thrust forward or thrust out — as far as possible, incredibly far, in exaggerated fashion, to the fullest extent, or to incredible length. Polack commented: 'The tongue was thrust out of the mouth with an extension impossible for a European to copy; early and long practice only could accomplish it.'[101]

Also perhaps exclusive to the war dance was a leap in which all of the performers jumped together to a height which observers found amazing. Again, there are numerous accounts. Two forms of leaping seem to have been extant. One was a perpendicular or vertical leap on the spot. The other was a swinging leap from side to side. Jumps of the first kind are reported by Cruise who says the manoeuvre was done 'as high and as frequently as possible';[102] by Polack who says it was 'often repeated in a simultaneous manner';[103] and by Bambridge[104] who observed it in 1843. The side to side jump was seen at Poverty Bay in 1769 by Gore and by Monkhouse who says 'each man jump'd with a swinging motion . . . to the right and left alternately'.[105] The missionary Richard Taylor saw the same at Lake Taupo in 1846 and Kerry-Nicholls about three decades later in the King Country.[106] The height of the leap must indeed have been considerable: Buller[107] says the dancers made the ground shake as they came down again.

The sideways jump: hari taua (war dance)

The leap: Ngaati Tuuwharetoa haka at Waitangi, 1934

Again highly characteristic of the war dance, and probably exclusive to it, was the custom of males dancing naked. After the middle of the nineteenth century, the missionary and travel literature shows a transition from absolute to partial nudity, doubtless as a result of adapting to European norms of behaviour. The early reports, however, are unequivocal. Cruise, who visited New Zealand in 1820, represents war dance performers as 'perfectly naked';[108] John Morgan, a missionary from 1836 to 1838, as 'nearly all naked';[109] and Buller, who lived in New Zealand from 1836 to 1876, as 'all in a state of nudity'.[110] Wilkes saw a mock exhibition of the war dance in 1840 in which some of the performers were 'entirely naked'.[111] Several writers from the 1820s through to the 1850s describe performers throwing off their cloaks, mats or garments for the war dance.[112] It was a custom which probably accounts for much of the opprobrium heaped upon the war dance by the early missionaries, and other visitors too appear to have been shocked by it. Augustus Earle's first experience of native New Zealanders on entering Hokianga Harbour in 1827 was a 'dance of welcome' which the 'lady passengers were obliged to leave, as when the dance began, each man proceeded to strip himself naked, a custom indispensible amongst themselves'.[113]

A rationale for nudity in the war dance is provided in reports of 1844 by Angas who says not only that the warriors 'dance naked',[114] but that they 'fight naked'.[115] Whether the Maori customarily fought naked or only in some circumstances is not clear. In his book *Maori Warfare*, Vayda[116] cites only secondary sources concerning Maori apparel in warfare. War belts, mats

Naked war dance performed in 1844 at Ohinemutu on the shores of Lake Rotorua. Body tattoo is visible on some of the warriors. From Angas The New Zealanders Illustrated

and, on occasion, war cloaks soaked with water to help them repel spear thrusts are said to have been worn.

Thomson[117] and others, nevertheless, are cited as suggesting that nothing was worn. Fighting naked would have had some merit. It would have left the warriors unencumbered in battle, and it would have been an absolute requirement for the display both of body tattooing and body paint. It may also have had implications in terms of phallic display. According to Buck,[118] the male organ was figuratively regarded as a symbol of virility and courage so that if the leader of a war party awoke with an erection on the morning before battle, it was taken as proof that his courage ran high and as an omen of success. Buck gives the opening lines of a Ngaati Raukawa war dance in which the enemy was taunted with the words:

> *Aawhea too ure ka riri*   When will your penis become enraged,
> *Aawhea too ure ka tora?* When will your penis become erect?

Vayda states that the Maori in general seem to have regarded an erect penis as a sign of courage,[119] and he recounts the story of Taketake whose upright penis so filled the enemy with admiration that they postponed an attack, giving their opponents an advantage and earning for Taketake's descendants the phrase '*ngaa uri o Taketake ure roa* — the people of Taketake whose penis was long'.

Naked dancing is reported as having taken place on occasion in modern times as well, but as a form of derision. In his biography of Sir Maui Pomare, Cody[120] tells of an occasion in 1917 when Pomare was met at the Waahi railway station by a hostile crowd and escorted to the riverside where, standing naked in the water, a group danced a haka in which, at appropriate times in the dance, they turned their bare bottoms towards the visitor. This was a revival of an old-time haka demonstrative of extreme contempt — 'the absolute in loathing and contumely'. Pomare is reported to have proved himself equal to the occasion by making himself comfortable on the riverbank and smoking pipe after pipe with every indication of enjoyment until the haka party was forced by the coldness of the water to give up. More recently, in 1983, and in similar vein, the Maori activist Dun Mihaka presented his buttocks to the Prince and Princess of Wales, provoking some controversy at the time.[121]

An adjunct of nudity, again characteristic of the war dance, was the use of body paint, alone or together with face paint. Generally charcoal seems to have been used on the face and red ochre and oil with or without charcoal on the body. Reports of this practice seem to be limited to the period between 1827 and about 1850.[122]

Unsurprisingly, a definitive characteristic of the war dance was its ability to inspire fear. Samwell, in his journal of 1777, considered it 'admirably calculated to strike Terror into their Enemies'[123] and Polack as 'calculated to excite the most alarming fears'.[124] Many early observers found it frightening to watch. Nicholas said it 'might inspire even the most resolute mind with terror and dismay'.[125] Others called it 'frightful'[126] or 'terrific'.[127] Bidwill thought it 'sufficient to strike terror into any man'.[128] Coote called it 'a most awful and terrorful experience'.[129] And when Maori crew from a whale ship exhibited a war dance in Tahiti in 1826, some of the Tahitians 'ran away in fear'.[130]

Some of the actions isolated above were explicitly recognised as components of dancing by the Maori themselves, as shown by the existence of terminology for them. As defined by Williams, terms used include moteko, pooteetee, whaakana, whakamoteko and whakamenemene (make grimaces), ngangahu (distort the features), puukana and tahu (stare wildly, distort the countenance), weru (pout or project the lips), whaatero or wheetero (protrude [the tongue]), whakapii (contort the body and features) and whakatea (show the whites of the eyes). Additionally, Best[131] gives 'whetee' for 'bulging out of the eyes' (defined in Williams as 'stare wildly').[132]

Tuutuungaarahu

A type of war dance which exploited the leap referred to earlier was the tuutuungaarahu (Waikato), whakatuuwaewae (Ngaati Porou), tuu ngaarahu (Ngaapuhi and Ngaati Porou), ngaarahu (Te Arawa and Ngaapuhi) or whakarewarewa (Te Arawa).[133] It was a divinatory dance to find out whether a war party was ready for battle. During the dance, the entire party leaped high in the air with both feet off the ground.[134] Old men, who acted as judges, crouched low and looked along the ground. If only one man in 500 was out of time, his feet would be seen to be down when all the others were up and this would be taken as an omen against success. In such a case, the war party would not set out and, according to Buck, 'the troops would be condemned to more training until their leg drill was perfect'.[135] Also divinatory in purpose, according to Best,[136] was the haka tuutohu or tuuranga a tohu (tohu = tuutohu, 'sign' or 'indication'). Best says it was performed without weapons in a wedge formation. When asked about the latter term, Arapeta Awatere[137] equated it with tuutuungaarahu. Other variants of the above terms include ngaarahu taua, ngaarehu, tuungaarehu, tuupeke, tuutuuwaewae and whakakite waewae, all of obvious derivation if Williams is consulted.

General characteristics of haka

Most haka, including war dances, share characteristics additional to those cited above for the war dance. They are common enough not to require detailed attribution.

A conspicuous characteristic of haka is the use of foot stamping. About a third of all accounts refer to it, running the gamut from the eighteenth century to the present day. Crozet,[138] who saw frequent dancing on shipboard in 1772, feared the dancers would break through the deck, as did Earle[139] and Markham[140] on different occasions more than half a century later. Maning described a war dance during which he 'felt the ground plainly trembling'.[141]

Again characteristic, and again mentioned in perhaps a third of the accounts, is body percussion. Thigh slapping and chest beating occur about equally. The former is first reported by Monkhouse[142] in 1769 and the latter in 1772 by Les Dez, who also mentions dancers striking themselves on the arms.[143] Sometimes both hands appear to have been used and at others one, probably depending on whether the other hand was occupied with holding a weapon or with a different action. Thomson[144] writes of dancers striking their thighs with the open left hand as do Shortland,[145] Buller[146] and Kerry-Nicholls.[147] Polack[148] writes of dancers striking the 'left breast with right hand flatted' but Hodgskin[149] of hitting the breasts alternately with each hand.

Quivering or trembling the hands in the haka is termed kakapa (lit. 'flutter' or 'quiver'). Williams also gives whaakapakapa and whakakurepe. Other terms for it are kapakapa and wiri or wiriwiri. Also used are aroarowhaki, aroarowhati and aroarokapa but these, according to Arapeta Awatere,[150] refer to actions generally, including finger trembling but not exclusive to it. Hand trembling in the haka is well attested in the literature but is seldom mentioned for the war dance. Seeming exceptions to the general rule are two King Country performances in the 1880s, one with all the trappings of

Maori war dance, Taranaki, c.1860. Pencil and watercolour by William Strutt.
PHOTO: *Alexander Turnbull Library, 69410¹/₂*

the war dance from Te Kooti and his men[151] and the other seen by Potts.[152] It would appear, nevertheless, that hand quivering is uncharacteristic of the war dance. Arapeta Awatere[153] was definite that it was not used in the peruperu or tuutuungaarahu.

If myth is a guide, the hand quivering movement was evidently regarded as essential to the haka by the Maori themselves. Best refers to the mythic origin of the haka 'in the *Haka a Taane-rore* (the dancing of Taane-rore), a name applied to the quivering appearance of the atmosphere as seen on hot summer days', also known as 'the *Haka a Raumati*, the dancing of the Summer Maid, and . . . the origin of all the *haka* of the world'.[154]

Hand quivering has been imported into the modern action song and, like the other movements used, is subject to rules which are formulated from time to time and applied to competitive dancing. In a 1971 interview, Arapeta Awatere[155] explained the approved movement at this time as 'rotational', i.e. done from the wrist and forearm with fingers and thumbs closed together. Moving the fingers by themselves he regarded as incorrect. The wrist had to be held not drooping or sticking up but level with the forearm. Also, the hands were not allowed to cross before the face, but had to move above or below. Even allowing for the imprecision of untrained observers, it is unlikely that such rules were followed in early performances. One account refers to quivering hands and arms.[156] Others, in about equal numbers, from Captain Cook onwards, refer to rapidly trembling or quivering fingers, hands, or both.

In the published accounts, arm and body movements used in the haka are referred to, as a rule, in general terms only. A notable exception is a description by Monkhouse of dancing seen by him in 1769. Although there are some elements of peruperu, the use of finger trembling and the wearing of clothing suggests that this performance was not a war dance.

> They first prepared themselves by passing some Cloth, which they borrowed for the occasion, round their loins, till now totally without any covering: then placing themselves back to back a little asunder the foremost begins, the others following his motions minutely, with lifting up his right leg, at the same instant raising his arms to a horizontal Position, and bending his forearm a little, he trembles his fingers with great quickness — begins a kind of song, and the right leg being raised as above, off they go, beating time singing & trembling the fingers in the most exact uniformity — the body is now and then inclined to one side or the other — sometimes they bend forwards exceedingly low and then suddenly raise themselves, extending their arms, and staring most hideously — at one time, they make a half turn and face one way, and in two or three seconds [return] to their former position, in doing of which they bend forwards make a large sweep downwards with both Arms, extended, and as they turn upon the left foot, elevate their arms in the curve, stare wildly, & pronounce a part of the song with a savage hoarse expiration — this part of the ceremony generally closes the dance.[157]

The uniformity of action alluded to by Monkhouse is a noteworthy characteristic of haka style, emphasised also by numerous later writers. Cruise wrote of a performance in 1820:

> It is singular how simultaneous even the slightest motion of the fingers is, with all the individuals in the group, be their number what it may; no irregularity is perceptible in the time and manner of their movements.[158]

Others also refer to simultaneity of movement.[159] Earle found 'the regularity of their movements truely astonishing'.[160] Maning writes of 'measured and uniform gesticulation'.[161] A frequent comment is that the dancers perform as if they are one person[162] or, more colourfully, as if 'actuated by one impulse'[163] or 'moved by one wire'.[164]

In tandem with unison or uniform body movement is precision of time-keeping which similarly impressed numerous observers. Most refer to it as 'correct', 'exact', 'excellent', 'marvellous', 'perfect' or 'proper'. Bidwill[165] thought it the most correct it is possible to imagine. Cook and his men sometimes heard haka (or perhaps paddling songs in similar style) from canoes and were again impressed with their timing. Paddles evidently served as a percussive device to supplement or substitute for the more usual body percussion, drawing a remark from Cook: 'and in their song they keep time with such exactness, that I have often heard above an hundred paddles struck against the sides of their boats at once, so as to produce but a single sound, at the division of their music'.[166]

The 'savage hoarse expiration' referred to by Monkhouse at the end of the dance appears also in a number of subsequent accounts, about as often in the war dance as in haka of a non-warlike nature. Descriptions of it are remarkably similar. In a 1770 account, Banks said each strain ended in concert 'with a loud and deep fetchd sigh';[167] half a century later, de Sainson called it a 'deep moan';[168] and 'an awful tremendous groan'.[169] Buller writes of the war dance 'ending with a long deep sough';[170] Thomson likewise said it 'terminated with a long, deep, expressive sigh'[171] and identical words are used by Kerry-Nicholls.[172] Talbot writes of chanting interrupted at intervals 'with a long gasping sigh'.[173] As can be seen, the moan, groan, sigh or sough typically ends the haka or a section of it.

When reference is made to the spatial organisation of haka dancers, they are described usually as arranged in rows, ranks or lines, though Thomson refers also to dancers standing in squares.[174] The number of rows would have depended on the number of dancers taking part, and perhaps also on the space available as, for example, when a haka was performed on shipboard. In one shipboard haka seen by George Forster,[175] there was only a single row. Three separate writers in the 1880s describe haka dancers as standing in two rows, with men in one line and women in the other.[176] Polack observed rows of dancers three deep on one occasion and four on another.[177]

Maori war dance at time of early missionaries, from a lantern slide. PHOTO: *Leon Clement Collection, Alexander Turnbull Library, F 127094¹/₂*

Dancers 'four or five abreast' are reported by Shortland,[178] and Hodgskin saw 200 dancers in rows six or seven deep.[179]

As earlier indicated, participation by women as well as men in haka performances, including the war dance, was not uncommon. It may, indeed, have been usual as it is referred to in reports almost as frequently as diagnostic haka traits such as body percussion and foot stamping. As early as 1769, at Tolaga Bay, Banks witnessed a war song in which both men and women joined, distorting their faces 'most hideously', rolling their eyes and 'putting out their tongues'.[180]

Nicholas saw a performance in a canoe which he found 'menacing and terrible':

> The women were no less violent in all their attitudes and movements than the men; they raved and roared with equal fury, and the distinction of sex appearing no longer visible, was completely lost in their convulsive excesses.[181]

Earle was astonished in 1827 to find that 'women mixed in the dance indiscriminately with the men, and went through all those horrid gestures with seemingly as much pleasure as the warriors themselves'.[182] The missionary Henry Williams, in a journal entry of 1833, complained about: 'The noise of the women in the *Pa* every evening quite unbearable, *haka*ing and dancing, like so many infernals . . . their shrieks and yells are truely dis-

'A dance of New Zealanders.' Lithograph by Augustus Earle

mal'.[183] And a decade later, Wakefield, like Earle, writes of women joining in the dance 'yelling and grimacing with as demoniacal a frenzy as any of the men'.[184]

Maori clothing was similar for both men and women, whether or not they were dancing. As observed by Cook, men wore a belt and women a girdle and sometimes no other clothing. When males did not dance entirely naked they seem generally to have stripped to the waist, and this practice was followed also by the females. Cruise observed that preparatory to the dance 'the upper mat or garment is laid aside for both men and women'.[185] Polack gives a more elaborate description of a dance in which the males were naked and the women 'had stripped themselves to the waist, leaving their budding charms exposed'.[186] The implication is that these women were young, but Polack specifically notes that married women and widows also took part.

When haka leaders are mentioned in accounts, they are generally stated to be male. However, females not only took part in haka but also acted as leaders, even in the war dance. In the latter case they seem almost to have been surrogate men, performing the same actions as the men including the use of the out-thrust tongue.[187] Customarily they were old, nude like the men, and made up to look as hideous as possible. Buller refers to 'old women, disfigured with red ochre, acting as fuglemen' in the war dance.[188] Thomson writes similarly of 'old naked women . . . acting as fuglers'[189] and Potts of 'blue lipped crones, that leaped with frenzied bounds'.[190] Best comments that 'few uglier sights could be imagined than these old hags when leading a *haka* or war-dance'.[191]

Usually, the leader of a haka shouts out a line or two of the song and is answered in chorus by a unison shouted refrain from the other dancers. The responsorial musical form, like all other haka traits, can readily be documented in travel and missionary literature. As good a description as any is provided by George Forster:

> . . . one of them sung some words in a rude manner, and all the rest accom-

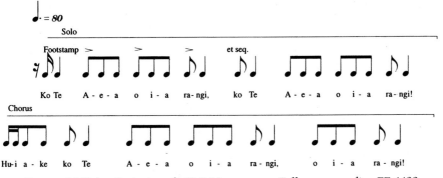

EXAMPLE 12 *Haka: Beginning of M&O 18 as sung on Folkways recording FE 4433*

panied the gestures he made, alternately extending their arms, and stamping with their feet in a violent and almost frantic manner. The last words, which we might suppose the burden of the song, or a chorus, they all repeated together.[192]

A good example of the responsorial form of haka is seen in Song 18 in McLean & Orbell, the famous 'Wairangi haka', beginning as in Example 12. The song is unique in its use of four leaders rather than the usual one. A full explanation, together with a description of the movements of the haka, is given in McLean & Orbell.

Haka nomenclature

Peruperu, puha, and the tuutuungaarahu or equivalents were the only posture dances in which weapons were used. These may be glossed by use of the English term 'war dance'. There is, however, no single term in Maori for them all. Nor is there a single unambiguous word, either in Maori or in English, to designate posture dances performed without weapons. Armstrong,[193] whose book is one of the few on the subject, makes use of the term 'peruperu' for the one and 'haka taparahi' for the other, but does not specifically reveal his sources. The distinction is tidy but is certainly wrong for peruperu and is true of haka taparahi only in so far as Armstrong's judgement has been adopted by others. It appears to have resulted from misunderstanding. The haka taparahi is indeed performed without weapons, but so are numerous other forms of haka which are not taparahi. Armstrong claims that peruperu and haka taparahi are *types* of haka under which all the others can be subsumed, whereas the other names designate *purpose*. Thus he speaks of the tuutuungaarahu as a peruperu and the maimai (see later) as a haka taparahi because the one is performed with weapons and the other without. In so doing he appears to have imposed a division of his own making. Taparahi is defined by Williams as 'A vigorous, ceremonial *haka*'. Best[194] lists it amongst types of haka practised by the Ngaati Porou tribe and states it was performed in a square with ranks of dancers, an arm's length apart, facing in the same direction. Arapeta Awatere, himself of Ngaati Porou, confirms it was a ceremonial dance, performed without weapons.[195] There is no reason to suppose, however, that all haka without weapons could be so designated. To the present writer, Awatere provided information contrary to Armstrong and consistent with that given by Best.[196] He said that the haka taparahi was performed by men with a broad front stance, i.e. with chests facing outwards. It was indeed performed without weapons but this, according to Awatere, was incidental as a broad front stance could not be adopted if weapons were carried.[197]

Armstrong may also have erred in his assumption of sub-classes of haka. By itself the term 'haka' is used loosely as an overall term for posture dances of all kinds, including war dances, and this usage is now well established whatever the case may have been in the past. Williams defines haka simply as 'dance' or 'song accompanying a dance'.[198] Best uses it as inclusive of the war dance or peruperu and states that it is a generic term.[199] However, by treating the separately named forms of posture dance as qualifiers for the term 'haka' instead of terms in their own right, Armstrong appears again to be in error. In common usage, a maimai is named simply as such, and not a 'haka maimai' as represented by Armstrong,[200] even though it makes use of haka movements; and, although a peruperu is a haka in the broad sense of the word, the term peruperu also stands properly alone rather than becoming 'haka peruperu' as Armstrong would have it.[201]

Types of haka

There are numerous separately named types of posture dance. Some appear to have been locally occurring equivalents of terms in use elsewhere. Others served specific needs and were named accordingly. Many are obsolete. Some appear in the literature as types of haka and others, as explained above, were evidently thought of as song types in their own right. For convenience, all will be treated here together.

The several forms of war dance have already been described, as has the haka taparahi. Others may be grouped according to whether the terms refer to function, manner of performance, or grouping of performers.

By function

Ngeri: In his *Games and Pastimes*, Best seems to restrict this term to derisive songs.[202] But in another publication, he reveals this usage as particular to the Tuuhoe tribe whereas elsewhere the term is applied to other classes of songs such as work songs and food-carrying songs.[203] Even amongst Tuuhoe it appears that the ngeri is no longer or possibly never was invariably derisive. Kino Hughes of Tuuhoe and Marata Te Tomo of Ngaati Tuuwharetoa confirmed the latter part of Best's information for their own tribes.[204] When asked about the ngeri, Kino said it was a heriheri kai (food-bearing song); Marata said that the ngeri, unlike compositions such as the maemae, 'is something that you use at all times — at any time. . . . Even these things you do when people are eating, harihari kai, they're called ngeri.' She agreed with her son, who was present, that compositions not called ngeri were used on more formal occasions. From these statements it appears that the term 'ngeri' can be used for any short informal composition in haka form performed with or without dance. Arapeta Awatere defined the ngeri as a short exhortation 'pepping up the party for action' and performed, as a rule, preliminary to another haka.[205] In a later interview he defined the ngeri as an exhortation addressed to one's own side: 'Come on boys, give it a go.'[206] Others take a similar view. Armstrong, who may have obtained his information from Awatere, says the purpose of the ngeri 'is to exhort warriors before

65

going into battle or commencing some noble endeavour'[207] and Karetu refers to it as a short haka with no set movements 'to stiffen the sinews, to summon up the blood'.[208]

Under the heading of ngeri, Best goes on to list hahani, tuutara, tumoto and kaioraora all as types of ngeri.[209] All are indeed abusive. But the kaioraora is a form of paatere, readily distinguishable from the ngeri by its characteristic rhythms. Hahani = hanihani is identified by Arapeta Awatere as synonymous with kaioraora and likewise a form of paatere.[210] The two remaining terms are, as stated by Best, forms of haka or ngeri:

Tuutara = kootaratara[211] are words identified by Awatere as denoting the action of the male penis entering the female vagina. The term means 'digging in' and the action is used as a form of sexual imagery to express derision. Awatere recited such a haka for the author; it contained the lines:

Ko te kootiritiri
Ko te kootaratara

The word kootiritiri is also indicative of digging, denoting the action of a spade entering the ground.[212]

Tumoto is defined by Williams as 'a virulent song chanted as revenge for some injury or defeat'. A complete tumoto, sung by Turau and Marata Te Tomo of Ngaati Tuuwharetoa, is transcribed and translated in McLean & Orbell as Song 34. The opening lines are as follows:

EXAMPLE 13 *Tumoto: Beginning of M&O 34 as sung by Turau and Marata Te Tomo*

Best[213] equates tumoto with kaioraora (see later) but, as already stated, the latter is musically a paatere rather than a haka.

Pirori: According to Best, the haka pirori was:

accompanied by an incisive, insulting, or virulent song, for the purpose of avenging an injury or insult received. The performers were absolutely naked and performed every act they could think of to express a desire to belittle and insult the party before whom they were performing. They exposed themselves by bending the legs, by turning their backs etc., so as to flout the visitors.[214]

Best saw one performed in 1898. Arapeta Awatere last saw one in 1926.

He said the term was from Ngaati Porou and meant 'swaying'. The Tuuhoe equivalent was piiwari. It was expressive of the pliability and weakness of the backbone of a tribe or person and the dance could be done in self-depreciation.[215]

By manner of performance

Haka horuhoru: Best says this haka was performed in a kneeling position by members of both sexes; the term 'horuhoru' describes deep grunting and rasping sounds made by the performers.[216]

Haka koiri: Given by Armstrong as a haka containing swaying motions.[217] The term may be a variant of haka koowiri or koowhiri, several of which have been recorded from Kurauia Tahuriorangi of Ngaati Pikiao (McL 741, 746–8 & 750–1). The term 'koowiri' refers to twisting movements of the hands and feet.[218] Williams (1975) says it means 'whirl around'. A haka kowiri appears in McLean & Orbell as Song 47, as sung by Kurauia Tahuriorangi. As in other forms of haka, leader solos alternate with a choral response, beginning as follows:

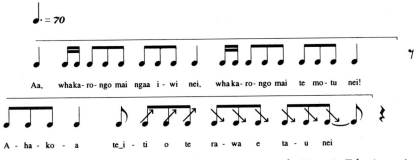

EXAMPLE 14 *Haka koowiri: Beginning of M&O 47 as sung by Kurauia Tahuriorangi*

Matohi: A kind of haka performed by men only (Williams) 'in which they stoop and elevate their posteriors in an absurd manner'.[219]

Haka pikari: From pikari 'shuffle the feet' (Williams), a haka implying certain movements of the legs not used in other forms.[220]

By grouping of performers

Haka aroaakapa: A haka with the performers in two or more ranks facing in the same direction.[221] Williams gives the term as meaning 'row, rank, front rank'.

Haka porowhaa: lit. 'four-sided, square' (Williams). A haka in which the performers form a square facing four ways.[222]

By virtue of their formation, the haka taparahi and the haka tuutohu also belong under this heading.

FUNERAL COMPOSITIONS IN HAKA STYLE

Maemae, manawawera, pihe and pookeka are names from different tribal areas for a type of composition performed at funerals. It has both song and action components. The song, which is usually quite lengthy, is shouted in haka style, in chorus, with a leader introducing each stanza. Haka movements are also performed but, except perhaps for the pihe, are done individually without the group uniformity characteristic of haka. Additionally, manawawera, pihe and perhaps pookeka have associations with warfare.

Maemae

An alternative spelling is maimai. Williams does not list the term 'maemae' as a song type but gives 'maimai' as 'a dance, or *haka*, to welcome guests at a *tangi* [funeral]'. Arapeta Awatere[223] has suggested that the one spelling may derive from mamae (pain) and the other from mai ('here' with connotations of welcome). The maemae is sung accompanied by the waving of green leaves as an expression of grief. Best[224] says it was a haka performed at an uhunga ceremony for mourning the dead. He adds that 'the women indulged in the swaying motions of the body and arms known as *aroarowhaki*, the men in somewhat more vehement *piikari* motions'.

The missionary Richard Taylor gives an extended description of a performance seen at Pukawa on the shores of Lake Taupo in 1846 which has all the hallmarks of the war dance but is identified by him as a maimai intended to express grief. The performers, who were both male and female, while uttering a 'kind of song', brandished spears, showed the whites of their eyes and jumped together with both feet first to one side and then the other, some protruding their tongues 'in a most unnatural way'.[225] It is clear that the maemae was less a form of mourning than an expression of anger at death.

After recording a maemae (McL 1116), the singer, Marata Te Tomo of Ngaati Tuuwharetoa did actions with puukana throughout a replay, explaining: 'That's how you dance for that sort of thing.' She added that both men and women did actions individually. 'There's always just one or two, just swinging, while the other hard cases do the puukana.' Marata went on to explain that several maemae may be strung together to make a longer song in performance. The song is performed at the tangi with the body present. The dead person is often addressed in the song with words such as 'Why have you died?' This, she said, is the formal use of the song, but it can be performed at other times, to start or finish a speech, as an introduction to a haka, or just for fun. A maemae is transcribed in full as Song 12 in McLean & Orbell as sung by Turau and Marata Te Tomo of Ngaati Tuuwharetoa. Example 15 is the final stanza.

Maemae in haka style are characteristic of Ngaati Tuuwharetoa tribe. A musically different but functionally identical form of maemae is performed

EXAMPLE 15 Maemae: Last stanza of M&O 12 as sung by Turau and Marata Te Tomo

EXAMPLE 16 Maemae: Beginning of McL 490 as sung by Tuku Bailey and Hannah Nicholas

by Taranaki tribes while the singers, again waving pieces of greenery, precede the corpse. Example 16, as sung by Tuku Bailey and Hannah Nicholas of Te Ati Awa tribe, is performed metrically in iambic rhythms, at a fairly slow tempo, with two phrases to each line of text and a uniform four beats in each phrase. It was composed by Pereni Ngaruaki, daughter of the Taranaki religious leader, Te Whiti-o-Rongomai, on the death of her father in 1907.

Manawawera

The manawawera belongs to Tuuhoe tribe. Best says it was performed to upbraid members of a defeated war party, by relatives of the slain who arrayed themselves for the purpose in old, ragged, dirty garments.[226] Elsewhere, Best glosses the term manawawera as 'seared heart' and says:

> As the defeated warriors marched into the village home they were met by a band of people, principally women, dressed in old disreputable garments (the sackcloth and ashes of the Maori), who pranced before them and indulged in those violent energetic movements termed 'whakapi' or 'pikari' the emitting of most distressing grunts and the exhibiting of the whites of the eyes.[227] They would perform and sing the haka, which . . . denoted grief for those slain and anger against the hapless who had lost the day and returned alive.[228]

John Rangihau of Tuuhoe defined the manawawera as meaning literally 'burning heart' and gave information amplifying that of Best as follows:

> The *manawawera* is a song sung by people who have survived the onslaught of an enemy, or on the death of a great chief or the death of a person by a particularly nasty accident. The song belittles the opposing people responsible for the death. Musically it is like a very vigorous *haka*. The actions are not uniform like a *haka*, but spontaneous; when the song degrades others, 'the more obscene the better.'[229]

In support of his statement, Rangihau said that he himself had performed a manawawera naked with a woman. Ideally several people should perform it.

It is possible that the manawawera has now lost its connotation of abuse of an enemy, becoming appropriate for deaths by other causes as well. Kino Hughes of Tuuhoe confirmed that the manawawera is performed by a group for a dead person. The only correct time to perform one is while coming on to the marae. Impromptu haka actions with puukana are performed by indi-

EXAMPLE 17 Manawawera: Beginning of McL 23A as led by Ira Manihera

viduals until the group gets near the dead body.[230] Later, he said that the manawawera is the Tuuhoe equivalent of the pookeka (see later) performed when anyone 'kua mate' (has died).[231]

Example 17 is the beginning of a manawawera as led by Ira Manihera of Tuuhoe in 1958. It is performed in standard haka style.

Pihe

This song type is glossed in Williams as a 'Dirge accompanied with waving of the arms in token of grief'. There is considerable attention to it in the ethnographic and travel literature, some reviewed by Oppenheim.[232]

The pihe is the northern tribes equivalent of the maemae and manawawera described above.[233] In 1820, the Bay of Islands missionary Thomas Kendall and the Cambridge University linguist Samuel Lee published their pioneer *Grammar and Vocabulary of the Language of New Zealand* in which appears the earliest known written text of a pihe ('Papa te whatitiri, i runga nei').[234] The song would have been obtained at dictation from the Ngaapuhi chief Hongi Hika or his brother-in-law, Waikato, who visited England with Kendall and collaborated with compiling the *Grammar*. A performance by a party of young men, very likely of the self-same pihe, was witnessed in 1821 by the missionaries Francis Hall and James Kemp when Hongi returned to Kerikeri from Thames with war canoes containing the bodies of two warriors who had been killed:

> They yelled and jumped, brandishing their weapons, and threw up human heads in the air in a shocking manner; but this was only a prelude to the horrid work which was about to follow. An awful pause ensued. At length the canoes moved slowly and touched the shore, when the widow of Tete and other women rushed down upon the beach in a frenzy of rage, and beat in pieces the carved work at the head of the canoes with poles. They proceeded to pull out three prisoners into the water and beat them to death. The frantic widow then went to another canoe and killed a female prisoner.[235]

In 1827, Dumont d'Urville visited New Zealand with a copy of Kendall's *Grammar* in hand and tested the people at each of his stopping places for their knowledge of this pihe which he thought to be a 'national song'. His efforts established it as known in part at Tokomaru Bay on the East Coast and in full at Tolaga Bay and the Waitemata. At Waitemata a chief, Rangi, was amazed to see d'Urville repeat the song after him from the grammar book. Unsurprisingly, the song was not known at Tasman Bay in the South Island.[236] D'Urville's interest in the pihe was shown also much earlier during a visit to the Bay of Islands in 1824 when he questioned a chief, Tuai, extensively about it in an attempt to establish the meaning of the text. In this he was unsuccessful, but a few scraps of information emerge which confirm the pihe both as a funeral song and as related to the war dance:

The *Pihe* is the solemn ode which warriors chant in chorus, sometimes after the fight, always by the fire that consumes the meal of the God, *Kai-Atoua*, and at funeral ceremonies . . . No doubt, when several hundred warriors clad in their war-dress, fully armed and standing in one or two ranks chant together this solemn hymn and accompany it with terrifying menacing gestures, the effect produced must be impressive, ominous and terrifying.[237]

Father Catherin Servant, a Marist missionary in the Hokianga from 1838 to 1842, gives another text of the Kendall pihe about which he writes:

. . . nothing is more striking than this *pihe* or chant of grief, which the natives perform in noisy, deep, harsh and plaintive voices: the animated, broken quality they give to this song in unison, invokes sadness. It appears they accompany their song of grief with rapid gestures.[238]

Dieffenbach calls the pihe a funeral ode and gives a text somewhat variant from that of Kendall. He explains that the song was modified according to the circumstances of death, whether in battle or by disease.[239]

Other extant texts of the same song include manuscripts by the Hokianga chief Mohi Tawhai and the Ngaapuhi tohunga Aperahama Taonui, dated 1885 and 1849 respectively. These are translated with explanatory notes by George Graham.[240] Quotations from the song are stated by Graham[241] to have been used in many of the laments in Sir George Grey's *Nga Moteatea*.[242]

Tregear gives a lengthy account of pihe without revealing when or where the event described took place:[243]

Over the corpse of a warrior especially if he had been killed in battle the war-dirge or scalp-dance (*pihi*) was chanted and executed. The manner thereof was as follows. An old chief rushed from the house of the deceased, clad only in a waist girdle of leaves, and drove his spear into the ground alongside the corpse, with the shout, 'That is one for Tu (the war god)!' The old men, at the cry, formed a solid square, each man holding in his hand a fern-stalk on which was fastened a lock of hair taken from the (preserved) head of an enemy. Advancing with even and solid tread towards the body, each held up the hair-decorated fern-stalk in the air repeating the *pihe* chant, commencing:
Tu is enraged and Rongomai descends.
(*Tu ka riri, Rongomai ka heke.*)
The points of the chorus were marked by the simultaneous lowering and uplifting of the fern-stalks, and in the middle of the chant the square of men divided into two parties, forming a north and south line on each side of the body. Again, to the accompaniment of the rising and falling hands, the *pihe* was sung to its conclusion, after which the old men stepped back and crouched down in their places.[244]

Buck mentions that 'In the north, the *pihe* dirge was performed by a number of men standing in a circle, facing inwards, and stabbing the ground with spears in time with the dirge.'[245] This, like the other accounts, has connotations of the war dance and is consistent with performance in haka style.

Arapeta Awatere, who was born in 1910, saw the pihe performed when he was 'a young fellow up North'. Weapons (mere) were used and passed from hand to hand. It was performed with tremendous force by men who ripped their shirts off as they became hot. To Awatere it seemed to be a test of stamina. The performance went on for at least an hour with 'one pihe after another'.[246]

By the time the present writer did his field work in the North, no one could be found who could perform a pihe. Hemi Manuera said the pihe was 'really a tangi'. It was performed by war parties after a massacre as an admission of defeat and as a direction to the victors to take away their dead.[247] As heard by Taawai Kawiti, pihe had evidently lost their associations with dance. He said they were a 'kind of mourning' performed like a haka but without the movements. They were performed by the South Hokianga people.[248]

A fragment of a song was recorded (McL 1017) which the singer called a pihe (or alternatively tiitiiwai)[249] but other recordings of it (McL 1029 & McL 1047B) identified it as a ngaarahu (war dance) and a mataara (watch song) respectively. It was stated by the singer of McL 1017 to have been performed at Rotorua by the Ngaapuhi for the Duke and Duchess of York in 1901. It was sung with the performers each jumping up and down and brandishing a stick, and one performer presented his tattooed behind to the duke. A description of the Ngaapuhi performance of the song on this very occasion is given by Loughnan[250] and quoted by Andersen:

> At length the impatient Ngapuhi, too long restrained, advanced with spears at the charge and yells of well-simulated rage. They rushed to the front in pursuit of a challenger who had approached them and thrown his spear (wero). Their ancient war-cry, one of the oldest of Maori war-cries, was raised as soon as they were in position:
>
> A ka e kei te wiwi
> Ka e kei te wawa.
>
> They leaped from side to side with tumultuous energy, swinging their spears and shaking the ground with the thud of their feet as the ancient war-cry of their race resounded, deep, peremptory, stirring. Painted faces, lolling tongues, fiercely-flashing eyes, and heads thrown from side to side in wild tumult of energetic movement; weapons poised quivering, or deftly swung to either flank; bare limbs and torsos moving together in perfect accord; the rattle of the piupiu heard with the thud of the stamping feet and the shouting of the war-cry; white feathers of the albatross shining on their black hair.[251]

The text, which is very short, is given also by Smith,[252] who calls it a ngeri; by Cowan who says it 'was used in ancient days before charging up to the assault of an enemy's fortification';[253] and by Kelly who cites it as a haka relating to the storming of a paa by the legendary Uenuku.[254]

EXAMPLE 18 McL 1017 as sung by Pakihi Peita

EXAMPLE 19 McL 1029A as sung by Piri Mokena

EXAMPLE 20 McL 1047B as sung by Matekino Wharemate

Versions of the song by Pakihi Peita (McL 1017) and Piri Mokena (McL 1029A) are both in haka style though they differ in rhythmic detail. The transcription of McL 1017 is somewhat conjectural because of pauses introduced by the singer. Matekino Wharemate (McL 1047B) transformed the haka rhythms of the other versions into a vigorous 2/8 time, though still in recited style (Example 20).

Although it is uncertain how the above song may once have been sung, it is clear from the historical evidence that it is not a pihe but most likely a ngeri performed as a preliminary to a peruperu. The confusion in calling it a pihe doubtless arose because both types of song are connected with warfare and both are performed in haka style.

Pookeka

The term appears in Williams only as 'a kind of chant'. It is the Te Arawa equivalent of the maemae, manawawera and pihe, found also in the Maataatua canoe area. Writing of the texts, Margaret Orbell comments that the pookeka 'is not so much a lament for a person who has died as a contemplation of death itself, and a kind of confrontation of it'.[255] Several have been recorded and the song type has been described by informants. It is performed with impromptu individual or non-uniform haka actions on the last night of a tangi to 'cheer up' those present. Mutu Kapa, who recorded a pookeka (McL 456), said weapon actions with the taiaha were performed while it was recited. From the manner of performance, Arapeta Awatere speculated that the derivation of the name is from poo ('night') and keka ('drunkish, not quite in control of one's senses or talkative in an incoherent manner'); thus pookeka ('night on which people speak in an incoherent manner to the departed').[256] Marata Te Tomo advanced a similar interpretation, saying the word 'means going silly, you're going mad' (referring to the actions).[257] Williams confirms that keka can mean 'mentally deranged'; however, it also has the meanings 'beside oneself with grief' (perhaps, in this sense, mad with grief) and 'dirge' or 'lament'. The latter suggests a more prosaic derivation than those invoking madness. The term 'pookeka' may mean simply 'night lament', referring to the custom of performing it on the last night of the funeral. Two pookeka appear as Songs 10 and 30 in McLean & Orbell. The following is the opening line of M&O 30 as performed by the leader, Turau Te Tomo of Ngaati Tuuwharetoa:

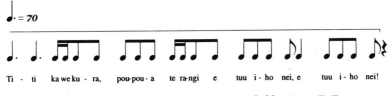

EXAMPLE 21 Pookeka: Beginning of M&O 30 as led by Turau Te Tomo

WOMEN'S DANCES

A number of references in the travel and missionary literature are unspecific as to the type of dance. Most can confidently be identified as either haka or war dance. The few remaining references suggest, however, that at first contact and before being overtaken by missionary disapproval, dance forms using movements of a different kind were practised by women or young girls.

In the journals of de Surville's visit to New Zealand to Doubtless Bay in 1769, there are several accounts of an incident in which three young women performed for over an hour a 'very lewd and immodest' dance with 'indecent gestures', 'sparing no efforts to overcome the indifference of the European spectators'. The dance was accompanied by a song with handclapping[258] from an old woman. Eventually, one of the girls seized de Surville round the waist and made 'lascivious movements' against him 'making it very clear what she wanted of him' until he shook her off.[259]

Dumont d'Urville remarks upon similar performances on shipboard at the Bay of Islands in 1824:

> Throughout the whole of the time we spent in the Bay of Islands, the thirty or so slave girls who had settled down on board to trade their charms gave us regularly every evening an exhibition of their love dances. Nothing could be more lewd or more obscene than their movements, gestures and poses; moreover everything made one think that the songs that accompanied them were, to say the least, quite as lascivious.[260]

Later, he refers more explicitly to the dance movements he saw:

> The women . . . have brought the functions they are designed to fulfil in this world into their games. Thus their dances consist of immoderate movements which cannot be described, and we will confine ourselves to noting one consecrated to *Oure* [ure] or *Phallus*.[261]

Another similar shipboard performance is described in some detail by Thiercelin, a French whaler who visited New Zealand in 1864. As happened to de Surville, the women dancers approached the men provocatively, blowing kisses and touching parts of their bodies with their fingers. The sailors reacted hilariously, 'laughing like madmen', but the Maori men who were present remained stern and sent the women away as soon as the performance was over.[262]

It is probable that the movements seen by d'Urville and Thiercelin and which embarrassed de Surville were those known respectively as onioni and kopikopi. Referring to haka leaders, Best says 'women were noted for their lascivious motions of the *onioni* type'.[263] Williams defines the word as 'move, wriggle' or 'copulate', 'used of the movement of the hips in some indecent *haka*'. As a dance movement, the term 'kopikopi' is not in Williams, but was supplied to the writer by Arapeta Awatere. 'Onioni' refers to the thrusting

Kopikopi dancing at Te Kuiti, 1971. PHOTO: *Jeremy Salmond*

movements of copulation and 'kopikopi' to rotational movement of the hips.[264]

Movements of the kopikopi kind are nowadays seen only when old or middle-aged women are engaging in comic dancing on the marae. Their exaggerated hip movements are guaranteed always to draw gales of laughter from the spectators. Salmond refers to this form of dancing as 'a local form of *hula* performed mainly by old women of the Waikato tribes':

> The Waikato area is the home of the Maori Queen, and when she visits her loyal *marae* she is usually accompanied by the King Movement's brass band. After the main meal of the *hui* the band assembles on the *marae* and starts up a lively quickstep. One by one the old ladies move on to the *marae* and begin to *kopikopi*. They gyrate their hips, roll their eyes and flirt comically with the elders, always to the great delight of the crowd.[265]

It is likely that the movements of this dance are not traditional but have indeed been copied from Hawaiian, Cook Islands or other Polynesian dancing fairly recently. The most probable origin is Princess Te Puea's famous Waikato concert party (see Chapter 20) which performed Hawaiian hula dances in the 1920s. Alternatively they may be a survival from an earlier form of Maori dancing similar to the Polynesian but no longer performed.

The latter possibility gains some support from a comment by Awatere that girls performing kopikopi would be singing love ditties (ruriruri).[266] However, references to ruriruri in the travel and missionary literature are somewhat obscure.

Ruriruri

Williams defines ruriruri as a 'song, ditty, generally of an amorous nature, accompanied by gestures'.

Edward Markham, who spent eight and a half months in the Hokianga and Bay of Islands in 1834, calls it a 'Roody Doody'. He describes it as recited by women, again on shipboard, 'in a kind of fixed time or Verse, Recitativo' with a text 'sometimes not of the most modest sort'. The woman who is going to 'take up the verse . . . keeps time with her fist or some lascivious movement *of her bottom*' (the italicised phrase crossed out). The texts, which must have been improvised, referred to 'the different abilities of their temporary Husbands, all the Scandal of the different Parrs [paas] or Native Villages and of the Europeans up and down the country'.[267] Father Servant, who was in the Hokianga a little later than Markham (1838–42), regarded the ruriruri as a game and did not recognise the vocal accompaniment as a song:

> To perform this game they sit in a circle or semicircle, and strike their thighs and chests at the same time, then they make rapid arm movements; high pitched whistles can be heard, words are spoken at the same time and at great speed by all the performers; the way this is carried out in unison — gestures, movements, whistles, cries — is a marvellous thing to the natives. But modesty is not well respected in these kinds of games: a chief one day said the *ruriruri* game had been dreamt up by Satan.[268]

In a diary entry dated 1840, the Bay of Islands missionary William Williams refers to both 'haka' and 'rurerure' as 'names for the native dances which are accompanied by obscene songs'.[269] Shortland writes of 'rurerure or haka', stating they were performed for amusement by young men and girls and 'frequently accompanied by gestures of the body of an immodest character'.[270] Best defines ruri or ruriruri variously as a haka of a comparatively mild nature, performed in a sitting position; 'Songs often accompanied by gestures'; and 'Song accompanied by arm action'.[271]

From the descriptions, the status of the ruriruri is uncertain. Best may have erred in calling it a haka, unless he was using the term as generic for all types of dance. Shortland's use of the term is ambivalent. It would seem probable that the ruriruri was a different form from haka but with some elements, such as body percussion, in common.

As used today, ruriruri is synonymous with pao and is not necessarily accompanied by dance or gesture. Piri Mokena, then in his eighties, told the writer that in the North old people used to sing ruri when he was young, and he sang one, in pao style, during the interview;[272] John McGregor's collection of Waikato song texts contains a number of ruri;[273] and the term is also used instead of pao by other tribes including Te Arawa, Tuuwharetoa and Ngaati Raukawa.[274]

Kanikani

The earliest accounts of kanikani describe it as ceremonial in nature. Later ones represent it as similar to the ruriruri. John Rutherford, who lived as a Maori for ten years between 1816 and 1826, gives a brief description of the 'Kane Kane' in his journal. It was performed at a marriage feast for the greater part of the night by women who stood in a row, several holding muskets over their heads, their movements accompanied by the singing of several of the men.[275] The following is an account of the kanikani as seen in 1834 by Edward Markham:

> The Third and last day we had a scene very different, Eighty women dancing a Slow Monotonous Step, but graceful movements of the Arms. The Mats were round their Middles and the Upper part exposed all their Breasts &c but I never saw a finer set of Women or Girls in an Opera Ballet. They were in two divisions Moyterra's Tribe, and the Tribes about the Heads, and also Apee set, their Visitors, Forty in each division, Ten in each row, two lines advancing about two inches at a time and two lines retrograding, Naked to the Middle and useing the Arms with slow but graceful Movements, The People on the Ground keeping up a Monotonous Chaunt in good time. The name of this Dance Jacky Marmont told me was Cunnu Cunnu [*kanikani*] and was Religious. All the Chiefs Daughters danced it, and no Slave Girl was allowed to enter the Ranks. It lasted for

Maori girls dancing. Pencil and watercolour by Edward Markham. Photo: *Alexander Turnbull Library, 126446¹/₂*

hours; till the Sun set they must not eat; during the dance I found that Madle Awattie was one and they had a master of the ceremonies, and fugle Man to each division; they kept it up till sun Down, but the last few hours one Division sat down for half an hour, and they releived each other; some of the women had flowers in their hair and even Combs as the European fashion of dressing the Hair is very prevalent, and some of the Women were nearly as fair as Europeans — when the Dance was over then the cooking began.[276]

Tregear mentions the kanikani, somewhat obscurely, as 'a sort of sea-saw dance'.[277] Burton records it as a dance performed by young people at Taumarunui.[278] Cowan describes the dance as seen in the Waikato during the reign of King Mahuta, performed, incongruously, to the strains of a Moody and Sankey hymn played by a Maori drum and all-girl fife band. First, said Cowan, the dance is performed by 'a couple of uncomely tattooed old dames . . . rolling their eyes and wriggling their bodies'. Then one at a time, the flute players stop playing and take turns performing a dance solo:

> She *pukanas* with her eyes, now set and glassy, now wild and rolling, throws her shapely head back, and gives herself up to the elemental passion of the *kanikani* . . . All the muscles of her trunk and lower limbs seem to be at work: the lascivious spirit of the untamed sex-instinct shines out in her.[279]

UNNAMED DANCES

The few accounts of unnamed women's dancing are consistent with reports of ruriruri and kanikani. One of the diaries of Crozet's visit in 1827 mentions dancing which may have been ruriruri:

> Often as we approached, we saw half-naked girls who ran together holding hands and then sang love songs and with a charming gaiety gave themselves up to dances full of grace and passion.[280]

Nicholas in 1814 was entertained by a dance of three young women whose movements he describes as 'easy and graceful';[281] in the 1830s, Walton mentions the 'amatory compositions' of women and the 'blandishments and gestures' seen in their dancing.[282] Polack writes similarly of 'smiles, gestures, soft hints and blandishments' in women's dancing, and accompanying songs that were 'extremely indelicate'.[283]

In 1864, Herbert Meade saw a dance which could have been a ruriruri. He gives an appealing description of young and old of both sexes meeting every evening to socialise and bathe near a geyser in the warm water on the shore of Lake Rotorua at Ohinemutu. Having joined the revellers, he had not been bathing long before one of the chiefs called on the girls to come and 'haka' to the strangers.

> . . . in a few minutes a number of the prettiest young girls in the settlement were seated in a circle in very shallow water, looking like mermaids, with the

Ohinemutu geyser. Chromolithograph by Herbert Meade

moonlight streaming over their well-shaped busts and raven locks.

They sang us a wild song, and beat their breasts to the changing time with varied and graceful gestures.

Others soon collected around us . . . and the choruses of the songs which followed were joined in by scores of voices.[284]

Also at Ohinemutu, a little over a decade later in 1876, the German doctor Max Buchner saw women, who were taking part in a haka, perform conspicuous movements which could well have been onioni, though Buchner himself found nothing in them of the 'repulsive explicitness' he was later to observe in the hulahula of Hawaii:

The most remarkable thing of all was that the women, especially the older ones, moved their bellies up and down to the beat with such suppleness that one would have believed they possessed a special type of joint for this purpose. This movement probably occurred in the especially elastic ligaments in the spine. I could find no other anatomical explanation for this phenomenon. In order to emphasize this virtuosity, above their skirts they carried their bellies, tied above and below with coloured ribbons, so that they bulged forth from these like round spheres.[285]

It is possible that the dances not specifically identified in the literature, including those seen by the Frenchmen de Surville, d'Urville and Thiercelin, were of some as yet undocumented type different from ruriruri or kanikani. With the possible exception of the kanikani, it is nevertheless clear that most were erotic in intent, and a gradual attrition has taken place since they were first described. Today the ruriruri has disappeared and the term 'kanikani' is used for European dancing, prompting speculation that this was always so and that the term itself may have derived from the famous French cancan.[286] This, at least, can be rejected as the cancan dates only from about 1840,[287] whereas Rutherford saw the kanikani before 1826. If, on the other hand, the reverse took place and French sailors introduced the name 'kanikani' to France, the dance itself did not survive the transition. The Maori dance must have been quite different from the cancan, which was danced in a line with much kicking and exposure of the legs to fast duple metre music as used for the quadrille.[288]

KARANGA

Karanga are marae calls performed by women. The usual context is during the ceremony of welcome to a marae, but they are also used on other occasions, even to announce such events as pulling a batch of bread from the oven.[289] Salmond observes that in some tribes, particularly the Waikato, karanga are used as a general mark of appreciation throughout a meeting:

> The old women *karanga* when gifts are laid down on the *marae,* when they enter the dining-hall and when they come out again. They *karanga* a concert party that stands to entertain them, and they *karanga* their friends as they start up the *kopikopi* (hula) . . . Visitors are *karanga*'d over to press noses or to come for a meal . . .[290]

The marae welcome ceremony (poowhiri) generally begins with an exchange of calls between the host women and women leading the party of visitors on to the marae. Salmond gives a detailed description as follows:

> As soon as the visitors begin to enter the *marae* an old woman standing in the porch of the meeting-house or out on the *marae* starts up the call of welcome. She usually stands to the right side of the meeting-house (facing out), dressed in black, and she beckons to the visitors with slow, graceful sweeps of the greenery she holds in her hand. Sometimes there are three or four callers on the *marae,* and as the visitors advance the old women retreat, calling and waving their greenery. Because they lead the visitors into the *marae,* they are called the *pae arahi* (leaders over the threshold). In front of the visitors walk their callers, also dressed in black, and all these old women call and answer as the party slowly advances. The *karanga* is a long, high call which sends greetings, invokes the dead, and brings an emotional atmosphere to the *marae.* The best callers have ethereal but carrying voices, in the words of an informant 'like a bird, high, light and airy'. Their calls are long and effortless, floating away to a sigh. The old women, sixty years old or more, usually give the *karanga,* and the best of them are known as 'bugles' for the clarion quality of their calls. They invoke the dead in language borrowed from mythology, and suit the words to the occasion.[291]

The 'sigh' referred to by Salmond at the end of a call is a long drawn out descending cry, often preceded by a kind of sob or catch of the voice. Ideally it serves as a cue for the karanga of reply to begin, with calls thenceforth overlapping and alternating between the groups, each call prompting the next and each timed to begin when the other begins its descent.[292] More often, as Salmond goes on to point out, 'the *karanga* mix and clash'.[293]

Local calls are sometimes distinguished as maioha (welcome) and visiting ones as tiiwaha, but generally the term karanga is used for both. Each marae has its recognised callers and visitors try to bring at least one caller with them so that the proper protocol will be observed. If they should fail to do so, the local people, rather than allow their calls to go unanswered, may send a woman of their own to bring in the visitors.[294]

Arapeta Awatere stated that the home people conventionally perform both the first and last karanga at a welcome and, at the most, three exchanges of karanga will take place with the visitors. The women performing the karanga time their calls, judging the pace of the approaching party, with the object of getting them right on to the marae aatea or marae proper.[295]

The karanga is seldom named by travellers in their accounts but is sometimes described by them. One early description is supplied by Nicholas:

The moment we were perceived, one of their women made a signal to us, by holding up a red mat, and waving it in the air, while she repeatedly cried out at the same time in a loud and shrill voice, *haromai, haromai, haromai,* (come hither,) the customary salutation of friendship and hospitality.[296]

The same words are still used in karanga of today, together with other stock phrases which are strung together in different combinations to suit the occasion. A selection is given by Salmond in which frequent reference is made to the dead:

Local callers welcome their visitors and summon the dead:
Haere mai rā i te reo o te rā, haere mai rā!
Come in the voice of the day, welcome!
Haere mai rā e kui mā, e koro mā i te pō
Come old women, old men from the underworld
E tama mā, i te karanga o tō tātou tipuna whare e tū mai nei
Come, children, to the call of our ancestral house, standing here
Huhuingia mai rā o tātou mate kia tangihia i te rā nei
Gather our dead to be wept over today
Haere mai rā!
Welcome!
Visitors address the ancestral house, and farewell the dead:
Karanga rā te tupuna whare ki te kāhui pani
Call, ancestral house, to those who mourn
Ki ngā iwi e, karanga rā!
Call to the tribes!
Haere rā ngā mate o te tau, o te marama,

Farewell the dead of the year, of the month.
O tēnei rā e! Haere atu rā!
Of today — farewell!

According to Hiwi and Pat Tauroa, the karanga of reply from the visitors should include advice to the tangata whenua as to who is in the group and where it is from. Sometimes the reason for coming is also mentioned and other information thought to be important may also be exchanged by way of the karanga.[297]

The rhythms of karanga follow their texts quite closely and there is no musical form beyond the standardised cry marking the end of the message. On this account they can be called recited although they are perhaps best described as intermediate in style between sung and recited. Four separate karanga recorded in 1963 at the Turangawaewae marae, Ngaruawahia, are transcribed as Song 38 in McLean & Orbell. Two of these are reproduced in the example following. All are recited on a single note except on the penultimate word. The texts, as on most such occasions, recall the deaths that have taken place since the visitors and hosts last met:

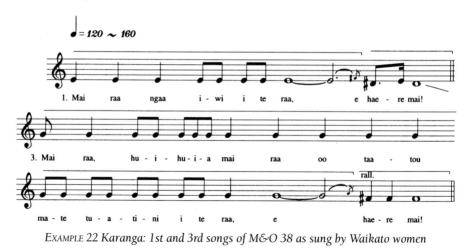

EXAMPLE 22 *Karanga: 1st and 3rd songs of M&O 38 as sung by Waikato women*

POOWHIRI

According to Kino Hughes of Tuuhoe,[298] the term 'poowhiri' (or poohiri) applies to the entire ceremony of welcome for visitors, beginning with the karanga, including haka and speeches and finishing with the hongi. The word is also used colloquially for the so-called 'action chant of welcome' performed with the waving of green branches after visitors have been called into the marae, but the correct term for the latter, according to Kino, is 'haka poowhiri'. The welcome chant is also sometimes designated as pao poowhiri and, when performed in poi form, is called poi poowhiri. There is support for Kino's view of poowhiri as a general rather than specific term in the dictionary definition of poowhiri (Williams) which means principally to 'wave', 'beckon' or 'welcome'.

Few haka poowhiri are now customarily performed and it is not known how widespread the practice may have been in former times. Salmond states that perhaps fewer than ten of these songs are now in popular use.[299] Of this number, only five have been recorded by the writer. The most common, heard indeed at almost every Maori meeting, is the canoe-hauling chant 'Tooia mai te waka', as explained in Chapter 1 in the section on 'rituals of encounter'. It is reproduced as Example 2.

Sometimes also used is the haka 'Utaina'. Like the better known and more often performed 'Tooia mai', it is a canoe chant with metaphorical associations indicative of welcome. As expressed by Armstrong, when 'Utaina' is performed 'the visitor knows that the canoe of good fortune is sailing before the wind and that all is well with the tribe and its guests'.[300] The transcribed example was recorded in 1958 by Pirihira Wikiriwhi of Ngaati Pikiao who said it was Ngaati Pikiao's chant of welcome to King George V and Queen Mary when they visited Rotorua as Duke and Duchess of Cornwall and York in 1901. In the recording it is followed immediately by 'Tooia mai'.

EXAMPLE 23 *Haka poowhiri: McL 8A as led by Pirihira Wikiriwhi*

Another haka poowhiri performed at the welcome of the duke and duchess makes use of transliterated English words which are changed on each occasion of welcome, according to circumstance. As performed by Tuuhoe tribe in 1901 and recorded by Kino Hughes (McL 1073C), it began:

Noo wai te kihi poti, e kupa mai te waitai?
Nou nei e te Kingi

Whose is the steam boat sailing through the ocean?
It is yours oh King

In 1943 it was performed at Ruatoria to welcome the vice-regal party of Governor-General Sir Cyril Newall at the Ngarimu Victoria Cross Investiture Meeting:

Noo wai te motokaa e topa mai ngaa rori?
Aue! Nou nei te Kaawana
Whose is the motor car speeding hither along the highway?
It is thine oh Governor.[301]

Nowadays it may be modified in similar fashion for a cabinet minister or other dignitary. The transcribed version of the song was recorded by Kino Hughes (as McL 1083A) and was taught by him at an Auckland waiata school in 1972. The song begins with the leader repeating 'Kei runga, kei raro' to set the time for the singing and the waving of green branches. Then all join in chorus, waving the branches up and down as indicated:

EXAMPLE 24 *Haka poowhiri: McL 1073A as sung by Kino Hughes*

Another version of the same song was performed, again at Rotorua in 1901, as Ngaati Raukawa's welcome to the duke. This time the reference is to the locomotive which carried the duke to Rotorua and the song is transformed into a poi:

Aue ii, noo wai te tereina e kupa mai Rotorua?
Aue ii, noohou nei, e te Tiuka
Whose is the train sweeping towards Rotorua?
It is yours oh Duke

Example 25 is the beginning of the song, as sung by Pairoa Wineera of Ngaati Raukawa, and the whole appears as Song 27 in McLean & Orbell.

A further example of a poowhiri was recorded by Marata Te Tomo of Ngaati Tuuwharetoa. As in 'Tooia mai te waka', there is reference in the text to haul-

EXAMPLE 25 Poi poowhiri: Beginning of M&O 27 as sung by Pairoa Wineera

ing a canoe and the implications of welcome are the same. The singer explained that while the wero (challenge) was taking place, the party which was to perform the poowhiri remained kneeling. On the command 'Whiti whiti e' from the man who had just completed the wero, they rose to perform the poowhiri, concluded by everyone performing 'Tooia mai te waka'.

EXAMPLE 26 Haka poowhiri: McL 1115 as sung by Marata Te Tomo

Another song, called a karanga by its Northland singer, Matekino Wharemate, is evidently also a poowhiri. It is performed like a haka and in its opening and closing lines uses the same words and rhythms as other poowhiri.

EXAMPLE 27 Haka poowhiri: McL 1046C as sung by Matekino Wharemate

87

Haka poowhiri which have not been recorded by the writer include three well-known East Coast ones called 'Te urunga tuu', 'Ka panapana' and 'Haukiwi hauweka', all performed by women of Ngaati Porou tribe.[302] The Ngaati Porou haka poowhiri is distinctive in two respects. The first is that it is performed exclusively by women rather than predominantly so, as elsewhere; the second is that it precedes rather than follows the more aggressive men's haka if this is performed. According to Arapeta Awatere, in Ngaati Porou the women's voice is expressive of hospitality and for this reason anything relating to the poowhiri was done by the womenfolk.[303]

The following is the beginning of 'Te urunga tuu' as recorded by the New Zealand Broadcasting Service at celebrations to commemorate the centenary of Rangiatea Maori Church at Otaki in 1950:[304]

EXAMPLE 28 *Haka poowhiri: AMPM RNZ 57.7*

The haka poowhiri 'Te urunga tuu' performed by Ngaati Porou women at Waitangi, 1934

'Ka panapana' was recorded on the same occasion as 'Te urunga tuu', beginning as follows:[305]

Aa-ra-ra   [i] ka pa - na - pa - na!   Aa - ha - ha!

Ka re - ka - re- ka to- nu ta- ku ngaa- kau   ki ngaa   ma - na ri - ri-ki_i   Poo - ha- tu [tu- a]

wha ka- pi- ri.   Ha- ra - mai te ta- ki - ti - ni,   ha- ra- mai te ta- ki- ma- no   pa- re - tai - to- ko-

ti - a ki Oo - ta- ki! Hi,   ha,   hou!

EXAMPLE 29 Haka poowhiri: AMPM RNZ 57.8

A version of 'Haukiwi hauweka', dating from about 1966, is available in a recording made by the New Zealand Broadcasting Corporation at a concert given in the Wellington Opera House by the Waihirere Maori Club of Gisborne.[306] It begins:

Hau - ki - wi, hau - we - ka   ka- we- a   he   koo - re - ro

ki- a wha - ka - ro- ngo mai   ngaa   i - wi   o   Ho - tuu - raau - a!

EXAMPLE 30 Haka poowhiri: AMPM 0260.1

As can be seen from the transcriptions, 'Tooia mai te waka', 'Ki okioki e', the Northland example and the first and last of the three East Coast songs are recited in standard haka style. 'Utaina' is also performed like a haka but makes use of duple instead of the more usual compound metre, as does 'Ka panapana'. 'Noo wai' has elements of both sung and recited styles. Although mostly sung, it nevertheless has haka rhythms.

HARI KAI

The final resolution of the 'rituals of encounter' outlined in Chapter 2 is the sharing of food by hosts and guests after the conflicts inherent in the process have been resolved and all potential threat removed. Erstwhile or potential enemies are now seated in amity enjoying together cooked food which traditionally is used as an integral part of whakanoa ceremonies for the removal of tapu. One would expect such an occasion to be joyful and the songs which are particular to it to reflect this condition. This, indeed, is found generally to be the case.

Traditionally, food was presented to guests accompanied by song and often dance. Maning writes of a train of young and middle-aged women appearing with food in smoking dishes, hot from the oven, held high in both hands: 'They advanced with a half-dancing, half-hopping sort of step, to the time of a wild but not unmusical chant'.[307] Kerry-Nicholls likewise mentions King Country women and girls, 'tripping along in Indian file, singing a wild refrain', bringing pork, potatoes, bread and kuumara in plaited flax baskets.[308] Potts gives an account of a 'Food Feast' seen at Hikurangi in the Waikato district in 1878 before which 'a great concourse of people of both sexes formed a procession . . . the women bearing baskets of various kinds of native food' each with 'its appropriate *ngeri* chanted with high-pitched voice, dancing and facial contortions';[309] and Cowan gives an extended account of a 'food-bringing' to guests which he names as hari kai or tuku kai:

> At a *tuku-kai* I witnessed not long ago, on the occasion of a large congress of the tribes, there first advanced a long line of merry girls and women, each carrying a plaited basket or *kono*, of green flax, containing a steaming 'first-course' of potatoes and pork, hot from the *hangi* [earth oven]. As they came they chanted a lively song, keeping time with a skipping dance, a kind of 'Here-we-come-gathering-nuts-and-may' turn, swaggering and swinging their plump bodies from side to side. Then they retired in good order for another course. Next a number of young men advanced in two long lines, yelling a *haka* song as they did so, each bearing a loaf of bread or a handful of biscuits, and others carrying buckets of tea, all of which were laid out on the grass in front of the visitors, a large party of Arawa tribespeople. Then a squad of Ngapuhi natives came forward carrying more bread, and pannikins for the tea. They, too, *haka*'d as they performed their share of the *tuku-kai*, and shouting a welcome song. 'Here we come,' chanted their leader, 'bringing our gift — the fifteen pannikins of Ngapuhi!' Next, half-skipped, half-danced forward, singing lustily as they came, a large party of Whanganui men, carrying baskets and dishes of boiled *kumara* and preserved pigeons. Then there marched up, bringing more *kai*, headed by a brass band of Maori youths playing a quickstep, a party of Ngati-Apa and Ngati-Raukawa people. Ngati-Apa were headed by an enormously stout woman, whose fat body quivered and shook as she danced along the

line, grimacing. The Ngati-Kahungunu people in their turn advanced, singing as they stamped, and turned this way and that, 'Here we come, bringing *kumara* and birds,' and swishing their flax waist-mats in Highland fashion as they swung up to the dining-table of the Arawa — the grassy green — and laid their offerings on the ground.[310]

More recently, but in strikingly similar terms, Buck describes food-bearing practice at his home village of Urenui in Taranaki. Women and girls, carrying a basket of food in each hand, marched in two lines towards the marae, the leading women singing songs, joined in chorus by those behind them. 'Every now and then, a short posture dance was performed to enliven the march, there being a number of songs and dances especially composed for processions carrying food.'[311]

Finally, under the heading 'Ceremonial Dancing', Best refers to 'the old custom of *heriheri kai*, or *makamaka kai*, the ceremonial bearing of food to a party of guests':

> The food-carriers, often a numerous party, each provided with an open bowl-shaped basket containing cooked food, marched in procession two deep from the cooking place. As they advanced slowly across the plaza towards the guests they executed a slow-time form of posture dance, accompanying it with a very euphonious and rhythmical chant.[312]

Common to all these accounts is a processional of some kind together with performance of songs and dances by women carrying baskets of cooked and other food. Best is alone in describing the songs as slow, but he is writing in the context of ritual which could have been solemn in nature and his use of the term 'makamaka', given by Williams as 'recite incantations', may also suggest that a form of ritual was involved. On the other hand, Best himself took part in the recording on a wax cylinder of a food-bearing song, glossed as 'makamaka kai' by the announcer of the song, which does not bear out his statement that the song was in slow time. The song was recorded by a 1921 Dominion Museum expedition at Koriniti, in the Wanganui area, from Rihipeti Aperaniko of Ngaati Paamoana.[313] The recording is too indistinct for much of the text to be discernible. However the performance characteristics are clear. Even allowing for a possible variation of speed of the cylinder recording machine, the song is fast, not slow, and its rhythms are identical with those of all other recorded food-bearing songs except the Tuuhoe example discussed next. It begins as follows:

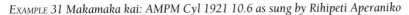

EXAMPLE 31 Makamaka kai: AMPM Cyl 1921 10.6 as sung by Rihipeti Aperaniko

An unequivocal example of ritual performance is from the Tuuhoe tribe where the term 'heri kai' is stated to have been restricted to food-bearing songs performed at the presentation of preserved birds or huahua.[314] John Rangihau said that amongst Tuuhoe such a presentation was ceremonial in nature. As many people as possible, 'a great host of people', carried the birds and performed haka dances as they moved forward slowly, led by a man and a woman. He last saw a performance at the opening of a meeting house at Waimana in 1968 when the people pretended to politicians and other Pakeha visitors that the preserved pigeons (which had become a fully protected species in 1921) were mutton birds.[315] Information about the ceremony was also given to the writer by Arapeta Awatere who said that Tuuhoe hari kai were performed 'at the time of eating the second fruits of the huahua [pre-served pigeon], Tuuhoe's most precious food'. The 'first fruits', explained Awatere, was a term for the first bird caught which was offered to Taane Mahuta, the god of the forests, by being either let go or left to rot in the bush.[316] Men formed up out of sight and carried the cooked birds in baskets to the rest of the tribe, meanwhile performing the hari kai which was in the form of a haka or ngeri.[317] One of the leaders of the ceremony, in his younger days, was Kino Hughes of Tuuhoe who last saw the ceremony performed at Rewarewa Pa, Ruatoki, around 1946. He called the song a heriheri huahua. According to Kino, the huahua were first served to the old people as other-wise the birds would fly away at night and never come back. The example which follows is the first stanza of a heriheri huahua as recorded by him in 1972. Confirming the information given by Rangihau and Awatere, it is sung in the style of a haka.

te ko - re, ko-re ra - wa_ a - ku i-wi ki te ma - hi kai e - ha hii,

ne - ke - ne - ke - hi - a hii!

EXAMPLE 32 Heriheri huahua: McL 1004 as sung by Kino Hughes

The Tuuhoe use of heri kai in solemn ceremony appears to have been exceptional. Food-bearing songs were elsewhere free of ritual associations and, to judge from the movements and demeanour of the participants in the descriptions above, were evidently festive and lively, as also are the performances which have been recorded. Except for the Tuuhoe heriheri huahua, all make use of rhythms much like those of paatere, performed in simple metre.

Terms already mentioned for food-bearing songs are hari kai, heriheri kai and tuku kai. Another term is whiu kai. Kai is the word for food. One of the meanings of hari is 'to carry' but it may not be without significance that others are 'dance',' joy' and 'feel or show gladness' (Williams). Heri is given by Williams as synonymous with hari; a meaning of tuku is 'present, offer', evidently referring in this case to the presentation of the food. Derivation for the term 'whiu kai' is less certain. It was given by Lucy Jacob[318] as the term for food-bearing songs in the Ngaati Raukawa area and one such song (McL 1113A) was recorded (in 1972), as a ngeri whiu kai, by Para Iwikau of Ngaati Tuuwharetoa. One of the meanings of whiu in Williams is to 'collect', 'assemble' or 'gather together' and another is to be 'satisfied with food', but the term may have derived rather from the first line of the particular song which began with the words 'Whiua a e'. A song with the same first line was recorded as a heriheri kai by Marata Te Tomo, also of Ngaati Tuuwharetoa, again in 1972:

Whi - u - a aa - e, whi - u - a aa - e!

Whi - u - a ta - ku pa - tii - tii ki te rae o te puu - ru e ngu - ngu - ru

mai nei, tuu a - ro pa - ki - ra - ra. Hei a - ha te puu - ru?

Hei wha- ka - paa- ru - re - ru - re   maa   te ni - ho mo - re.   Ngau   no - a,

ngau   no - a,   te   pa - hu - re!

EXAMPLE 33 Heriheri kai: McL 1107 as sung by Marata Te Tomo

Food-bearing songs are now obsolete and few have been recorded. Emere Pohatu of Ngaati Porou remembered hearing them when she was a girl. They ceased to be performed when the eating of meals was transferred from the meeting house to dining halls where the food could be set out in advance on tables.[319] The same explanation for the demise of food-bearing songs was given by Lucy Jacob.[320] Around 1913, when she was a little girl, meat was brought into the eating place in enamel dishes, and potatoes, pumpkin and other vegetables in kono (flax baskets). Most of the songs, according to Lucy, had 'dirty, smutty' words. Although she knew some, she was unwilling to record them because the words were 'too awful'. Fortunately a handful of other singers were not as reticent. The songs recorded indeed turn out to be highly ribald and must have been very entertaining in the context of conviviality within which they were performed; they also provoked some merriment during recording and dictation of the texts. Two examples of hari kai appear as Songs 48 and 49 in McLean & Orbell, as recorded from Kurauia Tahuriorangi of Ngaati Pikiao in 1964. There is obvious sexual imagery in seemingly innocuous texts about a rooster waking the singer up at dawn in Song 48 and a 'butting cow' and a 'rooter up' (pig) in Song 49. The songs begin respectively:

♩ = 80

Ee,   ko   te   hei - hei!   Hei   a - ha   te   hei - hei?

Ko   te   hei - hei!   Hei   a - ha   te   hei - hei?

♩ = 80

Ee,   ko   te   kau   tu - ki!   Kaao - re   i   a - hau!

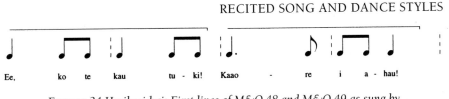

EXAMPLE 34 *Heriheri kai: First lines of M&O 48 and M&O 49 as sung by Kurauia Tahuriorangi*

A variant of M&O 49 was recorded by Marata Te Tomo as McL 1109. The opening words refer to a kettle of tea. As explained by the singer, if you 'drink too much tea you go out too much' but there is more to the song than this. Another singer revealed that a kuumara mentioned in the song in fact refers to the female organ.

EXAMPLE 35 *Heriheri kai: McL 1109 as sung by Marata Te Tomo*

Other heriheri kai have been recorded as McL 859, from Kiri Kaahaki of Te Whaanau-a-Apanui and as McL 1087, from Kino Hughes of Tuuhoe.

WORK SONGS

In his *Economics of the New Zealand Maori*, Firth distinguishes four main classes of rhythmic work songs: canoe-hauling songs, canoe-paddling songs, chants used during cultivation of kuumara, and songs known under the generic name of tewha.[321] They will be considered here in opposite order to that given by Firth.

Except for one, it is doubtful whether any of the song types named in Firth's last two classes were truly work songs in the standard sense of songs intended rhythmically to assist work. All are named in other sources as incantations. Best, from whom Firth may have obtained the term, does define tewha as a generic term for work song but he gives no further detail;[322] Williams gives 'tewha' only as a karakia (incantation) used when planting kuumara. Specific chants listed by Firth as 'used when digging the fields for cultivation' are 'koo kuumara', 'tapatapa kuumara' and 'whakatopatopa kuumara'. Best provides apparent confirmation of Firth's classification by referring to koo kuumara and whakatapa kuumara as 'work songs chaunted by those preparing the soil for the sweet potato crop',[323] but again the term 'work song' may be a misnomer: elsewhere Best himself gives 'koo kuumara' as 'a charm when planting crops'.[324] Firth's term 'whakatopatopa kuumara', evidently a variant of whakatapa kuumara, is defined by Williams again not as a work song but as an incantation.

The sole term above which could refer to a work song is 'koo kuumara' (lit. 'dig kuumara'). Arapeta Awatere said that in cultivating the kuumara, a karakia or incantation to Rongo (the god of agriculture) was first performed and then, when people started to dig, the koo kuumara. This was a true work song, performed with a leader. It was a form of ngeri (metrical song in haka style).[325] Tapatapa kuumara was a ritual concerning division of kuumara plots, i.e. cutting the boundaries for family plots. It was a karakia to Rongo to name the plots, performed either by a priest or by the head of the family. Next the whakatopatopa kuumara was recited. This was an incantation performed by the priest as he walked along the boundary of the kuumara plot. Neglect of this ritual was thought to bring disaster through failure of the crop. The tewha, according to Awatere, was a form of karakia asking for help from the departmental god concerned with the particular type of work.[326] This esoteric information was communicated to Awatere by his father.

In her book *The Old-Time Maori*, which draws upon her upbringing at Rotorua, Maggie Papakura (b. 1872) refers to songs which must have been koo kuumara:

> It was indeed a fine sight to see an ohu at work on a large kumara cultivation, with their long handled ko decorated with bunches of feathers near the top working and moving in unison to the accompaniment of a chant sung by a man who acted as leader of the party, the workers joining in from time to time.[327]

John Alexander Wilson (b.1829) comments in similarly nostalgic terms:

> . . . it was a pleasant sight to see them ranged in rows, and digging with their ko-es (wooden Maori spades) as they rose and fell, and their limbs and bod-

Preparing the ground for planting kuumara. Painting by G. Lindauer.
Photo: *Auckland City Art Gallery*

ies swayed rhythmically to the working of the ko, and the chorus of an ancient hymn, invoking a blessing on the fruit of their labours.[328]

In the index of his book *Maori Agriculture*, Elsdon Best refers to a number
of songs as 'working songs' which were clearly incantations. The sole exception again refers to songs which were evidently koo kumara, though Best
himself referred to them as 'tewha'. While impressed, like the above writers,
with the spectacle of the scene, Best, with his ethnographer's eye for detail,
adds a precise description of the manner in which the song coordinated the
movements of the workers:

The usual method of planting the *kumara*, or sweet potato, was that known as
whakarapa. When engaged in wielding the *ko*, the workers arranged themselves in a row, with proper intervals between them, and performed all actions
of their task in time with each other, such time being set and kept by the
chanting of the *tewha*, or working song. The sight of a number of men ma-
nipulating their long *ko* in unison, with the long, feather streamers waving,

97

the military precision of their movements accompanied by the weird chanting of the *tewha* or work song, was a striking one.

> In preparing the ground . . . each man . . . forces his *ko* into the soil with his right foot, then presses the shaft down and backwards until the point has loosened the soil sufficiently. He then withdraws the tool, places the point thereof a little distance from the hole, turns his body, and, placing his left foot on the footrest, again forces the implement into the soil and loosens it as before. On the completion of this process, the whole line of men take one pace to the rear, and the same actions are repeated, and so on until the ground is all prepared. In another method both thrusts of the *ko* into the soil are made with the left foot on the *teka* or footrest. The fugleman chants certain lines of the planting song, and the workers sing the others as they perform their task.[329]

Unfortunately no examples of koo kuumara have been recorded to settle the question of what they sounded like. Wilson's description is suggestive of a karakia and Papakura's of a ngeri as stated by Awatere. Best's description is plainly of a metrical form of song consistent with ngeri.

Hauling songs

Called rangi waka, tau waka, too waka, or tootoo waka, these songs were used to assist the heavy labour of launching the huge Maori canoes and of portaging them overland. They were also used for dragging logs of wood intended for other purposes, such as large tootara timbers for chiefs' houses and trunks of trees for paa fortifications,[330] as well as other heavy hauling tasks as shown in the following illustration.

Gable from Te Kaha storehouse at Auckland Museum showing people hauling in a whale

The missionary Samuel Ironside records the hauling of logs to a church site at Ngakuta (near Nelson) around 1841

> to tunes set by the fugleman (sailor fashion). Sometimes it was a school song, sometimes one of their old legends, more frequently a song improvised for the occasion.[331]

Hauling songs are long obsolete. Thus, when the Maori war canoe *Nga Toki Matawhaorua* was launched on 5 January 1974, in preparation for the first New Zealand Day celebrations at Waitangi, it is reported to have been put into the water: 'To the rhythmic chant of "heave-ho"'.[332]

Traditional hauling songs took the form of phrases performed alternately by a leader (kaaea),[333] while the pullers took breath, and a choral response during which the haul took place.[334] Shortland, in a statement echoed by later writers,[335] claims that songs of long syllables were used for sustained effort, as in pulling up hill, and short syllables for light weights 'when the impediment is overcome'.[336] Best characterises the kaaea as sometimes running back and forth as he performed his task and sometimes standing in the canoe as it was hauled along. His phrases were yelled out at the top of his voice; and if his vocal chords gave out he was relieved by another person.[337] According to Hare Hongi:

> In addition to the ropemen, a number of haulers were ranged along from end to end of the canoe itself. These men would, when the word was given by their fuglemen, extend one arm forward and one arm aftward, grasping the topsides, with chests pressed against the canoe-sides, simultaneously impel the canoe forward, and march along beside it.[338]

Best states that by the use of a tau waka or canoe-hauling chant, a heavy log 70 feet long has been hauled three miles in half a day.[339] Campbell gives an eye-witness account of the dragging out of the forest of an even larger log 3 feet in diameter and 80 feet long by a team of naked men. The head of the spar had been decorated with flowering branches and tufts of feathers and on it stood the oldest chief of the tribe brandishing a taiaha:

> He kept repeating a long string of words in quick succession, lifting up one foot and stamping it down again, the body thrown back on the other leg. Every moment his voice became louder and louder until almost reaching a scream; then he grasped the weapon with both hands, sprang into the air, and came down again as if smiting an enemy to the earth. At this instant, some eighty or more men, minus a flax mat like the chief, or even fig-leaf, yelled forth one word as ending chorus. As one man they simultaneously stamped on the ground, and then gave one fearful pull on the rope doubled round the end of the spar — a pull that you thought would snap the rope in two; but it stood the tremendous strain, and the huge mass forged ahead several feet.[340]
>
> Again and again the manoeuvre was repeated with intermissions for rest while young children brought kits of wet mud to smear on sleepers in front of the spar to make it slide more easily. Finally the log was brought to the brink of a hill down which it was pushed to crash to its destination at the water's edge.

The above incident furnishes a graphic illustration of the role of the leader in such efforts. Firth comments:

> . . . the antics of the chief, his prominent position on top of the object being hauled, the weapon which he wields in his hand, and the chant . . . are

patently devices of leadership by which he may impress his personality on the workers and secure increased control. His lofty post and the brandishing of the weapon keep the attention of the people concentrated on him and so enable him better to co-ordinate their activity. The rhythm of the chant also aids as a stimulus to effort.[341]

A putative hauling song is McL 74, performed as a peruperu by Arapeta Awatere of Ngaati Porou. Armstong gives a free translation of the text:[342]

Take the strain! Draw it hither! Drag it hither!
Haul the canoe from its resting place!

Armstrong suggests that, although the song has many times been performed as a peruperu, it was probably originally a too waka. The text he gives is in leader/chorus responsorial form. The haul would have taken place during the choral portions of the text (italicised below following Armstrong) at the end of each line and in the final lines of the song.

EXAMPLE 36 Peruperu: McL 74 as sung by Arapeta Awatere

The only song recorded specifically as a too waka is McL 846 (Example 37) as sung by Kino Hughes of Tuuhoe. Best gives the text and states that it is said to be part of the hauling song chanted when the ancestral Maataatua canoe was dragged from the forest.[343] It is in a neat 9/8 time with the haul presumably occurring on the last beat of each three.

As earlier noted, two other hauling songs, 'Tooia mai te waka' and 'Utaina', are still in the Maori repertoire and are used in the poowhiri ceremony of welcome because of their symbolic associations suggestive of hauling guests on to a marae. The two songs have been given as Examples 2 and 23.

$\bullet. = 85$

[Aa] tooi- a te wa- ka ee! Tooi- a te wa-ka ee!

Tooi - a te wa - ka ki ru - nga ki te mau - nga e tuu mai nei

(i), wha - ka - ta - ko - to - ri - a ki te nga-ro pa - ra-pa-ra ko - aa.

Me he tee - tee wa - ka, me he tee - tee wa - ka,

me he pii - tau wha - ka - re - i - a!

EXAMPLE 37 Too waka: McL 846 as sung by Kino Hughes

Paddling songs

Known variously as hautuu, hautuu waka, rangirangi, rangi waka, toiere, toitoi waka, tuki and tuki waka, canoe-paddling songs were observed and commented upon by numerous early European travellers to New Zealand.

George French Angas, who visited New Zealand in 1844, writes of Maori canoes arriving at the Waitemata Harbour from Thames carrying 50 to 60 men, all paddling together, singing a boat song in unison:

> their strokes and voices are timed by an individual who stands erect in the centre of the canoe, performing the twofold duty of conductor and prompter; beating each stroke with a staff which he holds in his hand, and prompting the words of the song. The voices of the crew, shouting in measured strain, may frequently be heard when the canoe itself is but a speck on the waves, and the distant sound falls on the ear with a wild and savage effect.[344]

Maori canoes, as ethnographically reported, have been classified by Best into three groups according to size;[345] Buck provides a summary.[346] Smallest were waka tiiwai, dugouts without sides, used in calm waters such as rivers, harbours and lakes; amongst them were canoes carrying no more than one to three persons. Next were waka teetee, seagoing canoes with strakes and figureheads and upwards of 50 feet long; they were used for fishing or coastal travel. Largest were the waka taua or war canoes, adorned with carved designs, paint and feathers. These canoes could be 80 or more feet long and could carry up to 100 persons; they are described as 'masterpieces of the builder's craft' by Buck who comments:

> Manned by a double row of tattooed warriors with their paddles flashing in perfect time to the canoe chants of a leader standing amidship with a quivering jade club, the speeding war canoe must have offered an inspiring yet awesome sight.[347]

The leader in the centre was called the hautuu, kaihautuu, kaakaariki, kaikaakaariki, kaituki, tangata hautuu, tangata kaakaariki or tiitiitai. Smaller canoes would have had no need for leaders, but in the largest canoes it must have been a task of some magnitude to keep the paddlers together; in these canoes there could be two or even three leaders.

One of the best eye-witness descriptions of the performance of paddling songs is that of Shortland:

> In the long war canoes two singers, called *Kaituki*, stand on stages placed on a level with the gunwale of the canoe, one near the bow and the other near the stern. In addition to their voices, they have in the hand some native weapon which they brandish in time, just as the leader of an orchestra brandishes the bow of his violin. Sometimes they sing alternate verses responding to each other, sometimes both together. By this means the time is remarkably well preserved. I have seen fifty or sixty paddles plunge into the water so exactly at the same instant that the eye could mark no difference between them. The singer frequently introduces into these chants extemporary jokes, or other matter, suitable to the occasion, to cause merriment, and enliven and encourage the crew.[348]

Maori war canoes entering a race at Te Papa, Tauranga, 1865. Drawing by H.G. Robley, 1880. Photo: *National Library of Australia*

A number of travellers' remarks about paddling songs are reminiscent of accounts of the war dance or haka. One reason may have been that some of the performances seen took place in war canoes manned by warriors who were battle ready. Another is that the paddling song itself appears to have been performed in the style of a ngeri[349] or peruperu and in the case of those performed in war canoes would have had the same objective of intimidating the enemy.

As noted earlier, the war dance was characteristically performed with weapons by men stripped for battle, wearing body and face paint. One early account shows that the occupants of a war canoe were sometimes similarly decorated. Cruise refers to a paddling song performed from a large war canoe 'impelled by the united force of ninety naked men, who were painted and ornamented with feathers'.[350]

Several accounts of paddling songs refer to the use of weapons by the leaders. Taiaha (long clubs), patu and mere (short clubs) are specifically mentioned and references to staffs, spears or swords doubtless apply to the same weapons.

Precision of time-keeping and the extraordinary uniformity of action achieved by the paddlers are also often remarked upon, again in similar terms to statements about the haka, and especially the peruperu. Shortland's remarks have already been quoted; Polack comments that 'the exact time kept by the paddles appears to the stranger as if one soul animated the group';[351] Hochstetter likewise refers to regular strokes of the paddles 'as if managed by one hand';[352] and Potts says: 'Time is kept with most wonderful precision — the thirty paddles in the canoe dash aside the waters at the same instant.'[353]

Some actions were evidently carried out less to aid the progress of the canoe than in the spirit of military drill to demonstrate the skill and virtuosity of the paddlers:

St John saw paddling songs performed when he was a passenger in a large Ngaati Whakaue war canoe called *Te Arawa*, on Lake Rotorua. There were 40 paddlers on each side with three fuglemen standing on the seats. The centre one wielded a taiaha; the others carried 'swords'. At intervals, at a shout from the fuglemen, 'every paddle was peaked simultaneously and struck by the oarsman with the palm of one hand in such perfect unison as to produce but one clap'.[354] The same manoeuvre was observed later in the Waikato by Cowan:

> The brawny-shouldered crew dipped their paddles, the fugleman amidships raised his wild canoe-song. 'Hoea te waka' ('Urge on the canoe') was the word, and the Kingite crew put their shoulders into it. Quicker and quicker came the strokes — '*Hūkere, Hūkere, Hūkere!*' Presently, '*Taringa whakarongo!*' ('Ears, listen!') shouted the captain; this by way of caution, or call to attention. Then — '*Hikitia!*' ('Lift up!') and at the sharp command every paddle was

lifted clear above the canoe-side, missing one stroke. '*Pakia!*' — and with a deft movement one hand, the inboard one, was slapped on the wet blade and clapped on the handle again, all in perfect unison. Then once more every man plunged deep his dripping *hoe*, and the captain began again his slow and measured time-song, '*Rite, ko te rite, rite, ko te rite!*' gradually quickening it as before . . .[355]

In the section above on haka, Captain Cook's remark has already been quoted about similar displays of virtuosity in which a hundred or more paddles were struck at the same time against the sides of a canoe. In both Cook's own Journal and in Banks's Journal[356] this information is given in the context of the war dance, provoking a puzzled editorial footnote from J.C. Beaglehole that either the sentence was unduly compacted or something was witnessed in the nature of posture dancing on canoes. In fact, the latter must have been the case. Cook himself explicitly made the connection elsewhere in his Journal:

> In most of their dances they appear like Mad men, jumping and stamping with their feet, making strange contorsions with every part of the body and a hideous noise at the same time, and if they happen to be in their Canoes they flourish with great Agility their Paddles and Pattoo Patoo's various ways, in the doing of which if there are ever so many boats and People they all keep time and motion together to a surprising degree.[357]

From this, however, it cannot be inferred that all references to war songs in canoes referred to paddling songs. Monkhouse's journal of 1769 gives an excellent description of a war dance performed from seven canoes which had chased the *Endeavour* and were evidently hove to at the time under her stern:

> . . . after being tired with threatning, they treated us with a kind of *Heiva*[358] or war dance performed by striking their paddles upon the gunwell, laid across for that Purpose, beating time in exact regularity to the parts of a Song which they chanted in a very martial tone. A Man in the headmost Canoe at the same time, standing erect, Shouldered, poized, & brandished his paddle with the true spirit of a Veteran. In some of his gesticulations great savageness was expressed — in bending forward, throwing his Arms behind him, elevating his head, staring wildly upwards, and thrusting his tongue forward, he exhibited a figure very like that expressed in the heads of their canoes.[359]

It would appear, nevertheless, that Cook's remarks about canoe slapping probably did refer to paddling songs, as Colenso refers to the same practice while again emphasising the unanimity of the performance:

> They paddled their war-canoes to inspiring songs . . . to which song the paddlers kept time, both in paddling and occasionally slapping the blades of

their paddles against the sides of the canoe, accompanying the same, at regular intervals, with their united voices, which arose together more like the voice of one *man*![360]

As earlier suggested, the canoe slapping seen by Cook can be regarded as the equivalent of body percussion in a haka performed on land and, in so far as it was applied to paddling songs, is further evidence of a close relationship between paddling songs and haka.

The position occupied by the song leader or leaders in a canoe appears to have varied according to the size of the canoe. Two early reports refer to a single leader who sat at the stern and also steered the canoe.[361] Usually, however, a single fugleman stood amidships. If there were two leaders they were generally placed at the bow and stern. A third, if present, stood in the middle. Colenso describes them as standing on the thwarts 'more like birds than men'.[362]

The form of the song was call and response, solo and chorus if there was a single leader, and either sung together with chorus or alternating verse by verse if there were two. Several writers refer to the leader solos as improvised and enlivened with extemporaneous jokes. Wade characterises the texts as consisting

of such matters as arise from the circumstances or feelings of the moment: grumblings for want of food, — complaints of small payment — remarks on the pakehas, (white men or foreigners,) in the boat, — rejoicing that soon there will be plenty to eat, — with occasional phrases and short sentences addressed to the rowers, bidding them to be strong, to let the oars dip deep, to pull all together, &c.[363]

The method was also employed when European boats supplanted the native ones and oarsmen took the place of paddlers. Campbell gives an account of rowing with a native crew on a 14-mile journey across the Hauraki Gulf during which boat songs were improvised with a one- or two-word chorus repeated by the crew as the oar was lifted from the water:

All the native village gossip of the day, whether social or political came to light in these extemporised boat or canoe songs; and if any new scandal was on the *tapis,* it was jubilantly given forth in terse and unmistakable language.[364]

Campbell took the trouble to obtain translations of two of the songs. They would have been easy to improvise as the verses are single line and couplets respectively. The one- or two-word choruses, referred to by Campbell, are 'Te naku mea' ('dig the thing [dip the oar]') after each verse in the first song with 'Tena' ('push') and 'Kumea' ('pull') alternating in the second.

Improvised texts were still being composed at the turn of the century,

The war canoe Taheretikitiki *on the Victoria lakelet at the Christchurch Exhibition*

when the Governor General of the time, Lord Plunket, and his entourage were taken for a canoe ride in the 80-foot Waikato canoe, *Taheretikitiki*, at the Christchurch Exhibition of 1906–07.[365] The scene can be imagined as onlookers in Edwardian dress strolled the banks enjoying the sight. James Cowan relates that a young, evidently corseted, Pakeha lady seemed to have caught the fancy of the hautu, who introduced into his paddling song the following, given by Cowan in translation only:

> There's a pretty girl yonder, sitting on the bank
> Ha, ha! She's smoothing down her gown
> (What a handsome gown!)
> What a splendid hat!
> See she's waving her handkerchief
> Ha, ha! What a small waist she has!
> A waist locked in so tightly!
> *Te hope rakatia!*[366]

By all accounts the songs were extremely effective in stimulating effort as well as keeping the paddlers together; many writers comment upon the resulting speed of the canoes. Polack remarks: 'The celerity with which a canoe is made to pursue its course often astonishes the stranger';[367] Hochstetter, with possibly little exaggeration, says the war canoe darted along 'almost with the velocity of a steam-boat';[368] when St John took his ride in *Te Arawa*, 'the canoe hissed through the water, a regular wave forming on each side of her bows';[369] and Potts wrote of feeling his craft 'bounding and quivering' while spray dashed over the sides.[370]

Like hauling songs, paddling songs as described in the literature appear to be long obsolete and efforts to tape-record them began too late for many to be salvaged.

A song named as a hautuu by Arapeta Awatere in 1958 is given by Best and Grace as the kawa of Maataatua, an incantation said to have been used for calming the sea during the voyage of the Maataatua ancestral canoe.[371] Although evidently associated with the sea, it does not seem a very suitable song for paddling; but nor does it seem to be a karakia. As sung, it is in fairly standard haka or ngeri style, beginning as follows:

EXAMPLE 38 *Hautuu: McL 71 as sung by Arapeta Awatere*

In most areas, no one in the 1960s and 1970s could be found who knew any paddling songs. On the Waikato river where canoe races are still occasionally staged, familiar ngeri such as 'Ka mate' are now pressed into service; in the Wanganui area, where canoes once plied the river, a fragment only of a single paddling song was recorded; and at Rotorua, where canoes were once plentiful on the lake, just one toiere waka was recorded.

The latter song was recorded from Hamu Mitchell of Ngaati Whakaue tribe and has been taught by him to culture groups. As the singer himself pointed out, however, it is unusual for a paddling song because it has a tune. As such, it does not conform with early descriptions of the genre. Possibly it is a sung adaptation of an earlier recited form. It is a brisk tempo composition in 2/4 time with rapid, syncopated paatere-like rhythms and a regular

EXAMPLE 39 *Toiere waka: McL 1254 as sung by Hamu Mitchell*

form of two bars to the phrase and two phrases to each line of the text. According to the singer, paddling was done by alternating several strokes on one side of the canoe with several strokes on the other. If so, from the form of the song, the strokes are likely to have occurred on the first beat of each bar, four to each side of the canoe, and sides would have alternated line by line with the song text. The song is a lengthy one, beginning as shown on the previous page.

Little can be said about the Wanganui fragment (McL 1158) as it was sung too hesitantly to be transcribed with certainty. However, it is essentially in haka style and, to this extent, is consistent with published descriptions.

The one song which can be offered as possibly typical of paddling songs is the following as sung in 1963 by Uehoka Tairakena of Ngaati Maahanga of Waikato. Although announced by the singer as a haka, it is flanked in the recording session by two other songs associated with canoes and its simple call and response structure is what might be expected of a paddling song. The relatively slow pace of 61 beats a minute is also consistent with paddling if one assumes a dip of the paddle every two beats, on the first beat of each phrase, i.e. about 30 strokes a minute or one every two seconds.

EXAMPLE 40 *Haka: McL 335 as sung by Uehoka Tairakena*

A variant of the same song was notated in 1973, though unfortunately it could not be recorded, from Arapeta Awatere. Awatere identified the song as a rangi waka with paddlers pulling on their paddles as speculated above at points marked in the transcription with quaver rests and, at the end of the song, with accent marks. All the paddlers yelled 'Hei' on the offbeat at the end of each group.[372]

EXAMPLE *41 Rangi waka: as sung by Arapeta Awatere*

The paucity of paddling songs in the repertoire is probably a result of their generally ephemeral and improvisatory nature. The texts would not have outlasted the occasion of performance, and the method of performance would be lost as soon as canoes ceased to be used.

CHAPTER 3

SUNG SONG AND DANCE STYLES

In contrast with recited styles, sung styles are melodically organised. The melody repeats line by line in tandem with the text, tempos are usually slower and there is more rhythmic variety. Unlike recited songs which are necessarily syllabic, more than one note can be assigned to a syllable. Margaret Orbell characterises the texts as more personal and contemplative than the recited ones, often taking the form of a communication from one person to another.[1]

WAIATA

By far the most frequently performed songs, accounting for more than half of all songs recorded and an even larger proportion of songs whose texts have been published in collections such as *Nga Moteatea*,[2] are those known as waiata. Although used loosely for all songs of a melodic nature, the term is properly a specific song type. It may be used by itself or a qualifying term may be added to indicate the use of the song or nature of the text. The most numerous of the waiata are laments (waiata tangi) and love songs (waiata aroha and waiata whaiaaipo). Other qualifying terms can be so specific that hundreds of songs can be recorded without finding another the same. Amongst common and uncommon waiata so distinguished are the following from the McLean collection:

Waiata aroha — love song (McL 1 and others)
Waiata hahani — song of disparagement (McL 1082)
Waiata kaipaipa — pipe-smoking song (McL D45)
Waiata kanga — cursing song (McL 702)
Waiata koororohuu — song with whizzer accompaniment (McL 1012)
Waiata koroingo — song of longing (McL 30)
Waiata matakite — prophetical song (McL 1060)
Waiata mihi — song of greeting (McL 201 and others)
Waiata murimuri aroha — song of yearning for the past (McL 1282A)
Waiata patupaiarehe — song composed by the fairy folk (McL 306)
Waiata poi — song with poi accompaniment (McL 110 and others)
Waiata take — song with a message (McL 226)
Waiata tangi — lament (McL 3 and others)

Waiata tohutohu — song of instruction (McL 35)
Waiata whaiaaipo — sweetheart song (McL 4 and others)
Waiata whakaihi — Northland term for waiata whaiaaipo (McL 1054)
Waiata whakamomori — song of despair (McL 54)
Waiata whakapapa — genealogical song (McL 1119)
Waiata whakautu — song of reply (McL 48)
Waiata whakawaha tupaapaku[3] — song demanding a body for burial (McL 267)

Others include:

Waiata aatahu — song of a love charm (NM 246)
Waiata ki mookai — song of degradation (NM 207)
Waiata makamaka kaihaukai — song for a feast presentation (NM 244)
Waiata manaaki — song of welcome (lit. 'to show respect')[4]
Waiata mate kanehe — song expressing affectionate desire[5]
Waiata puuremu — song bewailing a partner's adultery[6]
Waiata taunu — jeering song (NM 315)
Waiata tautitotito — song sung during a singing debate (NM 322)
Waiata tawhito — ancient song (NM 116)
Waiata tohu — prophetic song (NM 126)
Waiata wawata — song of yearning (NM 236)
Waiata whaiwhaiaa — sorcerous song[7]
Waiata whakamaanawa taonga — songs sung when receiving a formal present[8]
Waiata whakatangitangi — song of regret (NM 198)

Waiata are performed by groups of singers with a song leader who may be either male or female. The most common venue is at meetings where they are customarily performed as a kiinaki or 'relish' after speeches during the rituals of encounter described in Chapter 1. During the course of his speech an orator may pace up and down, often gesticulating as he does so with a walking stick (tokotoko)[9] as speakers might once have brandished a weapon. As Salmond explains:

> The best speakers . . . move freely on the *marae*, striding backwards and forwards, leaping on their turns (*pekepeke*), quickly stamping their feet and lunging into powerful gestures. They move like warriors, agile and strong.[10]

This activity ceases abruptly when it is time to sing. The speaker stands stock still, his supporters grouping in behind him to assist with the song. The speaker may lead the song himself or a woman from his group may start it for him. If the speaker makes the mistake of starting before his supporters are ready, or worse still, if they have failed to form into a cohesive group, the song may break down, an event everywhere regarded as a bad omen and at worst a sign of death or disaster for the speaker or his kin.

The topic of the song is meant to be appropriate for the occasion, demonstrating, for example, a connection between the visiting tribe and the home tribe. But nowadays even an action song is often regarded as accept-

A war speech in 1827. Lithograph by Augustus Earle

Hetekia Te Kani Te Ua (d.1966)
delivering a whaikoorero

Eruera Manuera (Ngaati Awa tribe) leading a waiata. PHOTO: *Jeremy Salmond*

able. As Hiwi Tauroa observes, it is 'the act of singing the waiata that is important . . . [and] the act of supportive singing that has most significance'.[11]

Another use of waiata, in former times more so than today, again related to oratory. Serious collecting of Maori song texts began in the late 1840s and early 1850s when Governor Grey became interested in them, having noticed to his surprise that chiefs, either in speeches to him, or in their letters: 'frequently quoted in explanation of their views and intentions, fragments of ancient poems'.[12] Shortland noted that the older persons in the audience 'always understand perfectly the application and meaning of the songs thus introduced in quotation, and on hearing them have no difficulty in judging the intentions of the speaker'.[13] The method and rationale of quotation is explained by Thomson:

> Orators at first selected quotations dimly shadowing forth their opinions. Such figurative language excited the curiosity and ingenuity of the assembly to detect their intentions. Quotation after quotation made their meaning more clear, and when the speakers were influential men, and held opinions in unison with the majority of the people, each quotation as it developed their meaning was received with murmurs of applause. To prevent mistakes, orators, before they concluded, almost invariably made their wishes known in some quotation not to be misunderstood. Then the whole assembly applauded the orators for their poetic knowledge, and their oratorical art in making manifest under beautiful metaphors their real opinions.[14]

113

If Best is to be believed, it would appear that messages were sometimes delivered exclusively by song, but his evidence for this is sketchy. Best claims that important communications 'were not seldom made in song' and cites an incident of 1793 in which two men who had been away were told of events that had taken place during their absence by means of a song.[15] Further, Philips quotes her informant George Graham of Auckland as stating that during the war waged by Hone Heke in the North, Heke sent messengers to South Auckland to ask the tribes there to join him in attacking Waitemata and communicated his purpose by means of a waiata.

> Although no direct statement or request was made, the hearers fully understood Heke's intentions and adjourned the meeting to prepare a suitable *waiata* in answer. This was delivered the following day, Potatau, later to become Maori king, being in this case the song leader. Potatau's reply was an expression of surprise that Heke should dare to threaten the *pakeha* who were 'within the shelter of his shadow'.[16]

It is possible that the story is either apocryphal or inflates the role of the waiata; Te Hurinui, who was an authority on waiata, in his book on the life of Potatau, refers to the event, quoting Potatau's reply to Heke, but makes no mention of song.[17] However, other such songs by Potatau are on record. In *Nga Moteatea*[18] are two songs of reply by Potatau (NM 195 and 196) to requests that he accept offers of kingship.

Laments and love songs

Although distinctions are made between laments (waiata tangi) and love songs (waiata aroha and waiata whaiaaipo), the two classes of song are functionally and textually often identical; musically, in common with other waiata, they are entirely so.

Best points out that although laments for the dead are called (waiata) tangi, so are songs bewailing lesser misfortune, even events as seemingly trivial as the loss of an eel pot or a fish hook.[19] One such song cited by Best was composed for a dead pig.[20] Similarly, because the word aroha means not only 'love', but also 'sympathy' and 'pity', amongst other meanings, a waiata aroha may be a true love song but can also be a lament or expressive of commiseration. Because love songs are invariably about lost or unhappy love, the term waiata aroha becomes interchangeable with waiata tangi although the converse is not necessarily true. Confirmation of this occurred often at recording sessions when singers were frequently at a loss to know which of the two terms to use. Because of this overlap, Margaret Orbell is able to say flatly:

> All waiata take the form of complaints. Most of them are waiata aroha, 'songs of yearning' in which women complain about gossip, or unrequited love, or

the way their husbands are treating them; and waiata tangi, which may bemoan an illness or some other trouble but usually lament the death of a relative.[21]

In another publication, Orbell provides more information about the content of the texts, the circumstances of composition, the occasions of use and the differences and similarities between waiata tangi and waiata aroha:

Waiata tangi (weeping waiata) were composed equally by men and women and were usually laments for the dead, though they might lament the loss of land or crops, illness, or some other loss. They were sung by individuals and by groups of people at funerals, and afterwards when it was appropriate to remember and mourn the person who had died; frequently as well they were later sung, sometimes in adapted form, to mourn other deaths. The second of these subgenres, waiata aroha (waiata of love, or longing), were composed exclusively by women and usually complained about unrequited love, the refusal of the poet's family to let her marry the man of her choice, or an absent or neglectful husband; occasionally too they lamented the poet's separation from relatives. They were sung in the first place by the poet, whose name and circumstances are sometimes still known, and they might later be sung by others, sometimes in adapted form. These others might be singing the song simply for entertainment, or in memory of the woman or the man she had loved; or they might see themselves as being in a comparable situation to that of the original poet, and adapt the words of her song to fit their own circumstances.

It was not only women who adapted these love laments to make them apply to their own situation. Men did so too, in the course of oratory: for example, a chief who regretted the absence of a man he wanted as a political ally might sing a well-known waiata aroha, thereby identifying himself with the poet and the other man with her absent lover. . . .

Between them, then, the waiata tangi and the waiata aroha lament and comment upon the experiences of separation through death, and separation in life. . . . in each case the poets speak mainly of their distress, and of the separation from a person (occasionally, persons) which has caused it. They are likely to refer to the accompanying circumstances, giving reasons for what has occurred. Frequently there is praise or blame: in waiata tangi the poet may praise the person who has died, attack and threaten enemies responsible, reproach the deceased for leaving, or blame himself or herself for not dying as well, while in waiata aroha the woman may complain bitterly about gossip and slander, and blame either the man or herself for the events which led to her present situation; sometimes too she asks her listeners not to blame her for her actions. These ideas reflect and give expression to major preoccupations in Maori society and thought. . . . it was a society in which persons of consequence were likely to complain publicly when they were in unhappy circumstances, and to name those responsible.[22]

Elsewhere, Orbell points out that the public singing by a woman of a clever, heartfelt waiata aroha could be a highly assertive act:

> For a woman in difficult domestic circumstances, it might well influence the persons to whom it was addressed and at the very least would improve her social position. And a girl's complaint about a man's indifference was an accepted way of declaring her love and encouraging a response.[23]

Waiata whaiaaipo (sweetheart songs) are evidently regarded as more personal and direct in their connotations than waiata aroha, though often the two terms are used interchangeably. It seems, too, that these songs could be less serious than waiata aroha. Orbell states that often in a waiata whaiaaipo a woman would claim to be in love with several men, addressing each in turn and sometimes sending herself on an imaginary journey to visit them. Such songs were mostly light-hearted and sung for entertainment 'though a poet might take the opportunity to speak her mind to someone with whom she had been involved, or encourage a man she particularly liked'.[24] The essential differences between the two song types are encapsulated by Orbell in the glossary to her book as: waiata aroha — waiata expressing longing and love; waiata whaiaaipo — love song, woman's waiata addressed to a man or men she loves, or claims to love.[25]

Half of the 50 songs transcribed and translated in McLean & Orbell are examples of waiata. Most take the melodic form of repeated strophes, each ending as a rule with a leader solo, performed either by prolonging the final syllable of the line or on meaningless syllables, called a hiianga or, in English, a 'drag'. The musical strophe divides usually into two phrases the second of which, because of the drag, may be longer than the first. Typically, each repetition of the musical strophe is coincident with a textual line and each musical phrase with a textual half line or phrase.

The example following is the beginning of a song of unknown tribal origin as sung by Turau and Marata Te Tomo of Ngaati Tuuwharetoa. It is transcribed in full as Song 16 in McLean & Orbell.

EXAMPLE 42 *Waiata: Beginning of M&O 16 as sung by Turau and Marata Te Tomo*

PAO

Pao (also called ruri, ruriruri or too[26]) are seldom referred to in the ethnographic and travel literature and, as Orbell observes, have been neglected also by scholars and translators.[27] If mentioned at all, they are generally dismissed as 'ditties'. Maori singers likewise tend not to value them, seldom thinking to offer them at recording sessions unless prompted to do so. Nevertheless, they are probably the most frequently sung and composed of all song types except waiata.

All pao take the form of two-line couplets, each couplet representing a verse or stanza. In contrast with the more elaborate and carefully composed waiata, pao were conventionally extemporised, their structure and manner of performance aiding the composition. The usual venue for performance would have been an informal occasion with a number of people present. While the composer thought of the next couplet, the company would repeat the previous one. At subsequent performances, if the pao are worth resurrecting, a similar format applies, each couplet continuing to be sung twice. Kino Hughes said that amongst the Tuuhoe tribe, pao are sung for entertainment after speech-making is over. Often they take the form of a competition, each person trying to match the others with another pao.[28]

As can be imagined, the songs sung on these occasions are only loosely associated. Pao composed on a single subject may later be sung together, but the order of verses may vary and additions and omissions may occur. Effectively, in contrast with the fixed order stanzas usual in longer compositions such as waiata, each couplet in a pao is a self-contained separate song.

Another characteristic of pao which aids improvisation and group participation is the use of all-purpose tunes or melodic stereotyping. The writer first became aware of this in 1964 when Rawinia Murray of Parikino stated that pao in Wanganui, unlike waiata in the same area, all have the same air.[29] The same was later found to be true of other areas. Additionally, individual singers may have favourite airs to which they will sing most pao known to them or group pao sung by others to different tunes. McL 1110, for example, is a set of unrelated pao with different tunes but all sung to the same tune by the singer.

Pao sung for entertainment are epigrammatic topical songs characterised by Orbell as 'offering comment, often witty and incisive, on love, sex, politics, and the vicissitudes of life in general'.[30] As such they tend to be ephemeral, becoming sooner or later forgotten along with the events which occasioned them. As a result, whether or not sung in traditional style, most pao still in the repertoire are of fairly recent composition. Few, if any, antedate the present century. Perhaps because of this, mention of European objects or possessions and the use of transliterated European words in the texts is common. Some pao also have European or transitional tunes.

Although seldom found in printed or manuscript sources, pao are well represented in the McLean collection of recordings. In all, more than 100 pao or sets of pao have been recorded. Some were composed by the singers themselves. For many of the others, as for waiata, the composers and circumstances of composition were known to the singers.

Pao composed by the singers include some composed spontaneously at the time of recording. McL 175B was sung by Te Kehi Kati of Ngaati Tuuwharetoa at the conclusion of a talk about the history of the area around Oruaiwi. The purpose of the song was to explain that although she was old now and feeble in body, her mind was still active. On replay of the item she clapped her hands in delight and shouted 'Hooray, hooray!' Another spontaneous pao, recorded by Uehoka Tairakena of Ngaati Mahanga, Waikato, was composed as a joke to farewell his own voice going the rounds of the tribes. After recording it, the singer thought of an additional verse and recorded this also. All was done in the space of one or two minutes:

EXAMPLE 43 *Pao: McL 278B as sung by Uehoka Tairakena*

Just as waiata can be sub-categorised by the addition of a qualifying term, so too can pao, with many of the main sub-categories of waiata (aroha, tangi, whaiaaipo, whakautu etc.) also represented. The most numerous of the pao are pao whaiaaipo (love songs), sung mostly, as stated above, for entertainment. Some are songs of romantic or unhappy love, similar in sentiment to waiata whaiaaipo. Many, by contrast, are ribald, referring in sexually explicit ways to their subjects. One example is McL 992 with references to the long strokes of sheep-shearing as representative of the sexual act. Others have been recorded for which the singers were unwilling to provide explanations.

Other types of pao, however, had a serious purpose. Those recorded include pao aroha — songs of sympathy by two widows for each other (McL 831); and pao poroporoaki — songs of farewell sung at a tangi on the last night of a burial (McL108).

In the Taranaki area, where former waiata have mostly been reworked into poi form (see next section), pao serve similar purposes to waiata elsewhere, as well as providing a record of historical events. Many are sung in association with poi and relate to the prophet Te Whiti. One Taranaki singer, Hamu Katene, never sang pao in isolation but only to illustrate points of history. Amongst such songs in the McLean collection are: pao poroporoaki — farewell songs for Maori prisoners taken to Otago at the time of Te Whiti (McL 478); pao tangi — lament for an uncle of the singer who had died (McL 485A); and pao whakautu — answer to a taunt (McL 550). Others include:

McL 483 — composed on the occasion of the return of the ashes of Maui Pomare to Manukorihi Paa

McL 521B — composed by the singers for tangi ceremonies

McL 548 — relating how the people were saved when British troops brought a cannon against Te Whiti at Parihaka

McL 628B — composed after the return of Maori prisoners exiled to Otago

And from other tribes:

McL 194 — composed by the singer's mother on her death bed

McL 628 — referring to the Bible

McL 898 — for 'boys' who went overseas in the Second World War

McL 1156 & 1157 — religious songs composed by a woman who got them in a dream

McL 1175 — a Tuuhoe song about the time Rua Kenana was in jail

Another category of pao, evidently sung, like pao whaiaaipo, mostly for entertainment, were dining-room pao;[31] singers say they were performed (like hari kai) when carrying food (kai), while visitors were having meals, or as a call to kai. The following is a call to kai as performed in 1964 by Kurauia Tahuriorangi of Ngaati Pikiao:

EXAMPLE 44 Pao: First stanza of McL 693A as sung by Kurauia Tahuriorangi

Also very much in the category of entertainment are 'billy-can pao' sung to the accompaniment of beating on a European tin billy or plate. The example following was recorded in 1970 from Raupare Werahiko of Ngaati Toa and Ngaati Raukawa.

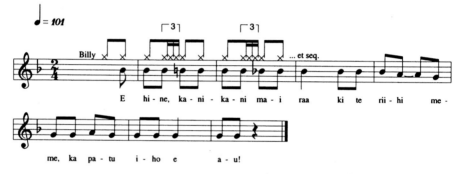

EXAMPLE 45 Pao: McL 824 as sung by Raupare Werahiko

Other billy-can pao have been recorded from Kino Hughes of Tuuhoe as McL 1088.

Pao structure

Pao are distinguished from other sung items most of all by their couplet structure and by a common rhythmic scheme. Perhaps a quarter of the pao in the McLean collection are performed with drags in mid line or at the ends of phrases, like waiata. Many in this category appear to be non-metric, again like waiata. Example 46 was recorded in 1964 from Meri Puata of Te Ati Awa.

Most of the remaining recorded pao are metric. Of these, a handful — only half a dozen in the entire recorded corpus — are in simple time (2/4 or 2/8). Two of these (McL 1128 and 1132) are Taranaki pao used formerly as marching songs for poi teams entering the marae. Example 47 is the beginning of McL 1128 as performed in 1973 by Kopeka Hawe and Miro Pokai of Ngaa Ruahinerangi tribe. The tempo of 98 beats/minute is at a steady marching pace.

EXAMPLE 46 *Pao: McL 628B as sung by Meri Puata*

EXAMPLE 47 *Pao: Beginning of McL 1128 as sung by Kopeka Hawe and Miro Pokai*

The rest of the recorded metric songs are all in triple time. A small group of the triple-time songs are in 3/4 time. They lack drags or ornament and have relatively fast tempos in the range of 100–115 beats/minute. The following, as sung in 1972 by Kino Hughes, is an example. It is the conclusion of a pao tangi composed by Titihooea, a woman of Ngaati Awa who went away on a ship with her lover, leaving her dog behind. The song is sung as if by the dog, sitting on a hill under the shade of a maahoe tree looking down at Te Mahoe where there is now a dam. The tune is similar to that of McLean & Orbell Song 3.

u - a, e - e - i, ki te wa - a kaa - i - nga, e ta - ku ma -

kau - he - a e - i.

EXAMPLE 48 Pao tangi: Beginning of McL 1103 as sung by Kino Hughes

The greatest number of pao by far are in 3/8 time. Characteristically, the 3/8 songs make use of iambic rhythms which, along with couplet line structure, occur in all tribal areas where recordings have been made. They are slower than the 3/4 songs, generally in the range of 50–80 dotted crotchet beats/minute.

The following is the beginning of a set of Taranaki pao poroporoaki in iambic rhythm. The singer said they were composed at Pungarehu as farewell songs for Maori prisoners taken to Otago. The first line refers to a military bugle. Although simple, the music is ingenious as it demands continuity over mid-line phrase breaks in the text. The song was recorded from Hamu Katene of Nga Rauru tribe in 1963.

E pi- ki mai Pu - nga-re-hu, ka ta- ngi mai te piu-ka-ra.

EXAMPLE 49 Pao poroporoaki: McL 478 as sung by Hamu Katene

Another very common characteristic of pao, particularly from female singers, and perhaps especially in the iambic songs, is an abundant use of rapid ornament, a device which makes these songs difficult to sing. Para Iwikau of Ngaati Tuuwharetoa, a notable exponent of both waiata and pao, commented about the latter that it took her longer 'to get into the way of them' than it did to learn waiata. One of her recordings (McL 96), exemplary of ornamented pao, is transcribed and translated in McLean & Orbell as Song 8. Another such song is Example 50, a pao whaiaaipo from Turau and Marata Te Tomo, also of Ngaati Tuuwharetoa. It is a love song by an unknown composer for Te Paerata.

Also from Marata Te Tomo is Example 51, recorded a decade later in 1972. It is an excellent example of pao style, demonstrative of the use of an all-purpose air. Except for the details of the ornament it is markedly similar to the previous example.

EXAMPLE 50 *Pao whaiaaipo: McL 138 as sung by Turau and Marata Te Tomo*

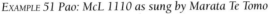

EXAMPLE 51 *Pao: McL 1110 as sung by Marata Te Tomo*

The above examples illustrate perfectly the common rhythmic scheme referred to earlier, which must also be regarded as diagnostic of pao style. An overwhelming majority of recorded pao contain exactly eight beats to the line. In about half of the songs, each eight-beat line is subdivided into two phrases of four beats each. This use of a standard rhythmic model explains the ability of singers to change the tune of a pao at will. Effectively, any pao text which conforms to the eight-beat pattern can be sung to any tune which also occupies eight beats.

POI

Not all poi can be described as sung, but there is a historical progression from recited styles of poi to the sung forms so it will be convenient to treat all together.

A turn of the century account of poi is the following from Elsdon Best:

The *poi* may be said to be allied to the *haka*, and is so styled by the natives. The *poi* dance (so termed) is performed by females. Each performer has a small, light ball made of leaves of the raupo tightly rolled, and having a string attached to it. In times past these *poi* balls were ornamented by attaching the long hair from the tail of the Maori dog, now extinct. The players hold the string, and, timing each movement to the *poi* song (*rangi poi*), twirl the light balls in many directions — now in front of the body, now over the right shoulder, then the left, &c. The players stand in ranks while perform-

123

ing. . . . This game has been revived of late years, and was one of the attractions of the Maori meeting at Rotorua at the time of the visit of our Royal guests in June, 1901.[32]

The royal visit referred to by Best was that of the Duke and Duchess of Cornwall and York who in 1910 became King George V and Queen Mary. The royal couple spent three days at Rotorua during which there was a large-scale reception from the Maori people who were represented by performing groups from all over the North Island. A report of the visit was published a year later under the editorship of Robert Loughnan.[33] It is valuable for its detailed accounts of haka, poi and other items performed at Rotorua, as described by Sir Apirana Ngata.[34]

Two poi teams, each of 40 women and girls, chosen for their beauty, performed for the duke and duchess on the second day. The girls of Ngaai Te Rangi wore long white cloaks and white albatross feathers in their hair. They began their poi to the accompaniment of a song alternating between two male leaders:

> The *poi* balls commence to spin; the deft hands twirling them move up and down, sideways, backwards and forwards, hovering now over the shoulders, now over and across the knee, the whirling balls appearing to surround, as with a network of gossamer, the bodies of the dancers as they sway from side to side, lifting alternate feet and throwing one across gently forward with a lilting motion, giving the general effect of a waltz step.[35]

The girls of Ngaati Raukawa, led by 'three little maids' and also with feathers in their hair, were dressed alternately in scarlet and white, creating picturesque patterns as they changed ranks from twos to fours and back again, anticipating by more than half a century the marching girls of more recent years. The accompaniment was equally innovative, consisting of flute, fiddle and jew's harp. Their finale was a *tour de force* 'to the soft strains of the waltz' during which the dancers performed with double poi, one in each hand, 'and with these they bewitched all who gazed upon them':

> And ever the white and scarlet changed places, or drew up into one long rank of alternate colours, or wheeled to right or left in fours, to no command other than the unwearied strains of the small band of Maori musicians.[36]

On the last day, the Ngaati Raukawa and Ngaai Te Rangi teams performed again as well as teams from Te Arawa and Ngaati Porou, but from Ngata's rhapsodical account of them it was evidently the former who stole the show.

Ngata says nothing about the music of the above performances beyond mentioning the 'strangely attractive monotone' of the Ngaai Te Rangi dancers, the use of the fiddle and other instruments by the Ngaati Raukawa group, and the waltz rhythms employed by both groups. Except for the use of monotone, it might well seem from this that, as early as 1901, poi songs were already Europeanised as they predominantly are today. Such an inference may not be entirely justified. The instruments were not necessarily playing European tunes, and the 'waltz' rhythms could have been 3/8 haka rhythms. Confirmation of the latter possibility is provided by Example 25, quoted earlier in the section on poowhiri. It is the Ngaati Raukawa welcome poi at the very event, as remembered over 60 years later by Pairoa Wineera, who was 19 years old in 1901 and very proud to have been chosen as one of the leaders of this item. The melody is mostly on two notes, but the endings of each verse are spoken as in haka and the rhythms also are those of haka. Another resemblance is the slap of the poi balls which can be heard wherever a foot stamp would occur in haka.

It is nevertheless true that European melodies were made use of in poi songs quite early. Ani Reweti Natana, of Ruatoki, who was two or three years old when Mount Tarawera erupted in 1886, remembered hearing poi songs when she was a girl, performed with accordion accompaniment. They were melodic and sounded about the same as they do now.[37] The first stanza of one such song composed *c*.1908, as performed by a Ngaati Tuuhourangi group in 1970, appears later as Example 100.

Accounts of poi dancing before 1900 are few and far between. As Mitcalfe points out, the earliest travellers such as Cook and de Surville and observers such as Earle and Cruise say nothing of the poi, although they provide detailed descriptions of haka and other dances.[38] The earliest reports of poi describe it not as a dance but as a game.

Nicholas refers to a present given to the missionary Samuel Marsden

> of a ball called a *poe*, with which the ladies amuse themselves by throwing it repeatedly backward and forward; it is somewhat larger than a cricket-ball, and made of their cloth or canvas, stuffed with the down of the bull-rush, having a long string attached to it, which they seize with the fore-finger while the ball is in motion, and are very dexterous in this practice.[39]

Dieffenbach likewise mentions the poi only as a game, doing so in the context of another game which seems to have been a form of juggling:

> They have a game with four balls, exactly like that of the Indian jugglers, and they accompany it with a song. Another game is with one ball (poi) suspended from a string.[40]

Colenso, too, refers to it merely as 'a pleasing and dexterous game' performed by young women with 'their light stuffed and ornamented handball'.[41]

However, Best quotes an 1841 report by Halswell[42] which refers to

> balls very neatly made of black and white plait, which are swung by the cord in a peculiar manner, whilst the performers, many in number, sing in excellent time. Most of the women excell in this, and the exact time, the

regular motion, and precise attitude which is observed by all the performers, are peculiarly striking.[43]

Here, for the first time, is an indication of an accompanying song. Mid-century accounts onwards, like the earlier ones, continue to call the poi a game, but do not fail to mention the song. Shortland gives the following information:

> Young women are very expert at a game called *pohi*, in which an ornamented ball fastened to a string three or four feet long is used. The string is held by one hand, while the ball is struck with the other repeatedly in different directions, but always in time with the measure of a song chanted at the same moment. When several seated together on the ground are thus diverting themselves, the graceful attitudes of their bodies present to the eye a group well adapted for the pencil of the artist.[44]

Shortland's reference to 'the pencil of the artist' may well refer to the accompanying (rather sentimental and over-idealised) painting by Joseph Merrett,[45] who is thought to have worked closely with Shortland.[46]

The painting formed part of an album presented to Eliza Hobson, the wife of New Zealand's first governor, when she returned to England in 1843. Also in the album is an account of poi, most likely written by Shortland, in which he describes the use of ornamented poi balls to convey messages. One use of the poi is said to have been as a 'love letter': a male suitor would send a poi to a young lady; if she favoured him she would play with the poi 'on all favourable occasions'; if she rejected him she would throw it away. Another use was as a message from chief to chief as a signal to gather forces. Playing with poi was stated to be accompanied by 'a kind of chant' and the ball was 'struck alternately with either hand the string being so managed as to cause the ball to describe a variety of figures'.[47]

Thomson provides further detail about the performers' movements:

> Poi is a game played with variegated balls, about the size of large oranges, to which strings are attached. The string is held in one hand and the ball is struck with the other. The hand holding the string is often changed, the string is shortened and lengthened, and the ball is struck from under the arms, and in a variety of ways. Poi is played in a sitting posture, and players sing songs applicable to the time. Much practice is requisite to play the poi ball properly, and when well played, with a handsome ball, and a good song, the effect is beautiful.[48]

Noteworthy in the accounts of both Shortland and Thomson, and illustrated also by one of the figures in Merrett's drawing, are statements that the poi was performed seated. Best is disposed to doubt this, claiming: 'Though this ball game might be practised to some extent in a sitting position, as of an evening, yet more important exhibitions were certainly given standing in

Joseph Merrett: 'The Maori game of poi', watercolour, pen & ink [1843].
PHOTO: *Hocken Library, Dunedin*

ranks.'[49] But he was probably thinking of performances such as those he saw in 1901.

The few accounts of poi are either inexplicit about the sex of the performers or, like Merrett's drawing, represent it as performed by females. Best is alone in stating that it was performed by females 'but sometimes youths took part'. He continues:

> It was a common pastime among the people at all times and was practised at intertribal social gatherings. Contests were sometimes held between different hamlets, when a party of *poi* performers from a village would visit another in order to play against a local team. Such visits also took place in connection with the *haka*, and other amusements calling for skill on the part of the performers.[50]

Best does not reveal his sources, but at the beginning of his account of poi he states:

> It is now viewed as being essentially an amusement for girls and women, but there is some evidence to show that, in former times, young men took part in it, at least among some tribes.[51]

Best and Buck both provide descriptions of the poi balls used in the dance.[52] Common ones were called poi kookau (unadorned poi). They were made by wrapping dry raupo leaves around some object to give them weight and form, and they had short strings. Superior poi were larger and had long strings. They were made of netting or with the taaniko technique and stuffed with raupo down or other soft material. They were usually decorated with tufts of dog's hair (awe) and hence called poi awe.

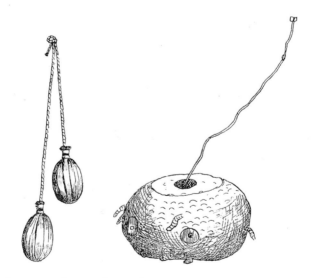

Common and ornate forms of poi. From Edge-Partington Album

In Ngata's description of the welcome to the Duke and Duchess of York in 1901, he characterises the long-string form of poi as the older of the two and goes on to provide information about former uses of poi:

> The old Maoris say that the *poi* dances of their time were even more effective; the strings used with the poi-balls being far longer, some six feet, and extending the picturesque gossamer effect of the twirling balls, the dancers being necessarily in extended order, and the display more imposing. The old dance was slower, and allowed more time for the display of grace and the elaboration of gesture. The ostensible object of the *poi* from the first was to give graceful welcome to strangers (*manuhiri*), visiting tribes, *tino rangatiras*, and other persons of distinction. But gradually there grew up another object, which was to attract the fighting men from other tribes, and invariably the best-chosen dancers and the best-ordered *pois* kept the ranks of the *tauas* [warriors] up to their full strength. To-day, of course, these *pois* are no more than what they were originally intended to be, the women's portion of the ceremonial welcome of a hospitable, high-minded, and punctilious people.[53]

Two matters for clarification emerge from this statement. First, whether or not earlier poi were performed seated, later ones were certainly performed standing and those performed with very long strings could have been performed in no other way. It may well be that the latter type of poi was not a particularly older form but merely antedated the performances of 1901.[54] Nevertheless, in view of the lack of firm evidence, it would seem sensible to accept an earlier statement from Best himself that poi were performed in both seated and standing positions.[55] Second, if the poi was used during the poowhiri or ceremonial welcome, then it might be supposed that it was, indeed, a form of haka, confirming Best's designation of the poi as haka poi.

There is no question that poi were sometimes composed in adapted haka form. The Ngaati Raukawa poi to welcome the Duke and Duchess of Cornwall and York in 1901 has already been quoted (see Example 25) and shown to be a form of sung haka. Additionally, McL 1097, a waiata poi by Kareko of Tuuhoe, though not well enough known by the singer to be transcribable in full, is also a sung haka, performed, like the Ngaati Raukawa item, with haka rhythms and a scale of two notes a tone apart. For some poi, however, the qualifying term 'haka' is a misnomer and, on this account, ought not be applied to all poi. Best or his informants may have been using the term 'haka' as generic for all forms of dance and, even though some poi songs are identifiable with haka, others were different.

Two written accounts have been found which refer to the poi or the song accompanying it as a haka. Lt. Col. St John was an amanuensis for a trader named Charles Marshall who arrived at the mouth of the Waikato River in 1830. He writes of the poi as follows:

One pretty haka they have, in which each performer holds a ball with a short piece of string attached, and the different motions given to it with great rapidity and in perfect time form a pleasing accompaniment to the monotonous dreary sing-song recital. At times the voice seems to proceed from the heels, it is so deep.[56]

Much later, in the King Country, Burton saw poi being performed by young girls to the accompaniment, with 'some hint of a *haka*', of music 'beaten out of a thin baking dish'. He found it a 'fetching' sight to see 'a pretty Maori lass — an adept in *poi* — throw the ball about in all directions, now striking her hands, now her bosom; now jerking it over one shoulder, now over the other, then upon her lap . . .'.[57]

This performance appears to have been akin to that of 'billy-can' pao, referred to earlier, and there is no reason to suppose that poi were not, on occasion, performed to pao tunes. Certainly they were sometimes performed to paatere. One extremely well known paatere, assumed to have been performed with poi, was that of Erenora, a high-born woman of Ngaati Raukawa (Example 6). Another is in *Nga Moteatea*: NM 131, a paatere — unfortunately not recorded on tape — cited by Best as a rangi poi or poi song.[58] In the introduction to this song, Ngata states explicitly that the tempo of paatere is suitable for poi dances. Finally, two poi songs recorded from Tuuhoe singers, one (McL 667A) designated as a waiata poi and the other (McL 1192B) as a haka poi, are both sung forms of paatere. The latter song was identified by the singer as composed by Monehu Tamehana, who was a Tuuhoe poi leader at the time of the royal visit in 1901. The following is the beginning of the song as recorded from Kino Hughes in 1974:

EXAMPLE 52 *Haka poi: Beginning of McL 1192B as sung by Kino Hughes*

Next is the first stanza of McL 667A as recorded in 1964 from Kino Hughes, Onewhero Te Ani and others of Tuuhoe tribe. No information was available from the singers on the history of the song.

EXAMPLE 53 *Waiata poi: Beginning of McL 667A as led by Kino Hughes*

When asked about Best's term 'haka poi', Arapeta Awatere said he never saw one though his clear memory went back only to 1914 or 1915 when he was four or five years old. However, he knew of two paatere besides 'Poia atu taku poi' (NM 142) in which poi actions were used.[59] Earlier, he was of the opinion that a poi is 'nothing but an accompaniment to a song' and a song was never written specially for it.[60] This may well have been the case until poi songs began to be composed for events such as the 1901 royal visit. It would appear that initially the poi was a game, most likely performed without vocal accompaniment. Songs later added to the game were adapted from haka, paatere and perhaps other song types, eventually becoming supplanted by songs in European idiom.

In the South Island, it is possible that the poi as a game survived longer than in the North. Murihiku informants told Beattie that the poi was at first performed without strings. Both long and short strings were later introduced and eventually the short form ousted the long. Both standing and seated forms of poi were played. One person said players knelt and used their hands to hit the balls about. Another said players stood in two rows facing each other and threw across balls and sang.[61] In Canterbury, the older form of poi was said generally to have been performed standing, with long strings, but to have been superseded from about 1890 by a style brought in by Te Whiti and Tohu of Parihaka (in Taranaki; see next).[62] In Nelson it was played with long strings in a style 'something like boxing'. The players sat or stood facing each other throwing the balls from one to another while others sat or stood singing a song.[63]

The Parihaka style of poi referred to above is of pivotal significance in the history of the poi. It was a late nineteenth-century development in which the poi became the emblem of a religious movement begun by the Maori prophet Te Whiti. These poi, too, appear to have followed a progression from recited through to sung forms, beginning, in this case, with the paatere.

Te Whiti addressing a meeting on 17 January 1880. PHOTO: *Canterbury Museum, Christchurch, ref. 6353*

Te Whiti and Tohu poi

Te Whiti-o-Rongomai (*c.*1831–1907) of Parihaka is an important historical figure in New Zealand, an early advocate of non-violence and passive resistance. In 1866, after his village had been burned by government troops, Te Whiti moved to Parihaka, between New Plymouth and Hawera in Taranaki, where, in association with his brother-in-law Tohu Kaakahi (?–1907), he established his own religion. Although he sympathised with the King Movement and Maori nationalism, he would not allow his people to fight. In 1879, when government workers began to survey unjustly confiscated land, Te Whiti launched a campaign of passive obstruction. Survey pegs were pulled up, fences were built across disputed land and farmers' fields were ploughed up as a form of protest. Settlers became alarmed and pressed for punitive action to which the government acceded by passing laws to permit imprisonment without trial. On Fireworks Day, 5 November 1881, a military expedition led by the Native Minister, John Bryce, marched on Parihaka with almost 1600 armed constabulary to arrest Te Whiti and Tohu. They were met by some 200 children, skipping, singing and dancing, and by women who offered bread to the soldiers. Te Whiti and Tohu gave themselves up peacefully and were kept in captivity for over a year, without trial, before being allowed to return home in March 1883. This less than glorious gov-

Maori boys performing the haka before British troops at Parihaka. Sketch by Private James Ledger (1881). PHOTO: *Hocken Library, Dunedin*

ernment victory inspired a satirical verse from a Pakeha poet: 'When can their glory fade? Oh! The wild charge they made!'[64]

Maori poets also commemorated the event. McL 533A and McL 548 are a waiata and a pao respectively, referring to a six-pounder Armstrong field gun that was dragged to the top of Fort Rolleston overlooking Parihaka and used to threaten the occupants with shelling if followers of the prophets from outside the area did not vacate the village by midday. As related by Dick Scott, this event occurred two days after the arrest of Te Whiti and Tohu.[65] The scene can be imagined as perhaps 2000 people[66] sat in silence watching the cannon, tension building slowly as the deadline drew near and no one obeyed the order to leave. Shortly before midday, a dog was seen slowly climbing the hill until it reached the top where it treated the British cannon with appropriate contempt by lifting its leg against the wheel.

In the years from 1866 onwards, before the above events took place, Te Whiti and Tohu had established at Parihaka 'a community in which the virtues of old Maoridom were united with the best of European civilisation':

> The land was farmed co-operatively; hard work and cleanliness were insisted upon; the mentally or physically handicapped were not made the butt of remarks: liquor was prohibited.[67]

In its heyday, Parihaka had a sealed road, its own bakehouse, abattoir, water supply and even electric lighting.[68] By 1891, there were four dining halls which could hold 300 guests at a sitting.[69] Te Whiti and Tohu also had

Parihaka in 1881 from Fort Rolleston. The European-style house overlooking the village was built to receive the governor, should he ever visit Te Whiti. The marae where Te Whiti addressed his followers is the open space where people are gathered. In the centre of the marae is Te Whiti's bank, standing on four uprights; at the back of it is the prophet's own house. To the right, on a slight rise, is the meeting house. The burial ground is on a small hill in the right foreground. Sketch by Private James Ledger (1881).
PHOTO: *Hocken Library, Dunedin.*

their own school for the children of Parihaka, having rejected European schooling 'as leading to folly and pride, while writing was condemned as the tool of the frauds constantly perpetrated by the Pakeha on the Maori'.[70] As late as 1962–63, some of the writer's Taranaki informants were illiterate as a result of Te Whiti's proscription against reading and writing.

In 1883 it was reported of Te Whiti that his only literature was the Bible.[71] In lieu of other writings in Parihaka was a large body of oral literature in the form of poi songs which together formed the liturgy of the Te Whiti and Tohu religion and served also as a symbol of peace.

Te Whiti's sermons, selections from the Old Testament and significant events in the prophets' careers were chanted while the singers, hair decked with white feathers, clad in white, twirled the poi.[72]

134

The three great symbols underpinning the Te Whiti movement were the Bible, the raukura and the poi. The Bible was supreme as the word of God; the raukura were feathers (traditionally three) from the underwing of the albatross, worn by followers to signify 'glory to God on high, peace on earth and goodwill to all mankind'; the poi stood for peace and hospitality.[73]

James Cowan gives a description of a Taranaki poi rehearsal seen by him at Parihaka, three years before Te Whiti's death in 1907,[74] at the express invitation of Te Whiti himself who was present at the performance. The event impressed Cowan deeply:

> The women and girls, numbering about thirty, wore a profusion of white feathers — the *raukura*, Te Whiti's badge — in their dark glossy hair. They gave one *poi* after another, some with long strings, an art requiring great skill and precision; they chanted and swung the *poi*, and swayed their supple forms for nearly two hours . . . There was something almost fierce about the delivery of this kind of *poi*, and the flashing black eyes, the tossing feathers, the high wild chant, combined to give a thrill to it all that the ordinary *poi* of the Maori amusement halls does not hold.[75]

The texts, Cowan explains, which referred to such topics as the coming of the ancestral canoes, land confiscations and other grievances and embodied the sayings of Te Whiti, were legendary, historical and ritualistic. One recounted an entire sermon given by Te Whiti.

In another publication, Cowan gives a similar description, again emphasising a perceived lack of European influence in the songs:

> The Maori prophet Te Whiti and his chief men at Parihaka village had their oracular utterances and their chants and prayers rehearsed and publicly sung by the *poi*-women. It was a very pretty sight to watch a large party of these girls and women, their heads all decked with white feathers — the *tohu* or emblem of Te Whiti-ism — going through the evolutions of the *poi*, with wonderful rapidity and deftness . . . for the Prophet of the Mountain did not look with favour on accordions and mouth-organs and other *pakeha* innovations.[76]

Less well known than the other events surrounding Te Whiti, though of long standing by the time of Cowan's visit in 1904, was a schism which had taken place between the followers of Te Whiti and Tohu after the exile of the two leaders from Parihaka in 1881. Differences between the two, which had begun as early as 1879, came to a head in the early 1890s when Te Whiti set about modernising Parihaka against the wishes of the more conservative Tohu. Followers of the latter became known as Pore (polled or dehorned) because they forsook the wearing of the raukura.[77] From this time onwards, each of the two men claimed to be the true prophet and, with their followers, went their separate ways. Each group thenceforth met on different days, composed its own poi songs, and maintained its own separate marae at Parihaka.

Poi dancers welcoming visitors to Manukorihi meeting house, Waitara

The present writer was privileged to record a large number of Te Whiti and Tohu poi songs, as performed by surviving singers of the 1960s and 1970s. The followers of Te Whiti, who live predominantly from Parihaka northwards, by and large had a freer attitude to sharing their songs than those of Tohu who live from Parihaka southwards as far afield as Wanganui.[78]

Women at Hiruharama, Wanganui River, performing traditional Aotea poi dance.
PHOTO: *Charles Hale*

Agreement to record in the Wanganui district was not obtained until most of the singers had died. As a result, there are few recordings from this area. The remaining Tohu singers nearly all placed restrictions on access to their songs, so their poi are unfortunately mostly unavailable for publication.

According to Rawinia Murray of Parikino, the Wanganui poi songs were led by men.[79]

The only Wanganui poi collected by the writer is McL 1167, recorded from Rangimotuhia Katene of Nga Rauru in 1973. Beginning as follows, it is a 2/4 song with rhythms resembling those of paatere:

EXAMPLE 54 *Poi: Beginning of McL 1167 as sung by Rangimotuhia Katene*

An early example of a Wanganui poi song was recorded on wax cylinder in 1921, at Hiruharama, by a Dominion Museum expedition.[80] It is in fast metrical paatere style. The singer was Te Hapai Rangitauira whose song was described as 'a whakatakiri poi, a time-song sung to give time to poi dancers'. There are six verses, one of which quotes from the well known 'Poia atu taku poi' (NM 142). The following is the first stanza:

EXAMPLE 55 *Whakatakiri poi: First stanza of AMPM Cyl 1921 29.2 (b) as sung by Te Hapai Rangitauira*

In South Taranaki, ten poi songs were recorded from singers of Ngaaruahinerangi tribe near Hawera, and 11 from singers of Ngaati Ruanui tribe at Pariroa Paa near Patea. As happens for waiata and pao elsewhere, the term 'poi' was sometimes qualified by these singers to indicate the purpose of the song. Thus poi karaipiture — scriptural poi (McL 513-4); poi karakia — an adaptation of the karakia for the birth ritual (McL 543); poi kawa — poi to open a meeting house (McL 544); and poi matakite — prophetical poi (McL 537).

One of the leaders of the Ngaaruahinerangi items was Kopeka Hawe who said that most of the sacred poi recorded from her group were composed before 1900. They used to be performed at Parihaka and at the time of recording were still being sung at tangi ceremonies in the district. The texts of many are based on the Scriptures.[81] All of the Ngaaruahinerangi poi were said by the singers to be performed to the same tune. This statement is borne out by analysis of the songs recorded which shows all to be in 2/4 time with scales of two notes, usually a major 2nd apart; leader prompts add a lower minor 3rd. A representative example is the following, recorded in 1973, a decade later than the singers' other songs, from Miro Pokai and Kopeka Hawe at Normanby.[82] Only the opening of the song is transcribed.

EXAMPLE 56 Poi: Beginning of McL 1131 as sung by Miro Pokai and Kopeka Hawe

Most of the Ngaati Ruanui poi recorded at Pariroa Pa appear to have been composed in the 1930s, many by Whareaitu, grandfather of one of the singers, Ngakirikiri Kershaw. Whareaitu's songs were composed for a poi team called Paopaokirangi. Some of the recorded Ngaati Ruanui songs have scriptural texts; others are adaptations of earlier songs.

The following transcription is of the first stanza of one of Whareaitu's poi songs for the Paopaokirangi poi team, as recorded in 1963 by Ngakirikiri Kershaw and Moerewarewa Reweti. The singers were leaders of this poi when it was performed by Ngaati Ruanui at the Queen's visit to Rotorua in 1954.

The tune, rhythms and tempo are almost identical with those of Ngaa-ruahinerangi poi.

EXAMPLE 57 Poi: First stanza of McL 534 as sung by Ngakirikiri Kershaw and Moerewarewa Reweti

The other poi songs recorded by the above singers are restricted to Ngaati Ruanui for copies so can be described in general terms only. There are at least three different structures; some of the songs, like the transcribed example, make use of the minor 2nd above the intoning note, some of the minor 2nd below and some of both. All appear to be in 2/4 time.

The followers of Te Whiti performed two styles of poi, an older style known as Ngaati Mutunga poi, and a newer one called Te Ati Awa poi. Ngaati Mutunga poi were performed by the tribe of this name from the village of Urenui. The last public performance of this style of poi prior to 1963 was said to have been in 1928, during the last visit of Maui Pomare to Urenui Pa, when the singers broke down. By 1963, few of the former performers remained and all had forgotten the songs. There was some disagreement amongst the singers as to the number of these poi. According to Pare Pirikahu there were six named Ngaati Mutunga poi interspersed with associated pao and each had five verses. She was able to give the names of three of the poi and to record a fragment of one of them with its pao (McL 551 and McL 548).[83] Pare Raumati, who had been one of the poi leaders, gave slightly differing information. She too was able to name three of the poi, but said

139

each had six figures.[84] Alone of the surviving singers, she succeeded in recording an entire song. Item McL 629 was described by her as 'the No.1 Ngaati Mutunga poi' and was the only one, after nearly three days of rehearsal, she was able to complete.

Ku-a ha-ri, ku-a ko-a, ku-a tuu te ti-ka-nga, ku-a hau - ra-ngi ka-to-

a mai te a - o. Ko te ku-pu a Te Whi-ti, ku-a tuu - haa - ngai

[h]a - na nei ta-ma-ri-ki ki ru-nga ki te whe-nu-a, naa - na i [h]aa - ki te [h]a-
Spoken in free rhythm

o, ta-na maa - ngai ka-ha! Ha-ri-a mai ko te ti-ro ho te po-no, e te i-wi, i hei-haa_ee!

EXAMPLE 58 *Poi: McL 629 as sung by Pare Raumati*

Several informants commented that Ngaati Mutunga poi were very quick and correspondingly difficult to perform. One said that they were chanted in paatere style.[85] Both statements are confirmed from the transcribed example. It is in metrical paatere style and, according to the singer, is meant to be sung faster than performed in the recording. Additionally, the singer was able to provide information about the composers and the manner of performance. There were two composers of Ngaati Mutunga poi: Ngaropi, who was a daughter-in-law of the prophet Te Whiti-o-Rongomai, and Rangitutahi who was an aunt of the singer. The verses were sung by alternate pairs of soloists until the end of the poi when the whole poi team joined in the chorus. The soloists did not take part in the dance and, except for the chorus, the dancers did not sing. This provides an explanation for the early demise of Ngaati Mutunga poi as the singers would probably have known thoroughly only the particular portions of each poi for which they were responsible.[86] Parts of the Ngaati Mutunga poi are stated to have been incorporated into the new Te Ati Awa style which eventually took its place.[87]

The Te Ati Awa tribe occupies territory immediately south of Ngaati Mutunga. Informants were agreed that the Te Ati Awa style of poi begun at Waitara. Some were adaptations of earlier waiata. According to Lizzy Paul there were seven Te Ati Awa poi.[88] These differed from the Ngaati Mutunga poi in a number of ways. One was the use by the dancers of double rather

Fife and drum band, Parihaka, 1898. PHOTO: *Taranaki Museum*

than single poi.[89] Another was an absence of solo singers; instead, everyone sang while at the same time performing the poi.[90] Most significant from a musical point of view was the unique feature of accompaniment by a flute and drum band playing in unison with the singers. According to Pare Pirikahu, when it was discovered that the band could not play the original paatere-type Ngaati Mutunga poi songs, the Te Ati Awa poi songs were devised expressly so that the band could accompany them.[91]

Evidence concerning the band is somewhat conflicting. It appears that there were two bands which may or may not have overlapped in tenure. One began at Parihaka at some time in the 1890s. The other, which was evidently the one used to accompany the Te Ati Awa poi songs, was started later in Waitara, at first with home-made bamboo flutes and makeshift drums made out of kerosene tins and subsequently using instruments transferred from the by this time defunct Parihaka band.[92] An undated photograph of the Parihaka fife and drum band shows a band of 31 uniformed players.[93] Another photograph in the Taranaki Museum, taken at Parihaka in 1898, has 29 players. This band is mentioned in a publication of the same date by Buck who refers to it as escorting visitors into Parihaka.[94] It appears to have been established in response to visits to Parihaka of an earlier brass band from Wanganui. The latter band belonged to the Tohu people and played at Parihaka but did not accompany poi dancing.[95] Buck says that the Taranaki followers of Te Whiti established their drum and fife band 'as the wooden fifes made a nearer approach to Maori instrumental music than brass'.[96] Be this as it may, it would seem that band music was not used to accompany poi

141

songs during the lifetime of Te Whiti. According to an elder named Awahou, who lived in Parihaka from about 1895, the Waitara band was formed for the amusement of the young people and at first was not permitted to perform on the marae at Parihaka but only in the meeting house during practices.[97] The band was called Te Puapua 'pretty flower' after one of the composers of the Ngaati Mutunga poi, Ngaropi, because of her beauty.[98] Pare Pirikahu said that at first it played only Pakeha tunes such as 'The Ship I Love', 'The Blue-bells of Scotland' and 'Gathering the Shells on the Seashore' and only later was the attempt made to use it for accompanying poi songs.[99]

EXAMPLE 59 *Tune of 'The Ship I Love'*

The Te Ati Awa poi songs were believed by at least one performer all to have the same tune,[100] but although the structures are very similar there are, in fact, melodic and other differences between them as recorded. The best known of them is the song 'Tangi a taku ihu', sung in Taranaki in both waiata and poi form. The complete words and music with a translation appear as Song 36 in McLean & Orbell, as sung by Hannah Nicholas and Tuku Bailey of Te Ati Awa, beginning as follows:

EXAMPLE 60 *Poi: Beginning of M&O 36 as sung by Hannah Nicholas and Tuku Bailey*

The above song is a remarkable example of rhythmic organisation. The additive rhythms follow the words closely while the slap of the double poi superimposes a regular 2/4 metre with exactly 16 beats of the poi to each line of the song.

Parihaka has recently undergone restoration by dedicated workers both Maori and Pakeha and some songs have been revived,[101] but it is doubtful whether the manifest skill of the older poi dancers and singers will ever be recaptured. By the 1960s, when the writer made his recordings, the Te Ati Awa poi had gone into decline like all the other Te Whiti and Tohu styles and were no longer being sung. The last public performances were said to have taken place some time after 1936 and were without band or even drums.[102]

ORIORI

In common with other song types such as waiata, pao and South Taranaki poi, the term 'oriori' was sometimes qualified to indicate the purpose of the song, though only, it would seem, for uses associated in some way with children. Thus oriori pootaka were top-spinning songs and oriori karetao were songs sung to the movements of the jumping jack.[103] Used by itself, the term 'oriori' refers to songs otherwise designated as oriori tamaiti or oriori tamariki (child's oriori or children's oriori). Other names for them are waiata whakaoriori, waiata poopoo (soothing songs), and whakatakiri (dandling songs).

Although generally glossed as 'lullabies', the standard view of oriori, as represented by Ngata and Best, has been that they were a highly important song type, confined to the children of chiefs and the nobility and used to educate them in matters appropriate to their descent.

Ngata states:

On the birth of a child, a child of chieftain and warrior lineage, a lullaby would be composed by the mother, the father or the grandparents. Some of the famous songs of the Maori are to be found here.[104]

Best gives an example of a textually complex oriori upon which he comments:

Here we have a composition that differs widely from what we would deem a suitable song to sing to an infant. The matters referred to in it could not be learned by the subject for many years, and would not be understood by her until she was well grown. We must conclude that this was a method employed in the preservation of tribal lore, also it would familiarise a child with names mentioned in traditions and myths which such child would be required to learn in later years.[105]

Elsewhere, Best is definite that oriori tamariki 'must not be confused with lullabies sung with the intention of causing a child to sleep' but are, on the contrary, educational or instructive in purport.[106]

The above judgements are made on the basis of published oriori whose texts are typically dense and, on this account, difficult to translate. Ngata's collection of translated and annotated songs *Nga Moteatea* Parts 1–3 contains 300 songs of which 25 are oriori. In the Preface to Part 1 of *Nga Moteatea* Ngata states of the oriori:

As a foundation to it recourse is made to distant Hawaiki: its traditions are related, its battles recounted; then the story of the migration to this country of Aotearoa is told, the genealogies are recited, and also the battles fought here.

If there should be some unavenged defeat in battle in respect of the child's lineage, the ritual appropriate to one destined for a warrior's life is included, the names of related warrior chiefs whose fame have gone abroad at the time of the composition are mentioned, in some instances defiant terms are used, also curses directed at the people responsible for a murder, or a defeat in battle.[107]

In the Preface to Part 2 of the same work, Ngata begins an analysis of the textual content of oriori in the first two volumes by stating:

> The beginning of a lullaby is always couched in terms of praise for the child for whom the lullaby has been composed, or is a recital of its aristocratic lineage; or laments the death of a parent or of a tribesman, or a time of famine, or a period of bitter cold; and in this way establishes the theme of the song. The child is then called upon to arise, or to awaken from sleep, and to proceed forthwith in search of its grandparents in places where they usually reside, if still alive; or if dead, the child is directed to the places where they died, or fell if killed in battle. At that stage the priestly-poet will embellish his theme with the child's aristocratic genealogy.[108]

Best likewise analyses the texts of several oriori, directing attention to the large number of proper names, references to myths such as the ascent of Taane to the heavens, an instruction to a child to avenge an insult, allusions to the mythological separation of earth and sky, to Polynesian ancestors before the coming of the canoes to New Zealand, to lines of descent over many generations and other such matters, all demonstrating 'the utter lack of the simple themes and simple language that mark our [European] nursery ballads and lullabies'.[109] Orbell outlines the overall tenor of oriori song texts as follows:

> Generally they serve as a vehicle for a survey of the child's origins, and of the tribal loyalties and feuds which he has inherited from his elders. Although the songs honour the boy for whom they are composed, it is typical of Maori poetry that they should often describe an unhappy political situation from which, when he becomes a man, he must rescue his tribe. Thus the boy, who is often said to be crying, is sent forth in the poem on a journey to his kinsmen, who will welcome him and give him their support.[110]

On the face of it, the received view of the oriori as a didactic song for aristocratic children[111] seems well supported. Caution, however, is in order.

The first European writer to have noticed oriori appears to have been Dieffenbach. He observes that Maori infants were unclothed but 'often took refuge in the warm blanket of the father or mother' where the child would be 'lulled to sleep by songs which are called *nga-ori-ori-tamaiti*'.[112]

There is nothing in Dieffenbach's statement to suggest that there was anything special about these songs or that they were confined to children of a particular social class. And the latter, indeed, appears unlikely. It would seem probable that only the most significant of these songs were thought important enough to be worth singing on public occasions and only these, accordingly, have survived in oral tradition and consequently in published collections.

Oriori are amongst the longest songs in the Maori repertoire, some, despite typically fast tempos and non-melismatic (syllabic) style, taking six or more minutes to perform. In contrast with the texts, the tunes are usually very simple. Leader solos take place not at the ends of lines, as in waiata, but at the beginnings of stanzas. The form follows a 'sandwich' principle in which melodic marker figures delineate the ends of two regular phrases within each textual line or musical strophe and a variable 'filling' appears between.

Because the length of the line could so easily be adjusted by the composer, the texts of oriori are less music-bound than those of waiata and other sung styles. As explained by Orbell:

> Since the melodic line is variable in length and shape, language is not as closely tied to musical form as it usually is in the case of waiata. The flexible lines and stanzas, the fast tempo, the simple melodies and swift, economical diction of the oriori make it a medium well suited to the rapid conveyance of complex ideas, with abrupt transitions and highly cryptic allusions to people, places and events.[113]

Two classic oriori are transcribed and translated in McLean & Orbell as Songs 9 and 50. Part of Song 9 is quoted as Example 1.

APAKURA

The apakura is a lament or dirge. But unlike the waiata tangi which can be about any misfortune, it is unequivocally for the dead. It is used only during the height of sorrow, is generally accompanied by wailing and is addressed directly to the body. Kino Hughes associated the apakura with the former practice during which women, especially, slashed themselves with 'sharp stones' (obsidian) in the presence of the body. Nowadays, he said, women may strike their chests for the same reason 'because they are deeply hurt for that body'.[114] The name apakura refers to the moaning of the ocean which represents the endless weeping of a mythical ancestress Apakura for her son, Tuuwhakararo. Few have been recorded or published and there is some disagreement amongst informants about the use of the term. Ngaati Porou singers treat it as a specific song type, distinguishing it from waiata tangi, with connotations as above. Kino Hughes was of the opinion that any waiata tangi could become an apakura if the singers were sufficiently deeply moved. The Northland singer Meha Tuoro named all her waiata as apakura but said she didn't know if this was correct. It would seem probable that Ngaati Porou is the area of origin of this song type. Four out of five apakura in Ngata and Te Hurinui's *Nga Moteatea*[115] are from Ngaati Porou, lending support to this view. Too few apakura have been recorded for definitive statements to be made about the music but, unlike other separately named song types, it would seem improbable that they are distinguishable in terms of musical style. One, published as Song 13 in McLean & Orbell, is in the style of an oriori. Others in the McLean collection appear to be in waiata style.

CHAPTER 4

GAME SONGS

The fullest descriptions of Maori games are in Elsdon Best's monograph *Games and Pastimes of the Maori*.[1] Sir Peter Buck's *The Coming of the Maori*[2] provides an excellent summary with additional information, and an accessible modern account, based in part upon that of Best, is *Games and Dances of the Maori People* by Alan Armstrong.[3]

Many Maori games had vocal accompaniment but few of the songs have survived into the present century. Tuuhoe and Ngaati Porou informants whose childhood spanned the late 1890s and early 1900s recalled no game songs of any kind in their home tribal areas. Even Moerangi Ratahi of Ngaati Awa, recorded in 1974 at a reputed 105 years of age, stated there were no game songs when she was a child. However, a few fragments of game songs have survived, some of whose texts appear in Best's book, and these allow a tentative reconstruction of some game song styles. Haka, poi and other dance forms are treated separately above.

BREATH HOLDING

In his *Games and Pastimes*, Best points out the narrow line between activities which while appearing to be games were also useful as exercises in preparation for adult life.[4] One such may have been the game known variously (from the word manawa 'breath') as tatau manawa, taki manawa, pepe taki manawa and whakataetae manawa.[5]

In the section on karakia, the importance attached to avoiding breaks for breathing in traditional singing has been mentioned. It was a skill evidently taken to heart even by children. The object of the tatau manawa game was to try to repeat a form of words for as long as possible in one breath. An example, called by the singer a whakataetae manawa, was recorded from Piri Mokena of Ngaapuhi tribe in 1972. Piri, who was 85 years old, explained that the performers would try to beat one another for the longest breath. When one person ran out of breath another would take over. In his time he 'never heard anyone get up to the finish'. An almost identical text to Piri's version of the song is given by Dieffenbach who says of it:

A very common sport amongst children consists in opening and shutting the fingers, and bending the arm in a certain manner, when the following words are said, the whole of which must be completed on a single breath.[6]

EXAMPLE 61 *Whakataetae manawa: McL 1026 as sung by Piri Mokena*

A variant of the same song was one of three 'nursery songs' recorded by Sir Apirana Ngata for the New Zealand Broadcasting Service in the late 1930s or early 1940s (Example 62).[7] He explains that it was performed as a breathing exercise by children who sang and at the same time counted the horizontal cross-battens of the lattice-work panels (tukutuku) inside a meeting house. The child would start at the bottom of the panel and count upwards as far as possible until breath ran out. Best refers to the batten-counting game as tatau kaho; anyone failing to repeat the whole song in one breath fell out of the game.[8] In both versions of the song, the rhythms are those characteristic of paatere, but regularly metred in 2/4 time.

Another game played to develop lung control was holding the breath while jumping feet first into deep water; it was known as rukuruku manawa.[9]

♩ = 107

Ka ta-hi ke, ka ru-a ke, ka no-ho mai ta-pa ti to-re-a wai

ka rau-a, ka rau-a mai, Kai a-na te whe-tuu, te ma-ra-ma, ko te pa-pa_i

a-ki-na e hu-i ta-re-re. Ko te ti-a_e re-re raa ru-nga raa te pe-ka - pe-ka

o hu-a kau-we-ra, tu-ra-ki-na ko to-re wi-wii, ke e-ke u-po-ko

ta-ma-ri-ki ta-re ro-a.

EXAMPLE 62 *Tatau kaho: AMPM RNZ D10867 as sung by Sir Apirana Ngata*

Detail of tukutuku panel (Te Honohononga) in Tane-nui-a-Rangi carved meeting house, University of Auckland. PHOTO: *Anthropology Department, University of Auckland*

DART THROWING

Known as teka (also neti, nuku and pehu), dart throwing was a competitive sport in which darts were thrown at a mound from which they would glance off in an upward direction. The winner was the player whose dart went the furthest. Charms or incantations were recited to make the dart more effective or to bring good luck. Best gives the texts of several of these charms but none has been recorded from singers.[10]

GIANT STRIDE

The giant stride (moari or moorere) was a tall pole erected as a rule near a river bank or lake shore with ropes attached to the top. Players swung out on the ropes and dropped off into deep water feet first.[11] Best gives the texts of two songs performed in association with the moari. The first is a short song of only four lines. Best says it was timed in performance so that, on the

The moorere or giant stride. From Angas The New Zealanders Illustrated

final word, players were correctly positioned to release the rope and drop into the water. The other song is longer and appears to have had a serious purpose. From information given by Best's Tuuhoe informant Paitini, it was part of a ceremony, involving the moari, for remembering persons killed by a rival tribe.[12] No moari songs have been recorded from singers so nothing can be said about the music.

HAND GAMES

Buck regards hand games as a type of military exercise which taught quickness of eye and hand.[13] The games are played by two persons who stand facing each other. As explained by Best:

> Certain movements with the hands are made by one player with great rapidity, and a certain phrase repeated. The other must make precisely the same movement and repeat the phrase so quickly that the two appear to be simultaneous.[14]

Movements used include handclapping, slapping the thighs or the chest, opening or shutting the thumbs or fingers, and jerking the hands right, left or up or down. The game is known generally as tii ringa. Different versions of it, named evidently from the first words of the associated texts, include 'hipitoi' (played with the thumbs), 'whakaropiropi' (played with the hands) and 'hei tama tu tama' (played with the arms). More complicated games include 'matimati' and 'mate rawa'.[15]

The whakaropiropi hand game

The following is part of a performance recorded by Kino Hughes of Tuuhoe in 1972 to illustrate the whakaropiropi game.

$\unicode{x1D153}\cdot = 145$

EXAMPLE 63 Whakaropiropi: Beginning of McL 1083 as sung by Kino Hughes

JACKSTONES

This game, played usually with five pebbles, is similar to the European game of knucklebones. Names for it include kooruru (Ngaai Tahu), kai makamaka (Ngaati Porou) and ruru (Tuuhoe). Full descriptions of game movements from each of the foregoing tribes are given by Armstrong.[16] John White calls the game tutukai and provides the text of a jingle which he says was sung by players.[17] It is a variant of 'Ka tahi tii, ka rua tii' — the same song transcribed above as a breath-holding song or whakataetae manawa. This song appears to have had multiple uses as it is cited by both White and Dieffenbach as serving also for the hand game tii.[18] A further version of it (McL 1063) has been recorded from Kino Hughes.

JUMPING JACK

The jumping jack — karetao or keretao (Tuuhoe), karaii (Ngaati Porou), tokoraurape (Northern tribes) — was a puppet, made from wood carved to represent a human, with a hand grip below the legs and strings which were manipulated to make the arms move. It was held and shaken by the left hand of the operator while the strings were alternately pulled and slackened with the right. By this means the puppet was made to quiver and move its arms as if performing a haka or posture dance. Best and Buck both state the performance was done in time to a chant called an oriori karetao.[19] However, consistent with the movements made by the keretao, the sole available recording of a jumping jack song is in haka style and was named by the performer as a haka keretao. It was recorded for the New Zealand Broadcasting Service at an unknown date from the Rev. W. Rangi.[20] The text is a variant of McL 1095 and part of McL 1012, both as sung by Kino Hughes of

Tuuhoe. It is doubtless ribald in intent as it contains allusions to women's genitals and, according to Buck, the movements made by the keretao provoked laughter.[21]

EXAMPLE 64 Haka keretao: AMPM RNZM 101 (Dub of P416) as sung by Rev. W. Rangi

Bennett says sometimes a whole row of performers in a haka or action song would be equipped with karetao, 'and as the rows in front knelt, the figures would be brought out and their movements displayed to the delight of the onlookers'.[22]

LAST MAN

In 1963, a paatere was recorded from Poihi Hikuroa of Ngaati Ruanui which another singer said was used at the village of Parihaka for a 'last man out' game. The participants formed a circle and were pointed to in turn as the singer reached the end of the song. Those pointed to were out, and the last one in was the winner. Example 65 is the concluding stanza of the song:

*Three karetao at
Auckland Institute &
Museum.*
PHOTO: *W.R. Reynolds*

 = *105*

Kaa - ta - hi ka wii, ka waa, Ka tu - ku ki Ma - ni - tii, Ma - ni - tai o Tuu -

rou - ro pa - re - a ko a - te rau - ri - ki ta - ra kai a te ma - nu. Hu - i - hu - i

kau mai e ti - ra, ee, ki ngaa ro - ro o te ra - ngi wii - wii, waa - waa,

e kai te ma - nu, hu - i ee, tai - ki ee!

EXAMPLE 65 *Paatere: Last stanza of McL 511 as sung by Poihi Hikuroa*

STICK GAMES

The game known as tii raakau took the form of rhythmically throwing and catching sticks from person to person. Alternative names for it given by Best are poi raakau (Ngaati Porou), tiitiitouretua (Tuuhoe) and tiitiitourea (Northern tribes). A.S. Thomson states that it was played with sticks three feet (0.9m) long by parties of 20 a side and the game was accompanied by songs.[23] Best gives details of the Tuuhoe and Ngaati Porou versions of the game, both played in a circle:

Tuuhoe players threw the sticks simultaneously in groups of four from one person to another across the circle, doing so to the accompaniment of a song which Best called a 'ngari tiitii-too-uretua'. By so syllabifying the term 'tiitiitouretua' Best draws attention to its derivation but discreetly leaves it untranslated; the name refers to a phallus.

Ngaati Porou players threw the sticks, often point first, to a single player who stood within the circle. The person in the middle caught the sticks as they were thrown, sometimes two at a time, and returned them to a stickless member of the circle. Again the sticks were thrown in time to a song chanted by the performers.

Even more than hand games, stick games served as training for future warriors. According to Best, the exercise was deemed an excellent training for youths who, in a few years time, would need to catch or parry the spears of enemies in battle.[24] Buck makes the same point in a detailed description of a Te Arawa version of the game, again played in a circle and again accompanied by a song:

> . . . the players knelt in a circle with two sticks each. In time to a chant, they beat the sticks together and then threw first one and then the other to the neighbour on the right, sticks being thrown in a vertical position. Each threw the first stick in the right hand, caught the incoming stick with the empty hand, threw the second stick with the left hand and caught the incoming stick with that hand. The passing of sticks, first right then left, continued for some beats and then the two sticks were beaten together. The tempo of the chant was quickened and great dexterity in catching and passing had to be displayed to remain in the game. Those who dropped a stick fell out and the circle lessened until the last one left in was declared the victor. The game taught dexterity in catching with both hands and made the catching of a spear in battle not so difficult.[25]

The oldest recording of a stick game song is a waiata poi raakau recorded on wax cylinder in 1921, at Hiruharama by a Dominion Museum expedition.[26] The singer was Ihaka Toitupu. His song is in all respects in paatere style except for the absence of additive rhythms which would interfere with the execution of the game. Standard paatere rhythms are regularised in the song into a steady 2/8 time. The song begins as follows:

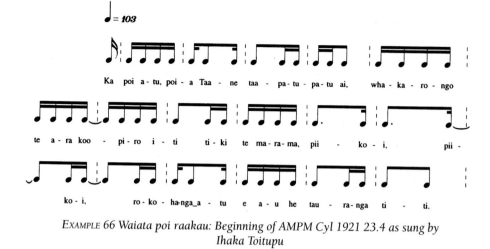

Example 66 *Waiata poi raakau: Beginning of AMPM Cyl 1921 23.4 as sung by Ihaka Toitupu*

Recordings of traditional stick game songs in the McLean collection are McL 1118 and McL 805A–C , the first as sung by Marata Te Tomo of Ngaati Tuuwharetoa and the others from a Tuuhourangi group led by Ngatai Bubb. They were named by the singers as tiitii toorea. The four songs represent a transition from older traditional through to modern. Marata's song is in fast metrical paatere style like the early Whanganui example sung by Ihaka Toitupu:

Example 67 *Tiitii toorea: McL 1118 as sung by Marata Te Tomo*

156

The first of the three Tuuhourangi songs is rhythmically similar to the Tuuwharetoa one, but is sung rather than recited. The song has four lines, each of 12 quavers, and a melody which departs from monotone at the end of each line.

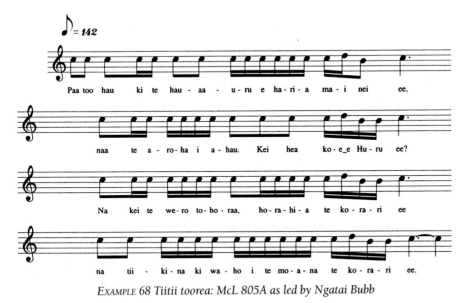

Paa too hau ki te hau - aa - u - ru e ha - ri - a ma - i nei ee,

naa te a - ro-ha i a-hau. Kei hea ko - e_e Hu - ru ee?

Na kei te we-ro to-ho-raa, ho-ra-hi-a te ko-ra-ri ee

na tii - ki-na ki wa-ho i te mo-a-na te ko-ra-ri ee.

EXAMPLE 68 *Tiitii toorea: McL 805A as led by Ngatai Bubb*

The second Tuuhourangi song is an excellent example of transitional style. It uses all of the notes of the European major scale beginning with a rising arpeggio on the tonic triad. Metrically it exhibits a blend of Maori and European. The following is the first of three verses, each with two lines of 16 quavers arranged in irregular groups of three and two.

Ma - te koe_i te a - ro-ha, ti - ti - ro ki - te mo - a - na,

puu - kai - ta - nga o a - ku roi - ma - ta ee!

EXAMPLE 69 *Tiitii toorea: McL 805B as led by Ngatai Bubb*

A modern version of the tiitii toorea game is performed universally to an acculturated tune as demonstrated in the final example sung by the Tuuhourangi group. The scale is hexatonic (lacking the 4th). Metrically the song is wholly European. Again there are three verses, this time in a straight-forward 6/8 metre:

E pa-paa wai-a-ri ta-ku nei ma-hi, ta-ku nei ma-hi he tu-ku roi-ma-ta.

E pa-paa wai-a-ri ta-ku nei ma-hi, ta-ku nei ma-hi he tu-ku roi-ma-ta.

Ee au-e-i, ka ma-te au, e hi-ne ho ki_i-ho raa.

Maa ku e kau-te oo hii-koi-ta-nga, maa ku e kau-te oo hii-koi ta-nga! hii-koi ta-nga!

EXAMPLE 70 Tiitii toorea: McL 805C as led by Ngatai Bubb

A modern stick game

STRING GAMES

The game of fashioning figures from string, known in English as 'cat's cradle', is a pastime found in many parts of the world, including most of Polynesia. The Maori name for it is 'whai'. Best says: 'Quaint stanzas, or jingles, were recited or sung in connection with some of the patterns of *whai*'.[27] One such, quoted by Best, relates to the mouti pattern.[28] It was recorded from the same Tuuhourangi group as the preceding examples, with a text which appears to be a corruption of that given by Best. The tune is Europeanised:

Mou - tii,   mou - tii,   mou - ha - re - re,   mou - ha - re - re.

EXAMPLE 71 *Waiata mo ngaa whai: McL 810A as led by Ngatai Bubb*

Best's text has three additional lines and is given also by Andersen who explains that the accents coincide with the movements made by the left hand of the player.[29]

Another whai song with the same tune was also recorded by the Tuuhourangi group:

Tuu - pe - ke   Koo - kaa   ki te ka - to puu - haa.

EXAMPLE 72 *Waiata mo ngaa whai: McL 810B as led by Ngatai Bubb*

A further mouti song, again with a modern tune, was recorded in 1971 from Kiri Kahaki of Te Whaanau-a-Apanui. The singer said it was popular right around the East Coast.

Tee- raa   Mou - tii, Mou - re-a, tee - raa   te a-o ee.

He - oi maa- na koe_i te   o - ti - ta - nga,   Ti - ro-ri - a   mai   raa   te mo - a - na.

(Tee) - raa   a - ra Mou - tii,   Mou - re - a, tee - raa   te a-o nei.

Ka   mau   te wa-hi-ne, te wa-hi-ne ra- re- ra-re, ra- we- ra- we te ti- hi o Mou - tii, Mou - re- a,

159

Example 73 Waiata mo ngaa whai: McL 860 as sung by Kiri Kahaki

A final example was recorded on wax cylinder at Koriniti, Wanganui River, in 1921.[30] It is associated with the string pattern 'Te Ara Pikipiki a Taawhaki' which depicts the climbing of the culture hero Taawhaki to the first heaven. It was performed by Heremia Rawiri of Oneriri. Unlike the above acculturated songs, it is recited in the style of a karakia. A text is given by Andersen[31] but differs considerably from the song as sung. The recording is too indistinct for a full transcription to be made but appears to begin as follows:

Example 74 Waiata mo ngaa whai: AMPM Cyl 1921 13.4 as sung by Heremia Rawiri

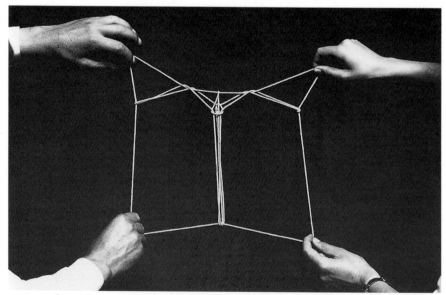

String figure: 'Te Ara Pikipiki a Taawhaki'. Photo: James McDonald, Museum of New Zealand Te Papa Tongarewa neg. no. C1576

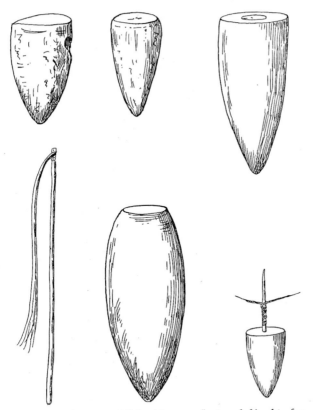

Maori tops: (top & middle) whip tops; (bottom left) whip for
whip top; (bottom right) pootaka huhu or humming top.
From Edge-Partington Album

TOP SPINNING[32]

Both whip tops and humming tops were used by the Maori, by adults as well as children according to Best. The generic term for them was pootaka. Some whip tops were made of stone but most tops of both kinds were made of wood (generally mataii or maapara). The whip top was sometimes called pootaka taa and was also known as kaihora, kaihotaka and kaitaka. A whip top pointed at both ends was termed pootaka kotore(rua), pootaka tikitiki (Arawa) or pootaka wherorua. A whip top with a flat instead of pointed top was called poro. The whip (taa or kare) was made by tying strips of green flax to a wooden handle. The top was spun by winding the lash of the whip around it and then pulling the whip vigorously. Whipping was then continued to keep the top in motion.

Humming tops were similar in appearance to the whip top except for a shaft projecting from the upper end around which a cord was wound. A stick was held against the top to steady it while the string was pulled to get the top spinning. Grooves or holes around the sides of the top caused it to

161

hum. Names for the humming top included pootaka taakiri, pootaka kukume and pootaka huhu. Humming tops made of gourd were called pootaka hue.

According to Best, 'short ditties were sometimes chanted by spinners of humming tops. As a rule two lines were sung, and then at a signal word, all players started their tops spinning'.[33] If, as Best indicates, these songs were sung in couplets, they are likely to have been in pao form.

A text is available for such a top-spinning song recorded on a dictaphone cylinder at Rotorua on 24 April 1920.[34] It was sung in pao style by Toki Wharetapu of Tuuhoe. The transcription is an approximation only of the performance as the recording is unclear.

EXAMPLE 75 Top-spinning song: AMPM Cyl 1920 12.3 as sung by Toki Wharetapu

The shouted words 'Hai tukua' at the end of each couplet gave the time for all to spin the tops. A similar top-spinning song recorded from a group of

Tuuhoe singers on the previous day[35] finishes with the same words.

The only top-spinning songs recorded from singers by the writer are McL 826 and McL 1108, the first from Raupare Werahiko and the other from Marata Te Tomo. Both of these singers had affiliations with Ngaati Tuuwharetoa and Ngaati Raukawa tribes. They described their songs as pao taa pootaka and waiata taa pootaka respectively. From Best's nomenclature, both of these songs would appear to have been associated with whip tops rather than humming tops. However, Raupare said the tops were humming tops, as did Marata. Again, both songs are in pao form.

EXAMPLE 76 *Pao taa pootaka: McL 826 as sung by Raupare Werahiko*

EXAMPLE 77 *Waiata taa pootaka: McL 1108 as sung by Marata Te Tomo*

163

An evidently highly serious form of song sung to the accompaniment of humming tops was known as oriori pootaka or whakaoriori pootaka. According to Best, they were performed in the Bay of Plenty area as an adjunct to the ceremony of mourning the dead, with the humming sound of the tops representative of wailing.[36] Bennett refers to them as laments sung as a form of respect for persons killed in battle, possibly last performed after the battle of Orakau (1864). The tops were made to sound between verses.[37] No examples have been recorded from singers and nothing is known of the musical style.

OTHER

Throughout Best's monograph occur song texts associated with minor games not considered above. Most are of charms or incantations employed either to aid the player or as a divinatory exercise to provide an omen of success or failure. The exceptions are skipping songs, a head-standing song (poroteeteke) which appears to have been a form of haka, hand games called upokotiti, tara-koekoeaa and hapii-tawa, and a game known as kurawiniwini played with string.[38] Again, none has been recorded.

SUMMARY OF GAME SONG STYLES

On the available evidence, it would seem that Maori children did not have distinctive music of their own, but rather shared adult styles. The oldest recording of a string game song is in karakia style, and charms (karakia) were also employed during games of skill such as dart throwing. Both recorded breath-holding songs are in metrical paatere style as is one of the stick game songs; the sole 'last man' song is also a paatere. All three top-spinning songs are pao and the one recording of a keretao song is a haka. Kino Hughes's recording of the whakaropiropi hand game is distinctive because of its brisk 6/8 rhythm, but this too could have derived from haka. The other songs are, in varying degrees, European in idiom and here, too, there is plenty of precedent in adult singing.

SECTION 2

MUSIC ETHNOGRAPHY

CHAPTER 5

MUSICAL INSTRUMENTS

Of the four customary classes of musical instruments, only idiophones and aerophones were common in New Zealand. Drums (membranophones) were absent. Stringed instruments (chordophones) are represented only by a single unconfirmed report from Canon Stack of a presumed South Island instrument called the kuu. It appears to have been a form of musical bow which, except for the presence of a string, was similar to the pakuru (see later). Best quotes Stack as follows:

> It was a one-stringed instrument made in the shape of a bow about ten inches [25 cm] long, out of a hard piece of *matai*. The string was of dressed *Phormium* [flax] fibre. It was held near the ear when played and the sound was produced by tapping it with a rod.[1]

If this instrument was like other musical bows in the Pacific area, such as the Hawaiian ukeke and Marquesan utete, it would have been held between the teeth, with the mouth used as a resonator.

IDIOPHONES

PAHUU

The most important idiophone was the wooden gong, which in New Zealand took the name (pahu) that was applied in Eastern Polynesia to the sharkskin drum. The pahuu was usually suspended above the platform of the watchtower in fortified Maori villages, and it was the watchman's duty to strike the gong occasionally to show that the people were on the alert. It was also used in wartime as a signal of hostilities.

There were two forms of pahuu. The first, which was probably rare, was hollowed out like the Polynesian slit-gong. Only one is known from written sources. It was made in Ruatahuna in 1899 and was four or five feet [1.2–1.5m] long. From Best's description, and his illustration, it seems to have been a true slit-gong with a large space in the interior hollowed out through a comparatively narrow slit.[2]

Most pahuu were essentially flat slabs of resonant wood. According to

Pahuu sketched at Ruatahuna by E. Richardson

Tregear, small ones were made of kaiwhiria wood and large ones of mataii.[3] The use of kaiwhiria is confirmed by Potts,[4] but mataii was probably usual as it is mentioned by most authorities. Sometimes tootara wood was used and in the Ngaati Porou tribal area the use of maire has been noted.

Some slab pahuu were unmodified; others apparently had a shallow depression in the centre, described as a 'groove' by Angas.[5] But most, according to Captain Mair, had an elliptical or oval hole pierced through the centre.[6] Sometimes the slab was rectangular; more often it seems to have been rounded off towards the ends.

Pahuu or war gong. From Angas The New Zealanders Illustrated

Some pahuu were of great length and could be heard for many miles. Dieffenbach records the length as about 12 feet [3.2m].[7] Thomson also says they were 12 feet long and states they could be heard over a distance of 20 miles [32 km] in still weather.[8] But this estimate of the distance may be an exaggeration. Captain Mair says that pahuu were two or three feet [60–90 cm] wide, six inches [15 cm] thick and were sometimes 30 feet [9 m] in length. According to Mair they could be heard in favourable conditions to a distance of six to ten miles [10–16 km]. He writes of an exchange of signals over nine miles [14 km] through the Waimana Valley in the Urewera country.[9] Hamilton knew of a slab-type pahuu that was 30 feet [9 m] long but he offers no estimate of the distance over which it could be heard.[10] Potts was told that the instruments were sometimes over 20 feet [6 m] long and could be heard for 12 miles [19 km]. He states that a celebrated pahuu on a hill in the isthmus of Auckland sounded the alarm for the whole isthmus.[11] Finally, Best quotes a statement from Sir George Grey that a pahuu on Mount Aroha-uta had been heard at Matamata which is 'not less than twelve or fourteen miles' [19–22 km] away.[12] The consensus amongst the several writers seems to be that slab-type pahuu were up to 30 feet [9 m] long and could be heard over distances of up to 12 miles [19 km]. Conditions favouring hearing the pahuu over such long distances would have occurred at night or when the listener was down wind, or when the pahuu was located on a hill, across water, or in a valley which would channel the sound.

Best, Andersen and Buck all quote nineteenth-century descriptions of the pahuu by Angus, Mair, Potts, Thomson, White and others.[13] A confirming description that does not appear in these sources is that of John Morgan, a CMS missionary who saw and heard a pahuu at Matamata in 1836. He writes:

> As night came on, the pahu or war bell rang. It was made of a piece of wood, oval, and partly hollowed out in the centre, and suspended by cords on a stage 15 or 20 feet high from the ground. It was beaten with a mallet by a man seated on the stage. The watchmen or kai wakaharas went their rounds and with a loud voice called upon the people to watch lest they should be surprised by the enemy. Young and old, chiefs and slaves, of both sexes, assembled within the pa, and there danced their savage dances and made the air ring with their horrid yells and obscene songs.[14]

According to an 1850 account of Sir George Grey, the reason for suspending the pahuu at such a height was to prevent it from being sounded without cause by children and others.[15] But while watchtowers may have served such a purpose, this could not have been the sole or even main reason for building them. Obviously the watchman had to have a good vantage point if he were to see the enemy, and the pahuu had to be mounted within reach of the watchman. Also the higher the pahuu was suspended, the greater the distance over which it would be heard and the more effective the alarm would be.

White says the pahuu was suspended from one end and struck with a stone,[16] but other writers agree that it was suspended from both ends and struck with heavy wooden beaters or mallets. Some writers claim that the wooden beater was rattled in the slot, but as Buck points out, such a method would 'not produce the volume of sound that would carry the number of miles credited to the instrument'.[17] The more usual method must have been simply to strike the gong heavily on the edge, or perhaps on the lip of the central hole. Unfortunately no specimens appear to be extant which could settle the question by an examination for wear. A putative pahuu at the Waikato Art Museum (TM63), is more likely to have been a water trough used for snaring pigeons.

Suspension of the pahuu was by means of ropes tied around the ends. These accordingly had either holes, grooves or knobs to prevent the ropes from falling off. The ropes were then tied either to trees or to a cross-piece which was supported by forked stick uprights.

Potts writes of a Hauhau call to prayers sounded by beating a pahuu.[18] However, as earlier noted, the most common use of the pahuu was in warfare by watchmen. Besides beating the pahuu, the watchmen would recite watch songs and blow upon the puukaaea or war trumpet. Angus states that at every stroke on the pahuu the watchman would call out the watchword of alarm.[19] The main object according to Buck,[20] Vayda[21] and others was to warn would-be invaders that the paa was on the alert, thereby discouraging an attack. Best claims that another object was to keep the occupants of a paa ready for battle by preventing them from sleeping too soundly,[22] surely a risky strategy if a siege were prolonged, although there is evidence that the pahuu was, indeed, beaten at night. The missionary Thomas Chapman wrote, for example, in his journal in 1836: '. . . we could distinctly hear the sound

Tree gong at Te Whaiti. From a sketch by Gilbert Mair, 1869

of the native pahu (I may almost say wooden gong) which they beat all night long in their pas when they expect an attack'.[23] But such uses would apply only if people were already in the paa and awaiting attack. Some paa sites, such as those on hill tops, would not have been fully occupied at all times. In the daytime the people would normally be working below, and when enemies were sighted the alarm would be given by the watchman on duty at the paa. This use of the pahuu is again documented by Potts who states specifically that the instrument was 'struck in cases of alarm, when the people immediately flocked in to the *pa*'.[24]

The sound made by the pahuu is evocatively described by Angas as 'a most melancholy one; the dull heavy strokes breaking with a solemn monotony on the stillness of the night: tolling, as it were, the death-knell of many to be slain on the morrow'.[25]

Best and Andersen conclude their accounts of pahuu by describing the use of hollow trees as gongs.[26] One side of the tree was open except for a long tongue of wood, sometimes ornamented with carved designs, that hung down and was struck with a wooden mallet kept there for the purpose. A tree gong at Te Kakau was struck by travellers to announce their approach to the village. Another on a hill in the Te Whaiti district was evidently used as an alarm gong. Captain Mair wrote that he was sent by General Whitmore to secure it in 1869 to prevent it from being sounded to warn of the approach of Whitmore's forces.[27]

Origin of the pahuu

As Buck points out:

The origin of the Maori war gong presents a problem. The application of the name *pahu* to a percussion instrument in New Zealand appears to indicate that the Maori ancestors knew the shark-skin drum in central Polynesia before they left. For some unknown reason, they ceased to manufacture the drum and developed a form of gong to which they gave the spare name of *pahu*.[28]

Buck goes on to suggest that the wooden slit-gong (which resembles the Maori pahuu) had probably not yet reached Central Polynesia when the Maori left this area for New Zealand and that the New Zealand form is likely to have been discovered independently by the Maori. In this conclusion Buck was almost certainly correct. Both the pahuu and the long wooden war trumpet or puukaaea (see later) were associated with the fighting stages of the late Classic period fortified village or paa. Fox gives carbon dates for timbers from paa fighting stages of between 1380 and 1583 and concludes that the elevated stage was added to rampart and ditch defences during the sixteenth century at the latest.[29] This places the invention of the fighting stage, and along with it the pahuu and the puukaaea, at upwards of half-way through the Classic Maori period which lasted from the fourteenth century until the eighteenth century.[30] In the South Island, where the Classic Maori phase began late,[31] the pahuu and long wooden war trumpet may have been absent. No one interviewed by James Beattie in 1920 had ever heard of a wooden drum in the South Island and the name puukaaea was applied not to a wooden trumpet but to the flax trumpet.[32]

OTHER IDIOPHONES

Other idiophones used by the Maori were an instrument related to the musical bow called the pakuru, and a form of jew's harp called the rooria. Also reported are clappers or castanets, called tookere.

Tookere

The sole authority for tookere appears to be Williams, who defines them as 'pieces of wood or bone used, a pair in each hand, as castanets'. Best quotes Williams and adds: 'A Tuhoe native informed the writer that bone clappers were formerly used by his people, and known as *tokere*, but no corroboration of this has been obtained.'[33] Buck echoes Williams but does not give his source.[34] Hamilton, Andersen and Mair, in otherwise comprehensive discussions, do not mention the instrument.[35] Best points out that there is no mention of tookere by early writers such as Parkinson and Forster, both of whom report clappers from Tahiti. He cautions it is not certain whether the Maori used clappers in former times and surmises that the idea may have been borrowed from Europeans.[36] The only extant specimen of tookere clappers known to the writer is a pair of plain wooden blocks at the Auckland Institute & Museum (AIM 752).[37] They are amongst items which Best commissioned to be made in the Urewera country and which subsequently found their way into various New Zealand museums. The particular item was purchased by the museum from Best in 1899.[38]

Pakuru

The pakuru,[39] pakure, pakakau or kiikiiporo was a musical instrument in the form of a thin strip of resonant wood such as maapara, kaiwhiria or mataii.[40] It was 12–18 inches [30–45 cm] long, 1–3 inches [2.5–7 cm] wide and about $1/2$ inch [1 cm] thick with one surface flat and the other convex. Williams says the kiikiiporo was played by pressing one slab of wood against the cheek and beating it with another. Most authorities say the pakuru was played by holding one end lightly with the left hand[41] and the other between the teeth with the flat side down.[42] The lips did not touch the instrument. It was tapped with a rod about 6 inches [15 cm] long held in the fingers of the right hand. The tapping was done in time to special songs which were generally called rangi pakuru. Several people could perform together as seen by Captain Mair:

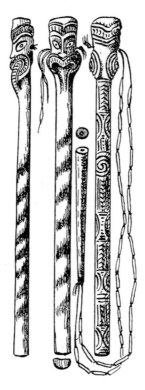

Pakuru with carved and burnt-on ornamentation. From Robley Collection after Hamilton

I have watched a number of skilled performers, standing in a row, their swaying bodies and little tapping mallets keeping the most perfect unison. Now rising shrill, or dying away in mournful cadence of some love song, the effect is remarkably melodious and pleasing.[43]

Sometimes the instrument was plain; sometimes it was elaborately ornamented with carving, notches, paaua shell inlays, or burnt designs.

From the published descriptions, it is not quite clear whether the pakuru was used simply to accompany songs or whether it functioned like a jew's harp or musical bow as a substitute for the vocal cords to suggest words. Colenso says the performer played the instrument while at the same time humming the tune;[44] White says variously that the beating of the instrument was 'accompanied by words emitted by the opening and compressing of the lips'[45] and that the player struck the instrument 'while he breathed the words of the chant, producing the higher or lower tones by closing or opening his lips';[46] Mair similarly states that the player struck the instrument 'while at the same time breathing the words of a song or chorus upon the wood causing the most pleasing vibrations or waves of sound';[47] Hamilton says 'the closing or separating of the lips causes different sound or notes to be emitted by the stick held in the teeth'.[48] Other writers say only that the tapping of the stick was done in time to the words of a song.

Kino Hughes of Tuuhoe provided information to the writer about an instrument he called a panguru but which conforms to the published descriptions of pakuru. He last saw the instrument played at Maungapohatu between 1908 and 1910. He said the instrument consisted of two sticks, one of tanguru[49] wood and the other of maire. The tanguru stick was about the thickness of the little finger and around 18 inches [45 cm] long. The other was a shorter beater, about 12 inches [30 cm] long, and the thickness of a piupiu strand. The longer stick was held lightly between the thumb and the forefinger at its mid point and tapped lightly with the beater while the performer whispered a song at the stick. Tapping the stick at different points produced different notes, high at the top end and low at the bottom. The tune of the performer's waiata was tapped out in this way, causing the stick 'to make the sound just like the human voice'. Singing at the stick was called 'whakatangi tanguru'. Three or four people would play in unison, each with an individual stick ('Kia teitei te rangi kia paapaku kia oorite ai te tangi awa a taatou panguru'). From this remarkably clear and detailed description, it is confirmed that the instrument indeed functioned as a substitute for the vocal cords.[50]

Rooria

The rooria (also known as kukau and tararii) was an elastic piece of supplejack (kareao)[51] 3–4 inches [7.5–10 cm] long, one end of which was held in the mouth or against the teeth and twanged with a finger. According to White, another form was made out of scraped mataii, tiitoki or maire.[52] The use of the instrument to suggest words is well documented. Buck says merely that the player made guttural sounds and movements of the lips helped to vary the sounds.[53] But according to Andersen the appeal of the instrument was not in its music but in the fact that it could so easily be made to speak. It was a common sight for Maori lovers, each with a jew's harp, to sit side by side and hold a quiet conversation on the instruments. A drawback of the indigenous instrument was that the supplejack was liable to crack with use, hence the proverb 'He arero kareao ka whati; engari te arero wahine kaaore kia whati — haere tonu ana' (A supplejack tongue will become cracked; not so the tongue of a woman — it goes on for ever).[54] No doubt partly for this reason, and also because the tone was preferred, European jew's harps soon replaced the Maori ones[55] and the name rooria became transferred to them. From his recollections of the 1840s, Colenso reports that they were highly prized and much care was taken in selecting them.[56] It was common practice to improve upon the tone of the European instrument by fixing a small lump of sealing wax or of kauri resin to the tip of the lamella. According to Colenso, the wax was to facilitate plucking within the mouth and with the tongue instead of the finger, but this seems unlikely.

Maori woman playing jew's harp.
PHOTO: *L. Hinge*

AEROPHONES

Most Maori aerophones were trumpets, flutes or, in the case of one instrument, the puutoorino, possibly both. Two instruments which fall outside these classes are the whizzer and the bullroarer.

WHIZZERS AND BULLROARERS
Koororohuu

The koororohuu (whizzer or cutwater) was a children's toy made from a small piece of thin, flat wood or pumpkin rind 3–4 inches [7.5–10 cm] long, pointed at both ends. According to Best, the wood used was heart mataii, maapara or kaiwhiria.[57] Two holes were pierced near the centre through which the two ends of a piece of string or flax (harakeke) were threaded and then tied. One thumb was inserted in the tied end and the other in the loop end; the disc was next swung towards the operator to twist the string and when it was sufficiently wound up an outward pull on the string caused it first to unwind rapidly and then, by its own momentum, to wind up again in the opposite direction. By timing the outward pull on the strings, the player could keep the instrument revolving rapidly in alternate directions, producing a whizzing noise during the unwinding parts of the cycle. Songs in pao style were sung to the accompaniment of the sound.[58] Alternative names reported for the whizzer include piirorohuu, porotiti, puurerehua, puuro-rohuu, takawairore, takawairori, tararii (used also for jew's harp), wairore and wairori.[59]

Puurorohuu

As described by Best, the puurorohuu (bullroarer) was made from a thin flat piece of wood, usually heart wood of mataii.[60] It was of similar shape to the koororohuu, but about 12–18 inches [30–45 cm] long.[61] A cord about four feet [1.2 m] long was tied to one end and the other end of the cord was attached to a wooden handle about three feet [90 cm] long. By means of the handle, the operator swung the instrument until it produced a deep boom-ing sound. In Polynesia, the bullroarer was used as a children's toy and the same use is attributed by Williams to New Zealand, but in the East Coast of the North Island it was reported by Best's Ngaati Porou informant, Tuta Nihoniho, to have been used ceremonially to produce rain. A karakia (in-cantation) was recited as the bullroarer was swung, and children were for-bidden to use the bullroarer in case it caused rain. In Taranaki, according to Hamilton,[62] bullroarers were called mamae and the whirling noise was used to dispense evil spirits at the lying in of a dead chief. Other names for the bullroarer were huhuu, puureehua, puurerehua, puurorohuu, rangorango, turorohuu and wheeorooro.[63]

As can be seen, there is some confusion in terminology for these instru-ments. Both had numerous alternative names and some are applied by dif-

Drawing of a bullroarer, 11½ inches (29 cm)
long. From Edge-Partington Album

ferent authorities to both instruments. 'Puurorohuu' is used for cutwater by both Best and Williams, but Best uses it also for bullroarer. 'Puurerehua' is used for bullroarer by both Williams and Best, but Williams uses it also for cutwater. However, the most commonly used terms for the two instruments are those adopted by Buck.[64] Buck's preferred term for whizzer or cutwater is koororohuu, which is the term currently used by members of Tuuhoe tribe, and his preference for bullroarer, despite William's ambiguous use of it, is the complementary term 'puurorohuu'.

The various alternative names seem mostly either to be simple variants of the primary ones or to have derived either from the appearance of the instrument or the sounds made by it. Thus, of the bullroarer terms, huhuu also means 'whiz or buzz' as does puurorohuu; rangorango evidently derives from rango, the word for a blowfly and wheeorooro means 'rumble or reverberate'. Similarly, of the terms for cutwater, porotiti also means 'disc', takawairore is 'to be in a state of agitation', tararii means 'whirligig' and wairori has the alternative meaning of 'to turn around or twist'.

Fischer points out that although the humming disc type of whizzer is found in Europe, China, Java and (South) America, it is unique in Oceania to New Zealand.[65] By contrast, leaf whizzers are widely distributed in Oceania, especially in the Solomon Islands and Micronesia but also in parts of New Guinea, Island Melanesia and Polynesia. In such circumstances one should not be surprised to find them also in New Zealand and indeed they are reported by Best for the East Coast, again from his informant Tutu Nihoniho.[66] As everywhere in Oceania, the instrument was a toy for children. Called a tiirango, it was made by bending a thin piece of supplejack (kareao) into the shape of a bow between the ends of which was fastened a strip of raupo leaf. A cord with a stick attached was fastened to one end and, using the stick as a handle, the tiirango was twirled around in the same way as a bullroarer, producing a whirring or humming sound. The name of the instrument, as suggested for the rangorango (above), derived from the sound of the blowfly (rango).

TRUMPETS

Four different Maori instruments have been described as trumpets. All were assigned by the Maori the generic name of puu, undoubtedly an onomatopoeic representation of the sound.[67] They were the flax trumpet, the shell trumpet, the long wooden war trumpet and an instrument called the puutoorino.

Additionally there are a few reports of trumpets made out of gourds. Tuta Nihoniho told Elsdon Best of this use in the Waiapu district;[68] Moser mentions another (see later under Rehu);[69] and Andersen gives information about a gourd trumpet about 12 inches [30 cm] long seen by his informant George Graham in use at Helensville.[70]

Teetere

The technically correct term for the so-called flax trumpet (puu harakeke or teetere) is leaf oboe. Its length, according to Andersen,[71] could vary from 9 inches [23 cm] to 24 inches [60 cm]. The instrument was made by winding a split half blade of flax (harakeke) in overlapping turns from a small mouth opening to a wider distal end.[72] It was a temporary instrument which was useable only as long as the leaf remained green. It was used as a toy by children and sometimes by adults as a makeshift to announce their approach to a village.[73] An example of the latter use was at Horahora before 1873 when the approach of the Maori King, Matutaera, was announced by the blowing of a teetere. Important as this event may have been, its use of the teetere would have been an expedient, prompted by the demands of the occasion and the availability of flax as a raw material.

> The first indication of the approach of the party was a long streaming flag float-ing high up in the air . . . and . . . in order to make a display and an impressive entry into the *kainga* [village], they were soon seen to emerge from amongst the *harakeke* and *toetoe*, a native in advance, carrying the flag. At a short dis-tance behind him came the trumpeter with a *tetere*, or trumpet, made of the leaves of the *harakeke*, or green flax; then the advance guard, of thirty men, three abreast, all armed . . .[74]

Other uses of the teetere are reported by James Cowan from the Hauhau wars in the 1860s. In 1865, at Pipiriki, the Hauhau attackers kept the gov-ernment forces awake at night by sounding bugle calls on teetere flax trum-pets in imitation of the soldiers; and in 1864–65, Ngaa Rauru warriors had a military drill, modelled on that of the British soldiers, which included bu-glers who blew calls on the flax teetere as an alarm to accustom them to attack.[75]

Again there is some overlap of terminology. The term puu harakeke from harakeke (flax) is unequivocal. However, teetere is used also as a synonym for the wooden war trumpet, and in the South Island, the term pukaaea, which elsewhere refers to the wooden war trumpet, was used instead for the flax trumpet.[76] As well, the terms puutara, puutaatara and puutaratara ap-pear to have been applied interchangeably to all forms of trumpet whether

A flax teetere made for Johannes Andersen by Paul Rokeno of Taupo

wooden, shell or flax.[77] A synonym for teetere given by Andersen, though not by other writers, is puukihi.[78]

Shell trumpet (puutaatara or puu moana)

The shell trumpet was made from a large Triton shell[79] with the end cut off and a carved wooden mouthpiece lashed on in its place. The lashing was secured through holes drilled in the shell and mouthpiece,[80] and gum[81] was used to seal the joint. A strip of dog-skin was sometimes attached as a handle or a string was used with tufts of dog's hair or feathers attached as ornamentation.[82] It was a signalling trumpet, admired, according to Andersen, for its volume of sound.[83] Early European visitors to New Zealand judged it according to their own less appropriate standards. Polack says 'the noise was as rude as can well be imagined'.[84] Banks, who heard the shell trumpet in 1770, compared the noise to that made by boys with a cow horn.[85] George Forster said of a 1773 performance: 'A hideous bellowing was all the sound that could be procured from this instrument'.[86]

From the above descriptions it would seem that the puutaatara did not in practice produce more than one note, and trial blowing of museum specimens confirms that few indeed are capable of overblowing like the European trumpet or bugle. However, the fundamental note is loud and clear, perfect for the uses to which the instrument was put.

As also in Polynesia, the instrument was associated with chiefs and leaders. Chiefs sometimes carried them when travelling and would sound them when approaching a village to warn the people to prepare for their coming. They were also used by a commanding chief for directing or rallying his forces during a fight. And in some chiefly families they were used to announce the birth of a first-born son. Another use was to announce visitors or as a signal to assemble the people on the marae.[87]

Puutaatara given to A. Hughes at Kawhia by Tawhiao. PHOTO: *M. McLean.*
Auckland Institute & Museum 37539.

Alternative names for the shell trumpet were: kaakara, potipoti (not in Williams), puuhaaureroa=puuwhaaureroa, puupakapaka,[88] puutara, puutaratara and puutoto.[89] Additionally, teetere (otherwise the term for flax trumpet) is given by Maning as the word for the shell trumpet as well as the long wooden war trumpet.[90] The term taatara, also on Best's list of alternatives, is given by Williams as the name for the *Charonia capax* shells from which trumpets were made, with equivalent terms puupuutara, puupuutaatara, and tuuteure, together with puutaatara, puutara and puutaratara, all of which are also terms for the trumpet itself. The derivation of puu moana from moana 'sea' is self-evident. Some of the alternative names presumably derive from the use of the instrument in war: pakapaka means 'quarrelsome', one of the meanings of tara is 'courage' and toto means 'blood'.

In view of an article by Gathercole,[91] who writes at length on the topic, comment is in order concerning an unusual form of puutaatara first described by Colenso. Only three such instruments are known to have existed. Colenso remarks as follows:

> Here I must notice a most curious plan which the old Maoris seem to have had for increasing, or altering, the power of the sound of their conch shell. An ancient trumpet of this kind (formerly belonging to the old patriotic chief of Table Cape, Ihaka Whanga, but now the property of Mr. Samuel Locke, of Napier,) has a thin piece of hard dark wood, of a broadly elliptical form, and measuring 5 x 3 inches, most dexterously fitted in to fill up a hole in the upper part of the body or large whorl of the shell; which piece of wood is also curved, and ribbed, or scraped to resemble and closely match the transverse ridges of the shell; and additionally carved, of course, with one of their national devices; besides being ornamented with strips of birds' skin and feathers; — the plumage of the *kaakaapo* or ground parrot, (*Strigops habroptilus*). At first I had supposed that the said shell, having been somehow broken, had been repaired by having this piece of wood set in; but on further examination, and also comparing it with the figure of a similar New Zealand shell trumpet in Cook's Voyages (*Second Voyage*, vol. I, plate 19,) which has, apparently, a precisely similar piece of dark wood let into it! I have concluded as above, that, in both instances, such was done purposely.[92]

The present location of the Locke instrument described by Colenso is unknown; the second known such instrument is figured by Oldman and is now in the Otago Museum.[93] It has a small oval of wood (3.8 x 2.9 cm) inserted in its bowl, held by flax bindings.[94] The Cook instrument referred to by Colenso is in the Cambridge Museum and is the subject of Gathercole's article. He states that 'the base of the bowl has been deliberately and evenly sliced off and replaced by a piece of wood carefully shaped to conform to its contours and firmly joined to it by ten flax bindings'. Along the line of the join is a string of flax caulked by an application of gum.[95] Another unusual feature of this instrument is a flax stopper attached to the carrying handle by a string. This stopper is described in the Museum register as a 'modulator' and has been carefully shaped to fit snugly into the bowl of the instrument.[96] Gathercole has an elaborate explanation both for the wooden patch and the so-called 'modulator'. Both Colenso and Oldman[97] — who may well have followed Colenso in the matter — surmise that the wooden inserts in their respective instruments might have been added to increase the volume of the sound. Gathercole agrees and states further that in such a case the efficacy of the wooden insert as a sounding-board would be enhanced by the use of the stopper as 'a muffler to help to vary the amount and quality of the sound'.[98] For such a view to be plausible it would need to be demonstrated either that the puutaatara was not a signalling instrument or that muffling it could in some way assist signalling. Gathercole ingeniously suggests that the sound of the shell trumpet was of symbolic as well as practical import. Also symbolic, he adds, were the dog-skin and kaakaapoo feather attachments which most writers have regarded as 'ornamentation'. Flocks of kaakaapoo had leaders who acted as sentries, a role analogous to that of the night sentry at a paa 'equipped with a trumpet to show that the defenders were alert'.[99] The shell trumpet, argues Gathercole, could have had a sacred function associated with Tupai, a thunder demon and mythical maker of the first shell trumpets, who could strike down offenders against tapu. But, says Gathercole, Tupai was capricious; to invoke his aid by sounding the trumpet could be dangerous so the sound had to 'regulated by modulation'. How 'modulation' could have done so is not, however, explained. A less esoteric explanation seems the more plausible. Gathercole himself points out that shell trumpets were both rare and treasured.[100] As such they would have been thought worthy of repair if broken, especially in view of the time, effort and care lavished upon carving and fitting the mouthpiece. A commonsense explanation is also available for the 'modulator'. A practical, if prosaic, use for it might have been to prevent vermin from entering the trumpet, while it was stored, and eating away at the wooden patch. Similar stoppers, as Gathercole acknowledges, were sometimes used to block the wooden mouthpiece when trumpets were stored and for these as well there is no need to invoke symbolic significance.

Puukaaea

The puukaaea[101] was a wooden trumpet 3–8½ feet [0.9–2.5m] long. Most were 5–6 feet [1.5–1.8m] long. They were made by splitting a piece of mataii wood longitudinally, hollowing it out, and then binding the two halves together again, usually with the aerial roots of the kiekie. According to Mair, glue to secure the binding was made from the tarata tree.[102] One end of the instrument had a carved wooden mouthpiece (koongutu) and the other was flared out to a diameter of 3–5 inches [8–12 cm], forming a bell-like shape (whara). Sometimes the bell was carved out of the body of the instrument and sometimes it was formed of several pieces, aptly described by one writer as fitted to each other like the staves of a cask.[103]

Again the use of the instrument is not in doubt. Writers are all agreed in calling it a war trumpet. The smaller, more portable instruments may have been used in the same way as the conch for rallying forces during battle. The longer puukaaea were obviously ill-adapted to carry about or even to hold while playing. They were sounded by watchmen on duty at the fortified village or paa to signal the approach of an enemy or to show that the paa was on the alert. They would have been used from a stationary position within the paa, supported, according to Angas, on the fence-work[104] of the paa from whence the instrument could be heard at a distance of several miles on a calm night. Another use was as a speaking trumpet or megaphone through which insults or defiance could be hurled at the enemy. One such curse was *'Too roro, too roro'* which means 'Your brains, your brains'.[105] It was a deadly insult, threatening the listener that the player would knock his brains out and eat them. Evidently as a magical attempt to aid the voice-production qualities of the instrument, the inside of the puukaaea at the flared end was often made to resemble the interior of the human throat by the insertion of carved wooden pegs called puutohe, tohe or tohetohe. These represented the uvula (tohetohe).

Non-military use of the puukaaea, while possibly rare, can be documented for at least two occasions. One was a Ngaapuhi event at the Bay of Islands in 1834 when William Barrett Marshall heard trumpet blasts announcing the arrival and departure of visitors. Conches could have been involved as Marshall mentions he was presented with one. But the instrument he describes was certainly a puukaaea:

> The trumpet, whose flourish was made to do honour to Pomare and his body-guard, was upwards of six feet long, formed by several pieces, curiously sewed together by threads of cane, and elaborately carved . . .[106]

Another example occurred in the Wanganui area in 1857, when the missionary Richard Taylor travelled in a canoe which had puukaaea trumpets on board. An entry in his diary for 16 October reads: 'My followers announced our approach with the trumpet, for they had brought two with them, each fully six feet long, which really made a very sweet and distinct sound.'[107]

Other estimates of the sound were not as flattering. Crozet, who visited the Bay of Islands in 1772, said the sound was a very disagreeable one similar to that of shepherds' horns.[108] Angas said it was loud and roaring.[109] Maning said it gave forth a 'groaning, moaning sound like the voice of a dying wild bull'[110] and George Forster said it made 'a very uncouth kind of braying'.[111] A good horn or trumpet player can get four notes out of the instrument and play a number of bugle calls on it,[112] but the Maori evidently

181

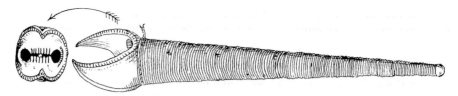

Drawing of a short puukaaea showing binding and a view of the tohe

did not exploit this feature. Forster was definite that 'they always sounded the same note', as was his compatriot James Burney.[113]

Best records 'titi matai' and 'wharawhara' as alternative names for the puukaaea in the Waipu district of the East Coast.[114] The latter name refers to the bell-shaped mouth of the instrument. Another synonym, given by Williams, is 'puutahoro'.

Puutoorino

The puutoorino[115] (or toorino) was an instrument about 1–2 feet [30–60 cm] long, widest in the middle and tapering at each end. Andersen refers to it as 'torpedo shaped'.[116] One end was usually not quite closed; the other had a mouth-opening for blowing. In the middle was a round, oval, or more usually, figure-of-eight, sounding hole. The sounding hole was generally representative of the human mouth and was surrounded by carving depicting a human face. In some of the more elaborately carved instruments, an entire head is carved in relief.[117] The puutoorino was made in the same way as the puukaaea by splitting a piece of mataii wood longitudinally, shaping and hollowing it out, and then binding the two halves together with split vines or kiekie roots.[118] A number of museum specimens of puutoorino are illustrated and described in detail by Andersen, Buck and, especially, Best.[119] Amongst them are specimens of rare double puutoorino, conjoined at top and bottom. One of these instruments is in the British Museum; another is in the Museum of New Zealand, Wellington.[120]

As Buck remarks,[121] the playing method of the puutoorino is in doubt. The earliest reports of the puutoorino from Cook's first voyage characterise it unequivocally as a trumpet which produced a 'harsh, shrill' or 'shrill, hoarse' sound.[122] However, it has also been described as a flute. Both Hamilton and Tregear say the instrument was a flute or a flageolet.[123] George Forster, in his account of Cook's second voyage, provides apparent support by stating 'it went by the name of a flute among our people'.[124] Other writers are unspe-

Carved puutoorino. Photo: M. McLean. *Auckland Institute & Museum 3450.*

cific about the playing method. Savage says merely that it was 'inflated at one extremity';[125] Newman calls it a 'nasal flute';[126] Buck was told it was a speaking trumpet, 'the player singing or reciting words into the instrument'.[127] The latter, if true, would explain reports that words could be breathed through the instrument.[128] Colenso, in common with a number of later writers, stated that the sound issuing from the central aperture of the puutoorino was 'modi-fied by the hand'.[129] Te Tahi-o-piripi of Ngaati Maniapoto told Buck: 'The left hand encircled the mouthpiece and the lips of the player; the right hand held the middle of the instrument, and the fingers were placed over the figure-of-eight hole to modify the sound.'[130] Andersen's Ngaati Porou in-formant, Iehu Nukunuku, said that the puutoorino made a murmuring sound like water bubbling into a calabash 'as the finger was moved not lifted' over the central opening.[131] Several writers say the sound could also be varied by fingering the pinhole which can be found at the pointed end of most of these instruments.[132]

The only one of the writer's informants able to provide information about the playing method of the puutoorino was Pairoa Wineera of Ngaati Raukawa and Ngaati Toa, who was 90 years old when last interviewed on 21 Novem-ber 1972. At the age of 12 she was taught to play the kooauau (end-blown flute) by her uncle Hemi Hohaea who was also able to play the puutoorino. According to Mrs Wineera the puutoorino was played in the same manner as the kooauau, as a mouth flute which played waiata tunes. It had a deeper tone than the kooauau and because of limited carrying power was played only indoors.

Resorting to experiment with museum instruments, the present writer has found that so long as the bindings are tight, the smaller puutoorino are best blown as flutes, but the larger ones can usually be blown only as trum-pets. In both applications, though not on all instruments, the pitch can be lowered by partially blocking the central sounding hole. But there are acoustic limits to this technique. Generally it is possible to lower the pitch in this way by a half tone, but attempting to lower the note further, or in some cases at all, stops the instrument from sounding. With few exceptions, fin-gering the small pinhole at the end of most instruments produces only minute variation of pitch or none at all. A peculiarity of all Maori trumpets with mouthpieces, whether puutaatara, puukaaea or puutoorino, is that the mouthpieces are almost invariably externally rounded in the same manner as the blowing ends of kooauau and nguru flutes. This aids flute-blowing but it is a disadvantage for trumpets. To sound the instruments in flute mode, the writer used the same oblique blowing technique as employed for kooauau or nguru flutes (see later). Mair confirms the use of this technique on the puutoorino with a statement that the performer blew into the large aperture obliquely.[133] It is also to be seen in a 1919 photograph of a puutoorino ap-parently being played. The performer is Princess Iwa who went to England with a concert party led by Maggie Papakura in 1911 and later performed in vaudeville. In the photograph, captioned 'Princess Iwa entertaining an ancestor', she is seen in a bizarre pose playing the puutoorino at the London Palladium to a dried head.[134]

As will be seen, a feature of the kooauau technique is that notes can be varied continuously downwards by portamento. When this was tried with puutoorino, a continuous portamento was found in some instruments to be available from the top note blowable, downwards by about a minor 2nd to major 2nd at which point there was an abrupt transition downwards by a full minor 3rd with no intervening notes playable. It proved possible to alternate rapidly between the two notes with an effect akin to yodelling. Amongst instruments which displayed this effect were Museum of New Zealand instruments WEB COLL 887 and WEB COLL 1768.[135] A possibly unique instrument is no. 51.572 at the Wanganui Public Museum. It has a fairly large mouthpiece at one end (diameter 1.8 cm) from which the instrument can be blown as a trumpet and a small mouthpiece at the other (diameter 1.1 cm) from which it can be blown as a flute.[136]

In view of the above results, Andersen's description of the puutoorino as a 'bugle-flute' may be accepted.[137] It is apparent that the puutoorino was a compromise instrument, perhaps explaining its early obsolescence. It was evidently not very effective in any of its applications. Even allowing for problems with loose bindings in museum specimens, as a trumpet it is far outstripped by the puutaatara and puukaaea. Except for instruments capable of the 'yodelling' effect, as a flute it could play only two or three notes within a tone or half tone of each other and could never have been as effective as the kooauau or nguru. As a megaphone it would have been poor indeed. Most were too short and all were the wrong shape for projecting sound the distance credited to its rival as a megaphone, the puukaaea. Finally, if proof were needed, Best is confirmed in his positive statement that the puutoorino 'was used as a mouth flute only and was never sounded with the nose'.[138]

An alternative name for the puutoorino, according to White,[139] was 'puu hoho', a name also given by Buck[140] as 'puu hoho ho'. Best and Buck both suggest that this name is imitative of the sound of the instrument.

FLUTES

As shown above, the puutoorino was sometimes a trumpet and sometimes a flute. The main instruments used solely as flutes were the kooauau and the nguru. Other flutes called porutu, rehu and whio have also been reported.

Kooauau

This instrument was a simple open tube, usually 5–6 inches [12–15 cm] long, with a bore of ½–¾ inch [1–2 cm] and three fingerholes. About a third of the koaauau flutes now in museums are made of human bone, a few of

Carved wooden kooauau.
PHOTO: M. McLean. Auckland Institute & Museum 29721.

whale-tooth ivory, and the remainder of wood.[141] When not in use they were often worn around the neck as an ornament and most have a corresponding additional hole for a suspension cord.[142] Some of James Beattie's South Island informants said the kooauau was sometimes made from bull kelp (*Durvillea antarctica*),[143] but this may have been a confusion as bull kelp is also called kooauau.[144] It is possible, nevertheless, that the name of the instrument derives from the kelp or vice versa.

The earliest instruments of the type — though of unknown name — are small flutes made from the wing and leg bones of another denizen of the sea, the albatross. Most such flutes have been found on surface sites in Canterbury, Otago and Southland in the South Island. One end is usually smoothed for blowing and the other has a hole for suspension. In addition to the suspension hole, there are three fingerholes, and many of the instruments are decorated with burned cross-hatched lines. The fingerholes are usually non-equidistant with the widest space conventionally between the top and middle holes. North Island flutes made of bone and wood reverse this convention and generally have the suspension hole bored not at the end but transversely through part of the body of the instrument or through a lug at the back. The placement of the three fingerholes resulted from the use of the finger joints to determine the spacings.[145] The human bone instruments are often carved in bands around the ends. They were made from the arm- or leg-bones of slain enemies as an adjunct of cannibalism. The object was to degrade the person killed.[146] Wooden flutes are usually either carved in the same way as bone ones or are intricately carved all over. Some have plugged fingerholes showing that sometimes the makers made a mistake with the tuning — probably by boring one or more fingerholes too large — and started over again rather than discard the instrument.

Maori albatross bone flute from Otago with incised decoration.
PHOTO: M. McLean. Auckland Institute & Museum 48393

Playing method

Although popularly believed to be a nose flute, the kooauau was traditionally blown with the mouth.[147] The method was learned by the writer from
the two surviving players of the 1960s and has since been used by him to
test specimens in museums throughout the world. Mouth-blowing the
kooauau is attested by eye-witness accounts from locations as diverse as the
East Coast, the Waikato, (most likely) Taranaki, the Wairarapa, Auckland
and the Bay of Plenty. Andersen describes the playing of Iehu Nukunuku of
Ngaati Porou on a flute he made from a gas pipe;[148] Best saw Hari Wahanui
of Waikato play on a flute from the Dominion Museum;[149] Kennedy watched
a Maori play near the Mokau River;[150] and the present writer's principal informants were Pairoa Wineera of Ngaati Raukawa and Henare Toka of Ngaati
Whaatua. Others who did not themselves play the kooauau but witnessed it
being played were Marata Te Tomo of Ngaati Tuuwharetoa and Ani Reweti
Natana of Tuuhoe, both of whom confirmed the instrument as a mouth
flute. Additionally, Uehoka Tairakena of Ngaati Maahanga of Waikato was
able to blow notes on the kooauau though he could not play a tune; he used
a blowing technique identical to that of Pairoa Wineera. Best says merely
that Wahanui blew into one end of the flute; Andersen says Nukunuku 'blew
sideways across the opening instead of directly across'.[151] Kennedy's player
held his instrument 'not vertically, but slanted to the right and blew into it
sideways'. In all cases the instrument was blown with the mouth, and the
'sideways' method described by Andersen and Kennedy is the same as that
learned by the present writer. The playing position of the instrument is not
vertical or horizontal but diagonal. From the point of view of the player, it is
held slightly downward and to the right, with the right-hand edge of the
blowing end resting on the lips. This puts the left-hand edge a little distance
from the lips and it is the stream of air striking this edge which causes the
instrument to sound. A peculiarity of this blowing technique is that notes
can be varied not only by fingering but also by manner of blowing. Henare
Toka was definite that this was part of the traditional playing method. It was
used where a slur or portamento was required between notes and it could
also be used to compensate for non-uniformities between instruments when
they were played together. The smaller the flute the greater the blowing
variability. North Island flutes of wood and human bone generally have a
blowing variability of about a major 2nd. By contrast, the smallest South
Island albatross bone flutes, which lack fingerholes and were thought by
earlier writers to be unfinished, proved to be practical musical instruments
with a range of a full octave.[152]

A curiosity of the kooauau, as also of the puutoorino, is an often repeated belief that words could be breathed through the instrument. Philips
offers the common-sense suggestion that the chief waiata airs would be so
familiar as to suggest the words when the tune was heard and surmises that

Unknown Maori playing kooauau.
PHOTO: *H. Webster. Alexander Turnbull Library, 15171¹/₂*

an ingenious performer might have combined fragments from well-known airs to form a new message.[153] Against this, Andersen is definite that he himself heard words on a cylinder recording of Iehu Nukunuku playing his gas-pipe flute in 1923. It was an event that evidently made an enduring impression upon him. From time to time in correspondence, and in at least three of his publications,[154] Andersen relates the following anecdote:

I have heard such a song whilst it was being recorded; but whilst I saw the movement of the old man's lips who was blowing into the flute, I did not know that the words as well as the melody were being recorded. It was not till more than a year later, when I reproduced the song for the sake of some Maori visitors to the Turnbull Library, that I learned that the words had been recorded. The Maori man who was listening intently, said softly: 'I can hear the words.' 'What words?' I asked. 'The words he is saying through the koauau,' said the man. I put the cylinder through again, and when he repeated the words, I could distinctly hear them coming from the instrument. Here the incredulous may smile, and say, 'Of course; when you know the words, naturally you can imagine that you hear them.' But I would remind the incredulous that if you have lost your place whilst the Psalms are singing in church you cannot catch the words of the singers, try as you will; but immediately you find the place you can hear every word. . . . When I asked the Maori if such flute-singing was customary, he said: 'Of course; and if you cannot get all the words the first time, you can get them all after one or two hearings; but it is not easy, and that is why a good flute player is so esteemed'.[155]

Iehu Nukunuku (with Elsdon Best and Paratene Ngata) playing gas-pipe flute at Waiomatatini in 1923. PHOTO: *James McDonald. Museum of New Zealand Te Papa Tongarewa neg. no. B2183*

'This', Andersen points out, 'explains another fact which till then seemed merely curious; That is, the fact that the Maori blew sideways across the end of the flute. . . . In blowing sideways the lips are free to move, and if the player is watched they will be seen to move — he is blowing the words into the *koauau*.'[156] Plausible as this may seem, it has been impossible to verify. Andersen identifies Nukunuku's song as the well-known oriori 'Pine pine te kura'.[157] But careful listening to the only cylinder recording of Nukunuku's flute playing[158] reveals that the song, whatever it may be, is not 'Pine pine te kura'. Nor are any words audible on the recording. Possibly Nukunuku recorded another song which has not survived. The present writer has tried to emulate Nukunuku by blowing words into a kooauau, but with only partial success. The flute sound can be broken into syllables and some of the consonants can be suggested, but vowel sounds seem impossible to produce. On these results, the best that can be said is that to hear the words the listener would still need to know the song.

Scales. Henare Toka and Pairoa Wineera both said the kooauau was used to accompany waiata singing and played the melody in unison with the singers. Kiwi Amohau and Iehu Nukunuku likewise told Best that 'all tunes had words',[159] and there is similar agreement on unison playing.[160] It follows that the kooauau should be capable of the same notes as used in waiata and

188

this indeed proves generally true. Andersen discovered from Amohau that traditionally neither partial fingering nor cross fingering was used.[161] By use of the 'simple' finger positions alone, the scale of the kooauau was therefore limited to four pitches, rather than the eight that would otherwise be available from fingering three holes.[162] The diagram shows the 'simple' finger positions and the most common kooauau scale produced by this fingering. In practice, portamento would probably also have been used, extending the range of the instrument within the limits of the portamento. Without portamento, the range of most flutes is a 4th or less. Small as such a range may seem, it is nevertheless adequate for playing most waiata. Further discussion of kooauau scales is in the section on flute scale typology below.

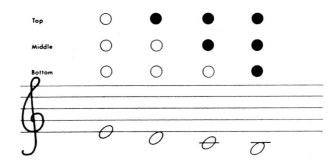

Nguru

In his *Endeavour* Journal of 1770, Joseph Banks illustrates a nguru[163] — though he does not name it — and describes it as 'crooked and shapd almost like a large tobacco pipe head'. One nguru excavated by archaeologists at Oruarangi, near Thames,[164] does, in fact, appear to have been made out of a clay tobacco pipe, so Banks's description is apt. Colenso speaks of whistles shaped 'something like a short thick tongue'[165] and this, too, is an excellent description of the shape of the nguru.

The nguru is generally shorter than the kooauau. Most are only 3 or 4 inches [7–10 cm] long. They are made of wood, clay, stone or rarely whale's tooth and are bored longitudinally like a kooauau. One end is open and rounded externally like a kooauau and the other finishes with a small hole in the centre of an upturned snout. Besides the snout hole there are usually two fingerholes on top and sometimes another one or two underneath the snout. Like kooauau, some nguru instruments have a hole bored through the back for a suspension cord.

Parkinson describes the instrument, which he also figures, as a whistle, worn about the neck, which yields a shrill sound.[166] Banks says of his 'tobacco pipe' instrument that 'it has hardly more musick in it than a whistle

Carved wooden nguru. PHOTO: *M. McLean. Otago Museum Oldman Collection 1025.*

with a Pea in it; but on none of these did I ever hear them attempt to play a tune or sing to their musick'.[167] Captain Cook writes in almost identical terms of what is presumably the same instrument. He describes it as:

> a small wooden pipe, resembling a child's nine-pin, only much smaller, and in this there is no more music than in a pea-whistle. They seem sensible, indeed, that these instruments are not musical, for we never heard an attempt to sing to them, or to produce with them any measured tones that bore the least resemblance to a tune.[168]

On the basis of these statements, Colenso suspected the instruments were only for the purpose of making a loud call 'as from a chief to his followers'.[169] Later writers, evidently following Colenso, call them 'war whistles', but there appears to be no eye-witness account of such a use.[170] It may well be that the instrument was obsolescent even in Cook's time and fell entirely out of use soon after. It is certain, at any rate, that Cook was wrong to suppose it was not musical. The writer's researches have revealed the nguru to be a mouth flute at least as versatile as the kooauau. Blown from the wide end in the same way as the kooauau, it produces scales identical with those of the kooauau, differing only in terms of distribution by date and area. Scales are discussed further in the section on flute scale typology below.

190

Origin of the nguru

The form of the nguru is unusual though not without parallel outside New Zealand. It needs explanation because nguru scales can be produced just as readily by the kooauau and the shape is therefore non-functional. Why labour to make an instrument of such a complicated shape when a straight tube would work as well?

Marcuse likens the nguru to 'an ornate sea cucumber' and cites Andersen as her authority for a statement that prehistoric specimens of this type of flute have been found in Peru.[171] Andersen illustrates a single terracotta flute from a prehistoric grave in Peru and speculates on this account on the possibility of Polynesian contact with the American continent.[172] Heyerdahl quotes Andersen at length in support of his well-known hypothesis for American settlement of Polynesia.[173] Except for a botanical opinion that the sweet potato may be of South American origin, Heyerdahl's theory is now largely discredited, though Bellwood concludes, after a review of the evidence, that some American contact with Polynesia could have taken place.[174] One nevertheless agrees with Buck that the Maori is likely to have invented the nguru in New Zealand 'without having received any suggestions from Peru'.[175] Aside from the coincidence of an upturned snout hole and the occurrence of some Oruarangi nguru which have been described as 'fashioned from baked clay',[176] there is no great resemblance between the Maori instruments and the Peruvian one which is much longer, has six fingerholes rather than three and is notched instead of rounded at the blowing end. An explanation for the coincidence is offered by Fischer[177] who quotes Izikowitz as stating that clay vessel flutes of South America simply imitated the form of flutes made from calabashes.[178] The same, Fischer suggests, might have happened independently in New Zealand.

Two other candidates as a nguru prototype are worthy of mention. One nguru is in existence which had been made from a broken clay tobacco pipe. A remote possibility, first suggested to the writer in 1967 by L.M. Groube and later also by D.R. Simmons is that the form derived literally from the Dutch clay tobacco pipe.[179] In 1642, the Dutch navigator Abel Janszoon Tasman lost three of his men to a canoe attack at Golden Bay near the present town of Nelson. The attackers took one dead body into their canoe and threw another into the sea[180] whence it could well have been washed ashore. If one of these men was carrying a Dutch meerschaum pipe it could have been found and fashioned into a flute. Early trading of European artefacts over long distances is known. A medal from Cook's second voyage was traded some 700 kilometres from Queen Charlotte Sound to Murdering Beach in Otago.[181] So it may have been possible, 130 years earlier, for a tobacco pipe to travel a lesser distance from Golden Bay to the Coromandel, perhaps following the route taken by greenstone which is known to have been present in the Oruarangi assemblage.[182] But the clay pipe nguru is unlikely to have

191

been Dutch. Clay pipe bowls and stems have been found close to Oruarangi at Kiri Island;[183] these are certainly late European[184] and it is uneconomic to postulate an earlier clay pipe if later ones are known to have been present.

A more likely protoform for the nguru would seem to be the whale tooth, and several ivory specimens are indeed extant. Six such nguru flutes are amongst those examined by the writer.[185] However, all but one have scales which the writer's typology shows to be late, and the remaining scale belongs to a flute which is undateable.

With the tobacco pipe and the whale tooth eliminated, the most likely protoform for the nguru remains the gourd. There is little in the ethnographic literature of relevance to the gourd as a protoform for the nguru. Much has been made of the appearance in Edge-Partington's *Album* of a gourd musical instrument attributed to New Zealand.[186] It is made from a small gourd with the stem cut off; there is a hole in the neck and three further holes appear in a row across the body of the instrument. Andersen, Best and Hamilton all appear to accept it as a genuine New Zealand instrument. However, Buck rightly rejects it as wrongly identified and more likely to be Hawaiian.[187]

Seemingly more germane are statements from Bauke about an instrument called a 'nguru' which was formed from a gourd and softly crooned into[188] and a statement from George Graham that gourds of suitable shape were used to make a toy nguru or puu.[189] In Graham's case, however, and (if Andersen's interpretation is accepted) in Bauke's also, the instrument referred to was a form of trumpet.

None of the above is convincing as evidence for a gourd protoform of the nguru. However, on a priori grounds, the stem end of a calabash is a good candidate because it is about the right shape; it would seem physically possible to make a nguru in this way; and, as perishable objects, flutes so made could not normally be expected to have survived in the archaeological record, accounting for the apparent lack of specimens. Moreover, the existence of the three-fingerhole Hawaiian ipu hokiokio as a possible Polynesian daughter form — despite the rejection of Edge-Partington's putative New Zealand specimen — somewhat strengthens the case. Finally, the Maori name for the holes in a flute, wenewene, is the same as for the calabash gourd, suggesting a connection. But, in fact, the matter has been put beyond doubt by a remarkable piece of work at the University of Auckland. One of New Zealand's best known archaeological sites is Kauri Point swamp, near Tauranga in the Bay of Plenty, which has yielded two broken puutoorino, thousands of obsidian flakes and numerous fragments of gourd. In 1984, Joan Maingay and Dorothy Brown succeeded in reassembling gourd fragments from this site into a recognisable small nguru, complete with fingerholes in the expected places, two on the upper surface and one at the snout end.[190]

The Kauri Point sequence ranges within an interval of 150–200 years

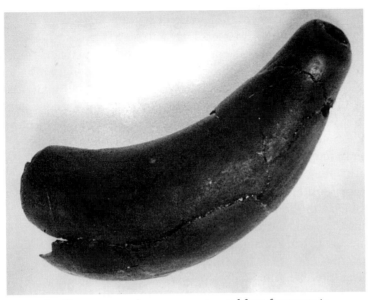

*Pre-European gourd nguru reconstructed from fragments in
1984 by Joan Maingay and Dorothy Brown.*
PHOTO: *Anthropology Department, University of Auckland*

beginning around AD 1500, establishing this nguru as antedating all known ethnographic specimens.[191]

Playing method

The absence of traditional accounts of the nguru has fueled speculation about the manner of blowing. Even more than the kooauau or the puutoorino, it has had bestowed upon it the sobriquet 'nose flute'. Andersen was sceptical of this description as was Buck,[192] but Best consistently accepts the instrument as a nose flute and, doubtless following Best, most museums so describe the instruments in their collections.

Early reports of the nguru neither give it a name nor make mention of nose-blowing. It is clear, nevertheless, that of Cook's fellow voyagers, Parkinson, at least, was in no doubt that the nguru was a mouth flute. His drawing of a nguru is accompanied by the remark: 'Besides the mouth-hole, they have several for the fingers to play upon.'[193]

The first published reference to nose-blowing the nguru, as of the name 'nguru' itself, appears to have been in Hamilton's *Maori Art* where Hamilton states: 'It is used by inserting the small end in the nostril, and, as the name implies, snoring or snorting through it.'[194] Hamilton obtained his information from Gilbert Mair who provided it in a letter written to Hamilton on 6 May, 1900.[195] As well, John White, a contemporary of Mair, is quoted by Best as stating: 'The flute made of a whale's tooth was termed a *nguru* and was played with the nose.'[196] The term nguru is now firmly established as the name for the instrument though precedent for it is absent. Mair's gloss, however, is wrong. Both Andersen and Buck point out that the term nguru, one of whose meanings is 'to murmur', seems to have been confused by Mair with ngoro 'to snore'.[197] The name does not therefore imply snoring or snorting. Nor could the instrument have been played by poking it up the nose, even by the small end. This could not possibly produce a note because there would be no blowing edge for air to impinge upon. In fact, the opening at the snout end of the nguru is a fingerhole and the instrument can be blown from the wide end in the same way as the kooauau. This ought in any event to be obvious as the wide end of the nguru is identically rounded to the blowing end of the kooauau, and the spacing of the three fingerholes also conforms to the kooauau convention.[198] Blowing from the wide end, and using the kooauau mouth-blowing technique, the present writer has blown over 30 nguru instruments from museum and other collections around the world in a study of Maori flute scales.[199] All nguru flutes can be blown with the mouth using this technique. When this is done they produce perfectly normal kooauau scales except for an extension downwards of one or two notes in the case of instruments with further fingerholes under the snout. Thus if, as is the case, the kooauau was a mouth flute, then so, it would appear, was the nguru. Recently, however, the manner of blowing the nguru has again been thrown into doubt. Notwithstanding the above, it turns out that nguru flutes can be blown from the wide end not only with the mouth but also with the nose. Richard Nunns of Nelson has given lecture demonstrations of the method which reportedly produces a 'rich, haunting tone' in contrast with mouth-blowing when 'the sound emitted was inferior'.[200] Aesthetics aside, it would seem unlikely that such a method was much used. The very largest instruments are probably incapable of nose-blowing and, with one thumb occupied to block a nostril, reaching holes under the snout of the instrument would become difficult or impossible. One may add that the holes under the snout would be quite inexplicable if the instrument were a nose flute played as described by Mair. When the nguru is played from the wide end, these holes have the practical advantage of serving as drip holes for condensation which accumulates in the bend of the instrument. But they are undoubtedly also intended for fingering even though they are hard to reach. Unlike the kooauau, most nguru flutes have little blowing variability. When fingered, the holes under the snout of the nguru duplicate the portamento ability of the kooauau by extending the range of notes downwards by a major 2nd or minor 3rd, overcoming the liability.[201]

Flute scale typology

In his book *Maori Music*, Andersen considered the diversity in the size and shape of the kooauau to be 'so great that it is difficult to see how any uniformity of sound could have been obtained from the various kinds'.[202] In his experiments with blowing the instruments he was baffled to find that no two flutes agreed in their intervals, and from albatross bone specimens he was able to obtain 'no more than a whistling suggestion of what the notes may be'.[203] He concluded that the albatross bone flutes might have been toys for children; and he explained away the apparent non-uniformity of intervals in other instruments, and the presence in some of plugged fingerholes, by accepting a suggestion from Peter Buck that each flute might have played only a single tune.[204] In fact, no such explanation is required. Andersen's problems occurred partly because he did not use the traditional oblique blowing technique and partly, as he himself recognised, because of lack of control over blowing variability.[205]

That kooauau are capable of uniform scales was demonstrated by the present writer in a study of South Island albatross bone flutes from the Otago Museum.[206] In a later paper, using a much larger sample of 145 mainly North Island flutes from ethnographic collections, it was shown that, except for known or suspected fakes and a few anomalous specimens, nine scales, in three groups of three scales each, account for almost the entire corpus of kooauau flutes in museums, and the two most popular scales for some 63 per cent.[207] With scales ranked according to their frequency order of appearance in the corpus, kooauau scale groups turn out to be distinguished by the interval between the two lowest notes of the scales. Group 1 scales have a semitone or m2 (S) between the two lowest notes, Group 2 scales a tone or M2 (T), and Group 3 scales a minor 3rd (m3). The same scales were found in the corpus of nguru flutes. However, the rank order of scales by frequency of appearance was different, a further (type 10) scale was found and some of the kooauau scales were absent.

Flute scale typology

Group	Scale type		Intervals (ascending)			% kooauau	% nguru
I	1	S	T	T		31.8	20.5
	2	S	T	S		30.8	20.5
	3	S	S	S		15.0	3.0
II	4	T	T	S		5.6	32.0
	5	T	T	T		3.7	0.0
III	6	T	S	S		3.7	3.0
	7	m3	S	S		3.7	0.0
	8	m3	S	T		1.0	0.0
	9	m3	T	T		1.0	3.0
	10	m3	T	S		0.0	9.0

All flutes were assigned to areas according to date and place of collection when known and on the basis of carving styles for the remainder. Ages were expressed as pre-nineteenth century, early nineteenth century and late nineteenth century. Kooauau areas were designated as Northern, Western, Eastern and Southern. Most nguru flutes were either Northern or from the Coromandel area. The age of kooauau flutes was found by and large to correspond with their frequency order in the table (above). Nguru flutes were found mostly to be older than kooauau.

The most revealing differences between the several flute populations was found to lie in the distinctive proportion of each scale type and in patterns of common absence. For example, of the two demonstrably oldest populations of flutes, the South Island series of albatross bone flutes lack type 4 scales and the Coromandel series of nguru flutes types 5 to 8, although both share type 9. The scales were found to have transformed over time following simple rules which enabled a chronological and geographical sequence to be worked out.

The accompanying figures show the proposed sequence beginning around AD 1600 at Coromandel with nguru flutes of type 10. With a transform to type 9, flutes migrate to the South Island and, with a change of form to albatross bone, the blowing-end convention reverses. Type 9 South Island flutes transform to types 8 and 5; type 5 changes to type 1, and type 8 changes

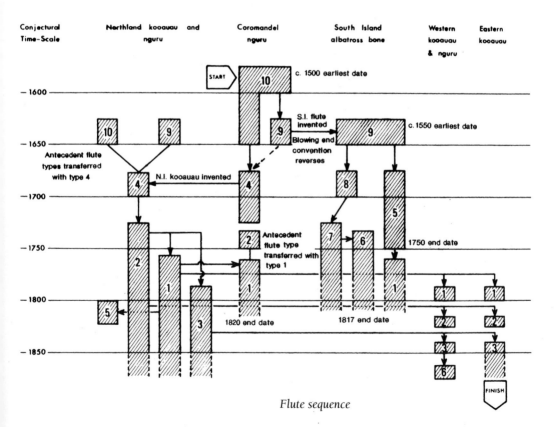

Flute sequence

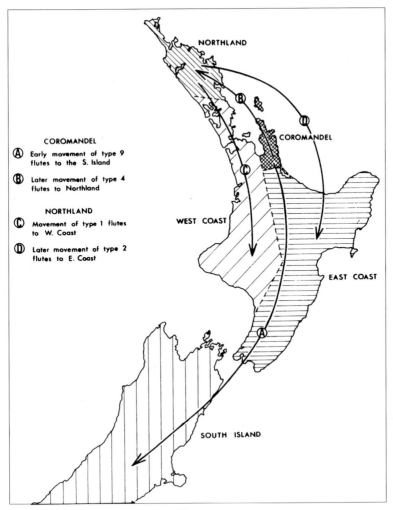

Map of flute migration

successively to types 7 and 6. The mutual presence of types 7, 6 and 1 at Murdering Beach (end date 1817) marks the finish of the South Island sequence. Meanwhile, back at Coromandel, nguru flutes of types 10 and 9 evolve to type 4 and migrate to Northland together with their still current antecedents. At this time, either at Coromandel or in Northland the discovery is made — possibly on the model of a South Island flute — that a section of human arm- or leg-bone pierced with three fingerholes will operate as a flute as effectively as a nguru. The nguru continues to be made, though in diminishing numbers, as it is supplanted by the kooauau. The two instruments develop in tandem and begin to be made in wood or wood and ivory respectively. Type 4 scales transform to types 2, 1 and 3, all three remaining current. Meanwhile, types 1 and 2 undergo a back migration to Oruarangi, type 1 migrates westwards and type 2 eastwards followed by type 3. Finally, some time after 1850, flutes become extinct in all areas, lingering longest in the East Coast, the last area to receive them.

Other flutes

Almost all Maori flutes in museums are identified as either kooauau or nguru. Some other names for flutes appear in the literature and will now be considered.

Porutu

The name is probably a transliteration of the English word 'flute'[208] and it is doubtful whether the instrument was indigenous. It seems simply to have been an extra-long kooauau, made to resemble the European flute. In the South Island it was remembered by informants of James Beattie as an instrument of tutu or mako wood with four to six fingerholes which was 'nearly as long as the pakeha flute'.[209] In the North Island, according to Mair, it was made from a young straight branch of porokaiwhiria, hollowed out by means of fire. It was elaborately carved all over, had three fingerholes like the kooauau and was about ³/₄ inch [2 cm] in diameter and 12–16 inches [30–40 cm] long.[210] In another manuscript, Mair gives the dimensions as even longer (18 inches to 2 feet [45–60 cm]).[211] Flutes of this description in museums are rare. Two such at the Auckland Institute and Museum, acquired in 1914 and 1890 respectively, are instruments 5886[212] and 100E.[213] The latter one was collected by Mair himself. Each has three fingerholes and both are made from hollowed tutu: one is 43.4 cm long and the other 41.0 cm. Unlike normal kooauau, the spacing between the fingerholes is widest between the top and the middle holes. Both flutes are carved all over in late nineteenth-century style and both have type 3 (chromatic) scales which analysis shows to be another late trait.

Rehu

In form the rehu seems to have been a side-blown porutu. The sole authority for it in this application is John White as quoted by Best.[214] White stated that the rehu was made from mataii wood or sometimes from tuupaakihi. One end was plugged and there were three fingerholes together with a mouth hole in the side.[215] Buller, quoted in full by Best, describes, but does not name, an ornately carved instrument of otherwise similar description which was 22.5 inches [57 cm] long and 1.5 inches [4 cm] wide in its broadest dimension.[216] Additionally, Moser mentions an instrument he thought might have been called a 're-hu' which seems to have been a form of trumpet. It was made from a calabash with two or three holes punctured in the side. A meeting was summoned by blowing into the mouth of the instrument, producing a 'most horrid noise' accompanied by the beating of a stick upon an iron pot.[217] Tregear applies the name rehu to albatross bone flutes.[218]

The writer has found only two instruments in museums matching White's description of the rehu. One is ME 197 in the Museum of New Zealand.[219] This flute is 36.3 cm long, has three fingerholes, a transverse blowing hole and has one end apparently plugged with a cork. The other possible rehu is no. 52555 at the Auckland Institute & Museum.[220] It is 34.5 cm long and carved all over. Again there are three fingerholes and a lateral hole for blowing, but the end plug which would enable the instrument to be played is missing. The only specimen found which is identified by a museum as a rehu (ME 414 in the Museum of New Zealand) is, however, end-blown. So blown, it produces a standard type 1 kooauau scale of STT (ascending). But it differs from a normal kooauau by absence of provision for suspension, lack of blowing variability, greater than usual length and the non-indigenous material from which it is made. It is 22.2 cm long and appears to be made from bamboo.

Whio

This instrument is unlikely ever to have been common. It appears to have been a compound of puutoorino and kooauau. White describes the instrument as made from two split pieces of mataii wood, hollowed out and lashed together with kiekie roots in the same manner as the puutoorino and puukaaea.[221] According to White it had three fingerholes on the upper side and a thumbhole on the lower. No instruments matching this description are known in museums but it is confirmed by Dieffenbach who equates it with the porutu.[222] This may also have been an instrument seen in 1772 by du Clesmeur who says:

> They also have a species of flute, made in two pieces, bound well together, into which they blow at the thick end. The smaller end and three little holes are closed with the fingers, and serve to vary the tones a little.[223]

An instrument of this description is illustrated but unattributed by White.[224]

Bauke gives a long description of the making of a similar flute which he once owned.[225] From the description it was evidently a whio, although Bauke calls it a puu. Like White's instrument, it was made of split mataii and had three fingerholes, but there is no mention of a thumbhole. It was 25 inches [63 cm] long with a bore of 7/8 inch [2 cm]. There is no reason to doubt Bauke's report of the instrument. But his description of the playing method is bizarre. According to him:

> To play this flute the musician sat upon his hams, clasped the flute between his knees, then drew up one foot until it touched the bottom of the open end of the

flute, and blew . . . across the open end — using the foot to open and close the bore.[226]

According to White,[227] the term whio was applied also to flutes (kooauau) made from human bone. Williams defines it as a 'whistle'.

The common feature of porutu, rehu and whio is that all seem to have been much longer than the kooauau, nguru or puutoorino. Were it not for du Clesmeur's solitary report of an instrument resembling a whio, this would suggest that all were late attempts at indigenising the European flute or fife which would have become familiar to the Maori from its use in military bands.[228]

CHAPTER 6

PERFORMANCE

PERFORMANCE TERMINOLOGY

Consistent with the importance attached to performance in Maori music, there was an extensive terminology; at least a hundred such terms have been identified by the writer. A large number are associated with leadership; many more relate to haka: examples of these are given later in this chapter and in Chapter 2 respectively. Additionally, a considerable number of terms refer to mistakes and singing faults. These faults are mostly concerned with breaches of a principle designated by Arapeta Awatere as whakaeke or sing-ing unison.[1] Faults named by Awatere are melodic, rhythmic or textual in nature. 'Rangi rua' (lit. two melodies) or parallelism was first heard by the writer at one of his first recording sessions, in 1958. One of the singers, a man, began singing at the interval of a 5th below the rest and was doubled at the octave by some of the women. This, the writer was told, was an example of bad singing, strongly disapproved of by the upholders of tradition and regarded by them as a sign of disaster.[2] 'Taupatupatu' is a fault in rhythm. It means literally 'up and down' or out of beat. Textual faults to which names have been give are 'hauaa whakahua' (faulty pronunciation), 'hauaa kama' (faulty articulation) and 'kuunanunanu' (uncertainty as to words). Conversely there are terms to indicate unison in singing such as 'wana' (perfect accord in singing, all together), 'reka' (pleasant to the ear, sweet) and 'ihi' (inspira-tion).[3]

Spirit voice

In his book *Maori Music*, Andersen comments on a performance phenom-enon known as the irirangi,[4] glossed in Williams as a 'spirit voice' and re-garded as a bad omen.[5] Arapeta Awatere said it was sometimes heard in a meeting house when a lot of people were singing. It was regarded in Maoridom as a sign of death. It was a voice 'away above the others' singing the tune but not the words.[6] Asked later if the phrase 'above the others' referred to the pitch or the physical location of the sound, he said the latter. It sounds as though it is 'up in the roof'.[7] Kino Hughes confirmed that the irirangi is still considered by Tuuhoe people to be an omen of death. He characterised it as 'an echo' in the roof of the meeting house or on the ridge pole.[8] Ngata and Te Hurinui call it 'a false note . . . an eerie or high pitched off key note' sung by a person under stress and about to panic and taken as an omen of lack of success for a war party.[9]

Andersen is at odds with some of the foregoing. According to him, the irirangi was not invariably thought of as an evil omen, as he was told by Te Rangi Hiroa that the effect was often deliberately sought by singers. Andersen claims to have heard it at Whareponga (in 1923); he explains it as a harmonic which appeared an octave and a 5th (or 12th) above the fundamental and which could occasionally be heard when the performers were singing an 'ng' sound. This would be consistent with Maori attitudes towards rangi rua (see above) which also takes the form of parallelism and is likewise regarded as a bad omen. Andersen's observation may be capable of explanation in terms of acoustic formant theory and, if so, the irirangi might show up if a recording could be made on a spectrum analyser.

BREATHING

In Chapter 2 it has already been mentioned that karakia or incantations had to be recited without break and the slightest slip was believed to have dire consequences such as death or disaster to the reciter. This belief extended to breaks even as small as those required to take breath. Because of this, shorter karakia were performed in one breath and longer ones were performed by two or more priests taking turns.[10] The process by which singers took over from each other as breath ran out was called kapo (lit. 'catch' or 'snatch').[11]

Training in breath control was practised in different breath-holding games called tatau manawa, tatau kaho and rukuruku manawa, played by children (see Chapter 4). Additionally, the term puu manawa is given by Best as a synonym for tatau manawa;[12] however, according to Arapeta Awatere, this refers not to a game but to a technique of breath control applied to karakia during recitation by two persons. Pupils were taught the precise word upon which one reciter had to take over from the other in order to maintain continuity of sound. If the takeover point was made somewhere else, this was a tohu aituaa, a 'bad omen': 'These are the things they guard against; there must be no flaw.' Other terms, again relating to karakia, are kawa rukuruku and taki manawa rere. The former applies to a solo reciter and refers to reciting a complete verse without pause on a single breath. The latter term means 'short-cutting'; it is used if a karakia is recited once only without observing repeats.[13]

Although care to avoid breaks for breathing probably originated with karakia, it is also characteristic of other forms of singing such as waiata, and similar sanctions apply. When the writer began his field work in 1958, mis-

takes in waiata singing were regarded with outright dismay by many singers, especially if there was a complete breakdown. This was taken to be a
whati or whaki (lit. 'broken'), again an omen of bad luck or, as in karakia,
even death.

In the next section, it will be seen that performance continuity in waiata
singing is achieved by the use of end-of-line leader solos, known as hiianga,
during which the other singers in the group can take breath. Because the
very structure of waiata favours continuous group performance, a person
forced to sing without the support of a group is faced with an insuperable
problem. As there are no breathing points built into the song, a soloist will
sing for as long as possible on one breath. The singer then snatches a quick
breath and carries on until forced by a shortage of wind to breathe again.
Since, ideally, such pauses for breath should not occur at all, they can appear anywhere in the song, even in the middle of a word. Persons learning
songs from tape recordings of individual singers need to be aware that these
breaks are not part of the song and will be absent if the song is performed by
a group. When two people are singing together, the difficulty is overcome
either by one acting as the leader and performing the leader solos or — for
the few songs, such as NM 46 'Ka eke ki Wairaka', which are conventionally
performed without leader solos — by taking care not to breathe at the same
time.

LEADERS

The prominent role played by the leader in responsorial songs such as haka,
digging songs, hauling songs and paddling songs has already been commented upon in the sections on haka and work songs in Chapter 2. For the
more restrained types of song such as waiata, leaders, though present, are
not as conspicuous and few writers appear to have noticed them.
Bellingshausen, who was at Queen Charlotte Sound in 1820, refers to songs
which may have been pao. They consisted of 'short couplets' and were led
by a precentor[14]. Thiercelin writes of similar songs performed by women on
shipboard.[15] And Thomson comments upon laments (waiata tangi): 'One or
two good voices commence, but all join in the chant.'[16]

Some insights into the role of the leader can be gained from the etymol-
ogy of terms used for leaders. Thus, according to Kino Hughes, a Tuuhoe
term used for taking the lead in a waiata is heri: 'Te heri o te waiata'. A
person might be asked: 'Ka heri taatau i te waiata' or 'Heria he waiata ma
taatau' (lead a song for us).[17] It can be assumed that the leader in this case is
seen figuratively to 'carry' the song (from heri 'to carry'). Similarly, Arapeta
Awatere gave kaihaapai (from haapai 'to lift up', 'to begin a song' or, again,
'to carry') as a term used throughout New Zealand for a waiata leader.[18] The
same term, glossed 'song raiser or leader', was given to Philips[19] by her informant George Graham (1874–1952) and is mentioned also by Andersen.[20]

Marata Te Tomo of Ngaati Tuuwharetoa called the leader simply 'te tangata tiimata i te waiata' (the man who begins the waiata).[21]

The prefix 'kai', which is used as above to form nouns denoting an agent from transitive verbs (Williams), appears also in several other terms used for leaders and in each case the significance of the term can be derived from the meaning of the word to which the prefix is attached. Examples are kaituki, kaihautuu and kaikaakaariki[22] for leaders of paddling songs, and kaiwhakahau for the leader of a hauling song. Additionally, Armstrong gives kaitaki and kaitaataki as an alternatives for kaikaakaariki and kaaea (the usual term for the leader of a hauling song), all of which are now used as terms for leaders in haka and action songs;[23] and Williams gives pooteeteke as a term both for a fugleman and a haka leader. Arapeta Awatere says that the latter term is used for a haka leader only in the Tokomaru, Aotea and Kurahaupo canoe areas. Unlike the kaaea of other tribes, who operated from behind or amongst the performers, the pooteeteke led from in front.[24] Williams defines both tuki and hautuu as 'to give the time to paddlers/for the rowers in a canoe'; another meaning of tuki is 'to attack'; whakahau means 'to command' and taki and taataki 'to lead'. The reduplicated form of taki is takitaki, which Andersen defines, along with haapai, as the 'act of starting a song'.[25] Arapeta Awatere points out, however, that Andersen's usage is correct only in the sense that one cannot lead a song without starting it. The word tukituki means 'to lead a song'; for example: 'Ko ahau te kai takitaki i te haka' (I am the leader of the haka); or 'E takitaki ana ahau i te haka' (I am leading [or reciting] the haka). As well, takitaki is used for the leader solo which begins a haka and it can also be applied to the leader solos in waiata.[26]

Like kaikaakaariki, the word kaakaariki, without the kai prefix, is defined by Williams as 'to act as a fugleman in a canoe' but it is also the word for a native parrot. According to Arapeta Awatere, the parrots had a leader which the rest followed, hence the application of the word to song leaders.[27] It may be significant that the word taki is applied in the same way in the phrase manu taki 'a bird acting as a sentry or leader of the flock'. The term kaaea also has an avian counterpart. Williams gives it for the leader of a flight of parrots (kaakaa) and this would seem derivation enough. Arapeta Awatere, however, was given an alternative explanation by Ngaati Porou elders; they told him that kaaea is an abbreviation for the kaaeaea or sparrow hawk. This bird is a small hawk which catches its prey towards evening and its call (eeee, eeee), which it makes during the day, is similar to the sound which a fugleman or a haka leader makes to urge on the paddlers or dancers.[28]

On the above evidence, the leader, then, is the person who gives the time, attacks, begins, carries or commands the song. The multiplicity of leadership terms appears, in part, to be a product of tribal variation.[29]

The most obvious reason for having a leader is that most Maori songs are performed by groups rather than individuals and, when there are a number of singers, a leader is needed to keep the group together. The leader sets the tempo for recited items and both pitch and pace for sung types of song. In waiata singing, an equally essential task is to ensure performance continuity by means of the hiianga or leader solo. This provides a bridge between successive lines of the text, allowing members of the group time to breathe without risk of breaking the song, as well as an opportunity to think ahead to the next line.

Usually a song leader will perform half a line or so of a song solo before being joined by the rest of the group and, having begun the song, is expected, as a rule, to hold the lead throughout. The writer's first indication of this was in 1964 at a Ringatu meeting held at Te Rere Pa near Opotiki. When the writer began a well-known waiata by Te Kooti to illustrate the use of a song transcription, everyone immediately joined in and, to the writer's horror, stopped singing at all the leader breaks to allow the writer to perform them by himself. Fortunately the writer was able to complete the song, but if he had been unable to do so, a whati (break) would be deemed to have occurred and ill luck would be expected to follow. The act of beginning the song, in this case, was a signal to those present that the writer considered he knew the song and was competent to lead it.

Notwithstanding the above, there were a number of occasions upon which transfer of leadership was observed to take place at recording sessions[30] and at least one informant noticed the same: Bob Mahuta of Waikato said that at the King Movement's Turangawaewae marae women often took over the lead from a male singer and many of the men had come to rely on this. Several told him that it was necessary to know only the first two or three lines of a song because the women will then take over.[31] It is possible that this practice is also followed elsewhere when the singers are accustomed to performing together. The host people (tangata whenua) at a marae generally have a repertoire of songs which can be performed after speeches from their own spokesmen, and they may also have a number of nominated leaders each of whom customarily leads particular songs. According to Arapeta Awatere these leaders must be at hand at all times to lead songs and in consideration of this take no part in duties such as lighting fires or cooking.[32] Unless their numbers are large, visiting groups necessarily have less choice of songs to sing and persons to lead them than the tangata whenua, but they have an opportunity to decide which waiata they will perform and who will lead before entering the marae. In each case, a speaker either leads the song himself or, if he is unable to do so, someone else may be asked to lead the song on his behalf. At a tangi (funeral ceremony), according to Arapeta Awatere, when a song is to be performed which is appropriate to a particular deceased person, generally it is the closest relative or next of kin who is nominated to lead the song.[33]

Qualities of leaders

The main quality sought in a song leader, according to Kino Hughes, is that the leader's voice must be heard amongst the others, i.e. it must stand out.[34] Arapeta Awatere likewise assigned first priority to power and clarity of diction, followed by sense of pitch, memory for words and sense of rhythm.[35] At a later interview, in a discussion of criteria applied to haka leaders at cultural competitions, he similarly stressed clear enunciation and ability to keep the tempo and rhythm; also the leader must position himself where he can be heard by his team. A good position for the leader, according to Awatere, is in the middle of the group at the back.[36] But the position of the leader is of equal importance during the performance of traditional songs. It is noticeable on the marae that women and other supporters will group in behind a song leader before beginning to sing, often having to traverse some distance to do so. Nobody attempts to sing at a position from which they will be unable to hear the leader. Again the present writer is able to illustrate from personal experience: The very first song learned by the writer was NM 46 'Ka eke ki Wairaka'. It was recorded as McL 1 from Arapeta Awatere as a test of the writer's ability to transcribe a song into music notation. A fortnight later, Awatere had the writer perform the song with him at a meeting, with gratifying results. Later, however, at another meeting when Awatere was not present, another singer decided on the spur of the moment to repeat this success. He began the song from the other side of the meeting house from the writer's position, having asked the writer to sing with him. Unfortunately this singer didn't know the song well, mumbling the parts with which he was unfamiliar so that at these points the writer was unable to hear him and lost track of the song. The other singer was able to keep going, but the writer broke down. This embarrassment might have been avoided by the simple expedient of standing next to the leader.

All of the above attributes of leadership are consistent with an overriding primacy accorded by Awatere and others to song texts and the leader's role in assuring that the message of the song will be clearly heard.

PITCHING OF SONGS

One of the responsibilities of song leaders is to choose a pitch best suited to the majority of singers. Pei Te Hurinui of Ngaati Maniapoto tribe said a song must be pitched low if women are to join in but otherwise can be set high.[37] The most likely reason for this recommendation is that although Maori women tend to sing an octave higher than the men in group songs, older women, in particular, seem able to sing comfortably within the male tenor register. Singing at the octave is likely to force such women beyond the limits of their range if the song is pitched too high by a male leader. The word for low pitch, according to Arapeta Awatere, is 'paapaku' and for high pitch 'teitei' or (amongst West Coast tribes) 'ikeike'. Thus: 'he paapaku te rangi' (the tune or pitch is low); 'he teitei te rangi' (the pitch is high); and 'he tino teitei te rangi' (the pitch is very high).[38] Other terms which may be used are 'raro' and 'runga' for low and high respectively. Thus: 'hikitia te rangi ki runga' (lift up the tune higher) and 'whakahokia te rangi ki raro' (bring the pitch of the tune down).[39]

In both group and solo singing there may be drift in the pitch of the intoning note. Generally this takes the form of flatting. Often there is a gradual drift downwards of up to a semitone during the course of a song. Exceptionally the drift may be greater, and very occasionally there will be a rise of pitch instead of a fall. Drift upwards or downwards in pitch is involuntary; accordingly there is neither a Maori word for it nor is it part of the style,[40] though one singer who recorded for the writer was aware of it and would allow for it by starting his songs high.[41]

The writer did not uncover any evidence that different registers were recognised in Maori singing and this, indeed, would seem unlikely as traditional song types are performed entirely in unison or at the octave. Herries Beattie, whose field work was conducted in 1920, was told by his principal South Island informant that in the days before white people came, four kinds of voice were recognised, two men's and two women's. The highest was called reotakiri and the next reomaru, but he could not remember the other two.[42] It would seem likely that these were not pre-European song terms as stated but names for parts in hymn singing.

RIDING IN

This is the writer's own term for a device commonly used by a singer who has temporarily dropped out of a group song and wishes to rejoin the singing. It is also used by solo singers in songs normally sung by groups when taking up the song again after an enforced break for breath. When performing a waiata with a group, such a singer will often 'ride in' to the note the rest are singing by beginning a 3rd or 4th above the target note and filling in to the unison. In recited forms such as paatere, riding in takes place, as a rule, from below. Arapeta Awatere speculated that this happens in paatere most likely because the singer has performed a terminal glissando on ceasing to sing and begins again at the finishing pitch.[43] In neither case are the riding-in notes regarded as part of the song. Although singers are often aware of the device, there is no Maori term for it.[44] Kino Hughes was of the opinion that riding in should not be done and singers should come in on the note.[45] Arapeta Awatere inclined to the same view, attributing the use of the device in paatere to shortness of breath on the part of old singers. Middle-aged singers in good health would, he thought, 'get right on the note'.[46]

AMBIGUITY OF SONG BEGINNINGS

Very often, singers require a phrase or two to establish the melody. In both solo and group performances, the beginning of a song may seem rhythmically vague and uncertain in comparison with the remainder. Not infrequently the beginning differs from the basic melody, as later established, melodically as well as rhythmically. In such a case the beginning tends to be narrower in range. The tendency is common enough for it to be considered part of the style. Again, however, it appears to be involuntary on the part of singers or leaders and, so far as the writer is aware, is not recognised by them.[47]

GESTURE, POSTURE AND STANCE

Dance styles as such, with their performance characteristics and associated terminology, have been considered in Chapters 2 and 3. Reference is also made in these chapters to gestures accompanying song types not normally designated as dance, such as paatere. Haka and associated song types such as pookeka and maemae are the pre-eminent recited dance styles, and the only dance form with sung accompaniment is the poi. By and large, action is most frequently associated with recited forms of song. In the performance of sung styles such as waiata, gesture — if it occurs — is generally restrained and appears mostly to be an involuntary response to the music. An exception to the general rule was the deliberate use of head movement by one singer as an aid to obtaining volume (see Chapter 10). The same singer was of the opinion that performers sing better standing than seated because body movement helps them to sing correctly.[48] The general preference in singing is undoubtedly to stand rather than sit, but probably because this reflects standard behaviour on the marae. As noted in the section on waiata in Chapter 3, although a speaker will customarily pace up and down between remarks, he will stand still as soon as he begins to sing and is then joined by his supporters who will group in behind him.

MALE/FEMALE SPECIALISATION

In April 1991, a dispute erupted in Maoridom about a haka performed at a World Cup rugby match in Cardiff by a team of women. A former All Black said the haka breached Maori cultural protocol, and the chairwoman of the Auckland District Maori Council also criticised it as 'not proper', saying the women were entitled to play rugby like men if they wished, 'but they shouldn't be allowed to do the haka'. The women footballers' use of haka was defended by the then Maori Language Commissioner, Sir Kingi Ihaka, who pointed out that Ngaati Porou women of the East Coast had performed the haka for many years, as had women from other tribes.[49] Ihaka's rebuttal was, as it happened, flawed because haka of this type are haka poowhiri or welcome haka, far removed from the aggressive types of haka appropriate for a football match. On the other hand, his opponents in the argument may not have been aware that women traditionally took part even in the war dance, often as leaders (see Chapter 2) . The controversy is, nevertheless, an excellent illustration of polarities between the sexes in Maoridom which may have had their origins in simple division of labour but have become strongly imbued with cultural overlays of what is or is not 'proper'.

Firth makes the point that division of labour in Maori society was 'firmly rooted in custom' but 'not altogether arbitrary and incomprehensible'. In general, he says, 'men attended to the more energetic, arduous and exciting occupations, while the women engaged in the more sober and somewhat more monotonous tasks'.[50] This, however, provides only a partial explanation. Strong elements of tapu entered into many male activities such as carving, house-building, the manufacture of canoes, the working of greenstone and tattooing.[51] The manufacture of musical instruments was also exclusive to men[52] and the most likely explanation is that this too was a tapu activity. The performance of economic magic, in particular, was reserved to men. Thus, although women had their own karakia for occupations such as weaving, the most potent spells were recited by male experts.[53] Today, as in the past, karakia are performed predominantly by men.

On the marae, which remains so central to the Maori way of life, there is a strict spatial delimitation of tama taane and tama wahine (lit. son and daughter) or male and female sides, both on the marae aatea (ceremonial courtyard) and in the meeting house. This division also demarcates the sacred (tapu) from the common (noa). The whare whakairo (carved meeting house) represents the body of a male ancestor lying face down with the ridge pole representing his spine and the rafters his ribs. In most tribal areas, the left-hand side of the meeting house facing outwards, where the window is located, is male and tapu, while the right-hand side with its entrance-way is female and noa.[54] Local people occupy the right-hand side of the meeting house; visitors, who have tapu upon them, occupy the left. If a body, itself tapu, is brought into a meeting house, the coffin is also placed on the tapu left-hand side.

The male/female dichotomy, and its associations with tapu and noa, permeates marae proceedings. In the rituals of encounter described in Chapter 1, the waerea (protective incantation) of the visitors and the wero (challenge) of the host people are the prerogative of males, performed outside the gateway and at the gateway respectively. Women alone of both sides exchange karanga, the host women doing so either from the porch of the meeting house or from the tama wahine side of the marae. Women take a prominent part in the hosts' poowhiri (welcome chant), stationing themselves in front of the meeting house, and women alone wail. But, in all but a few tribal areas, men have the sole right to engage in whaikoorero (formal speeches); in consequence, only men perform tauparapara (recitations preceding a speech). Finally, men and women together perform the waiata at the end of each speech.

As indicated earlier, women sometimes took part in war dances, especially old women who behaved like men when they acted as leaders. Women even on occasion fought alongside men when, for example, the inner defences of a paa were under threat.[55] Warfare was nevertheless a characteristically male activity as indicated by the proverb: 'He puta taua ki te taane, he whaanau tama ki te wahine' (Battle for men and childbirth for women).[56] Accordingly, the peruperu and other war dances, as well as all but welcome haka, are today performed exclusively by men, as are whakaaraara paa (watch songs) and other song types associated with war.

Again, notwithstanding Best's claim that young males sometimes took part in the poi dance,[57] within living memory the poi has been exclusively the province of women, complementary as such to the male haka. This reciprocity is plainly one of the principles governing performances by modern concert parties. Arapeta Awatere extended the connotation of marae spatial organisation to distinguish tama taane and tama wahine styles of singing, the one urgent, driving, powerful and masculine (and evidently associated with aggression and war), the other feminine and graceful.[58] When asked why the poi is restricted to women he replied immediately: 'A poi won't kill an enemy!'[59]

CHAPTER 7

COMPOSITION

In his book *The Anthropology of Music*, Alan P. Merriam distinguishes three sources for the creation of music: the supernatural or superhuman, borrowing, and individual composition.[1] All three are recognised by the Maori, but pride of place is reserved for individual composition.

SUPERNATURAL COMPOSITION

The patupaiarehe or tuurehu (fairies) were fair or white-skinned beings, malign or beneficent, thought to frequent misty forests and hilltops. A few songs are attributed to them but not in a general way. In such cases, the name of the patupaiarehe composer forms part of the oral record just as it would if he or she were human. The patupaiarehe seem to have been regarded, in this respect, simply as another, though non-human, tribe. A well-

Mount Pirongia, one of the locations said to be frequented by fairy folk

documented patupaiarehe song is Song 25 in McLean & Orbell, by the fairy chief Te Rangipouri who fell in love with a human woman named Tawhaitu. Another is *Nga Moteatea* Song 37 by Parearohi, the daughter of Te Rangipouri, who took a human husband.

A handful of songs are attributed to dream composition. Amohia Te Rei Tuhua of Hamilton recorded a waiata (McL 209) composed by another singer in a dream; Marjorie Rau of New Plymouth recorded a pao (McL 1123) learnt in a dream from a deceased singer who had appeared to her; the singer of McL 214, another pao, said it was composed by her mother in a dream; Moa Pokiha of Whanganui recorded several pao with 'spiritual' meanings which he said were composed about 40 years previously by a woman who obtained them in a dream, and McL 861, a waiata, was composed by Arapeta Awatere's great-grandfather, Hemi Ratapu, in a dream.[2] The famous composer of action songs, Tuini Ngawai, is also said to have received songs in dreams.[3] Dream composition, nevertheless, appears to have been relatively uncommon and, along with other forms of supernatural composition, is insignificant in New Zealand compared with individual composition.

BORROWING

The process of borrowing is explicitly recognised by the use of the term kaupapa to distinguish the original of a song from a parody or later adaptation.[4] Elsdon Best claims that early this century songs such as laments were 'mostly composed of fragments culled from earlier ones'. He himself witnessed the composition of such a song by a man and his wife. 'The task of composing a short song occupied them about three quarters of an hour, but an examination of it showed that it was largely the result of plagiarism.'[5] And Sir George Grey, writing of much earlier practice, likewise believed: 'It is the custom of the natives to compose their poetry rather by combining materials drawn from ancient poems than by inventing original matter'.[6] Such views are at the same time an overstatement and an oversimplification. There is no doubt, however, that both small-scale and large-scale borrowings were commonplace.

On the one hand, Maori song texts are partly composed of formulas and formulaic expressions.[7] As in many English folk songs, such formulas are especially common in the opening lines of waiata. Additionally, both intertribally and within single tribal areas, composers often borrowed and adapted even quite long passages from existing songs: 'Thus the words of a waiata tangi [lament] may be changed so that it laments the death of another person, who is now addressed in it, and other passages, especially those containing place names and personal names, may be altered accordingly.'[8] Whole songs were also reworked to suit new circumstances. Song 13 in McLean & Orbell is known to have passed through a series of such transformations, and is itself based on passages from earlier songs.

It is probably no longer appropriate to regard such reworkings as 'plagiarism', given the now negative or even pejorative connotations of this term. Arapeta Awatere observed that although ownership of songs by tribe was acknowledged, there was nothing to stop people from other tribes learning the songs and making them their own by adapting or reworking them. 'After a while they will really believe the song is theirs'.[9] Such adaptation, thought Awatere, definitely made the song that of the borrower and was accepted as a legitimate form of composition by the adaptors if not by the donors. Thus an adapted song was in no sense 'wrong' and, as reworking was an accepted form of composition, it was incorrect to call it 'plagiarism'.[10] In effect, he agreed, reworking was a means of composition. In Awatere's view, old songs were reworked for two reasons: because the melody and symbolism of the words were liked, and to make the song appropriate in a new context.[11] Whatever the case, it is certain that adapted songs could be speedily absorbed into the repertoire of the borrowing tribe and soon became indistinguishable from other songs. Sometimes an adaptation would replace the original version; or, more usually, the original would continue in one area and the adaptation would be the 'received' version in another, complete with a song history appropriate to its new circumstances. However, not all adaptations would catch on and there must have been many such songs which disappeared after their first performance. Evidence of this can be found in the numerous Maori newspapers of the late nineteenth and early twentieth centuries which are full of modified song texts of this kind, some of which have continued to be sung in their original form.

The above refers to song texts but applies equally to tunes. When a song transfers to another tribal area, whether or not in textually modified form, the original tune may or may not survive the transition. Additionally, a tune may be borrowed and have completely different words composed for it even within a tribal area. The result can be, on the one hand, tune variants of songs which are textually the same or nearly the same and, on the other, textual variants of songs with similar or identical tunes. An example of the first process is Song 15 in McLean & Orbell which is given with two tunes, one as sung by Ngaati Tuuwharetoa tribe and the other by Ngaai Te Rangi. Another is the popular and widespread song 'E paa too hau'[12] which has at least three different tunes in different parts of the country. Examples of songs with the same tune but different texts are Songs 5 and 23 in McLean & Orbell. Perhaps even more than the modification of a borrowed text, the borrowing of tunes to serve as a vehicle for new words must be regarded as a compositional device.

INDIVIDUAL COMPOSITION

The detailed references to authorship in song after song of published collections such as Ngata and Te Hurinui's *Nga Moteatea* provides seemingly irrefutable evidence that composition by individuals was the norm for most Maori songs. Borrowing is an overlapping category as the individual responsible for a reworked song would claim authorship. Nevertheless, most songs must have been original compositions if the song histories provided for them are correct.

Two means of individual composition can be distinguished: the first is spontaneous composition or improvisation; the other is the making of a song to which prior thought has been given. Of the song types discussed in Section 1, only karanga, pao and paddling songs appear to have been conventionally or typically extemporised. As has been shown, the use of standard textual phrases in karanga and the structure and manner of performance of these song types assisted improvisation. The texts of other song types mostly display such maturity of thought and complexity of construction that improvisation can be ruled out. The conclusion seems inescapable that most songs were carefully crafted compositions. Evidence of the degree of importance attached to composition is provided in a mid nineteenth-century passage in Maori which may have been the work of Governor Grey's Te Arawa informant, Te Rangikaheke. The statement, translated by S.M. Mead, is a note about the composition of a paatere by a woman composer. To avoid distraction she placed herself under tapu or ceremonial restriction, avoiding food and the company of kinfolk until the task was complete:

> In order to be able to think she retired to a house by herself and remained there until the tune [rangi] of the composition had been worked out. No food was eaten during the act of composition. When the chant was completed she came out of voluntary isolation, washed her hands and then touched a fern root or potato. The offering was cooked and then thrown to the gods. After this brief ritual the composer was *noa*, that is, free of restriction, and free to resume her daily activities.[13]

The task of producing a satisfactory song was evidently taken very seriously, so much so that composers appear often to have recruited others to help. This may, indeed, have been usual.

GROUP COMPOSITION

According to Arapeta Awatere, it is erroneous to think that each song in *Nga Moteatea* was the work of one person. Ngata told Awatere that the longer esoteric songs, especially, were group efforts and that lesser tohunga experts helped the Ngaati Porou composer Rangiuia with some of his songs; another example was the famous oriori 'Pine pine te kura'[14] which is too complex to have been the product of one brain and is reputed to have taken 25 years to compose. Most songs, according to Awatere, were composed as a 'group effort', even though a particular person was credited with the song. The same, he pointed out, is still happening with the composition of action songs. Tuini Ngaawai, for example, was helped in some of her songs by her brother Hori, by Awatere himself, and by Ngoingoi Pewhairangi, her niece.[15] Written sources provide further evidence. Johannes Andersen was told by Maori informants that songs were a product of collaboration: 'the final form being ascribed to one person though it was the work of several'.[16] In Part 4 of *Nga Moteatea*, Ngata gives detailed information:

> A composition was generally the work of a group, but centred round the person whose passion, resentment or grief was its inspiration. This might be expected of a people which had a strong sense of cooperation. The group helped to select the appropriate words or recall references from the tribal traditions which should be woven into the stanzas. It assisted further with the air to which the lines as they were formed were sung. The members of the group would memorise words and air and take these to their respective places of abode and by constant repetition test them for modification and improvement. In the end the composition, as a communal effort, was recorded in the memories of a wide circle of men and women, and of the youth of the community — words, air, enunciation, action and all. Thus it has been transmitted down generations of an unlettered people, sometimes added to or adapted to suit outstanding incidents in the tribal history.[17]

Some songs, notably karakia, tauparapara and whakaaraara paa, stand apart from other compositions as seemingly authorless. As most such songs are old, it could be that the composers have simply been forgotten. The composers of karakia, however, according to Arapeta Awatere, were the priests of the traditional schools of learning or whare waananga (see later).[18] The esoteric songs they composed were by their nature secret and on this account may have been kept anonymous by design. Another possibility, judging from the length and complexity of the texts, is that the priestly composers of karakia, like their secular counterparts, may have composed collectively. But unlike the latter they would have had no occasion with which to link the song and no reason, in consequence, to attribute it to an individual. Whatever the case, no attempt appears to have been made by the composers to attribute authorship to supernatural agencies. Rather, the useful impression was conveyed that all karakia are of equally ancient vintage, allied with those thought to have been brought to New Zealand by the occupants of the ancestral canoes.

Assigning successive lines of the song to different members of the group would have relieved the burden of memorisation which would otherwise stand in the way of composing a long song. Arapeta Awatere was well aware of the merits of this method, referring to it as the composer's 'Grundig'— an allusion to the writer's Grundig tape recorder used during his Bay of Plenty field work in 1958 when he was a guest of Awatere.[19]

It is not known how many of the songs recorded by the present writer were a product of group composition though attributed to individuals. It can be assumed that about the same proportion fall into this category as songs in published collections. A number of Taranaki songs, however, were explicitly stated to have been composed by two or more persons, bearing out a statement by one Taranaki informant that group composition was common when Te Whiti was alive.[20]

CHAPTER 8

OWNERSHIP

Alan P. Merriam points out that once music is produced 'it becomes property of one sort or another — property of an individual, of a particular group, or perhaps of the society at large'.[1] It has already been noted that in the Maori case ownership of songs by tribes was acknowledged and group composition was common. The latter practice can reasonably be supposed always to have conferred ownership by the tribe. But even when group composition was not involved, ownership would ultimately devolve to the tribe if the song became popular enough to enter the group repertoire. Arapeta Awatere was definite that once composed, a song became part of the oral literature of the community and at this point no longer belonged to the composer but to the group.[2] Tribal ownership of the song is established by references to places and people in the song text, and adaptation of a borrowed song is accomplished by inserting local references to replace the original ones. Additionally, in all tribes, importance is attached to knowing the name of the composer of a song and the circumstances of composition. It is by this means, along with the internal evidence of the text, that the ownership of a song, and hence an individual's right to sing it, is established. At recording sessions, singers were conscientious about providing this information if it was known to them, although disputes were common and agreement was not always reached. In 1958 recording sessions, discussions of the history of each song could occupy up to three quarters of an hour before it was sung.

Some songs, such as the well-known 'E paa too hau',[3] have universal currency. Others are of unknown or uncertain origin, and these are less likely to be subject to ownership restraints. For most songs, however, a strict protocol applies.

An important, highly practical and obvious reason for preoccupation with ownership of songs has been with their use to help prove ownership of tribal land. In 1865, the Native Lands Act established the Native Land Court to adjudicate rival claims to land, using evidence from tribal tradition as proof of title.[4] Land Court records contain the texts of many songs cited in support of claims. The method was used successfully as recently as 1957 when the waiata 'Taku tuuranga ake ki runga ra' was sung in court during a hearing in which the Maori of the far north claimed ownership of the famous Ninety Mile Beach. Mutu Kapa, who recorded the song as McL 450 in 1963, says this lament was composed by Tohe for his daughter when he arrived in Ahipara and looked back at the way he had come; the singing of this song in court was the reason the government lost its claim for the toheroa shellfish on the beach.

But the importance attached to ownership of songs runs deeper than land claims. It is very much a product of agreed performance practice. In earlier chapters it has been noted that the usual venue for waiata singing is as an adjunct of speech-making at tribal and intertribal meetings (hui). The song customarily performed at the end of a speech is normally one belonging to the speaker's own tribal group. But there are exceptions. On occasion a song belonging to the host group may be performed instead as a compliment to the hosts. The principle to be observed is that the song chosen must be appropriate to the particular event. A Whanganui singer, Rawinia Murray of Parikino, explained that she was careful always to study what was said by speakers at a tangi to ensure that the waiata sung would have a connection. It was important to know chants suitable for different areas so that one could 'sing back something that will belong to them'.[5] Rangi Pokiha, also of Whanganui tribe, explained that one's own songs could be sung anywhere, but other people's songs could be sung only on their own marae. Thus a Whanganui person, for example, could perform a Tuuwharetoa song in Tuuwharetoa territory but not in Waikato.[6] In either event, because the singing of waiata is a public act, singers like to be sure of their right to perform a song whether doing so on the marae or at a recording session. Force of public opinion in this matter is very strong and there is widespread fear of repercussions should a singer overstep the mark by singing a song to which he or she is not entitled.

A reason advanced by Lucy Jacob, a Ngaati Raukawa singer, for not singing other people's songs was anxiety over being criticised for mistakes.[7] But other singers, in their turn, deferred to her. Erenora's famous paatere 'Poia atu taku poi' (M&O 4) was known to numerous singers besides Lucy Jacob, but most did not record it, recognising that the prerogative was hers as she had it in direct line from the composer who was her grandmother. However, this was probably a special case.[8] Ownership rights are still observed even when a singer knows the song well and this appears to be usual in all tribal areas. In the Bay of Plenty area, for example, one singer of Ngaai Te Rangi recorded two songs from his own area but refrained from singing a good Ngaati Pikiao waiata known to him 'because it might be stepping on their toes'. Ngaati Pikiao, in turn, were as scrupulous concerning songs from outside their area as were a Ngaati Whakaue group recorded in 1964 at Ohinemutu who took great pains at the recording session not to sing other people's songs. Kurauia Tahuriorangi, a notable singer of Ngaati Pikiao who recorded numerous songs from her own tribe, knew many Tuuhoe songs as well but did not offer to record them. She thought other singers had been wrong to record songs which did not belong to them and did not wish to be criticised herself for the same thing. In her case, the proscription extended right down to the local area so that she felt unentitled to record songs even from the adjacent Te Arawa area of Tuuhourangi. She also knew songs belonging to a local group within her own tribe which for the same reason she chose to leave to them. Other Bay of Plenty tribes were similarly circumspect. A Tuuhoe group recorded in 1964 at Ruatahuna, for example, sang only the songs belonging to their own area of Ruatahuna, demurring at singing songs from elsewhere within Tuuhoe. Further afield, in Taranaki, Mohi Ririkore of New Plymouth was very particular to give out only songs for which he had a right so that he would 'not get blamed'. Hamu Kaatene from the same area was likewise unwilling to sing songs belonging to other people, as was Pare Raumati of Otorohanga, because of what people belonging to these tribes would say. Additionally, singers when recording would sometimes omit part of a song out of regard for proprietorial rights elsewhere. Thus Tame Naera of Ngaati Whakaue who recorded *Nga Moteatea* Song 61 in 1958 left out the first section as appropriate only for the Tuuwharetoa descendants of Te Heuheu.

Supernatural sanctions also sometimes apply. A well-known Waikato elder's breakdown during the singing of an oriori at Turangawaewae in 1963 was attributed by another singer to his not having a right to the song: 'That thing doesn't belong to Tainui. That's why he break down!' And in 1958 in the Bay of Plenty area, the writer was told that many of the older people believed they would die if they sang their songs to anyone other than members of their own tribe. Some, indeed, took this attitude further, believing that a death, most likely their own, would be caused if a waiata was sung at any time other than a funeral ceremony. Such proscriptions go beyond ownership and enter the realm of tapu. Many singers refused to give out songs for this reason and others were recorded only with difficulty. In 1963, Henare Iti of Ngaati Maniapoto recorded just one song, a King Movement song which he regarded as his most important, after four hours of discussion and debate which included tearful speeches from his wife and daughters who thought he would die if he recorded any of his songs. A cousin of Henare Iti was later astonished to hear that he had recorded the song as he had earlier refused his own sons as well as numerous representatives of the Mormon Church. Sanctions of this kind have been a potent cause of song loss in some communities and are further discussed in Chapter 18.

Some songs, notably karakia, are not performed by groups but by individuals who in this case appear often to assume ownership to themselves. Dieffenbach comments that although:

> Most songs live in the memory of all . . . certain karakia or incantations are less generally known and a stranger obtains them with difficulty, as they are only handed down among the tohunga, or priests, from father to son.[9]

Gudgeon states specifically that such karakia were the personal property of the tohunga and his disciples and in many cases were known only to them. Because of this, they

> had a real market value in the eyes of the tribe, so long as there was no doubt as to the efficacy of his *karakia*, which same depended very much on the personal *mana* of the *tohunga*.[10]

The writer was told by Dick Wetere, a Waikato informant, that many karakia, for example to cure choking by removing a fish bone from the throat, were strictly personal and were handed down secretly within families. But karakia associated with the ancestral canoes belonged to the tribe and approval for passing these on had to be gained from the chief. In Weetere's view, it would be best if the karakia were forgotten as approval wrongly given would cause a curse to fall on the chief.[11]

As time went on, it seems probable that attitudes towards secular songs such as waiata became more and more like those applying to karakia. For the vast bulk of secular songs, traditional ownership by tribes was sustainable only for as long as songs remained in the repertoire. As the singing tradition went into decline, ownership of songs appears to have transferred in a *de facto* way from the tribes to the only individuals remaining who could sing the songs. As the status of such singers was undoubtedly enhanced by their proprietorship of the songs, there was a disincentive to pass them on to others, especially if the singer's reputation was not fully deserved. Requests from other members of the tribe for the songs might then be refused either for selfish reasons or from fear of being found out as less expert than supposed. All of this made collecting difficult and the actions of the many who recorded their songs the more admirable. Maoridom has abundant cause to thank all who did so.

CHAPTER 9

LEARNING AND INSTRUCTION

Alan P. Merriam has noted that the simplest form of learning music is imitation, which tends to be especially characteristic of early learning. In most societies, he suggests, the casual performer tends to learn in this way 'while the future specialist must always undergo some form of instruction'.[1] Both propositions hold true, with qualifications, for the Maori.

INCIDENTAL LEARNING

When the singing tradition was in full flower, it is probable that most Maori songs were learned not by means of formal instruction but simply by listening to others sing. Buck gives the usual method for learning waiata as follows:

> To keep their own memories green, the old people in the evenings or early mornings sang through their repertoire of songs while reclining in the tribal meeting-house and the older children learned them so as to join in with the community singing. Speeches were always brightened with appropriate songs or historical dirges, and the speaker often called upon his people to give volume to the song. When the chorus stood up, it was a matter of pride to the younger people to be able to join in. Thus there were both opportunity and incentive for the adolescents to improve their knowledge of classical language and acquire an extensive repertoire of figures of speech, proverbs and sayings, and chants and songs which would be appropriate for various occasions.[2]

Such learning, however, could be less casual than it seemed. According to Ngoi Pewhairangi of Ngaati Porou:

> If you are born on a marae, there are certain qualities about you that are recognised by elders. They don't actually teach you. They select you and place you in a situation where you absorb knowledge. When you're asleep on your own, they're singing waiatas or reciting genealogies in the next room. As you're lying there in the dark, you absorb everything that's going on. And before you realise what you're doing, you've learned how to recite too, or you've learned the words of a certain song. And this can go on for three or four years. But you don't realise that they're putting you into the situation to learn.

> Suddenly, later, they take you to a meeting house and they recite these genealogies or sing these waiatas and deliberately forget a line. And you find yourself singing by yourself because you've recited and learned these things by heart. And you sing this line they've left out. And after a while they say to you 'Why don't you learn other songs or other genealogies?'[3]

Arapeta Awatere, when asked the meaning of the word 'korokii', said it referred to the song of the birds in the early morning but also to songs such as paatere and oriori sung as described above. They were sung in order to teach history or tradition to young children who slept with their parents and grandparents.[4] Awatere himself learned in this way from his Ngaapuhi grandmother who would wake up at about two in the morning and sing songs and recite genealogies long before he could understand them:

> This got the air or tune into my ear. I began to develop a feel for the *waiata*. By the time I was three I was able to sing a few words. Then by the time I was five I was able to sing simple things she had taught me — onomatopoeic jingles. By the time I was five I was able to sing with her.[5]

When he was three or four years old, his grandmother taught him the following song by singing it to him over and over:

He rau tutu e pua i te ara   A tutu leaf blossoms along the way
He rau mahara e pua i te manawa e   A hundred thoughts blossom in the heart

This form of instruction was plainly very effective with an apt pupil. By the time Awatere was five years old he was chanting the names of the canoes and knew his own genealogy without volition on his part: 'It just came; no mental effort; no nothing.'[6] The present writer believes he absorbed something of waiata singing style in the same way, not only by listening to songs at meetings, but at night during his Waikato field trip in 1963 while lying semi-awake in the early hours listening to his host, Uehoka Tairakena, softly rehearsing his songs in the next room.

The above, whether intentionally or otherwise, was a means of indoctrinating children especially. Because no conscious effort was required from the learner, it was effective only in situations such as marae living where waiata were frequently sung and heard. For adults learning from choice, a method still used is simply to stand up to join the elders when they sing and in this way gradually to learn the song. Para Iwikau of Ngaati Tuuwharetoa, for example, stated that she learned pao by getting in behind the old people and copying them.[7] The writer knows of one person who persisted with this method for more than 20 years, at first attracting some ridicule because of his inability to sing but ultimately earning admiration as a competent singer of numerous waiata.

After the advent of literacy, which occurred soon after missionisation, the above methods were supplemented and, to a degree, supplanted by the use of written texts. The most recent aid has been sound-recording technology. When singers were asked in the 1960s how they had learned their songs, some said they just picked up their songs by 'listening to the old folks'. But, by a ratio of more than three to one, most stated they had learned their songs from particular individuals. It is possible that some learned incidentally rather than by intent from the persons named and failed to make a distinction when answering the question. Nevertheless it would appear that learning from individuals by this time predominated over incidental learning.

INDIVIDUAL LEARNING

Firth summarises former practice concerning the transmission of magic. Spells of lesser importance such as charms to avert bad luck were imparted without much ceremony on hunting trips and the like by an elder to a younger relative. Family spells were communicated to descendants only, and the magic associated with handicrafts was given as a part of practical instruction to anyone being taught.[8]

Traditionally, some individuals were, and still are, chosen at an early age to become receptacles of tribal knowledge, which can include songs, and in such a case are 'apprenticed' to an elder kinsman. The arrangement might be informal, or the person concerned might go through a tohi ceremony similar to that undergone by entrants to the whare waananga (see next), with appropriate incantations to assist learning and ensure success.[9] Individuals not so favoured who wish to learn songs evidently simply ask other singers for them. The songs are then either supplied or refused at the discretion of the person asked. Many singers, even those who have been through the ceremony, possess manuscript waiata books in which they have written down the texts of songs known to them or which they wish to learn. Some have inherited waiata books from earlier singers. In most cases, one supposes, a song is obtained by copying it from another singer's waiata book and rehearsing it if need be with the donor until the air is learned. Songs can also be picked up piecemeal from more than one source. Turau Te Tomo, for example, obtained the text of McL 128 from one source and the tune from another.

FORMAL INSTRUCTION

Whare waananga

Some forms of knowledge were singled out as too important for their acquisition to be either informal or left to chance, and these were traditionally the subject of special instruction in schools or 'houses' of learning. The house of learning was known as the whare kura[10] (treasure house), whare maire (in some tribes said to be an inferior school devoted to the evil arts) or whare waananga (house of knowledge). Other names for house of learning were whare takiura[11] and whare puuraakau. The name did not necessarily denote a separate building but rather different curricula.

In Eastern Polynesia, similar schools of instruction are documented for Hawaii, the Marquesas Islands, the Society Islands and Easter Island. In Hawaii, as outlined by Barrère et al., training was offered in halau schools of dancing in the latter days of the Hawaiian monarchy. The schools were conducted under strict rules of tapu including abstinence from sexual indulgence.[12] In the Marquesas Islands, music students worked under a similar strict tapu in a special house. Painting with saffron, spitting, conversation, sexual play and all unrelated activities were forbidden.[13] In the Society Islands, chant was a vehicle for instruction in 'houses of learning' devoted to subjects such as myths and history, genealogy, geography and astronomy.[14] Finally, in Easter Island, according to Métraux, knowledge of the famous Easter Island tablets was the prerogative of a class of reciters called tangata rongorongo who knew the chants and genealogies and taught them in special schools.[15]

Reports of the Maori schools of learning are similar to those of the Polynesian ones, suggesting that such schools may have been held in pre-European times, as Maori traditions of early schools would indicate. The only documented schools, however, are post-European. The standard work on them, from which most later summaries derive, is Elsdon Best's monograph *The Maori School of Learning*.[16]

The best known post-contact school of learning was held by Te Matorohanga and Nepia Pohuhu in the Wairarapa area in 1865. Its proceedings were written down by the Maori scribe Te Whatahoro,[17] and used later by S. Percy Smith as the basis for his compilation *The Lore of the Whare-Wananga*.[18] The reliability of this work has been questioned,[19] and Best based much of his account on it, throwing doubt on some of this also. Nevertheless, there is enough information about the schools of learning themselves, without joining debate on what was taught by them, for a summary of some of their salient features to be offered.

According to legend, the original house of learning, known as Rangiaatea, was situated in the uppermost Maori heaven. From it the god Taane obtained the traditional three baskets of knowledge, together with two sacred stones (whatu). As listed by Buck the baskets were:

- The *kete uruuru matua* of peace, goodness and love
- The *kete uruuru rangi* of prayers, incantations and ritual
- The *kete uruuru tau* (or *tawhito*) of war, agriculture, woodwork, stonework and earthwork.[20]

Best gives the names and contents differently as follows:

- The *kete aronui* of good containing all knowledge of benefit to humans
- The *kete tuatea* of evil including black magic and the art of war
- The *kete tuauri* of ritual or ceremonial.[21]

Te Whatahoro (1841–
1923). PHOTO: *James*
McDonald. Museum of
New Zealand Te Papa
Tongarewa neg. no. C229

The baskets appear to have formed the basis of the curriculum for later mortal houses of learning, details of curriculum and of house nomenclature and procedure differing from area to area. The schools are stated to have been held during the winter months in houses set aside for the purpose or, in a few cases, specially built and maintained. Only young men of high rank and tested powers of memory who had gone through the tohi ritual were admitted.[22] Other preliminary ceremonies were also performed.[23] Instruction took place only during the morning hours while the sun was still rising in the sky.[24] On graduation, students were given stones called whatu kairangi (doubtless symbolising those obtained by Taane) as certificates of proficiency.[25] The subjects of instruction, according to Stack, included myths relating to the gods and demi-gods; charms, incantations and the rules of tapu; history; national and tribal laws; genealogies; treatment of diseases; astronomy; and agriculture.[26]

Best says the object of the whare waananga was 'to preserve all desirable knowledge . . . and to hand it down the centuries free of any alteration, omission, interpolation, or deterioration'.[27] In pursuit of this end, the schools, as in Polynesia, were conducted under conditions of the strictest tapu. Because of the tapu of the place, students had to enter and leave the house naked; women were not allowed in the house; scholars and teachers alike

225

fasted throughout the teaching session; and when the school was over students went through a ceremony of biting the paepae or horizontal beam of the latrine to remove tapu which had accumulated upon them.[28]

At the Wairarapa school of learning conducted by Te Matorohanga, manuscript books kept by some of the pupils, like the pupils themselves, were likewise considered to have become charged with dangerous tapu. The tapu was removed at the end of the session by means of another ceremony, described by Best, termed 'umu whakahoro'.[29] The vital necessity for this protective measure is illustrated by a story which Best tells about one of the students who foolishly declined to have the tapu removed from his book. He took the book home with him and isolated it by placing it in a box which he suspended by means of a rope from the ridge pole of a special hut. One day when he was consulting his book he was called outside and when he returned found children eating food on the sacred box. There could be but one result of this appalling mischance: '. . . in three brief months the owner of the book was insane, in four he was dead'.[30]

The only traditional song type taught in the whare waananga, consistent with its esoteric status, appears to have been the karakia. Precautions to protect against the dangers of tapu continued to be taken with these even after the demise of sacred houses. Samuel Locke, for example, mentions getting back, after 17 years, manuscript books he had left with old chiefs to write in as they felt inclined. As many incantations were so sacred they could not be repeated in a common dwelling house, they had to be written down in the open air.[31]

Closer to modern times, it is noteworthy that in Taranaki, when the sacred poi songs were taught, the instruction was again formal and conditions of tapu similar to those of the old whare waananga were observed. Moerewarewa Reweti of Ngaati Ruanui said she was given knowledge of song interpretation, history and legend after first undergoing a maka (dedication) ceremony during which her head was three times sprinkled with water. The aim of this was to improve memory so that songs would be quickly learned. The pupils were not permitted to eat or smoke while learning.[32] The same prohibitions were applied during a recording session on the day of interview when both of the singers involved refrained from smoking or eating until the session was over. An earlier experience of the present writer seemed to show additionally that books with sacred songs in them are still in some quarters considered to be tapu as in the days of the whare waananga. However, although the book concerned was probably tapu, so too, in this case, was the act of writing itself. When the writer wished to copy the text of a Taranaki song (McL 187) from the singer's waiata book, he was given approval only on condition that he did the copying alone and handled the pen himself. Everything was first removed from the table to be used for the copying except flowers and the table cover and the table was sprinkled with water to purify it. Only then was the waiata book taken down from its position in a flour bag overhanging the table and given to the writer. Later the singer explained her belief that if she wrote a song down for anyone, this would cause her literally to lose it and she would then be unable to recall it. Singing the song on to tape, she thought, would not have this effect. It would appear likely that this belief was an outcome of the prohibition on writing by Te Whiti and Tohu.

The term whare waananga is no longer used strictly for schools of the kind conducted by Te Matorohanga but has been applied also to lesser tribal schools in subjects which are not always esoteric and which may or may not be taught under conditions of tapu. Weekend waiata schools, 'seminars' and other instructional groups are formed from time to time in different tribal areas, organised sometimes by tribal committees or executives or other organisations, and sometimes by individuals. Subjects such as genealogy, marae etiquette and local traditions, as well as waiata singing, are commonly taught and frequent use is made of modern aids such as tape and cassette recorders. The most recent application of the term waananga is for large-scale community colleges, such as one called Te Wananga o Raukawa, conducted by Ngaati Raukawa tribe at Otaki, offering short courses, diplomas and three-year bachelor degrees in various aspects of Maoritanga.

Karanga

Besides karakia and other sacred songs such as Taranaki poi, another song type important enough to require formal instruction was the karanga. Arapeta Awatere said old people would get the young ones together on the marae and teach them. In a 'carry over' from the pure (tapu removal ceremony), prayers would first be performed to guard against evil and to make sure the teaching was taken seriously. In modern times the prayers are Christian; in former times they were karakia. But only the best pupils were permitted to call on the marae. At first the learner would be paired with an older singer, perhaps for years. She would take over temporarily if the senior caller was absent and would assume full status when the older person died.[33]

Merimeri Penfold learned to karanga from an old Taranaki woman named Moana whom she and several other women had approached to teach them. The old lady was horrified at the idea of doing so anywhere except on the marae, and invited the women to come with her the next time she called. They did so and six of them followed the old lady around the marae while she 'karanga'd as she'd never karanga'd before', meanwhile totally ignoring her followers as she went about her duties. The next time they were on the marae the old lady said 'Mary!' and expected Mary to karanga. When she began, the old lady joined in to help. Later she gave instruction in appropriate phrases for different occasions and the separate calls for local and visiting parties.[34]

Whare tapere

Best and other authorities make it clear that the term whare (house) was qualified according to the activity taking place in the house, but a single building could have multiple uses. Thus an ordinary whare puni (sleeping house) became a whare tapere (house of amusement) when used for recreation. Best says that young folk would meet in any sufficiently large dwelling house or guest house in order to pass the evening in story-telling, singing and playing games and the house would be called a whare tapere while so used.[35] Other names for the whare tapere were whare maatoro, whare ngahau, whare pakimairo, whare roopaa and whare taakaro.

Although the whare tapere was a house of recreation, it was also used as a venue for secular instruction. Arapeta Awatere said jingles and ruri were taught there, as well as waiata, tauparapara and non-tapu activities such as mat-making;[36] and Best states that during the evening in the whare maatoro, in times of peace, old men would teach young folk how to perform on musical instruments such as the rooria (jew's harp), 'speak of famous performers of former times, and teach the songs that pertained to the different instruments'.[37] Because of the above uses, Arapeta Awatere preferred to think of the whare tapere as an 'arts and crafts' school rather than a house of amusement. As explained by Awatere, anyone could attend except top-grade tohunga (experts) who were too tapu to enter. If the whare waananga is likened to a university, the whare tapere could be thought of as a secondary school. The equivalent of the primary school was the whare o reehii (Ngaati Porou, Rongowhakaata and Ngaati Kahungunu tribes) or whare reehia (Tuuhoe tribe and others). It was a 'house of pleasure', for children only, and children learned counting games there.[38]

Kino Hughes of Tuuhoe gave the term whare whakaako (lit. house of instruction) for a meeting house or other house in which songs were taught: 'Ki te ako ngaa waiata' (Nothing else was taught there — only songs).[39]

Methods of instruction

Information about methods used during a Ngaati Porou school early in the present century was given by Arapeta Awatere.[40] The school was conducted by Aperahama Te Whainga, the leading tohunga in the Hauiti whare tapere, south of Tolaga Bay in the East Coast. Awatere began attending the school when he was seven years old and continued until he was nine or ten.

One of the methods used by Te Whainga was to teach in the dark. He would arouse his pupils from sleep in the meeting house between one and three o'clock in the morning when, as he said, 'the mind is free'. 'This', said Awatere, 'is really what granny did too. I was half asleep.' Another technique used by Te Whainga was to stand behind his pupils to avoid distracting them.

Considerable effort went into ensuring that the students understood the meaning of songs learnt. Key words were explained along with the history of the song so that 'as we sang we felt with the thing'. Situational teaching also took place. Awatere recalled, for example, actually being taken to watch the moon rise when learning 'Teeraa te marama ka mahuta i te pae'.[41] And on the morning after a learning session, Te Whainga would take his pupils on horseback to visit sites mentioned in the song.

Learning of the song itself was strictly by rote. Sessions lasted for one or two hours during which the learners would go over and over the song. After this, no further singing was allowed. Questions were not allowed during the session and no effort was to made to focus on mistakes. Instead, the pupils would be taken back each time to the beginning of the song. 'You don't start half way,' said Awatere; 'you don't even talk about mistakes.' In effect, in Awatere's estimation, Te Whainga's 'whole idea was to turn himself into a sound machine'.

Prompting

A technique which is widely used for learning waiata takes advantage of the leader solo 'drag' or hiianga which occurs in this song type at the ends of verses. While the drag is being sung, one of the singers prompts the others a phrase ahead by saying the beginning words of the next verse. During the writer's field work the method was used for the rehearsal of McL 144 and 733 and is exemplified by McL 346. According to Kino Hughes, the term for prompting during leader solos is 'kama'.[42]

Te Whiti and Tohu poi songs do not have drags. For these a different method is used, not just in rehearsal but in performance as well. The singers are prompted at the beginning of each verse by the leader who sings the first word solo and then repeats it with the poi team joining in. If the song is later written down, singers generally include the prompts. Thus the presence in manuscript song texts of doubled words at the beginnings of verses is an indication that the song concerned is most likely a poi.

Especially intensive use of prompting appears to have been made in the whare waananga. Best states that when there were three instructors in the whare waananga, two of them would act as prompters (kaituruki) to the one teaching.[43] Arapeta Awatere gave similar information. He said the word for prompt was 'makamaka', a reduplication from the word 'maka' (to throw). The person who did the prompting was called the 'kaimakamaka' and was also referred to as 'turuki' (lit. 'to support') and 'wetewete' (lit. 'to untie'). The tohunga in charge who checked on stance, pronunciation and so on was called the 'tohunga ahurewa' and two others who supervised points of detail and took it in turns to prompt were called 'tohunga turuki' or 'tohunga wetewete'.[44]

SECTION 3

MUSIC STRUCTURE

CHAPTER 10

MANNER OF SINGING

J.S. Polack, who was resident in the Bay of Islands in the 1830s, described Maori singing he heard there as sung in a 'whining, drawling, disagreeable tone', the soporific effect of which soon 'composed [him] to sleep'.[1] The same writer contrasted the voices of the women which he found 'pleasing, feminine and flexible' with those of the men which he described as in general 'harsh and inharmonious' as well as sometimes given in a 'drawling, nasal twang . . . discordant to the ear of a European'.[2] James Cook, writing 70 years earlier, made no comment on men's voices but, like Polack, singled out the voices of the women as 'remarkably mellow and soft' with a 'tender and pleasing effect'.[3]

As heard today, waiata singing is performed in unison by mixed groups with song leaders who may be either male or female. A distinction can be made between the qualities required of a leader and those displayed by the rest of the group. The quality evidently sought in a group is tonal blend. At a waiata school held in Auckland in April 1972, the Tuuhoe elder Kino Hughes stated that both men and women should be in a group, with the women standing never in front of the men but alongside or behind them. Nobody's voice in the group should stand out from the others. Kino illustrated this principle by asking:

> K. 'If a dog finds some pigs in the bush, which pig will he catch?'
> Response (from audience) 'The fattest one?'
> K. (scornfully) 'A dog doesn't know a fat pig from a thin one. He will catch the pig that leaves the group and tear its ear. And that's what will happen to you if you stand apart from the group. You will be talked about [Your ear will be torn].'

In all tribes it is noticeable that group singing is indeed performed with a high degree of tonal blend except for leader solos which are, necessarily, distinctive. In 1958, during his first field trip, the writer noticed that Tuuhoe song leaders at Ringatu meetings tended to have very penetrating voices, often a result of nasal quality as much as power. However loudness is also regarded as desirable. At a 1972 recording session, Kino Hughes referred to the composer of McL 991 as having a good voice which (possibly meant metaphorically) could be heard a mile away. Kino himself characteristically moved his head in emphasis while singing and used the method knowingly as an aid to obtaining volume. He was critical of leaders who 'just stood there like a post'. The leader, he said, must shake his head. 'When you move your head, that waiata come straight to you. You wouldn't miss it. That's how you get that volume when you move your head.'[4] Earlier, in 1958, Arapeta Awatere also told the writer that leaders need to have powerful voices. He said that singing from the stomach, called reo hotu, was the traditionally approved method and singing from the throat (reo pararaa) was condemned. According to Awatere, this method of voice production was carried over to singing from the technique of speaking on the marae where power of voice was essential to ensure that a voice would carry.[5]

Besides exhibiting a high degree of tonal blend, group singing is characterised by an open-throated rather than constricted quality of voice, in some tribes more than others. Of groups recorded by the writer, a spectrum can be observed. Te Arawa and some Waikato groups sang with an almost European quality of voice, perhaps indeed as a result of influence from European music. Tuuhoe groups had a noticeably harsher tone. Tuuwharetoa and Ngaati Porou were somewhere in between. In no case was vibrato or portamento used in traditional waiata singing, in marked contrast with the style adopted, even by the same singers, for hymn singing. Rasp is generally absent, again except for Tuuhoe where it can be heard especially from older singers within the group — in most cases those who are prominent as leaders in some if not all of the songs they sing.

Tuuhoe singers, in common with Ngaai Te Rangi, Whaanau-a-Apanui and Te Arawa tribes, also make use of a device which the writer has called the Bay of Plenty sforzando. Characteristically, it is performed by confident singers who are enjoying the song. It takes the form of a stressing or forceful accenting of certain syllables of the song text, particularly those beginning with the letter 'h'. Kino Hughes was aware of it and stated it was called 'he whakatumatuma' (defined by Williams as 'to act defiantly').[6] In a 1971 interview, Arapeta Awatere equated it with his term 'hotu' which he said means literally 'a throbbing of the voice'. Again he said it was performed from the stomach rather than the throat. The effect is to drive the tone right out so that words can be heard clearly.[7] Possibly this use of the term is an extension of its dictionary meaning 'to pant'. A different but evidently erroneous interpretation of the term hotu is given by Andersen in his book *Maori Music*. He seems to be referring to the same phenomenon as he says it occurs most often on the letter 'h'. However he defines it as an emotional break or 'heart note', consistent with the alternative dictionary meaning of 'hotu' (to sob or sigh).[8] Awatere volunteered that the word is used for spasmodic moaning as a result of extreme weeping and is used idiomatically for deep longing as in the phrase 'e hotu nei te manawa' (my heart throbs). However, this is not the meaning as applied to songs and, although the hotu is in effect a kind of break, Andersen had evidently became confused by the two meanings of the word.[9]

In haka, powerful voice production is considered essential, especially for the peruperu or war dance as performed by warriors. It was remarked upon very early by visitors to New Zealand. Anders Sparrman, who sailed with Cook on the HMS *Resolution*, referred to the 'revolting harshness and hoarseness of voice and gesture' in the war and dance songs which he linked with fighting lust 'and a desire to tear their enemies' limbs apart with their teeth'.[10] Another early visitor who was impressed by the vocal style of the haka was M. de Sainson who came to New Zealand with Dumont d'Urville in 1826– 27. He describes a haka in which words and actions became progressively more intense — building to an 'incredible crescendo . . . sublime and terrible' and culminating with a 'delirium of howls and contortions'. Over a period of two hours he witnessed several such performances, all marked with the same degree of precision and energy.[11]

CHAPTER 11

SCALES

To ethnomusicologists, a scale is simply an inventory of all of the notes in a composition, arranged in ascending or descending order. Recited Maori styles such as karakia and haka, which are forms of stylised speech, cannot be analysed in terms of scales. The sung forms including waiata, pao and oriori, on the other hand, contain notes that are definite enough in pitch to be arranged in scale form, and it is with these that the present analysis is principally concerned.

TONIC

An important concept in scale analysis is that of tonic or tonal centre. In the Maori case, melodic organisation centres around a fixed intoning note or durational tonic known, according to Andersen who elicited the term from a Ngaati Porou informant, as the 'oro'.[1] Philips calls it 'paorooro' or 'patiorooro',[2] probably on the authority of George Graham. The dictionary definition of oro (Williams) is 'rumble' or 'sound'. Arapeta Awatere, whose upbringing was principally Ngaati Porou, said the word 'oro' refers to a continuous sound such as the sound made by a waterfall or the rolling or sustained sound of thunder. He had not heard the term 'patiorooro' but knew 'paorooro' which refers to the resounding or continuous rolling quality of thunder. An allied term is 'ororangi' (lit. 'the sound in heaven'),[3] again used to describe the sound of thunder.[4] On the face of it, the usage reported by Andersen is an excellent example of a general term adopted as a metaphor for specialised use. The oro or intoning note of a waiata is continuous in nature, like the rolling of thunder or the sound of a waterfall. The term, however, is not applied to music in all tribal areas. It was unknown to Marata Te Tomo of Ngaati Tuuwharetoa;[5] Kino Hughes had also not heard of it as a musical term but said that amongst the Tuuhoe the word refers to the sound of an axe being sharpened on a grindstone.[6] As applied to the intoning note, it is possible that this graphic and useful term was coined on the spot by Andersen's informant as a response to Andersen's own questions.

If the notes of a waiata are written out consecutively in the form of a scale, the oro will nearly always be found close to the middle. Since each melodic departure from the oro is ordinarily followed by a return to it, the oro is invariably the most frequently occurring note of a melody. In most cases it is also the final[7] and often it starts the song as well. The oro thus qualifies as the tonic and the scales containing it are of the kind known by ethnomusicologists as centric.

RANGE

In traditional sung items, range from the lowest note to the highest seldom exceeds the musical interval of a 4th. Not quite three-quarters (74.4%) of songs analysed by the writer have ranges of a 4th or less.[8] The unit of range for traditional Maori songs is thus the tetrachord rather than the octave.

NUMBER OF NOTES

One way of classifying scales is according to the number of notes. A conspicuous characteristic of Maori music, reported by missionaries and others in locations from north to south in New Zealand, is the presence of scales with few notes. Thomas Chapman (1792–1876) was a lay missionary for the Church Missionary Society (CMS) who began work in the Bay of Islands at Paihia in 1830. Not long after his arrival, he complained in his journal of the 'tiring and troublesome' sound of women who, as soon as it was dark, began singing 'rude and noisy songs' which they continued until almost midnight. These, he wrote, 'could hardly be said . . . to contain more than three or four notes'.[9] Another CMS missionary, Richard Taylor (1805–73), likewise noticed that native airs in the Wanganui area in 1839 embraced 'no more than three or four notes'.[10] Sarah Selwyn said the same of Maori hymn singing in the Manawatu in 1845.[11] And Herries Beattie (1881–1972), who collected Maori lore throughout the South Island three-quarters of a century ago, described songs he heard at this time as 'all minor key' and sung on 'one or two notes'.[12]

The single-note songs heard by Beattie were possibly paatere, which are performed substantially on one note and, as such, are the only recited songs which can be regarded as possessing a scale, albeit the simplest possible. More elaborate Maori scales seem likely to have grown by extension from the single note or pure tonic nucleus exemplified by the paatere. The addition of a major or minor 2nd above or below the tonic results in four possible ditonic or two-note scales, all found frequently in practice. Combining these and/or adding further notes above and below generates tritonic (three-note), tetratonic (four-note) and other higher order scales which again are amongst those most frequently found.

A detailed analysis of 651 Maori scales has been published, representing all sung items of the first 800 songs recorded by the writer.[13] The main tribes represented in these recordings are Ngaati Tuuwharetoa, Waikato tribes, Taranaki tribes, Te Arawa tribes and Tuuhoe. Tribes not represented are Ngaati Kahungunu and Hauraki tribes, whose singing traditions are almost extinct, as well as Northland tribes, the East Coast tribe of Ngaati Porou, and Wanganui tribes, all of which were recorded later. Too few Wanganui songs were obtained for analysis of them to be practicable. For purposes of the present chapter, a supplementary analysis was undertaken of a sample of 64 Ngaati Porou songs recorded by the writer and by the Maori Purposes Fund Board,[14] and results for Northland rely upon an analysis by van Waardenberg[15] of 131 songs, again from the McLean and Maori Purposes Fund Board collections. The two latter studies bring the total number of scales analysed to 846.

The first step in the 1969 analysis was to prepare melodic interval diagrams according to a new method worked out by the writer (see Chapter 12). This made possible two approaches to analysing the scales. One was the conventional method of including all pitches sung; the other was the construction of skeletal scales containing only those notes essential to song structure as determined by the amount of melodic movement involving each note.[16] Both approaches were followed and the results compared. The latter method proved productive in terms of penetrating the underlying system. By examining the melodic interval associations of each scalic note with each of the others in the entire body of material, it was possible to determine the most often used or strongest associations and from these isolate composite

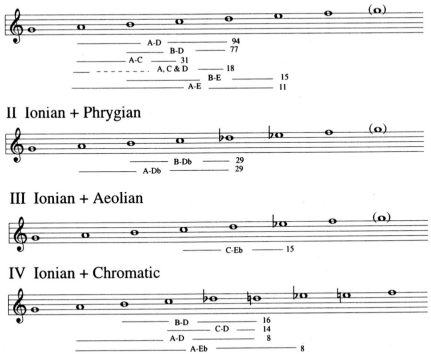

EXAMPLE 78a *Scale family: Scales with Ionian lower tetrachord (tonic on C)*

V Aeolian + Ionian

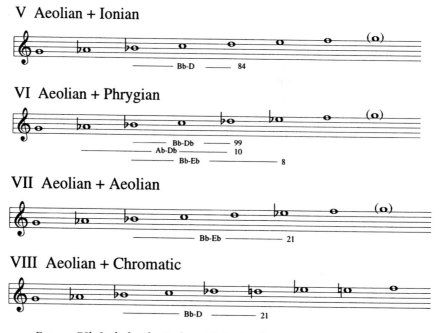

VI Aeolian + Phrygian

VII Aeolian + Aeolian

VIII Aeolian + Chromatic

EXAMPLE 78b Scale family: Scales with Aeolian lower tetrachord (tonic on C)

scales. Three such scales and a possible fourth were identified in the 1969 study. Re-examination of the data adds four further scales; they are written out in Example 78 with their tonics on C.

As already noted, the *oro* or tonic of a Maori scale is most often to be found in the centre. The scales are therefore centric or, in terms of conventional analysis, plagal. In terms of interval associations, it turns out that there are just two possibilities for the tetrachord below the tonic and four for the tetrachord above. Either of the two lower tetrachords can be combined with any of the four upper tetrachords, resulting in the eight scales shown. The complete family of eight composite scales accounts for all but a handful of the individual Maori scales found in recordings, together with all of the flute scales reported in Chapter 5.[17] In Example 78, the most common three-, four- and five-note scales are shown together with the number of times they appear in the corpus. To avoid cluttering the diagram, the most frequent ditonic scales are shown separately in Example 79. It will be seen that these are subsumed by the tritonic scales marked in scales I , II, V and VI of Example 78.

Ionian   Aeolian

EXAMPLE 79 Most frequent ditonic scales

MODE

Scales in Western music, as exemplified by the white notes of the piano, have seven notes, and mode is determined by the disposition of semitones within the scale in relation to the tonal centre or tonic. The most familiar Western modes are the common major and minor scales; the former is known technically, from a Greek name given to it in medieval times, as the Ionian and the latter, with lowered leading note, is the Aeolian. Other medieval modes such as Dorian and Mixolydian are extant as a result of their use in church music and folk music. Traditional Maori music hardly ever has as many as seven notes, but Ionian and Aeolian modes both occur as composite scales (Scales I and VII in Example 78) as does the Phrygian mode (Scale VI). The other composite Maori scales are wholly or partially made up of tetrachord segments of the Ionian, Phrygian or Aeolian. In the article earlier referred to,[18] missionary hymn and psalm singing were ruled out as influences upon the Maori in adopting these modes, as was any possibility of historical connection. The most likely explanation is that the Maori and the medieval modes evolved from shared principles of some kind which have yet to be demonstrated.

CHROMATIC SCALES

Two of the skeletal scales (scales IV and VIII) make use of both major and minor forms of 2nd and 3rd above the tonic. All-note scales fill out the core structures by means of infix and affix, extending range and resulting in numerous fully chromatic scales as shown in Example 80.

DIFFERENCES BY TRIBE AND SONG TYPE

In the writer's 1969 study, tritonic skeletal scales were found to be the most numerous for all tribes, accounting for almost half the total (47%). Tetratonic scales were the next most frequent (31%), followed by ditonic scales (17%). When results for Northland and Ngaati Porou are added, the results change hardly at all, with tritonic remaining the same, tetratonic standing at 32 per cent and ditonic somewhat down to 14 per cent. Small but statistically significant differences show up in distributions by tribe and song type. In the 1979 study, Tuuwharetoa and Waikato tribes were found to have relatively more tetratonic and fewer ditonic scales than other tribes and the reverse was the case for Tuuhoe and Taranaki. The Taranaki result was mirrored by that for poi songs, most of which were recorded in Taranaki. These songs exhibited a dramatically low proportion of tetratonic scales and a correspondingly high proportion of ditonic scales. As a group, oriori contained an unusually high proportion of tetratonic scales at the expense of tritonic. The supplementary Ngaati Porou sample and the scales in van Waardenberg's Northland study turn out to be essentially complementary. Common fea-

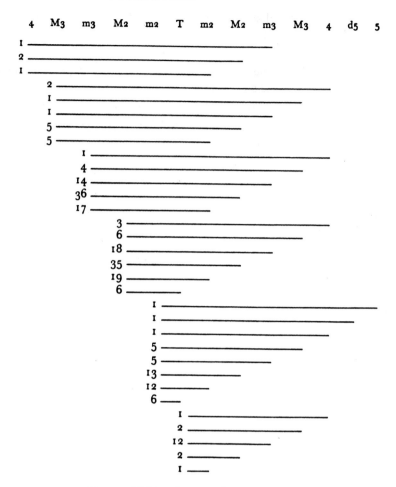

4	M3	m3	M2	m2	T	m2	M2	m3	M3	4	d5	5

EXAMPLE 80 Most frequent chromatic scales

tures are absence of poi songs and a predominance of waiata. But the Northland sample wholly lacks ditonic skeletal scales in contradistinction to Ngaati Porou which has somewhat more (20%) than the 1969 sample (17%). Ngaati Porou, on the other hand, has fewer tritonic scales (36%) than the 1969 sample (47%), exactly balancing out Northland which has more (53%). Excluded from the Northland count are a significant number of scales (17% of the total sung corpus) designated by van Waardenberg as containing ambiguous tonics. These scales may be regarded as either Ionian or Aeolian in type depending on which of the central notes is designated as the tonic.

A count of the commonly occurring scales marked in Example 78 shows that these represent almost three-quarters of the entire sample. Ionian-type scales outnumber Aeolian by 2:1. An overwhelming proportion are Scale I or pure Ionian. This has resulted largely from the addition of Ngaati Porou and, especially, Northland songs to those of the 1969 corpus. In both areas there appear to be more waiata than elsewhere with a European cast of melody, even to the extent of the quite diagnostic major 3rd above the tonic. It should not, nevertheless, be too hastily assumed that this is evidence of direct European influence upon the songs. Rather (especially in view of the coincidence of flute scales with vocal ones), as van Waardenberg points out for Northland: 'It seems likely . . . that scales already containing a European nucleus, such as m2 T M2, came gradually to be preferred over those that did not.'[19]

CHAPTER 12

MELODIC INTERVALS

The most casual listener to Maori waiata soon becomes aware that the melodic steps or intervals between the notes of a song tend to be small compared with the much larger skips that often occur in European music. The smallest interval between one note and the next in European music is a half tone or semitone. Except between phrases, most Maori chant melodies have steps no greater than one, two or three semitones or, in musical terms, the intervals of minor 2nd (m2), major 2nd (M2), or minor 3rd (m3). Even the m3 occurs seldom in comparison with M2s and m2s which together carry nearly 90 per cent of the melodic movement.[1] This characteristic was noticed by Joseph Banks who, like many observers since, was reminded of European cathedral singing. In a journal entry of 10 October 1769, he commented: 'They then sung a song of their own, it was not without some taste like a Psalm tune and contain many notes and semitones . . .'[2] Sydney Parkinson had the same impression, describing the singing he heard as 'very much like the chant which the popish priests use at mass'.[3]

In a paper entitled 'A New Method of Melodic Interval Analysis', a detailed interval analysis is given of all of the sung items in the first 800 songs recorded by the writer.[4] Diagrams were drawn using the pattern following. The scale appears on the left of the diagram. Lines in the form of arrowheads represent rising and falling intervals with intervals of each kind appearing together: m2s in column 1, M2s in column 2, m3s in column 3 and so across the page. Counts of each melodic interval are entered against the arrowheads. In the diagrams, a circle around a note indicates the tonic, a leftward arrow the finishing note and a rightward arrow the starting note. A completed diagram contains all of the information needed for an interval analysis of the song in a compact graphical form recognisable as easily by the non-specialist as by a person trained in music. The following are diagrams of the common ditonic scales involving steps of M2s or m2s above and below the tonic. It can be be seen that in the diagrams the M2 and m2 are distinctive in appearance, resulting in unique patterns for each structure.

By itself, a scale shows only the notes of a song and provides only limited information about the melody from which it may have been derived. In

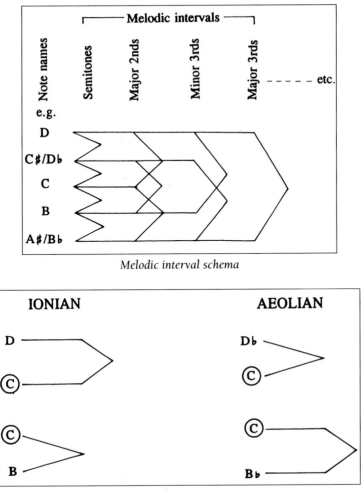

Melodic interval schema

Common ditonic structures

principle, melodic steps can occur between any note of a scale and any other. In practice, in a given music system, some choices are preferred over others and these are revealed by the interval diagrams. When there are more than two notes in the scale, the number of choices available at each step in a melody, rising or falling, multiplies. Even the three or four notes typical of Maori songs allow for numerous different melodies. These show up in the diagrams, as in songs McL 106 and McL 120 which have the same scale but quite different melodies.

Both songs are laments (waiata tangi) of uncertain origin: in the one case most likely from Ngaati Maniapoto and in the other from Ngaati Awa. In each case, the scale is the most commonly occurring tetratonic scale consisting of m3 and m2 scalic intervals below the tonic and a M2 above. Superficially, the melodic interval diagrams look the same. But the interval count

243

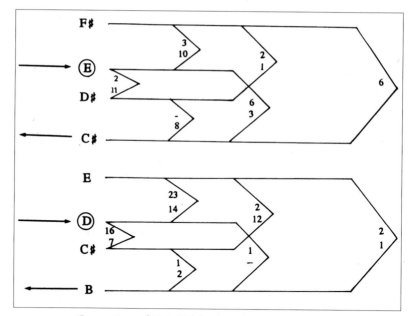

Comparison of McL 106 (top) and McL 120 (bottom)

reveals that the paths taken by the two melodies diverge. Both songs begin on the tonic and end on the lower m3, but in McL 106 a rise of a M2 to the note above the tonic is followed by a fall of a 4th to the lower scalic m3 and then, usually, a rise by way of a conjunct M2 and m2 back to the tonic. In McL 120, by contrast, the lower m3 is important only as a finishing note with most of the melodic movement confined to the notes immediately adjacent to the tonic: the most common path taken by the melody in this song is a fall of a m2 from the tonic to the note directly below, followed by a rise of a m3 to the note above the tonic and a fall from there of a M2 back to the tonic. In the one case, the predominant direction of movement to and from the tonic is 'up-down-up-up' and in the other 'down-up-down'. Comparing diagrams for all of the songs in the corpus permitted an analysis of interval preference by tribe and song type.

INTERVAL PREFERENCE BY TRIBE

Similarities between tribes were found to far outweigh differences but a few distinctions emerged:

- Waikato was distinguished by a preference for m3s below the tonic whereas with other tribes the m3 tends to span the tonic.
- Arawa had a preference for the m2 above the tonic and the M2 below.
- Tuuhoe favoured M2s both above and below the tonic.

INTERVAL PREFERENCE BY SONG TYPE

• Waiata used M2s and m2s about equally both above and below the tonic.

• Pao favoured intervals above the tonic. This occurs because the tonic tends to be the lowest note of the scale in contrast with waiata and other sung forms in which the tonic is usually centric.

• Oriori have a preponderance of intervals below the tonic, particularly the m2.

THE QUARTER-TONE MYTH

In 1820, the Ngaapuhi chiefs Hongi Hika (1772–1828) and Hohaia Waikato (c.1790–1877) visited England with the missionary Thomas Kendall. While in England they assisted Kendall and the Cambridge linguist Professor Samuel Lee with the compilation of a *Grammar and Vocabulary of the Language of New Zealand*.[5] Thirty-five years later, perhaps inspired by this early visit, another Cambridge scholar, James A. Davies of Trinity College, wrote an article 'On the Native Songs of New Zealand' as an appendix to Governor George Grey's book *Polynesian Mythology*.[6] It is not known who Davies's Maori informant might have been but, with such a lapse of time between 1820 and 1855, Hongi or Waikato themselves are unlikely to have been involved. In his article, Davies included the music of four Maori songs which, with the aid of a graduated monochord, he had transcribed into musical notation. The monochord appears to have seduced Davies into over-precision as he notated the songs in enharmonic notation, having persuaded himself that the 'natural music' of the Maori could be identified with the quarter-tone enharmonic genera of the ancient Greeks. His assumption of quarter tones has been echoed down the years to the point that it is now something almost everyone 'knows' about Maori music. But there is little reason to believe the popular notion to be true. Indeed, Davies's own observation that his singer 'did not always repeat the musical phrase with precisely the same modulation'[7] indicates the exact opposite. Nor, as Davies supposed, was it proof of quarter tones that his singer accepted the notations when they were sung back. This shows only that the notations were within limits of variability acceptable to the singer.

Whether the enharmonic genera is even a possibility in Maori music is also open to doubt. According to the first edition of the *Harvard Dictionary of Music*, the enharmonic genera of the ancient Greeks was derived by lowering the upper of the two middle notes of the tetrachord A G F E until it became identical with the lower. The remaining interval was then halved to produce quarter tones thus: A F F - E or M3 + $\frac{1}{4}$ tone + $\frac{1}{4}$ tone descending.[8] As has been seen above, the tetrachord used here as a starting point is identical with the most common Maori tetratonic scale assuming a tonic on F.

No. 1.

HE WAIATA AROHA: OR, THE BRIDE'S COMPLAINT.

Marks or signs: ¼ sharp x, sharp ⤬ or ½ above note, ¾ sharp ⤬.

¼ flat ♭, flat ♭ or ½ below, ¾ flat ♭.

* The pages refer to Sir George Grey's collection of New Zealand Songs, " Mau Konga moteatea, me nga Haki rara."

NM 229 'Teeraa te puukohu' as notated by James A. Davies

The two consecutive quarter tones in this case would need to bisect the semitone which commonly appears immediately below the tonic in Maori scales. Quarter tones can occur in this position, and M3s are most likely to occur above the tonic. Neither, however, is frequent and, so far as the writer is aware, they do not occur in association.

Modern recordings are of no assistance in determining how accurate Davies's transcriptions might have been. Three of the four songs transcribed by Davies have been recorded[9] but the tunes bear no resemblance to his transcriptions.

Aside from Davies's contribution, the sole piece of evidence for Maori quarter tones is an equally unconvincing, though much quoted, anecdote concerning Hare Hongi and Alfred Hill. According to Andersen, Hill remarked to Hongi, who had just finished singing a song, that the whole was within the interval of a tone (M2):

'Surely not,' said Hare Hongi. 'Yes; sing it again.' He sang it again. 'Yes, it is within a tone.' 'Do you know,' remarked Hongi in telling me of it, 'I felt that I had been ranging over the octave.'

'So it is,' concludes Andersen, 'these minute subdivisions of a tone do not, after a time, seem minute at all.'[10] Unfortunately it is not revealed what song Hongi might have been singing and there is not the remotest evidence, whatever Hongi's own subjective impression of range, that he was indeed singing in microtones. A nice counter-anecdote is told by Haami Rangiihu about a time when he and a Maori group performed a Maori chant in Australia in the presence of an expert European musician. They told him about the 'quarter tones' in Maori chant and how, as a result, it could not be realised on European musical instruments. The musician asked them to sing the chant again and confounded them by correctly playing it on the piano![11]

The ethnomusicologist Edwin Burrows anticipated the present writer's caveats more than half a century ago, though he felt obliged in his publications to accept Maori quarter tones on Andersen's authority. In a letter to Andersen, he correctly and sensibly pointed out that the question is not simply about the occurrence of small intervals but how consistently they are repeated in different versions of the same song. In transcribing Polynesian songs he found that variations were not confined to a quarter tone but could be as much as a major 3rd or perfect 4th in one version compared with another.[12] Though he did not say so specifically, he had plainly, and again correctly, concluded that small variations of pitch were insignificant if they fell within the limits of variability of the performers. It was not a matter Andersen was competent to check as he had transcribed no Maori songs whatsoever, much less analysed them.

The present writer's corpus of recorded Maori songs nearly all use intervals close to the tempered values with deviations no greater than those commonly met with in European vocal music. Microtones which do occur are both readily explainable and, as a rule, fail the consistency test. Most frequent are neutral 2nds appearing as a lower auxiliary to the intoning note. They tend to stabilise later in the song as unambiguous m2s or M2s. Sometimes a singer will microtonally flatten a note on some appearances in a melody but not others, or will consistently flatten a note each time it occurs but match this by adjusting the intoning note downwards at each repeat of the melody. The result is a steady dropping of pitch throughout the song. In neither case can the microtones concerned be considered structurally significant. Rather they are examples of performance variability.

The same is true of inflected microtones sometimes to be heard in solo performances or in the leader solo performed at line endings in waiata. An example of the latter occurs in Song 14 of McLean & Orbell where the leader's note at the end of each line is decidedly variable in pitch, sometimes appearing as a D-flat, sometimes as a D-natural, and sometimes in between. It is likely that in this case the intended note was a D-flat throughout.

A few singers have been recorded who perform little crescendos on long-held notes, unconsciously raising the pitch of their voices slightly as they do so. In a group situation they would be obliged to conform to other singers. A similar such example was recorded at one of the writer's first recording sessions in 1958 and necessitated the invention of a special transcription sign to indicate it. On occasion, while sustaining a long note on the tonic, the singer, Waina Te Hoeta, raised the pitch very slightly towards the middle of the note, returning to the original pitch at the end.

247

Hae-re　　raa　　　ko-u-to-u　　　ngaa i - a　　　hu-ri ki-no.

EXAMPLE 81 Line 7 of McL 36 as sung by Waina Te Hoeta

The inflected note in this case was an incipient rise to a full M2 above the tonic which was performed elsewhere in the song at identical points in the melody.

He ma-u - nga　　tuu no - a　　　ngaa hi - wi　　　i ru-nga　　raa.

EXAMPLE 82 Line 3 of McL 36 as sung by Waina Te Hoeta

Inflections of this kind can also occur on occasion in group singing. An example is McL 647 in which, on successive repeats of the melody, there was at first the merest suggestion of a change of pitch at the point in question, from a few of the singers. Over the next four repeats, this was taken up by the rest of the singers and eventually appeared as an unequivocal non-microtonic note. In a prescriptive transcription, unintentional deviations of this kind would not be shown as they are non-essential to the song.

The few cases of positively articulated microtones used consistently are usually also readily explainable. Quarter tones sometimes occur when a passing note is required by the song text and the range is too small to permit the use of semitones.

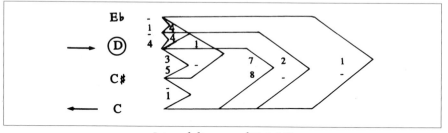

Interval diagram of McL 245

In at least one such case the singer later expanded the range of the song he was singing and substituted standard semitones for his earlier quarter tones.

The sole case found by the writer of apparently unequivocal quarter tones used structurally in a melody occurs in a song recorded by W. Ngata for the Maori Purposes Fund Board. The song is 'Te ao o te Parera', recorded from a group of singers led by Hati Nepia at Manutuke, near Gisborne, on 2 December 1953.[13] The song is fundamentally ditonic on the interval of a M2, with the tonic appearing as the upper of the two notes. The tonic is somewhat unstable, sometimes drooping in pitch before recovering to its former level. After the leader solo at the end of each line, the singers join the leader strongly on the tonic at whatever pitch it happens to be, and then elevate the note by approximately a quarter tone before returning to the tonic via the lower M2. It may be that the quarter tone in this case is an incipient rise to a full half tone. However, no other recordings of the song are available so it is not possible to find out whether other singers would perform the song in the same way. Whatever the case, a single example is insufficient to admit quarter tones to the system as currently practised. Finally, a study by the writer of pre-European albatross-bone Maori flutes ought to have turned up evidence of microtones if these were in use when the flutes were made. Careful measurements of pitch were made using a highly stable specially calibrated audio oscillator and a cathode ray oscilloscope. Quarter tones were indeed found to be possible on some of the flutes but with no implication that they were necessarily used.[14] The reverse is likely as the most frequently occurring scales did not involve microtones.[15]

On the available evidence, one must conclude that although quarter tones do sometimes occur in Maori music they are not, as popularly supposed, integral to the music system. The notion of Maori quarter tones has persisted essentially out of ignorance both of quarter tones and of the rules of Maori music. Although Maori intervals are usually close to the European tempered values, they are used in unfamiliar ways: especially, the mode is often neither major nor minor. The listener is likely to notice only that the melody sounds strange and, having heard the term, seizes upon quarter tones as an explanation.

CHAPTER 13

RHYTHM, METRE AND TEMPO

SUNG ITEMS

In commenting upon his 1855 transcriptions of Maori waiata, Davies states:

> One word as to *time*. Though I have timed the airs I have given, I am free to
> confess there was neither metre nor rhythm of any marked character discern-
> ible in them; and even in the divisions of the lines or verses, the singer seemed
> to stop indifferently now at one, now at another word.[1]

Davies's singer would, in fact, have stopped only because he or she ran
out of breath, as solo singers are still prone to do today.[2] Line and stanza
organisation are present in waiata as sung by groups, and are discussed in
the next chapter, on form. The above conclusion about metre and rhythm,
however, remains as true today as it was in 1855, except for transitional
songs with some degree of European influence. Traditional waiata are
heterometric or without time signature. In other words, they lack the regular beat which is a feature of most European music. To the Western ear it
may appear that rhythm or metre is lacking. Alternatively it may seem to be
present in the form either of continual syncopation or of constantly changing time. In fact, the rhythms are additive rather than divisive and should
not be thought of in terms of Western metre. As represented in most of the
writer's transcriptions of waiata, the basic rhythmic unit is an eighth note or
quaver and the rhythms appear as irregular groups of two or three units
beamed together. In Western terms, the 'beat' is sometimes two quavers long
and sometimes three. Sustained notes of greater length may also appear at
prescribed points in the melody. Occasionally, regular time changes occur in
a song such that a true additive metre emerges, again unusual in Western
music. Two songs in McLean & Orbell are of this nature. They are Song 6
'Ka eke ki Wairaka', a waiata, which is in 7/8 time, and Song 50 'Pine pine te
kura', an oriori, which is largely in 5/4 time.

The reader may wonder how groups of singers manage to keep together
in songs where metre is absent. There is, in fact, a governing principle at
work in many songs which may assist the singers; it is a form of textual
metre (discussed in Chapter 15).

Because waiata, especially, are typically non-metric in musical terms, tempo or pace cannot usually be expressed in the conventional way as beats per minute. A convenient alternative measure is syllables of text per minute. When songs are timed in this way, it is found that tempos of sung items range from about 50 syllables per minute for the slowest songs to 240 or more syllables per minute for the fastest, averaging 100 for Tuuhoe tribe through 110 for Waikato/Maniapoto, 120 for Tuuwharetoa, 130 for Arawa and 140 for Taranaki. Particular songs tend to be sung at or near the same tempo no matter where or by whom they are sung, showing that each song has its own preferred tempo which singers remember.

A category of sung item for which extensive rhythmic analysis has already been provided is the pao. As noted in Chapter 3, about a quarter of recorded pao are performed with end of line drags like waiata and many, again like waiata, are non-metric. The remainder are mostly in 3/8 time with characteristic iambic rhythms and a common rhythmic scheme of eight bars to each line of text.

RECITED ITEMS

Recited songs differ from the sung styles primarily by absence of stable pitch organisation, by their necessarily through-composed rather than strophic form and, again necessarily, by their syllabic rather than melismatic style of singing. They are also more likely to be metred, with the probability of metre increasing according to the amount and type of body movement involved. Karakia, which are performed by individuals and have no formal movement component, are usually unmetred. So are tauparapara and other recited songs performed by individuals, such as whakaaraara paa. Paatere, which are traditionally performed by groups of singers with self-accompanied individual use of movement, could be described as semi-metred. Hari kai, which were performed in procession by women bearing food, are invariably metred, as are recited game songs that involve regular or uniform movement. Metre at its most conspicuous is the hallmark of haka and dance forms with their vigorous use of foot stamping and drilled uniform movement. Maori terms for metre in a haka, referring evidently to the foot stamping involved, are 'patupatu' (lit. 'strike', 'beat' or 'pound') and 'takahi' (lit. 'stamp').[3]

Tempos of recited songs are about 100 syllables per minute faster than sung items, ranging from 120 to 380 syllables per minute. Haka, regulated by foot stamping, are the slowest with an average of 170 syllables per minute; paatere are next at an average of 240 syllables per minute; and karakia can rattle along at an extraordinary 300 or more syllables per minute. Generally tempo remains steady throughout a song, whether sung or recited, though there are some early reports of tempos getting faster during the progress of a haka as excitement mounted.

A similarity between sung and recited forms is their common use of additive rhythms. Karakia make the most extensive use of these with rhythmic groupings which, while not slavishly following the words, are more obviously text-based than those of other song types. In effect, a karakia is a form of extended or heightened speech. Dieffenbach characterised them, not inappropriately, as possessing 'no modulation of the voice [i.e. recited rather than sung], but syllables are lengthened and shortened, and it produces the same effect as the reading of the Talmud in synagogues'.[4] A short karakia, as sung by Hamu Katene of Nga Rauru tribe of Whanganui, is transcribed as Example 83. It is an incantation that was used during the cultivation of the ground with the koo (digging stick) in preparation for planting kuumara. Except for a descending glide on the last three syllables, it is sung throughout on a monotone.

EXAMPLE 83 *Karakia: McL 479A as sung by Hamu Katene*

In paatere, there is a tendency toward duple metre, but the divisive rhythmic groupings are often modified in such a way as to become additive. Song 20, 'E noho ana anoo i te papa tahi' in McLean & Orbell, as led by Makarena Mariu of Ngaati Tuuwharetoa, may be taken as exemplary of paatere rhythms as follows:

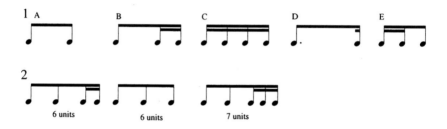

EXAMPLE 84 Paatere rhythms from M&O 20 as led by Makarena Mariu

The rhythmic groups A, B and C appear many times in the song; the dotted figure D, and E which is the inverse of B, occur less frequently. By the addition of extra semiquavers, these may be modified from a count of four units to five, six, seven or even eight units: A as in (2), B as in (3), C as in (4) and D as in (5). Similarly, semiquavers can be dropped so that groups of four units become three as in (6).

Of the metred forms of recited song, hari kai, which are invariably in 2/4 or 2/8 time, make use of the same rhythmic building blocks as paatere but in different proportions, as shown in Example 85, where rhythms are ranked in order of frequency of use.

2/4 TIME	2/8 TIME	%	REL. FREQ.
		27	100
		19	70
		16	59
		12	44
		6	22
		5	19
		2	7

253

2/4 TIME	2/8 TIME	%	REL. FREQ.
♪ 𝅘𝅥𝅭	𝅘𝅥𝅮𝅘𝅥𝅭	2	7
𝄽 𝅘𝅥𝅘𝅥	𝄾 𝅘𝅥𝅮𝅘𝅥𝅮	2	7
𝄽 𝅘𝅥	𝄾 ♪	1	4
𝅘𝅥𝅘𝅥 𝄽	𝅘𝅥𝅮𝅘𝅥𝅮 𝄾	.5	2

Example 85 Hari kai rhythms

Some haka have the same rhythms as above, but most are in compound metre with characteristic rhythmic groupings as shown in numerous transcriptions throughout the present book. A favourite haka device is to syncopate the beat, introduce a rest to coincide with the foot stamp on the first pulse of a group of three, or provide a driving emphasis with a trochaic rhythm instead of an iambus. Additionally, even in haka, additive groupings may be used to the extent that the metre allows by introducing a string of syllables which together add up to a multiple of three. Such groupings have the effect of syncopation, as the underlying beat provided by the foot stamp is not disturbed. The following is taken from the famous 'Wairangi' haka (M&O 18):

ka wha - ka - koo - pu - ra   Ru - a - ra - ngi - ha - pe   te - i - na -

Example 86 Haka extract from line 3 of M&O 18 as sung on Folkways recording FE 4433

CHAPTER 14

FORM

TEXTUAL FORM

Sung items are organised by line and stanza. Waiata have long stanzas containing irregular numbers of lines. Each line typically contains two phrases. Pao, by contrast, take the form of two-line couplets, each couplet representing a verse or stanza. In both cases the lines are of uniform length. As has been seen, pao verses or couplets are all effectively separate songs and may be sung in any order or even in isolation. The order of stanzas in waiata is usually fixed, though occasionally a verse may be left out by singers or a different verse order will become established. Recited items have no line organisation and are best represented as prose. In contrast with other recited songs, haka are typically responsorial, with leader solos and choral responses.

Andersen provides terminology he obtained from a Ngaati Porou informant. According to Andersen, the Ngaati Porou term for stanza is 'whiti', and divisions within the stanza are known as 'upoko' (lit. 'heads').[1] Williams likewise gives both 'whiti' and 'upoko' as meaning a verse or division of a song. Arapeta Awatere confirms the use of the term whiti by Te Arawa, Tuuhoe and other tribes besides Ngaati Porou and provides additional information on the meaning of upoko. According to Awatere, upoko is a sense unit referring to the subject matter of the song. If one were to regard a song as a book, the term whiti would refer to chapters and upoko to paragraphs. The tune must fit, with the end of an upoko coinciding always with the end of a musical line. Thus, in the well-known oriori 'Pine pine te kura' (M&O 50), the first upoko ends at line 4 on the word 'Tuhaepo' (rendered up to this point by Orbell as one long sentence). Another example given by Awatere is the waiata 'Ka eke ki Wairaka' (M&O 6) which is one long whiti with no upoko or changes of subject. The term for a line in a song text is 'raarangi',[2] used also for lines of psalms. The terms upoko, whiti and raarangi are used not only for traditional songs but are also in current use by the Ringatu church for their sung liturgy.[3]

MUSICAL FORM

Consistent with the prose nature of their texts, recited songs have no musical form except for haka and related styles in which form tends to follow the texts sentence by sentence and phrase by phrase.

Sung items mostly make use of the varied repetition of a basic melody or strophe. With few exceptions, the end of each strophe of a waiata coincides with the end of a textual line and is marked by a melismatic leader solo known as the 'hii' or 'hiianga' (the drag).[4] Typically, each repetition of the musical strophe is coincident with a full textual line and each musical phrase with a textual half line or phrase. The leader solo either prolongs a syllable of the text or, more usually, is performed on meaningless syllables or vocables, generally *e* or *ei*. Because of the drag, the second phrase is usually musically longer than the first. As explained in Chapter 6, the hiianga links successive lines of the text, providing a temporary resting place for group performers during which they can take breath and think ahead to the next line. Effectively, the action of the group during the hiianga is opposite to that of the leader. While the leader performs the hiianga, the other singers take a rest, referred to as 'whakataanga'.[5]

In a few songs, melodic continuity is achieved by an ingenious departure from the standard pattern of co-occurring musical and textual lines. The leader solo occurs as usual at the end of the musical line but coincides with the beginning instead of the end of the textual line. As a result, the music demands a continuation at the end of the textual line and the text cannot stop at the end of the musical line. Thus continuity can hardly be avoided and the singers must keep singing from beginning to end.[6]

The end of a structural division, such as a verse or stanza, and the end of the song itself, as well as dropouts by individuals in group performance, are all marked by a device the writer has called the terminal glissando. It takes the form of a characteristic expulsion of breath accompanied by a glissando drop of the voice over the interval of a 3rd or 4th. Judging by the remarks of early writers such as George Forster, who described it in 1774 as 'resembling the sliding of a finger along the fingerboard on the violin',[7] it has been a feature of Maori music for more than 200 years. It is doubtless even older, as similar trailing cadences have been documented in both Eastern and Western Polynesia.[8] Throughout his book *Maori Music*, Andersen erroneously applies the term 'hiianga' to the terminal glissando rather than the leader solo,[9] probably by wrongly interpreting Best whose explanation of the term is ambiguous.[10] The correct Maori name for the terminal glissando is 'whakauu' which means 'a confirming'[11] as in the phrase 'Ko te whakauunga o te hiianga'[12] or 'whakamutunga'[13] (lit. 'to bring to an end').[14] As applied to karakia, the term is 'whakatau'[15] (lit. 'to cause to alight').

Pao differ from waiata not only in terms of their couplet line structure but also their distinctive manner of performance in which each couplet is traditionally first performed solo and then repeated as a chorus. Drags may occur in mid line or at the ends of phrases as in waiata but, because the soloist performs an entire verse which cues the choral repeat, they are not essential. Non-lexical syllabifying on *e* or *ei* may still occur at the ends of lines but it generally takes the form of a sustained single-note cadence rather than melisma.

Taranaki poi songs also differ substantially from waiata in form. In common with waiata is the use of a basic melody or strophe repeated line by line throughout the song. There is, however, no drag to mark the end of the line. Instead, each song is performed continuously without break from beginning to end. Performance cues are given by the leader at the beginning of each stanza by prompting the other singers with the first word.

Oriori also tend to be structurally different from waiata. Performance is again continuous as in waiata, but leader solos take place, as a rule, not at the end of each line but at the beginning or end of each verse or stanza. As explained in Chapter 3, the textual lines of oriori are of non-uniform length with melodic figures marking each end and a variable 'filling' between.

CHAPTER 15

SONG/TEXT RELATIONSHIPS

As shown in the last chapter, there is a close relationship between textual and musical form in waiata and other traditional songs. Line and stanza organisation, in particular, are in one-to-one correspondence, though this is not always obvious in published song texts where often, as noted by Orbell, songs with long lines 'have been printed in what are in reality half-lines, so that the movement of the language and thought has to some extent been obscured'.[1] A different approach to song texts was followed in McLean & Orbell where, for the first time, an attempt was made to represent song texts exactly as sung. This proved productive in many ways. Especially, the fixing of text boundaries by reference to the musical phrase allowed speech particles to be assigned to their correct half lines, removing ambiguities and explicating translation.

THE RULE OF EIGHT

A further breakthrough came some years after publication of the McLean & Orbell volume. The linguist Bruce Biggs was one day browsing through it when he made a remarkable discovery. In song after song and line after line, if a long vowel was counted as two and a short vowel as one, there were 'just eight vowels to each half line of the text'.[2] Biggs had found what has become known as the 'rule of eight', establishing such Maori texts as governed by a quantitative or numerical metre as absolute in its way as that of Greek or Latin verse, though dependent on vowel rather than syllable count. Technically, Maori is known as a 'mora timed' language and Biggs's discovery establishes the mora (one-count quantitative unit) as the basic unit also in Maori prosody. The principle will be familiar to most readers from English (accentual) prosody where stressed and unstressed syllables replace the long and short ones of Greek and Latin verse, and a count of eight is again common. In light of this, it may be wondered whether the rule of eight is truly indigenous or rather is a Maori adaptation of the more familiar English system as used, pre-eminently, in hymn texts. Although some rule of eight songs appear to be pre-European, the latter possibility could not be ruled out until recently. Now, however, it can confidently be dismissed. Recent work indicates that the rule of eight is of at least Eastern Polynesian provenience and may well date back to Proto-Polynesian times. Kevin Salisbury has demonstrated multiples of six morae as characteristic of a Pukapukan song type called mako[3] and, using the New Zealand discovery of the rule of eight as a starting point, Steven Fischer has verified its use in the oldest witnessed chants from Tokelau, Mangareva, Hawaii, Mangaia, the Tuamotu Islands and other Polynesian islands and has used it to provide a tentative reconstruction of a Rapanui (Easter Island) song text until now regarded by scholars as incomprehensible.[4]

A detailed analysis of 15 rule of eight waiata has been published by the writer[5] and a condensed version is also available.[6] The following is a summary only of some of the salient points:
- The rule of eight applies not to all waiata but only to those exhibiting two-phrase music structure, with or without drags.
- Meaningless particles of all kinds, including but not limited to drag vocables, are excluded from the rule of eight count.
- Several particles such as *e, ka, me, ra* and possibly others have ambivalent status, sometimes counting as one for purposes of the rule of eight and sometimes two.

Although Biggs's discovery makes it possible to determine the line structure of rule of eight waiata without reference to the music, the music remains a useful guide in the following cases:
- Articles essential to meaning are occasionally left out in performance, evidently to achieve the required count of eight vowels to the half line. Their retention in published song texts can inflate the apparent vowel count beyond eight.
- The rising diphthongs *-ai, -ei,* and *au-* often count as one instead of two but in general may do so only when assigned to a single note in the music. If the component vowels are separately articulated as sung, the count is two.[7]
- Pseudo-diphthongs are sometimes formed in performance by attaching a single-vowel particle (usually *e, i* or *o*) to the final vowel of the preceding word. Rather more than half of such diphthongs count as one for purposes of the rule of eight. They can readily be heard in performance and are indicated in the McLean & Orbell transcriptions by a ligature joining the two vowels.
- Like adjacent vowels are often run together in performance and may similarly count as either one or two for purposes of the rule of eight. Again they are indicated in the McLean & Orbell transcriptions by ligatures.[8]

Like-vowel Ligatures

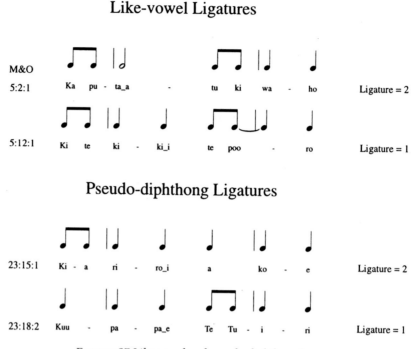

EXAMPLE 87 Like-vowel and pseudo-diphthong ligatures

Application of the rule of eight

Because vowel length is phonemic in Maori, it would be an advantage to translators if a rule could be found relating vowel length to musical length. Cases of doubt could then be referred to the music and translation would be aided. Analysis of rule of eight texts has allowed such a rule to be formulated. Because short vowels outnumber long vowels in the texts by eleven to one, it is not to be expected that musical length will follow linguistic length in every case. In practice, it is the 'marked' linguistic feature, namely the long vowel, which is found to correspond 95 per cent of the time, and short vowels are sung long whenever the music demands a long note. Thus, although note duration is an unreliable means of identifying short vowels, the correspondence of long vowels and long notes is high enough to permit uncertain long vowels to be identified with confidence from the music, especially if the words concerned appear more than once in different songs. It is noticeable that when a count is short in a rule of eight song, the half line concerned often contains an obsolete place or personal name whose pronunciation is currently unknown. The short count indicates that one or more vowels in the name must be long, and the coincidence of long notes with long vowels allows the actual vowels to be identified. An example involving the word 'Moria' occurs in Songs 19 (line 11) and 29 (line 9) of McLean & Orbell:

EXAMPLE 88 *Extracts from M&O 19 & 25*

In each case the phrase count is seven instead of eight, showing that one of the vowels written as short must be long. In Example 88a, the first and last vowels of 'Moria' are the only possibilities for the extra count because these are the only vowels that are musically long. In Example 88b, only the first syllable of 'Moria' is musically long so 'Mooria' is established as the correct pronunciation of this place name.

Structure of rule of eight songs

So far it has been seen that the rule of eight applies only to waiata exhibiting two-phrase music structure. Each pair of phrases consists of both a line of text and a musical strophe which is repeated throughout the song with or without 'drags'. Drags, if present, occur at the end of the second phrase and do not count for purposes of the rule of eight. The two phrases of the musical strophe are coincident also with textual phrases or sense units and each such unit contains eight morae.

Examination of rule of eight songs in McLean & Orbell reveals that most exhibit a pattern of four long notes or drags, two to each phrase, occurring regularly throughout the song. These long notes and/or drags occur in musically stressed positions at fixed points within the song. Other long notes may occur in the song but are normally subdivided, becoming long only when required to accommodate a long vowel. The fixed long notes, by contrast, are independent of the text, remain long at all times and form the basis of a rhythmic scheme common to nearly all rule of eight waiata. Example 89 reproduces a single strophe of each of several rule of eight songs.

Each strophe, as already noted, consists of two phrases. Each phrase can be seen to consist of two bars preceded by an optional anacrucis, and the four fixed long notes in each strophe are seen to occur in each case at the beginning of a bar. Unmetred or semi-metred songs are represented with beats of variable length. Regardless of whether a song is metred or unmetred, the following rules apply to produce a count of four musical units to the phrase or eight to the strophe:

	PHRASE 1					PHRASE 2			
	Anacrusis	Drag	Rem. notes	Drag	Rem. notes	Anacrusis	Drag	Rem. notes	Drag	Rem. notes

M&O
5
37
42
6
19
24
11
22

EXAMPLE 89 Formal scheme of rule of eight songs

• Each musically stressed long note or melismatic drag counts musically as one unless there is no remainder in the bar.

• If there is no remainder in the bar, a long note or drag counts musically as two.

• Each unstressed remainder counts musically as one.

• An anacrusis takes its time from the final or preceding bar and is not counted.

Given the existence of beats of variable length, rule of eight waiata are thus found to be governed not only by textual metre but also by musical metre, albeit of an unconventional kind. The half line or phrase remains the unit for the rule of eight text, the entire strophe becomes the unit for the corresponding rule of eight melody and the hiianga or drag is restored to importance as counting for purposes of musical metre though not towards the textual count. A practical consequence of this pattern is that any rule of eight text can be fitted to any rule of eight melody as demonstrated in Example 90 where lines from three different songs are fitted to the rhythmic scheme of Song 6 in McLean & Orbell:

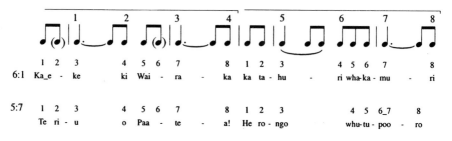

262

29:11	1	2	3_4		5	6		7_8		1	2	3			4	5	6	7		8
	Hoo	-	mai		he	ma	-	taa		ki - a		ha		-		e - ha - e		a	-	u

42:2	1		2_3		4	5	6	7		8	1	2	3			4	5	6	7		8
	I	-	naa		i	-	a	te	ko		-	re	he ma	-	na		ko ma - i		ho	-	ki

EXAMPLE 90 *Song lines fitted to the rhythmic scheme of M&O 6*

With the half line as the unit for the text and the whole line for the music, both text and music are seen to exhibit rule of eight metre and to do so within the confines of a single rhythmic model.

CHAPTER 16

SUMMARY OF STYLES

Despite some regional differences, especially in terminology, traditional Maori music is stylistically highly homogeneous both geographically and through time.

Named categories of song turn out to be as distinguishable in musical style as they are in terms of song use and textual content. Song types can accordingly be classified into recited and sung. Recited styles have no melody or line organisation and are differentiated mostly in terms of rhythm. Sung items, by contrast, are melodically organised and distinguishable mostly by their musical form. With few exceptions, both recited and sung types of song are performed in unison by groups of singers with a song leader. Performance is continuous without pauses for breath. Additive rhythms are characteristic. There are nine principal styles, four recited, four sung and one semi-sung.

RECITED STYLES

Karakia are incantations or invocations. When recited as an introduction to a speech they are known as **tauparapara**. They are performed by males either solo or, to ensure an unbroken flow of sound when performed in ritual context, by relays of two or more singers. The style is a rapid speech rhythm monotone punctuated by sustained notes and descending glides at the end of phrases.

Paatere (songs composed by slandered women) may be performed either solo or by mixed groups and are intoned mostly on one note but with prescribed continuous rises and falls of pitch near the ends of stanzas. Tempo is rapid, though not as fast as karakia, and characteristic rhythmic groupings, which otherwise would be 2/4 or 2/8, are modified to become additive. Songs in the same style but with especially virulent texts are called **kaioraora**.

Haka are posture dances with shouted accompaniment. Some, particularly haka poowhiri (welcome haka) are performed by both men and women but most, especially the **peruperu** or war dance, are nowadays performed only by men. Unlike karakia and paatere, they are strongly metric, in conformity with a beat marked by foot stamping and body percussion. Most are in compound metre. Cross rhythms can emerge as a result of additive textual groupings running counter to the foot stamp. The form is usually a responsorial alternation of leader solo and choral refrain. Funeral compositions in haka style from different tribal areas are known as maemae (Ngaati Tuuwharetoa), manawawera (Tuuhoe), pihe (Northland) and pookeka (Te Arawa). Also performed in haka style were work songs such as canoe-hauling songs, paddling songs and digging songs.

Hari kai are food-bearing songs performed by women. Like haka they are metred. They use the same rhythms as paatere but in regular 2/4 or 2/8 time.

Karanga are marae calls performed by women. Although essentially recited, they may be regarded as semi-sung. The texts are improvised using standard phrases and their rhythms follow the texts closely. They are performed on a monotone with a short melodic figure and a standardised descending cry marking the end of the message.

SUNG STYLES

Sung styles have scales with few notes, small melodic intervals, range within the musical interval of a 4th, and a strong emphasis upon a central intoning note, known as the oro.

Waiata are songs performed by mixed groups, usually in marae context as a kiinaki or relish after speeches. Most are laments. In Northland they are known alternatively as apakura. They take the form of repeated strophes, each coinciding with a textual line and ending, as a rule, with a leader solo, called the hiianga, performed usually on meaningless syllables. The musical strophe typically divides into two phrases, each consisting of a textual half line. Most waiata are musically non-metric. Many, however, have texts which exhibit quantitative or numerical metre. In 'rule of eight' waiata, the syllable count of a half line of text is exactly eight if short vowels are counted as one and long as two. Rule of eight waiata are characterised by a single rhythmic model such that any rule of eight text can be fitted to any rule of eight tune.

Pao are epigrammatic topical songs sung, generally for entertainment, by both men and women. Unlike waiata they are frequently metric. Most metric pao are triple-time songs with characteristic iambic rhythms. Also characteristic of many is an abundant use of rapid ornament. All pao take the form of two-line couplets, each couplet representing a verse or stanza. Frequently the line subdivides into two phrases, as in waiata. In contrast with waiata, the texts were conventionally extemporised, the composer making up the next verse while the previous one was being repeated by the chorus. Also different from waiata is the use in particular areas or by individual singers of all-purpose airs to which any pao can be sung. Swapping at will from one tune to another is aided by the use of a single metric scheme common to most pao. Effectively it is another 'rule of eight', consisting of eight standard (accentual) beats to the line and four beats to the half line.

Poi songs accompany the well-known poi dance in which the performers manipulate light balls attached to strings. The earliest poi songs appear to have been composed in recited haka and in paatere style. More fully documented poi songs are those developed after 1866 at Parihaka by followers of the Taranaki prophets Te Whiti-o-Rongomai and Tohu Kaakahi. Several styles emerged, of which the latest appears to have been that of the Te Atiawa people. As in waiata, there is a basic melody or strophe repeated line by line throughout the song. Each song is performed continuously from beginning to end, pausing only at the beginnings of stanzas where the leader provides a prompt by repeating the first word.

Oriori, as currently performed, are long, highly allusive songs whose texts are addressed, as a rule, to high-born children. Lesser such songs, which appear to have been simple lullabies, have not survived in the oral record. Again the form is different from waiata. Leaders perform solos not at the ends of lines, as in waiata, but at the beginning or end of each stanza. The lines are of variable length, following a characteristic 'sandwich' principle in which melodic figures mark the beginning and end of each phrase and a variable 'filling' appears between.

Game songs and some others are not unique in style but are performed in the style of other song types such as karakia, paatere, haka and pao.

BOOK 2
THE IMPACT OF
EUROPEAN MUSIC

CHAPTER 17

TYPES OF INFLUENCE AND CHANGE

SEALERS AND WHALERS

The first sealers in New Zealand began operating as early as 1792 at Dusky Sound in the South Island. The industry, however, was short-lived as seals were hunted almost to extinction within 30 years.[1] Pelagic whaling vessels began visiting New Zealand at about the same time, doing so in great numbers from 1805 onwards, by which time they were calling regularly at the Bay of Islands for food and water, and Maori crew were occasionally being taken on. Pelagic whaling began to decline after 1840 as did shore-based whaling a few years later.[2]

Both sealing and whaling stations were concentrated mostly in the far south of the South Island where there appears to have been only limited

Whalers at anchor off Kororareka in the Bay of Islands. Sketch by Louis Le Breton from Dumont d'Urville Atlas Pittoresque *1837–40.* PHOTO: *Alexander Turnbull Library, 26 MNZ¹/₄*

impact upon the Maori population.[3] The visits of whalers and other trading vessels to the Bay of Islands were of greater importance. They lasted much longer, triggered significant social changes and, as a result of trade in muskets and powder which they initiated, led ultimately to the devastating musket wars of the 1820s and 30s. However, there is no evidence that either sealers or whalers influenced Maori music. Few of the songs sung by them have survived even in the European repertoire, much less in the Maori.[4] To judge from remarks of the French navigator Duperrey, it would seem, indeed, that at the time in question, the Maori and European music systems were different enough to be mutually incomprehensible. Like other Europeans before and since, Duperrey, who visited New Zealand for two weeks in 1824, judged Maori music to be monotonous, but adds the significant observation: ·

> . . . if their singing was far from having the advantage of pleasing us, ours certainly did not win their approval. They received our most popular ballads with the coldest indifference, and the tough fibres of their souls were not in the least shaken by the martial airs which delight and excite a European.[5]

MISSIONARIES

Missions in New Zealand

Most of the early missionaries in New Zealand were sent by the Church Missionary Society (CMS) which represented the evangelical movement within the Church of England. The CMS remained alone in the field from 1814 when Samuel Marsden landed in the Bay of Islands until 1823 when the Wesleyans established their first mission station at Whangaroa. Roman Catholic missions did not begin until 1838 and were so beset with difficulties that little progress was made until after 1880. By this time, the CMS had achieved such a lead that it could not be overtaken. In 1840 there were 19 CMS, eight Wesleyan, and two Catholic missions in the North Island. The later relative status of the three main missionary societies can be gauged from the education grants to church schools during Sir George Grey's first New Zealand governorship (1845–53): half went to the Anglicans, a third to the Wesleyans, and a sixth to the Catholics.[6] Today, the Anglican church still has more adherents among the Maori than any other.[7]

Missionary influence

If sealers' and whalers' songs had little impact upon Maori music, the opposite was true of the missionaries. Their influence was profound, in terms both of activities which they discouraged and of those, especially hymn singing, which they introduced. Amongst activities interdicted by the missionaries were some, such as murder, theft and prostitution, which were acknowledged as evils also amongst Europeans. Maori practices which they strove to eradicate included cannibalism, infanticide, polygamy, slavery and warfare, together with associated customs and beliefs such as muru and utu, the 'law of tapu', tattooing and the war dance. As early as 1819, Samuel Marsden was enquiring of Thomas Kendall and the other missionaries at the Bay of Islands whether the natives had 'in any degree laid down their ferocious habits, such as shouting, dancing naked and sham fighting to inflame their passions, and to kindle their warlike ardour'. Kendall replied, perhaps prematurely, that they were not as addicted to their habits as formerly, though a year earlier he had confessed to having himself 'listened to and been partly infected with the profane and obscene rubbish contained in heathen songs'.[8] Kendall's ambivalent attitude was not shared by the other missionaries. According to A.S. Thomson:

> As many of the laments, songs and stories referred to love, war and superstition, several influential missionaries tried to bury them in oblivion, by describing them as heathenish compositions incompatible with Christianity.[9]

One of the missionaries referred to was undoubtedly Henry Williams of the CMS. In a letter to his brother-in-law in England, he wrote: 'I feel it necessary to prohibit all old customs; their dances, singing and tattooing, their general domestic disorders.'[10] In 1830 he commented, with evident self-satisfaction: 'Quietness and good order has succeeded to their native wildness, and now we never hear anything of their songs or witness their dances.'[11] The Waikato missionary Robert Maunsell was likewise happy in 1835 after hearing a Maori group repeating catechisms throughout the greater part of a night:

> It is gratifying to reflect that their native songs, most filthy and debasing, are fast giving way to a form of words not only more agreeable to the ear in sound but calculated to convey saving and edifying truths . . .[12]

Robert Maunsell (1810–94)

Wesleyans evidently concurred with the efforts of their CMS brethren. Similar sentiments to those of Williams and Maunsell were expressed in 1851 by the South Island Wesleyan Charles Creed who wrote to his mission headquarters from Waikouaiti:

> Christianity has indeed accomplished wonders amongst this people . . . The musket and the tomahawk have been laid aside for the spade and the reaping hook. The obscene and horrifying war songs and war dances have yielded to the songs of Zion and assemblies for the purpose of worshipping the true God.[13]

Charles Creed (1812–79)

The self-evaluations of the missionaries nevertheless need to be treated with some caution. The above passage was written only a month after Creed had written in his journal of an incident in which haka had been 'boldly taken up' and practised for three consecutive nights in the house of one Kahuti. The occasion was in the nature of a protest after Creed had refused to help pay for a boat whose purchase had been negotiated on the Sabbath. Sadly for natural justice, the outcome was victory for Creed. Kahuti was unable to pay for the boat and had to give it up, after which Creed helped the 'well behaved natives' to purchase the same boat. Later the 'haka men' applied to Creed for their 'case to be passed over' which he agreed to on condition that they provide him with a written statement that they would 'give up the haka'.[14]

Throughout Polynesia, one of the results of missionary intervention was the enforced abandonment of prohibited items, including song and dance. Another was the deliberate filling of the vacuum so created by substituting a repertoire of hymns whose texts, sentiments and tunes were of the missionaries' own choosing. These two topics are taken up in succeeding chapters.

THE COLONIAL REGIME

Large-scale colonisation in New Zealand began with the arrival of Edward Gibbon Wakefield's first New Zealand Company settlers at Port Nicholson, now Wellington, in January 1840. Thereafter, the European population grew rapidly. Within two years it is estimated to have reached 10,000. By 1851 it was 27,000. In 1861 it reached 98,000 and by the end of 1864 it exceeded 171,000.[15] The Maori population, by contrast, went into decline. Whereas in 1858 about half the population was Maori, in the next 30 years it dropped to only 7 per cent. By 1886, Maori people numbered fewer than 44,000[16] and were regarded officially as 'a dying race'.

In his book *The Oxford History of New Zealand Music*, John Thomson devotes two chapters to music in the first settlements and to related topics such as colonial balls and military and brass bands.[17] Some of the musical activities of the settlers are unlikely to have affected the Maori. Events such as balls, soirées, theatrical performances, opera and oratorio, instrumental recitals and orchestral and chamber music concerts were largely urban and, in colonial times, were probably exclusively European. There were nevertheless plentiful opportunities for Maori listeners to hear and begin to assimilate European music. Instruments such as fiddles, accordions, concertinas

Maori brass band, Rotorua, late 1890s. Photo: *Rotorua Museum of Art & History Te Whare Taonga o Te Arawa, Rotorua*

273

and mouth organs or harmonicas would have been heard very early. The same would be true of popular songs sung socially or informally in taverns and other venues. Brass and military bands were unquestionably influential. Thomson mentions that the enthusiasm of the Maori for bands led them to form numerous ensembles of their own such as the Parihaka fife and drum band of the 1890s.[18] Some were adopted from the Salvation Army which visited Maori settlements in the latter part of the nineteenth century teaching instruments such as the cornet and tuba.[19]

Another major influence was the music of the dance hall, particularly waltzes and polkas. A striking number of popular Maori songs of the early 1900s are in waltz time, and reference to Maori fondness for waltzes can be found earlier still in travel literature. Max Buchner, who visited Rotorua in 1876, wrote that at this time the younger generation at Ohinemutu preferred waltzes and other European dances to haka, and almost every evening a ball took place in an empty hut. He participated on one occasion at a moonlight dance, held in front of a meeting house to music provided by a soldier on a concertina, at which he said the girls danced extremely well, though he found the unevenness of the ground troublesome and was worried about treading on the girls' bare feet.[20]

THE MODERN ERA

Politically, the colonial era can be said to have ended in 1907 when New Zealand became a Dominion. In social terms it ended earlier, merging imperceptibly into what may be called the modern era during which the Maori population overcame the 'dying race' appellation and came more fully to terms with the European culture.

In earlier chapters it has been demonstrated that the traditional Maori music system was incompatible with the European. When such is the case, there are only a limited number of ways in which an intrusive music system can be accommodated.[21] All but one are exemplified by the Maori adjustment to European music. The exception concerns chordal structure or harmony which is absent in the Maori system but is a central, if sometimes only underlying, feature of European music. Central features of a music system are those essential to it. As such they are highly conspicuous and can only be knowingly adopted by the recipients. The Maori could have transferred or grafted harmony on to the traditional system but chose not to do so.[22] Instead, harmony is used only in genres such as hymns (Chapter 19) and action songs (Chapter 20) whose music is in acknowledged borrowed European idiom. The central elements of the two systems thus remained intact and mutually exclusive.

Non-central traits in a music system can be adopted into another music system only if they are compatible with it. Because they are non-central, such traits can be borrowed involuntarily and without the recipient being aware that change has occurred. A contemporary example of such a process at work is unknowing imposition of European scales and metre when young and middle-aged Maori try to learn traditional waiata without first becoming familiar with the style. This process is further discussed in Chapter 21.

When the elements of two different music systems are both non-central and non-compatible they are unable to interact. In such a case, the only possible relationships are either independence from each other or abandonment of one in favour of the other. Independence can take the form either of rejection of the intrusive system or of co-existence with it. Rejection occurred in the early stages of missionary attempts to teach hymns with European tunes. Co-existence began when Maori became bimusical in both the traditional Maori and the European systems (Chapters19–20). Abandonment manifests itself by song loss or diminution of repertoire (Chapter 18) or by substitution when a new form replaces an old one, as when missionaries finally succeeded in replacing indigenised hymns with European ones (Chapter 19) and, pre-eminently, when Maori became proficient enough with European music to practice it on equal terms with Europeans. The latter process belongs with the history of European music in New Zealand and is beyond the scope of the present book to document in full. It is germane to note, however, that it began early amongst those who had the benefit of a mission education. Lady Martin, writing primarily of the 1850s, said it was quite common at this time for young New Zealanders to play the harmonium and act as organists in their native churches.[23] Thomson comments upon the fine tradition of Maori singers in New Zealand.[24] Two of the earliest, Princess Te Rangi Pai and Princess Iwa (Chapter 20) were associated with Maori concert parties at the turn of the century. Later singers have been prominent in European art music: the bass Inia Te Wiata (1915–71) became a leading opera singer at the Royal Opera House, Covent Garden; and the best-known living New Zealand singer is undoubtedly soprano Dame Kiri Te Kanawa (1941–). Other Maori singers and instrumentalists in the European classical tradition have remained undocumented by scholars but there have doubtless been many of them. One such was John (Hoani) Halbert (1890–1958) of Invercargill who, though nearly blind from unsuccessfully treated cataracts, taught the present writer the violin in 1944–47. He was a fine virtuoso violinist who delighted in playing the great violin concertos and the most difficult works by composers such as Paganini, Sarasate and Wieniawski.[25] Lastly, mention must be made of the numerous Maori musicians and performing groups who have contributed to New Zealand's popular music industry.[26]

After a music system has gone through a period of abandonment, a belated awareness of its value may lead to attempts at revival. Because it necessarily follows some form of break in continuity, revival is seldom able to replicate the original style exactly. Maori efforts at revival are discussed in Chapter 21.

CHAPTER 18

SONG LOSS

When the writer began field work in 1958, traditional Maori music was everywhere in decline, except amongst members of Tuuhoe tribe where the Ringatu religion had helped to keep waiata singing alive. Even at this date, almost 40 years ago, it sometimes happened that at funerals and meetings no older songs were performed and it was left for action songs to fill the gap. A number of reasons for this decline have been identified in two articles by the writer.[1] Some of the causes were found to be recent but others were in the nature of continuing influences which applied as much in the past as they do now.

Missionary impact on Maori music has been discussed in Chapter 17 where it was shown that the missionaries discouraged traditional singing and successfully introduced hymn singing. The missionaries, however, were by no means exclusively to blame for the demise of songs which their hymns appeared to replace. Song loss was already a well-established process long before the missionaries arrived. An examination of early song collections reveals that many of the songs in them were recent at the time of collection, showing that, in common with other Polynesians, the Maori people had a vigorous composing tradition with new songs regularly displacing the old. In such circumstances, when composition is ongoing, it is the style that survives rather than individual songs. Song loss in Maoridom became a problem only after the singing tradition declined to a point where few new songs were being composed. At this stage, the older repertoire became in effect 'classical' or moribund, a shrinking resource invested with tapu associations that, far from protecting it, contributed in time to its further decline. Some of the components of this decline have been documented in earlier chapters. It has been shown that Maori songs were always sung for a reason. Songs deemed no longer appropriate for an occasion simply ceased to be sung. Loss of function also caused the disappearance of some or all of the songs in some entire use categories (e.g. paddling songs and food-bearing songs). Others might have followed were it not that new uses were found for them. The haka, for example, has become a staple of modern concert parties.

Reinforcing the frequent reluctance to sing except when there is occasion to do so is the widespread belief that to sing a waiata tangi (lament) except on the occasion of a death is to invite a death. In Northland this has caused the virtual extinction of waiata singing, because too few singers were willing, for fear of the consequences, either to teach or record songs.[2] Fear of supernatural penalties has also created other barriers to transmission. In Chapter 9, it was explained that to improve memory and as a precaution against memory lapses, conditions of strict tapu were observed when esoteric songs such as karakia and Taranaki sacred poi were being taught. Such songs had to be performed word-perfect if disaster were to be avoided. An example is given by Grace who quotes the karakia 'Tena tapu nui' and the story that Tuuhoro, the son of Tama-te-kapua — captain of the ancestral Arawa canoe — died as a result of reciting it incorrectly.[3] And, most consequential of all, because a single word was omitted from the karakia at the naming of the great culture hero Maui, he failed in his attempt to win immortality for humanity by crawling up the vagina of the mythical goddess of death, Hine-nui-te-poo, in order to slay her.[4] Although it probably began with karakia, the same attitude to mistakes seems eventually to have transferred to nominally secular songs, such as waiata, so that memory lapses came to be regarded in the same way as omens of death or disaster. Inability to finish a waiata is especially feared: 'It's no good', said one informant, 'if you can't finish it; it's a bad luck'.[5] And even more dire consequences can ensue: 'If you make the least little mistake they say you die.'[6] A few young people in the 1960s told the writer they did not dare to learn waiata for this reason.

Another cause of song loss has been decline of memorising ability coincident with literacy and increasing dependence on printed texts. Few singers today know many songs; certainly there is no one of the calibre of one of Best's informants who is said to have given him no fewer than 380 songs![7] Equally, it is doubtful if any present-day singer has the ability, formerly said to be commonplace, of picking up a song aurally after just one or two hearings. So long as this could still be done, songs could be learned in context, on the occasion of their use, and the beliefs that precluded their performance at other times would not have affected their transmission. Today, by contrast, when most Maori live not in rural communities but in large cities, there are few opportunities to hear traditional songs at all, much less the requisite number of times for casual learning to be possible.

A further potent barrier to the effective transmission of songs is ownership. Details have been given in Chapter 8 of sanctions which restrict songs to their own tribal areas and, when song loss has progressed beyond a certain point, to individuals who may prefer to die with the songs rather than pass them on to persons they consider unauthorised. Sometimes an individual actually identifies himself with the songs known to him and may believe that if a song is given to anyone else he will literally lose it. The song is like a piece of material property which, once given away, will be forgotten by the donor. When he has given away his last song, the singer becomes an 'empty barrel', no longer able to sing.

For a time in every community which is undergoing song loss, the effects may be masked by the dynamics of group performance. The most frequently performed traditional songs, and as such of perhaps greatest utility, are waiata which are sung by groups of singers at meetings as a kiinaki or 'relish' after speeches during the rituals of encounter described in Chapter 1. So long as a group has a competent leader, a song can be reasonably well sung even if no one else in the group knows the whole song. The leader provides cues at appropriate points in the song, and words or lines which particular individuals do not know can be carried by the leader and other members of the group. When a group becomes depleted in numbers, and particularly if a leader dies, this process breaks down and the songs formerly sung by the group can no longer be performed. At this point it becomes possible to recover fragments only of the singing tradition from a few scattered individuals until, with their death, the song tradition of the area comes entirely to an end.

CHAPTER 19

HYMNODY

HYMN SINGING IN NEW ZEALAND

Perhaps the first hymn ever heard on New Zealand soil was the familiar Old Hundredth, as sung by Samuel Marsden at a Christmas Day sermon at the Bay of Islands in 1814 when he introduced Christianity to the Maori.[1] Marsden's own thoughts at the time are on record:

> I rose up and began the service with singing the Old Hundredth Psalm; and felt my very soul melt within me, when I viewed my congregation, and considered the state they were in.[2]

The response of his Maori congregation was less favourable than Marsden might have wished. It appears to have been one of uncomprehending wonder, as Marsden was the first white man the listeners had ever seen:

> When he stood up to pray they all said, 'O friends, he stands up!' When he commenced singing a hymn, they exclaimed to one another, 'O friends, he opens his mouth!'[3]

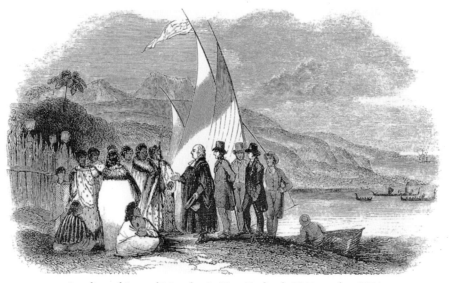

Landing of Samuel Marsden in New Zealand, 19 December 1814

By 1823 at the latest, however, Maori were themselves singing hymns: there are two references in Samuel Marsden's diary of that year (on 9 and 24 August) to natives singing hymns in their own language.[4] Hymn singing soon, indeed, became an integral part of CMS services as shown by numerous references to hymns and hymn singing in missionary journals and by the following outline of a Sabbath day service held at the Waimate mission, which was established in 1831:

> A native hymn is first sung; the liturgy of the Church of England, which has been translated and printed in the language of the country is then read; which is followed by another hymn . . .[5]

By 1833 — only 19 years after Samuel Marsden preached his first sermon — hymn singing among the Maori was certainly widespread and was diffusing faster than even the missionaries had believed possible, often by former slaves who had gained their freedom as a result of missionary intervention.[6] An illustrative incident in 1833 was described by the missionary Henry Williams:

> We assembled all (about one hundred and fifty or two hundred) to evening service. . . . We commenced, as usual by singing a hymn; but what was our surprise when we heard our whole congregation join and sing correctly with us! In the prayers, also, the responses were given by all, as the voice of one man.[7]

According to the missionary William Williams, the people on this occasion had not previously been contacted by missionaries but had received instruction from three youths who had lived with mission families at Paihia.[8]

Another person who was impressed by Maori congregational singing was Edward Markham, who wrote in 1834:

> The service began and there were full 300 in the Chapel. The whole of the congregation joined. There are few Country Churches in England where it is performed half so well. No noise or bustle. The lessons were read and the Psalms sung to Familiar Church Tunes. I could have fancied myself in England but for the Motley group before me.[9]

Such excellence seems to have been unusual, however, and at this date may have been limited to one or two places in the Bay of Islands where missionisation first began. William Brown, for example, was more impressed by Maori enthusiasm for hymn singing than by their aptitude for it:

> The missionary natives are now [1840] very numerous. . . . They sing hymns every morning and evening — a species of devotion in which they appear to take great delight, notwithstanding their utter want of all musical talent.[10]

Others also gave testimony of Maori devotion to hymn singing. According to William Williams, natives of Wairoa in 1840 were so eager to obtain hymns that they made their own manuscript copies. One copy given to Williams was written in gunpowder, evidently on a wooden slab which had first been rubbed with oil and then dusted with gunpowder to make a surface upon which the words of the hymn could be scratched.[11] Edward Jerningham Wakefield observed in 1841 that all were 'mihanere' or converts at Patea, where 'They sang hymns night and day, almost incessantly'.[12] William Puckey described the following incident in 1845 at Kaitaia:

> . . . attracted by the sound of singing we went to the spot from whence the sound proceeded and found that a number of the Missionary natives (perhaps about sixty) had assembled and were having their evening prayers. They were singing the praises of their Redeemer, and some of the sailors only a few yards off were singing songs, some very obscene.[13]

On 28 November 1847, William Williams mentions in his journal how the natives commenced family prayers with a hymn: 'This practice is without exception among the professed Christians. How different this is from an English community.'[14] And Captain David Rough, first harbour master in Auckland, observed in 1849 how in Maori encampments:

> Before wrapping themselves in their blankets for sleep, the New Testament was invariably drawn from a bag which some old man or young teacher carried, a hymn was sung, the glad tidings read with reverence, and prayer offered to the Father of all with as much apparent earnestness and devotion as may be observed in any assembly of Christian worshippers.[15]

By the middle of 1842, according to the biographer of the Wesleyan missionary James Watkin, a knowledge of hymns, prayers and catechism had spread at the hands of converts to every native settlement south of Moeraki in the South Island: 'Night and morning in every village one could hear the sounds of song and prayer.'[16] The same was observed by Charles Heaphy (1820–81) while exploring the West Coast of the South Island in 1846:

> The natives, by their chattering during the night, prevented our getting any sleep. They passed it in an incessant row of singing, chanting, and talking; one only giving over and lying down to be followed by the commencement of another. When they had exhausted the news and finished their songs, for want of other occupation they commenced anew with the recital of the morning service, not for purposes of devotion, but merely as a pastime, and perhaps, to show their proficiency. Before morning we thus heard repeated four litanies, and the whole collection of their version of the Psalms, together with three or four creeds and a marriage service. These were repeated with every variety of intonation of voice; and finally they recited the whole morning service in grotesque pronunciation and manner of delivery, which with these natives is a species of never-tiring amusement.[17]

Paihia Mission Station from an original by Lt Thomas Woore RN

The rapid spread of hymn singing throughout the Maori population was undoubtedly aided by the manifest ability they displayed in learning to read and write and by the publication of immense printings of hymns from the mission presses, often in editions of many thousands.[18] The first mission presses were set up in 1834 by William Colenso for the CMS at Paihia and in 1836 by William Woon for the Wesleyans at Mangungu.[19]

Mangungu Mission Station, rear view c.1850s. PHOTO: *Alexander Turnbull Library, F 5432¹/₂*

PRINTINGS OF HYMNS AND PSALMS
Church Missionary Society

As early as 1827, 400 copies of a book containing seven hymns in Maori was printed in Sydney by Mr. R. Davis (W5),[20] and other books containing 19 and 27 hymns respectively followed in 1830 and 1833 (W6&9). In 1839, the Paihia Press in New Zealand issued a Maori edition of the Book of Common Prayer which included 42 hymns in Maori (W31). By 1860 the number of hymns available had risen to 52 (W321) and by 1876 to 56 (W214). The definitive CMS collection of hymns (W649), called *He himene mo te Karakia ki te Atua [Hymns in the Maori Language]*, was first published in 1883. Edited by Archdeacon W.L. Williams, it superseded the old inset hymnals and is still in use by the Anglican Maori church. It contained 172 hymns, with further editions in 1887 (W735), 1896 (W911) and 1905[21] raising the number of hymns to 175, 183 and 187 respectively.

In 1840, 16,000 copies of a Maori translation of the psalms by William Puckey were printed by the CMS mission printer Colenso under the title *Waiata a Rawiri [Songs of David]* (W38). In the same year the psalms were bound in with the first complete edition of the CMS prayer book (*Ko te Pukapuka o nga Inoinga*) (W39) and in later years continued, with revisions, to be printed with the prayer book.

Wesleyan

The earliest publication of hymns in Maori by the Wesleyans appears to have been in 1837 when 35 hymns, including 14 taken from the CMS hymnal, were printed together with prayers and extracts from the Gospels (W23). In a diary entry of 10 April 1837, at Mangungu, William Woon refers to this work as 'A Harmony of the Gospels', stating: 'Young and old, rich and poor, are desirous to possess a copy and ere long we hope hundreds of copies will be in circulation.'[22] Another diary entry, of 29 September 1838, refers to printing a second edition of the hymns (W23a), and from 1839 onwards, hymns were published as a supplement to the Wesleyan Maori prayer book, beginning with 30 hymns (W36) and rising by 1894 to 114 (W878). From the 1879 edition onwards (W559), the Wesleyan prayer book also contained the Psalter, printed from the same plates as the 1848 CMS prayer book (W169). A revised Wesleyan Maori prayer book containing 121 hymns together with the psalms was published in 1927 and reprinted in 1938 with the title *Ko te Pukapuka o nga Inoi me era atu Tikanga* and abbreviated cover title *Nga Inoi me Nga Himene*.[23] This, though long out of print, is still in use by the Methodist Maori Mission.

THE AUTHORS

The 1894 Wesleyan Prayer Book and hymnal (W878) contains a unique list in which the authors of the hymns are named 'as far as known'.[24] Eighty-one of the 114 hymns, including 19 which are also in the 1883 CMS hymnal, have the authors thus identified. The Wesleyan missionary John Hobbs emerges as by far the most prolific of the authors, with 28 hymns to his credit, followed by Edward Marsh Williams[25] with 14. The next greatest number of hymns were composed by Bishop William Williams of the CMS (8), and the Wesleyans Thomas Buddle (6) and Nathaniel Turner (4). Seven of Hobbs's hymns and 11 of Edward Marsh Williams's are retained in the 1938 Wesleyan hymnal. According to Herbert Williams in a note about the 1883 CMS hymn book (W649), a large number of the new hymns in it were translated by E.M. Williams.

John Hobbs (1800–83)

Nathaniel Turner (1793–1864)

Thomas Buddle (1812–83)

Edward Marsh Williams (1818–1909). Photo:
Alexander Turnbull Library, 111124¹/₂

John Whiteley (1806–69)

William Williams (1800–78) at age 52.
From a lithograph by Charles Baugniet

Missionary journals occasionally mention the composition of hymns: John
Hobbs, in an 1825 diary entry at Wesleydale, refers to composing one of his
hymns in the native language, possibly the first of the many which he was
later to write. It is of special interest because of his decision to abandon
English singing 'to allow the domestic boys and girls to sing in the native
language'.[26] Hobbs, as a Wesleyan, was here adopting 'the position of the

285

Church Missionary Brethren in the Bay of Islands'. On 16 December 1826, he writes of composing another hymn in Maori which he hoped was 'more spiritual than the others I did before'.[27] It was 'E ihu, e te Oranga', later to be printed as Hymn 79 in the Wesleyan Maori hymnal (1938). His daughter Emma wrote glowingly of his Maori hymns as follows:

> Hymns written by Father in 1825 are considered by those who understand the language to be among the best. There is such a natural simplicity of expression. They are favourites with the natives and will last as long as the Maori language.[28]

The Wesleyan missionary William Woon, in a letter written on 24 February 1837, mentions Nathaniel Turner, John Whiteley and himself as having written nearly 30 hymns of various metres.[29] John Bumby, writing from Mangungu in 1840, refers to a hymn 'Me haere taatou nei' (Hymn 48 in the Wesleyan Maori hymnal (1938)) composed by Nathaniel Turner which 'was powerfully sung and with great unison'.[30] But many of the earliest hymns fell by the wayside, failing to survive hymn-book revisions which purged the less popular hymns from the repertoire in favour of new compositions; some never reached the hymnals at all. As an example, William Marshall attended a service in 1834 at which he heard a hymn in Maori, 'Whakapono mai e Ihu', whose composition he attributed to William Yate of the CMS; later he gives the text of another early hymn, 'Hoomai ra pea, e Ihu', but neither appears to have entered the repertoire.[31] Similarly, the Wesleyan James Watkin, who was at Waikouaiti, Otago, from 1840 to 1855, 'composed a few hymns for congregational singing' but having acknowledged that some were of imperfect scansion he disclaimed the possession of the poetic gift.[32] None of his hymns, as far as is known, is in the published Wesleyan hymnals. Saddest of all is the story of the CMS missionary Thomas Whytehead who went to Waimate in 1843, only to die there in the same year. He introduced to the Maori his translation in rhyming verse of the evening hymn of Bishop Ken ('Glory to Thee, my God, this night') beginning 'Hei korooria ki te Atua'. His followers used to sing it under his window, calling it the 'hiimene hoou' (new hymn) of the sick minister.[33] In a diary entry of 1–8 May 1843, Sarah Selwyn refers to Whytehead's dying effort as a legacy the Maori people 'were greatly pleased with' although they could not at first catch the tune.[34] The hymn was printed in leaflet form without date or imprint (W96) but was never admitted to the printed collections.

CMS missionaries appear to have been much more conservative in retaining hymn texts than the Wesleyans. Of 42 CMS hymns extant in 1840, four-fifths were still in the hymnal in 1905. On the other hand, of 83 hymns in the Wesleyan Maori hymnal of 1848, no fewer than 60, or 73 per cent of the total, had been dropped from the repertoire by 1927. Even allowing for the greater time span in the latter case, the trend seems clear. The most likely explanation is that the early CMS hymns were truly more popular and more enduring than most of the Wesleyan ones. Confirmation of this can be found by comparing the two repertoires for hymns in common. Only one hymn of Wesleyan origin, namely 'Tapu, Tapu, Tapu' by Thomas Buddle, a translation of the well-known 'Holy, Holy, Holy' by Dykes, seems ever to have been adopted into the CMS repertoire, but the Wesleyans, by contrast, borrowed heavily from the CMS: of 58 hymns common to the 1894 Wesleyan hymnal and the CMS hymnal of 1905, all but 'Tapu, Tapu, Tapu' were taken by the Wesleyans from the longer established CMS repertoire.

THE TUNES

In considering which English hymns and psalms were most likely known and sung by the CMS, one must remember that these missionaries belonged to the Evangelical branch of the Anglican church and that New Zealand missionisation began in 1814. The Evangelicals were in sympathy with Methodist ideas and practices, one of which was the adoption of hymn singing rather than the metrical psalms which Calvin had prescribed as alone suitable for Christian worship. The repertoire of hymns available to them was the same as that later to be used in New Zealand by the Wesleyans.

At this time, there was no standard approved hymn book. The definitive *Hymns Ancient and Modern* (1861)[35] was still almost half a century in the future. The hymns sung by the Evangelicals came from earlier, mostly Methodist, collections and compilations such as Madan, *A Collection of Psalms and Hymns Extracted from Various Authors* (1760). There was, nevertheless, a well-established system of naming and classifying hymns and hymn tunes with which all of the missionaries would have been familiar. The standard practice was to apply a unique name to each hymn tune, and to indicate a textual metre for each hymn specifying the number of syllables in each line. The most common method of naming tunes was after the place of origin following a precedent set in Est's Psalter of 1592 and Ravenscroft's Psalter of 1621. Alternatively the tune might be named after the composer, a saint or some other person or by the use of a word or phrase associated with the particular hymn.[36] The system of tune metres was devised in the days when words and music were seldom printed together. In principle, a tune composed for a hymn of a particular metre could be used for any other hymn with the same metre. Hymn books still customarily include a metrical index in which tunes of the same metre are grouped together, facilitating tune substitution. As will be seen, the composers of hymns in Maori made full use of both systems. Each hymn in Maori was composed to conform to a chosen metre and the metre was indicated at the beginning of the text as in English hymnals.[37] In later Maori hymnals a tune was also designated.

One difficulty in addressing the problem of which hymns might have been sung in nineteenth-century New Zealand is that missionary practice cannot be assumed to have been uniform. The available evidence seems to show that it did, in fact, differ from time to time and from place to place.

During the 20 years after 1830, Henry and William Williams's Paihia mission had the benefit of a barrel organ, built by A. Buckingham of London and sent in 1829 from England as a gift from the Williams brothers' maternal uncle, the Rev. E.G. Marsh. It was operated by turning a handle at the rear and was equipped with three interchangeable barrels, each capable of playing five tunes.[38] Henry Williams's journal records that an organ — evidently a different subscription instrument[39] — had been written for in 1828,[40] and the reactions of the Williams family to the gift organ two years later are also on record. On 27 August 1830, Henry Williams wrote:

> We were some time before we learned the particulars of the organ. They were most gratifying and I trust it will add much solemnity to our psalmody. It has come without the slightest injury, and the first evening all were delighted with its sound . . . We shall send an order for some more tunes. I should very much like to have the Te Deum and a chant or two.[41]

His brother William was favourably impressed with the sound:

> The organ has reached us safely . . . We put it together the first night it was landed, and have ever since found it to answer exceedingly well. It is sufficiently powerful to fill a much larger chapel than our own.[42]

General view of Williams's barrel organ. The display pipes are gilded flat-backed wooden dummies.
PHOTO: *Wanganui Regional Museum*

Henry's wife Marianne was overcome with nostalgia for her homeland, England:

> All the females as well as the males met in the chapel to hear the new organ the first week it arrived, and I was glad the overpowering sensations which its full and melodious sounds produced and all the recollections it aroused were a little moderated before the Sabbath.[43]

Tunes known to have been played by the organ include Bedford, Hanover, Manchester, the 'Old Hundredth' and the National Anthem.[44] Hymns accompanied by it included 'O God our help in ages past', 'Christ the Lord has risen', 'Come thou everlasting spirit', 'O, for a heart to praise my God', 'A charge to keep I have' and 'O worship the King'.[45]

The Williams barrel organ was heard in 1834 by a traveller, William Barrett Marshall, who commented that the chapel at Paihia had 'a well-toned hand-organ, which New Zealanders as well as English, accompanied with their singing'.[46] In a journal entry written at Paihia on Sunday 22 March 1840, it was commented upon also by Sarah Mathew, wife of the first surveyor-general of New Zealand, Felton Mathew:

> The church is a very neat little building like a schoolroom with a sort of pulpit at one end and a small organ at the other; it is a barrel organ and plays the Psalm tunes very well.[47]

The organ remained with the Williams family until 1898 when it was acquired by the Wanganui Museum.[48]

So far as is known, the Williams brothers were the only early missionaries fortunate enough to possess a barrel organ. For the remainder, whether CMS or Wesleyan, the need for hymn tunes was met by recourse to tune books, some published in the late eighteenth century and others which began to proliferate early in the nineteenth century. A number of tune books likely to have been used by missionaries are now in the archive collection of the Kinder Library at St John's College, Auckland, including three which were owned and personally autographed by John Hobbs.[49] Firm evidence concerning the use of tune books appears in the diary of William Woon who wrote from Mangungu in 1837 pleading: 'we are badly off for a selection of tunes and the collections of Leach, Rippon & others would be a acquisition to the mission'.[50] The books he wanted were James Leach's *New Sett of Hymn and Psalm Tunes* (1789) and John Rippon's *A Selection of Psalm and Hymn Tunes* (c.1791).[51] Later in Woon's diary is a reference which allows the hymn book he used to be identified absolutely. On 3 June 1841 appears the entry: 'Sung that beautiful and incomparable hymn, "Let earth and heaven agree" 37th page of our hymn book this evening at family worship.' The hymn book was John Wesley's *Collection of Hymns for the Use of the People Called Methodists . . . with a Supplement*, first published in 1780. An undated copy

William Woon (1803–58).
Photo: *Auckland City Libraries*

(London: Mason) in the Kinder Library indeed has the hymn 'Let earth and heaven agree' '4-6's & 2-8's', on page 37, confirming this, or a reprint with identical pagination, as the edition used by Woon.[52] In a later edition of the same hymnal with tunes (1877), it appears as Hymn 34 to the tune Darwell's.

On 23 June 1845, in Woon's diary, is the entry:

> In the evening . . . Sung a sweet Tune out of the Centenary Tune Book, called 'Holy Mount'; 4-7s to 'Holy Lamb — who thee receive', Garland[53] playing the seconds on the Flute, and we had a delightful harmony. This is an admirable collection, and worthy of the 100th year of Wesleyan Methodism.[54]

The same hymn and tune are referred to on 25 August, this time attributed to the *Union Tune Book*.[55] The two passages are important because they confirm that both tune books were used by Woon.

In 1847, the problem of finding tunes was solved for Methodists by the publication of *A Companion to the Wesleyan Hymn-Book*[56] with 228 tunes for use with the *Collection*. Another passage from Woon's diary, dated 18 May 1858, proves that he made use of the *Companion* once it was available:

> That beautiful hymn in our Collection comforted my mind while with streaming eyes from time to time my son, and precious wife, played on the piano, and she sung, that exquisite composition by Arnold, St. Paul's, to the words 'Prostrate with eyes of faith I see' &c in the Companion to the Wesleyan Hymn Book.[57]

The number of tunes available to Wesleyans was later increased to 338 with the publication of *The Wesley Tune Book* (1871),[58] and finally to 1008 by the publication in 1877 of the complete *Collection* with tunes, including many from sources such as *Hymns Ancient and Modern* (1861), the *Congregational Hymn and Tune Book* (1862), the *Bristol Tune Book* (1863), the *St. Alban's Tune Book* (1877) and the *London Tune Book* (1877).[59] This book continued to be used until 1904 when it was superseded by *The Methodist Hymn-Book with Tunes*.[60] A specifically New Zealand contribution was the *New Zealand Hymnal* (1862)[61] which contained 222 hymns without tunes, followed by *The Tune Book for the New Zealand Hymnal* (1866) and the *New Zealand Hymnal with Tunes* (1871), both compiled by Dr A.G. Purchas of St John's College. Purchas's effort was, however, wasted as, according to his namesake, Henry T. Purchas, the work never achieved widespread use and was soon driven from the field by *Hymns Ancient and Modern*.[62]

A few tunes and/or hymns are specifically named in early travel accounts or missionary journals, and of the former about a third are used in later Maori hymnals as tunes for hymns in Maori. The others were evidently either found unsuitable or failed to become popular and dropped out of the repertoire. An example occurs in an 1826 journal entry of William Williams who mentions singing 'the 9th hymn in Newton's Collection, "Jacob's Ladder"'.[63] The reference is to the collection known as the *Olney Hymns* by John Newton and William Cowper (first published 1779). The ninth hymn, entitled 'Jacob's Ladder — Gen.xxviii.12' and beginning 'If the Lord our leader be / We may follow without fear' is one of the many excluded from modern hymnals. Another example is the hymn in Maori composed by John Hobbs in 1825, set by him to the English tune 'Auburn' which likewise does not appear in modern hymnals.[64] Hobbs records the interest taken in attempting to sing it as 'truely gratifying' but it would have been dauntingly difficult for his mission 'boys and girls' to manage, ranging as it does over an entire octave with numerous leaps of 5ths and 4ths to negotiate.

EXAMPLE 91 *The hymn tune 'Auburn'*

Additionally there is indirect evidence of attrition. One of the first missionaries in New Zealand was John Gare Butler (1791–1841) who served as superintendent of the CMS mission from 1819 until he was dismissed by

Samuel Marsden in 1823.[65] His principal contribution was the compilation of a hymnal of no fewer than 425 hymns and four doxologies entitled *A Selection of Psalms and Hymns from the Best Authors*, published in 1828. In it are many well-known hymns which are still sung today such as 'All hail the power of Jesus' name' (A&M 217) and Bishop Ken's Morning Hymn 'Awake my soul' (A&M 3); also there are less well known but still extant hymns by the Wesley brothers and others. Most noteworthy are the large number of hymns which have ceased to be sung during the century and a half since publication. Many of the latter were selected from the collections of Philip Doddridge (1702–51), some of whose more than 300 hymns were published in 1755;[66] John Newton (1725–1807), co-author of *The Olney Hymns* (1779) and one of the founders of the Evangelical School; and Isaac Watts (1674–1748), known as 'the Father of the English hymn',[67] who is said to have written over 600 hymns.[68] Most of the hymns by these authors had already been dropped before Butler compiled his hymnal, as well as a majority of the 6500 hymns attributed to Charles Wesley[69] and all but a tiny proportion of the 400,000 hymns listed in Julian's *Dictionary of Hymnology* as having been written by the end of the nineteenth century.[70]

ST JOHN'S AND TAUPIRI

In 1842 New Zealand's first bishop, George Augustus Selwyn (1809–78), arrived in New Zealand on the ship *Tomatin* with a small party of ecclesiastics and their wives. It has been said of him:

Bishop Selwyn (1809–78)

Sarah Selwyn (1809–1907) in 1841 two years after her marriage. Steel engraving by F.C. Lewis after a painting by George Richmond. PHOTO: Hocken Library, Dunedin

Selwyn found Anglicanism in New Zealand in a string of mission stations and left it a properly constituted province of the Church of England. He was the missionary bishop *par excellence* . . .[71]

A less flattering view is that before Selwyn came to New Zealand,

perfect harmony obtained between the Wesleyan mission and the Anglican mission . . . Christian natives [of both missions] . . . sang the same hymns, recited the same creed, and used the same form of service. The converts of the two missionary societies looked upon one another as belonging to one body. When Bishop Selwyn and other High Church clergy arrived in New Zealand, all this was changed.[72]

There was, in fact, a profound conflict between Selwyn's high-church aspirations and conduct and the evangelical values held dear by most of the missionaries. In the end there was open hostility between him and Henry Williams, ostensibly over land, which culminated in the latter's dismissal from the CMS and reinstatement five years later after complaints against him had been heard in England.

Amongst the passengers on the *Tomatin* were several with training in music. The bishop, in a letter written on board, refers in one passage to his wife, Sarah:

You would be pleased with our church . . . Sarah leads the Hymns and Psalms, which are sung well, as four of our gentlemen are practised singers, and several of the steerage passengers join in good tune.[73]

Sarah, in one of her own letters, ascribed the leadership role to Charles Reay (*c*.1808–46):

Mr. Reay was made Precentor of the Tomatin Cathedral and under his auspices we got up a good deal of music, Psalm singing and chanting in a very creditable manner. Mary's[74] book has been of use, and Sarah Cotton's also,[75] and had there been more music books on board, we shd. have got up a good deal — for we had a base,[76] 2 excellent altos and a tenor — with a knowledge of music.[77]

Two of the remaining 'gentlemen' referred to would have been William Bambridge (1819–79) who later taught singing at Waimate,[78] and Seymour Spencer (*c*.1812–98), an American later described by Sarah Selwyn as the 'main stay' of the choir at Waimate.[79] Also on board was Elizabeth Dudley (d.1845)[80] who was 'a gifted pianist . . . [later] much in demand for musical soirées [at Waimate]'.[81]

In 1838, as a Fellow of St John's College, Cambridge, Selwyn had published a 114-page polemic entitled 'Are Cathedral Institutions Useless?' in which he argued in favour of centres for church education. Soon after arriving in New Zealand in 1842, he put his ideas into practice by establishing his own antipodean Theological College of St John's to provide instruction

Henry Williams (1792–1867)

for young men of both races studying for holy orders. Selwyn began his college at the tiny Waimate North Mission House but, as a result of conflicts with the CMS concerning lease of the site, moved it within two years to Tamaki, Auckland.[82]

From the beginning, singing was evidently part of the curriculum, and the chanted form of service was being tried. Even before the move to Auckland, the bishop reported from Waimate, in July 1843:

> Many of our Students are able to sing; so that we have the Psalms chanted Morning and Evening; but at present we have no organ. The effect, however, of our 9 or 10 voices, with the ladies and school-boys is far from being displeasing.[83]

Within a few years, at Auckland, high standards of choral singing were reached as a result of the efforts of Dr A.G. Purchas (1821–1906) who was appointed to St John's as a medical officer in 1846 and ordained as a deacon a year later.[84] Sarah Selwyn described the arrival of Dr Purchas at St John's as follows:

> About this time, Mr. and Mrs. Purchas arrived from England to join the staff. Besides his profession of medicine, Mr. Purchas brought with him a knowledge of music which was a great gain. He . . . was an excellent teacher and ere long we had singing in the chapel which was popular and greatly enlivened the service. I should not say the Maoris are musical, but the people are excellent timists. They soon learnt many catches and glees; used to sing 'Bacon and Potatoes'

St John's College, Auckland, as painted by the Rev. John Kinder in 1874. Photo: *Auckland City Art Gallery*

(Fra Martino) as a dinner bell in default of a real bell or gong. So the summer and early autumn passed.[85]

On 17 August 1846, she commented:

Music is really beginning to flourish among us. The English boys cannot yet sing in parts as well as the Maori lads. We have a chanted grace with the Amen in parts sung every day in hall now. When the Bases are not out plowing the effect is very good.[86]

In 1850 there is further reference to Dr Purchas:

He taught the boys both English and Maori to sing and the chapel services were greatly enhanced by their music. They learned to sing in parts, my friend the cook being very musical. . . . Mr. Purchas had classes for secular singing also, and all about we used to hear snatches of old familiar catches, etc.[87]

Arthur Guyon Purchas (1821–1906).
Photo: *Auckland City Libraries*

In his history of St John's College, J.K. Davis gives a detailed account of the daily routine and other activities during Purchas's tenure:

> At 7 a.m. the day was begun with Morning Prayer in the chapel. The prayers were intoned. The lessons were read by the scholars, the first in English, the second in Maori. The canticles were chanted, one in each language. The versicles were sung, sometimes in English, sometimes in Maori. No metrical psalms or hymns were used, excepting a Maori hymn after the first collect . . . Until a harmonium was procured, the musical part of the services was led off with a tuning fork.
>
> On Monday, Wednesday and Friday evenings, a singing class conducted by Dr. Purchas was held . . . This was attended by the two boys' schools with their masters, and by as many of the lay associates as were free at the time.
>
> The routine on Tuesday was always different . . . The Harmonic Society met each Tuesday evening. Glees and other kindred music were practised one week, and anthems and other church music the next.[88]

Purchas's success in teaching singing at St John's was aided by his introduction of a figure notation form of sol-fa with notes running from 1 to 8 for the major scale and 6 to 6 for the minor. The system is explained in an appendix to a publication by Purchas in which he provides figure notations of 31 hymns for use in his singing classes at St John's.[89] The figures were sung to the syllables Ta Ru To Wha Ma No Tu Wa which were abbreviations of the Maori numerals from one to eight (tahi, rua, toru, whaa, rima, ono, whitu, waru).

ST. ANN's.   C. M.

Key I.   Time 4.

5 : | 3 6 5 8 | 2 7 8 ‖ 5 | 8 5 6 *4 | 5 : ‖

2 : | 1 1 1 3 | 4 2 3 ‖ 2 | 1 3 3 2 | 2 : ‖

5 : | 5 6 8 8 | 6 5 5 ‖ 5 | 6 7 8 6 | 7 : ‖

7̄ : | 1 4 3 6 | 2 5 1 ‖ 7̄ | 6̄ 3 1 2 | 5̄ : ‖

7̄ : | 8 6 2 7 | 8 6 7 ‖ 5 | 6 8 2 7 | 8 : ‖

5 : | 5 4 4 5 | 3 *4 5 ‖ 3 | 4 5 4 2 | 3 : ‖

2 : | 8 8 2 2 | 3 2 2 ‖ 8 | 8 8 6 5 | 5 : ‖

5 : | 3 4 2 5 | 1 2 5̄ ‖ 1 | 4 3 2 5 | 1 : ‖

The hymn tune 'St Ann's' as written by Purchas in figure and conventional notation (Purchas [1848] No.3 and Purchas 1866 No.39)

Lady Mary Ann Martin, who came to New Zealand in 1842 with the Selwyns,[90] was actively involved both with the work of St John's College and that of the nearby St Stephen's School for Native Girls (established in 1846). From the following account by her of a Maori wedding at which pupils performed, it would seem that the Purchas figure system was used at both institutions:

The Maori boys and girls between the speeches sang English glees and catches with great spirit. It was a pleasant surprise to find that the New Zealanders, when properly taught, had much musical talent and very good voices. We had noticed, from the first, the perfect time that they kept, not only when responding in church, but when singing songs as they paddled. But their native music, when they chanted their old songs, was harsh and monotonous, and their attempts to follow our hymn-tunes most deplorable. No sooner, however, were the young people in the school taught to read music by the figure system, and trained by regular practices weekly, than we found out the gift of song that was in them. The girls used to sing some of Mendelssohn's Chorales with great spirit and accuracy.[91]

The Purchas system was also successfully used in the Waikato at the Taupiri mission of Benjamin Ashwell (1810–83) who attended St John's College before being ordained in 1848.[92] Ashwell wrote in 1852 of both Selwyn's institution at Auckland and his own at Taupiri:

> The children at both schools sing and chant English tunes in parts — and to hear the children of cannibals singing first seconds tenor and bass to some of our beautiful tunes and hymns causes a thrill of joy which only a missionary can know.[93]

Ashwell listed singing as one of the subjects taught at his Taupiri school and gave the credit for any proficiency 'to the Rev. A.G. Purchas who introduced the figure system' and to his wife Harriet who, as a result of her thorough understanding of music,

> was able to carry out the plan efficiently. In a short time our school took four parts in singing, and chanted a part of our beautiful service on Sundays, and could sing in English, glees, rounds, anthems, and hymns.[94]

Richard Taylor visited the Ashwells early in 1851 and again just over a year later. On the first occasion there were 26 girl and 10 boy boarders whose

Woodcut by Eduard Ade of Ashwell's Maori School at Taupiri

progress in singing was described as 'very creditable'. On the second, there were 'near fifty boarders male and female, young and old', who sang 'with great precision'.[95] By 1858 the standard of singing was remarkable indeed. Mrs James Stack, who visited the Ashwell's Taupiri establishment in that year, recorded in her diary:

> After tea we spent a very enjoyable time listening to the school children sing-ing. I was more surprised by their knowledge of music than by anything else I had yet witnessed. They sang correctly in parts difficult music by Mendelssohn and other composers, such as 'Sleepers Awake', 'To God on High', 'Dark Shade of Night', and the 'Hallelujah Chorus'.[96]

Two points arise out of the descriptions of singing at St John's, St Stephen's and Ashwell's Taupiri mission. The first is that in a privileged, closed, board-ing-school environment, with a rigid daily routine, trained musicians were able to achieve high standards of European singing with Maori young peo-ple.[97] The second is that references to 'chanting' show this form of the Eng-lish service to have been practised at both St John's and Taupiri after 1846. This was at the same time consistent with Selwyn's high-church aspirations and a natural outcome of the advanced musicianship practised at St John's. The following remark by William Bambridge in his 1842 diary indicates that the chanted service was probably also tried at St John's in the Maori language:

> In the evening studied Maori after practising with Mr. Spencer[98] some chants set to Maori words. The effect was tolerably good.[99]

There is no evidence, however, that Anglican chanting was practised at Maori missions anywhere else in New Zealand at or before this time.[100] Most missionaries, in fact, would probably have condemned it as 'Puseyism'.[101] Henry Williams, indeed, specifically repudiated it, and had a long-running dispute with Selwyn concerning it. In 1847, after a visit to St John's, he wrote to Selwyn suggesting that the Wesleyans and Presbyterians might choose to have their children educated in Anglican church schools if this were not regarded by them as too great a sacrifice. He added:

> It seems therefore to be the more desirable to avoid any unnecessary cause for offence, such as I believe the practice of intoning to be . . . It is true that in our cathedrals at home the service is always chanted . . . but I much doubt whether it can be asserted that it leads to edification . . . The practice of intoning the service has of late been introduced in many churches at home together with other novelties of crosses, candlesticks and the like but . . . has convulsed the church to its very centre.[102]

A month later he confided in a letter to his fellow missionary Alfred Brown:

The more I see of the Bishop the more I feel that he is unsound at bottom . . . I relieved my mind before I came away by writing a letter upon intonation and candlesticks. He made an allusion to it afterwards and expressed an intention of modifying matters.[103]

But the bishop did not do so. A year later, when Williams again visited St John's, and even 20 years afterwards at St Paul's Church,[104] Auckland, he was 'grieved' to find the responses still being sung.[105]

EARLY DIFFICULTIES

In areas where mission stations were first established, and in contrast with the eventual successes with young persons at St John's and Taupiri, there is evidence that adult Maori at first experienced difficulty with European music and their standard of performance in it was poor. The not very flattering opinions of William Brown, Sarah Selwyn and Lady Martin have already been noted.

The Auckland pioneer John Logan Campbell, who arrived in 1840, commented in his book *Poenamo* upon the singing of a Maori psalm to a tune which he supposed had been taught by a missionary. He claimed to find nothing either European or Maori about it. Any Maori lament, chant or song 'save the war song', he said, 'would have been better than the hideous incongruity into which the ill used psalm tune had drifted'.[106]

Dr Henry Weekes (1804–94), surgeon-superintendent to the Plymouth Company, visited a Maori chapel at Cloudy Bay in 1841 where he heard the Old Hundredth sung

in loud bass, all singing in unison and slow. They invariably ended in a key or two lower than the one they commenced in, which was caused by their frequent use of a flat semitone, instead of a natural. There was a touch of the savage about it altogether strange and peculiar.[107]

W.H. Lyon was incredulous at the rendition of another familiar tune, Tallis's Canon, at Ohinemuri in 1873:

How the ghost of the poor old composer must have shuddered and groaned as they sang!! Each note was dragged out to at least five times its right length and the number of false notes was legion. They sang with loud but tremulous voices, and a good deal of uncertainty I thought. I should hardly like to say positively that they all sang the same tune, though they were quite at one to time, there were dischords here and there that were increased perhaps, by the harshness of the voices. I have heard the good old tune executed, 'often still oftener' have I heard it 'murdered' but such a 'diabolical outrage' upon it as this, is surely unparalleled![108]

'NATIVE AIRS'

Inability to sing European music is to be expected where, as in the case of the Maori, the indigenous music system is markedly different. Moreover, it is to be expected that in such circumstances the first attempts to sing European music would bear more resemblance to the indigenous system than to the European one. Naturally the Maori preferred to wed the Maori hymn texts, composed by the missionaries, to familiar Maori tunes. This process was well understood by Richard Taylor, who wrote on 26 April 1839:

> . . . the lads are very fond of singing but certainly they have no notion of music. Their native airs embrace no more than three or four notes and they carry no more into the hymns they sing, indeed it is the most discordant singing I have ever heard, no country choir in England being worse . . .[109]

In November the same year, Henry Williams wrote of a service at Waikanae: 'We sang two hymns, the tunes of which are purely native — quite original.'[110] A few days later he met a chief who said he knew several hymns but could not catch the airs so had composed his own, again 'quite original'.[111] In 1845, Sarah Selwyn went on a canoe journey up the Manawatu River, and wrote the following after spending Sunday on shore at a large village:

> The hymns were sung, not with English tunes but after their native notions which are peculiar. The scale did not seem to contain more than three or at the most four notes, the precentor holding fast to one of them as each verse was ended. The choir which was the congregation, after he had howled his note for

Richard Taylor (1805–73)

the first few words of the next verse, all struck in simultaneously and sang (?) to the end, breaking off suddenly, all but precentor who howled on.[112]

The passage is important because it proves that not only Maori scales but also the traditional manner of performance, with leader solos and chorus, were carried over into the singing of hymns. The same form of hymn singing was observed eight years earlier at Waiapu, East Cape, by George Clarke, who accompanied William Williams on his first missionary visit to the area in 1837. They found that returned slaves who had been released in Northland had already introduced Christianity and their own form of hymn singing and had assembled for them a congregation of more than a thousand people. 'It was then,' says Clarke, 'a common custom for the "leader" [of a hymn] to sing the first line by himself, and then the people joined in with a roar.'

> Mr. Williams struck up the 'Old Hundredth', but when he got to the second line not a soul fell into the tune, and on all that sea of upturned faces there was a look of blank surprise and unmistakable disgust. The 'Teacher', however, rose to the occasion, and stepping up to the pulpit, said, 'They don't know that tune, sir, let me start one they can sing.' So he made his *start*, and every face began to lighten. With a sound like the bursting of thunder, they took the second line out of the leader's mouth, and, as it were, carried off in a roar, like the noise of many waters, all the rest of the singing.[113]

CMS missionaries seem universally to have disapproved of the war dance and to have done their best to discourage it. Generally, however, they did not object to songs, and this explains their tolerance of hymn singing to Maori airs. Even Alfred Brown, who referred in his journal both to 'obscene dances' and 'filthy native songs',[114] liked native hymn singing when he heard it at Oputao in 1845: 'Being unable to sing European tunes, they had adapted some plaintive native tunes to the hymns, which they sang with pleasing effect.'[115] And in the following year he enthused: 'The hymn was sung to a native tune in which the whole congregation joined and the effect was perfectly thrilling.'[116]

Hymn singing to Maori airs can also be documented at Pukehika in the Wanganui area in 1848, at Otaki in 1880 and at Hukatere, near Patea, in 1891. John Hobbs wrote in his diary on 29 October 1848: 'The teacher asked me to take the sermon and he read the prayers. Their singing was in native tune.'[117] Elizabeth Colenso mentioned a service at Rangiatea church in Otaki, where 'the Maoris sang the hymns with a kind of Maori chant'.[118]

And, at Hukatere, Taranaki, on Christmas Day 1891, as reported by the Rev. W. Gittos, who was visiting the area:

> . . . the first hymn given out by a Maori local preacher was an old Maori chant, in which all joined most heartily, the women taking up the chorus in real Maori style.

Interior of Rangiatea church at Otaki

These chants, Gittos went on to note, had the advantage of most European tunes in simplicity and elasticity 'as they answer alike for long short or peculiar metres'.[119]

It is to the missionary John Whiteley that we are indebted for the only notation that the writer has so far found of early Maori hymn singing. On Wednesday 14 July 1841, at Harihari in Taranaki, he recorded:

Was much interested in hearing a native tune sung to one of Brother Turner's hymns; the simplicity and suitability of both induced me to attempt the music which is as follows:[120]

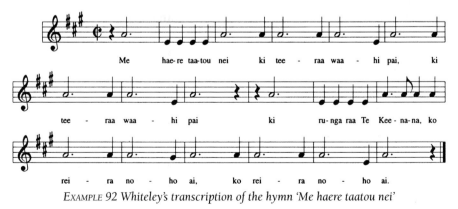

EXAMPLE 92 *Whiteley's transcription of the hymn 'Me haere taatou nei'*

The text can be found as Hymn 48 in the Methodist Maori hymnal[121] but it is the tune which is of greatest interest. Containing, as it does, clear evidence of both Maori and European characteristics, this notation is a revealing example of acculturation at work. Purely Maori characteristics are the strong durational tonic and the use of only three notes. European influence can be seen in the use of regular metre and, most uncharacteristic for the Maori, the interval of a perfect 4th throughout the song instead of the smaller intervals of major 2nd, minor 2nd and minor 3rd. This leads one to suppose that the first characteristic of the European music system to be picked up by the Maori may have been the tonic-dominant relationship. Perhaps only the bass line was heard and the melody ignored.

Another Maori hymn (McL 395) is notated below. It is the writer's own transcription of a hymn recorded in 1963 from Henare Toka of Ngaati Whaatua tribe. According to the singer, this hymn was an early one adapted from a waiata air in 1814. It can be seen that there are many non-European characteristics. The scale could pass as European, but its centric organisation around a strong durational tonic is typically Maori. Moreover, the scale has only four notes, its range is limited to a 4th, and the final is not on the tonic.[122] Other Maori characteristics are the absence of metre, the presence of meaningless syllabifying at the ends of lines, and a marked terminal glissando at the end of the song.

EXAMPLE 93 *Hiimene: McL 395 as sung by Henare Toka*

The hymn is probably the best known of all Maori hymns,[123] sung nowadays, however, not to a chant tune, but most often to the following unequivocally European melody:[124]

Ta - ma ngaa- kau maa - ri- e, ta - ma a te A - tua,

tee - nei to - nu ma - tou, a - ro-hai - na mai.

EXAMPLE 94 *Hiimene: The modern tune of 'Tama ngaakau maarie'*

Hymn singing to native airs was by way of an interregnum. Its appearance in Taranaki as late as 1891 was exceptional.[125] In most areas, missionaries persisted with the use of English tunes for congregational singing, forcing the Maori effectively to become bimusical. The European system became the approved standard for hymns and the Maori one was sidelined for traditional use. Only a handful of hymns to traditional tunes have been recorded, all in the 1950s and 1960s from the few persons who still knew them. One, in pao style, recorded in 1966 from Eruera Stirling of Ngaati Porou,[126] seems to owe its survival to being adopted into customary context. According to the singer, it was sung when Sir Apirana Ngata was dying and was often sung by Ngaati Porou elders when persons were dying. It is Hymn 175 in the Anglican Maori Hymn Book,[127] sung elsewhere to the quite different European tune, 'Maidstone'.[128]

Taa - ku nei e koa_a - i au, ko ngaa wha - re o te A - tu -

a, aa - taa - hu - a_a - na mai ee - nei to - hu o te pa - i.

EXAMPLE 95 *Hiimene: AMPM 0232.9 Beginning of Hymn 175 as sung by Eruera Stirling*

PSALMS AND RESPONSES

In English churches, after the sixteenth century, there were two principal forms of psalm singing. Used mostly in cathedrals, and replacing the more elaborate plainsong of the Middle Ages, was a modified form of Gregorian chant known as Anglican Chant. The alternative metrical psalms, brought together in the so-called 'Old Version' Psalter of Sternhold and Hopkins in 1562[129] and 'New Version' of Tate and Brady in 1696, had simple tunes and strict time suitable for congregational use. With the rise of the modern hymn, they fell progressively out of use in England in the nineteenth century except for a few, such as the Old Hundredth, which remained popular enough to be retained in hymn books. There are occasional references to them in

New Zealand missionary and travel literature, of which some have already been quoted.

As happened for hymn singing, there is a strong possibility that before 1838 some psalm singing in New Zealand was to native waiata airs in communities Christianised by converts. According to Arthur Thomson, although two-thirds of the natives at this time had never seen a missionary, masters of whalers reported that the 'aborigines' far away from the mission stations 'prayed night and morning in nasal psalmody, and chanted Christian psalms to heathen tunes'.[130] Additionally, Charlotte Godley, during a visit to Otaki in 1850, mentions hearing the Maori in Rangiatea church 'sing a Psalm to one of their own airs' which she said was 'exactly like the chanting in the Roman Catholic cathedrals when it is performed by the priests and without accompaniment'.[131] No Maori psalms of this kind appear, however, to have survived in the oral record.

In missionary times, as has been seen, the chanted form of Anglican service, including psalmody, appears to have been practised principally at St John's and at Taupiri. Most CMS missionaries would not, in any case, have had the musical training to be capable of teaching or performing Anglican Chant. Even in England, chanted psalms were sung primarily in cathedrals and collegiate churches until the advent of the Oxford Movement which influenced Selwyn in New Zealand. In ordinary churches, the psalms of the day were not chanted but read or spoken alternately, either by minister and clerk or, in parish churches, by minister and congregation.[132] There can be little doubt that this method was used also by missionaries in New Zealand. Indications of it can be found in entries in both CMS and Wesleyan missionary journals which refer to 'repeating' the psalms.[133] Moreover, from the first printed collections of hymns and psalms in Maori onwards, psalms are called waiata and hymns are called himene. The latter word is a transliteration of the English word 'hymn'. 'Waiata', however, is the Maori word for song, and it is noteworthy that Maori psalm singing of today takes the form not of organised melody with different pitches but of monotonic chanting. The same is true of the responses. At a Maori service observed in All Saints Church, Auckland, in 1969, the Ten Commandments and the psalms took the form of alternation between minister and congregation.[134] The singing was monotonic, with some of the congregation singing at the 3rd above. Sometimes a few of the women added an inverted 5th so that the chanting appeared throughout to be on a chord. At the end of each phrase — as marked by commas in the text — there was a descending glissando. Other parts of the service, such as the Lord's Prayer and the general confession, were performed by the congregation alone in the same style, but with sustained notes at the end of each phrase and the glissando reserved for amens. The introduction of harmony stems from European influence, but a terminal glissando is traditional in waiata singing and is purely Maori.

The above style of monotonic church singing is one which the Maori people have evolved for themselves, and the most likely progenitor is spoken or quasi-spoken delivery. Evidence for this can be found in a footnote statement Henry Williams made in 1833 about Maori congregational responses in prayer:

> The responses of a Maori congregation are most gratifying to a cultivated ear. They fall naturally into monotone, while the native perception of 'time' is so keen that the words sound 'as the voice of one man.' We have something to learn from them in that respect.[135]

'Nothing,' said Sarah Selwyn in 1845, 'could be finer than the responses and most of all the creed. It was like one great voice.'[136] Numerous other writers, from 1828 onwards,[137] although often critical of Maori hymn singing, also praised the 'perfect time' and unanimity of Maori responses in the service, surpassing, according to several, anything to be heard in England. Arthur Thomson commented: 'The liturgy in the Maori dialect is singularly beautiful, and the effect of a large congregation uttering the responses indescribably impressive.'[138]

LATER HYMNODY

A landmark event for Anglican Maori hymnody was the publication in 1883 and reissue in 1905 of *He Himene mo te Karakia ki te Atua* [*Hymns in the Maori Language*] in which, for the first time, a tune as well as a metre was designated for each and every hymn.[139] The Wesleyans followed suit with their combined prayer book and hymnal of 1927 and 1938[140] and the Presbyterians with the issue of their own Maori hymnal *Nga Waiata me Nga Himene a Te Hahi Perehipitiriana* in 1933.[141] In each case, the tunes chosen came mostly from the hymn books in current use by the respective parent churches: namely, *Hymns Ancient and Modern* by the Anglicans, *The Methodist Hymn-Book with Tunes*[142] by the Methodists and *Church Praise*[143] by the Presbyterians. Additionally, a few tunes in the Anglican Maori hymnal were drawn from *The Bristol Tune Book*[144] and *The Hymnal Companion*[145] and from Sankey's *Sacred Songs and Solos*. The Methodist hymnal was likewise supplemented from Sankey and the Presbyterian hymnal both from Sankey and from other Gospel collections such as *Alexander's Hymns No. 3*.

TUNE SUBSTITUTION

Without confirmation from early sources, it cannot be known for certain whether any of the tunes designated for Maori hymns in the later collections are the same as those employed when the hymns were first sung. It is especially difficult to determine what tunes might have been used by the Wesleyans because so many hymns were dropped from the hymnal before 1927. The only tunes known to have been used by them as early as 1848 are

'Calcutta' for the hymn 'Ko a mua ra a Ihu'[146] and 'Rule Britannia' for the hymn 'E Ihu, e te Kingi nui'.[147] By 1927, the former was no longer in the hymnal and the latter was being sung to 'St Matthias'.[148] For the more conservative Anglicans, who were much less prone to change the tunes of established hymns, it is possible to determine what tunes might have been used in 1840 by ruling out those whose dates of composition post-date the corresponding texts. Of 42 CMS hymns extant in 1840, only eight (19%) had gone from the repertoire by 1905 and of the remainder, no fewer than 23 of the 34 (68%) could have been sung to the same tunes in 1840. It is nevertheless clear that both denominations practised large-scale tune substitution, in part by taking advantage of new tunes as they became available, albeit the Wesleyans more than the CMS. As well, tune substitution was forced on them when different standard hymnals were adopted by the several denominations and not all of the earlier tunes were available in them. Both types of change can be illustrated by examining a list of 35 hymns common to the three main Maori hymnals as adopted from the CMS (1905) by the Wesleyans (1938) and the Presbyterians (1933). The Wesleyans changed to a different tune ten times from choice and three because the tune was not in the Methodist hymnal (1904). The Presbyterians changed seven times from choice and four times because the tune was not in *Church Praise* (1907). Since this time, older tunes have continued to be replaced by new ones, especially from revivalist hymnals, and some of the younger people are even reported to be experimenting with rock tunes.

HYMN-SINGING STYLE

Transcription into music notation of hymns in Maori from recordings reveals the tunes — and, in most cases, harmonies as well, if sung — to be remarkably faithful to the same tunes as notated in standard hymnals; often even the key is identical. The main features distinguishing Maori performances from European ones, are the Maori texts, the characteristic timbre of the singers' voices, generally slow tempi, and a conspicuous use of portamento between notes.[149]

CHAPTER 20

THE MODERN GENRES

For most people, Maori music is synonymous not with the older traditional forms such as waiata, but with modern songs whose melodies are not Maori in origin but European. Most familiar of all are the most recent: those known generally in English as action songs and in Maori as 'waiata kori' (lit. 'action songs') or 'waiata-a-ringa' (lit. 'hand songs', referring to the characteristic hand gestures). Amongst the antecedents of these songs were the hymns taught by the missionaries. Others may now be considered.

TRANSITIONAL SONGS

In previous chapters it has been noted that the central elements of the Maori and European music systems are incompatible and have remained mutually exclusive. The opposite is true of European traits which are non-central to the Maori system. These could and did intrude into traditional forms such as waiata and pao as well as poi and game songs, resulting in historically transitional songs with elements of both the European and the Maori. Most such songs appear to have emerged towards the end of the nineteenth century and at the beginning of the twentieth.

Of the traditional song types, pao appear always to have been more ephemeral than waiata. As a result, more tend to be of recent composition and they are correspondingly more likely to have European-type melodies. As well, their simple two-line structure lends itself to European melodies in simple binary form of eight bars per line. An example with an unequivocal European air is the well-known 'Hoki hoki tonu mai',[1] recorded (Example 96) from Kino Hughes with verses 1 and 2 in opposite to usual order.

Further examples are two pao (Example 97), again in waltz time and again in regular four-square form, from a 'Round Robin' of five such songs recorded from a Tuuhourangi group in 1970.

Game songs are another category which make frequent use of European airs, as shown in Chapter 4.

A sure indication of European influence in Maori songs is the presence of major tonality, as in the examples below. Even when a melody conforms in most respects to traditional norms, European influence may still be revealed

EXAMPLE 96 Pao: McL 1190 as sung by Kino Hughes

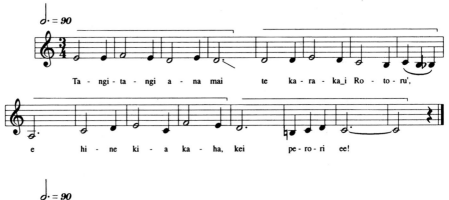

EXAMPLE 97 Pao: McL 822 B&E as sung by a Tuuhourangi group

EXAMPLE 98 Pao: McL 21 as led by Te Mamaeroa Hanuera

310

by the tonality as in Example 98, another pao,[2] in which a major 3rd predominates as a structural interval.

Another indicator of European influence is the presence of metre, again as in the above examples and in the following, composed in the 1880s, from a song about football as sung by Para Iwikau of Ngaati Tuuwharetoa.[3]

EXAMPLE 99 *Waiata: First stanza of M&O 5 as sung by Para Iwikau*

A distinguishing characteristic of many transitional songs is that their use of European elements is often partial or incomplete. Such songs strike the European listener as unpredictable or 'quaint' because the non-Maori elements are incompletely integrated and some of the rules of European music have, in consequence, been broken. Similar 'irregularities' have been documented for acculturated styles from elsewhere in Oceania.[4]

Phrase structure may be non-standard, as in the following poi (*c.*1908) which has a Europeanised melody in 2/4 time but with three-bar phrases, rather than the conventional four, and a spoken two-bar ending:

EXAMPLE 100 *Poi: McL 814 as sung by a Tuuhourangi group*

Most revealing as evidence of transitional status are time changes which, while appearing to be completely natural when the song is sung, run counter to the European convention of uniform metre. A good example is the following pao[5] which the singers said became popular during the decade of about 1890 to 1900. The tonality is strongly major though the scale lacks the 4th degree. The time is 2/4 with interpolated bars of 3/4:

EXAMPLE 101 Pao: First stanza of McL 20 as led by Te Mamaeroa Hanuera

SONGS IN EUROPEAN IDIOM

Amongst the predecessors of action song are songs with European melodies composed from the late nineteenth century onwards. Perhaps amongst the earliest are some reported by St John who writes of the bodyguard of the second Maori King, Tawhiao Matutaera (1825–94), singing 'Maori songs to English tunes' at Horahora.[6] The date is not stated but must have been during the decade from 1863 to 1873, most likely in 1871, when St John accompanied Donald McLean on a tour of the Waikato.[7] Of about the same vintage, and possibly the very same, were temperance songs in Maori published in 1873 and 1885 by C.O. Davis (1816–87) who composed his verses in rhyme and set them to popular English hymn and secular tunes of the day such as 'Pembroke' and 'Home Sweet Home'.[8]

Other early Maori songs with English melodies were first and foremost a product of the entertainment industry. Concert parties employing them most likely originated in the 'thermal wonderland' of the Rotorua area where, long before the establishment of the town in 1881, tourists came to view the nearby world-famous Pink and White Terraces[9] and to bathe in the hot

Maori children performing a haka. Photo: *Alexander Turnbull Library, Tesla Collection 16753 ¹/₁*

springs. Concerts are said to have begun at the starting point for the terraces, Te Wairoa village, in the 1860s[10] and were commonplace by the 1870s. At Ohinemutu village and elsewhere, visitors were entertained with 'haka parties' and, after the Puarenga Stream at the Maori village of Whakarewarewa was bridged in 1885, children regaled the visitors with 'penny hakas' and by diving for pennies from the bridge. At first only poi songs and haka appear to have been performed by entertainment groups, as at the Rotorua welcome of the Duke and Duchess of Cornwall and York in 1901, and it would seem likely that poi songs to European-type melodies were amongst the earliest progenitors of the later action song.

ALFRED HILL

Although born in Australia and resident there for most of his adult life, Alfred Hill (1870–1960) achieved a reputation not only as New Zealand's first professional composer of art music but also, if largely by default, as an authority on Maori music. He published two collections of early European-ised Maori songs which he himself had collected and arranged.[11] His childhood was spent in Wellington. When he was 15 years old he went to Leipzig to study music at the conservatorium there. Five years later he returned to Wellington where he wrote a pageant, *Hinemoa*, first performed in 1897, based on the well-known Maori legend of Hinemoa and Tutanekai. Subsequently he composed other works based on Maori themes, notably a Maori Symphony (1899), an opera, *Tapu or the Tale of a Maori Pah* (1902), a 'Maori'

313

Alfred Hill (1870–1960) at
about 36 years of age

Quartet (1913), a cantata, *Tawhaki* (1931) and a number of songs including 'Waiata Poi' which became immensely popular. With others of Hill's songs, it was adopted enthusiastically into the repertoire of Maori concert parties and remained a staple for at least 40 years.[12]

MODERN POI

One poi of about 1908 vintage has been referred to in the chapter on poi,[13] where it was shown that European melodies were already being used for poi songs before 1900, particularly, it would seem, in the tourist area surrounding Rotorua.

Like action songs (see later), modern poi songs sometimes use ready-made melodies of European origin. An example is Princess Te Puea's poi song of tribute to the fourth Maori King, 'E Rata e noho',[14] composed in 1917 to a tune which, like one of the tunes of the well-known 'Hoki hoki tonu mai', has more than a passing resemblance to 'Little Brown Jug'. The rhythms are in fast metrical paatere style. Example 102 is the first stanza of a rendition, recorded in 1938 from Te Puea's concert party, with banjo accompaniment, at the opening of Turongo Meeting House, Ngaruawahia.[15]

A possible survival of earlier seated poi is the well-known canoe poi of today which depicts the paddling of a canoe and is accompanied, as a rule, by a European-type song. Familiar to most New Zealanders, from the first line of the chorus, as 'Come Oh Maidens' or 'Come Ye Maidens' is the waltz-time 'Hoea ra te waka nei', by Paraire Tomoana (1868–1946) of Hastings,[16] composed during the First World War[17] and first published in 1919.[18] It was sung at Gisborne in 1919 to welcome Maori soldiers back from the war[19] and a year later it was performed by a group called the Hawke's Bay Maori

EXAMPLE 102 Poi: First stanza of AMPM RNZ 2.1 as performed by Te Puea's concert party

Entertainers, doubtless Tomoana's own, at Rotorua during the visit to New Zealand of the Prince of Wales.[20]

Del Mar provides an eye-witness account of a possibly different canoe poi performed by about 40 girls in the Rotorua area during the First World War. More so than the performances of today, it mimed a complete canoe journey from the launching to the beaching of the canoe, with a storm and capsizing en route.[21] A similar presentation with lighting effects depicting a sunset and a thunder storm was staged in Wellington at the Grand Opera House in 1914 as part of a 'Grand Entertainment' by the New Zealand Natives' Association.[22]

A variation of the same idea is for the paddling actions to be done without the poi. A well-known Arawa canoe song of this kind, again in waltz time and again reminiscent of 'Little Brown Jug', is 'Uia mai koia'. Example

Tuuwharetoa women performing 'Uia mai koia' at Waitangi, 1934

315

EXAMPLE 103 Beginning of canoe song as performed by Guide Rangi's concert party

103 is the beginning of the song as performed by Guide Rangi's Concert Party in 1949.[23]

The earliest performances of the canoe poi were before 1905. The Rotorua guide and entertainer Maggie Papakura[24] said the genre was invented by her sister, Guide Bella.[25] The statement seems credible as a canoe poi was performed at the Christchurch Exhibition of 1906–07 by an Arawa group led by Bella[26] and again later by Maggie Papakura's own group which went to England in 1911. The accompanying song at this time was performed by the soloist of the group, Princess Iwa (see later), and may not have been in European idiom. A review of a performance by the group at the London Palace in October 1911 describes the item as follows:

> One of the poi dances represents the arrival of the Arawa tribe in New Zealand about ten centuries ago, and is called the 'Canoe Poi'. Six Maori maidens sit in the direction of one side of the stage, and six others are posed the reverse way. They then bend to and fro — in imitation of paddling a canoe — and respond to the chanting of Iwa. They use their pois in such a way they appear to produce the sound of the water being cleaved by a boat.[27]

Arawa poi girls performing the canoe poi at the Christchurch Exhibition

316

OTHER EARLY SONGS

Possibly New Zealand's most familiar Maori song is the former Channel 2 TV close-down or 'Goodnight Song', 'Hine e hine'.[28] It was composed by Fanny Rose Howie (née Porter) (1868–1916), a contralto better known under her stage name of Princess Te Rangi Pai. In 1903, the composer toured as a singer in the British Isles where her rendition of 'Home Sweet Home' in Maori captivated audiences. 'Hine e hine' achieved acclaim in New Zealand during the singer's last tour of the North Island in 1907.[29]

A number of early songs, erroneously supposed by several writers to be action songs (see later), are associated with Sir Apirana Ngata (1874–1950) and his parliamentary colleague, Hone Heke (1869–1909). Heke entered parliament in 1893 and Ngata in 1905. According to Peter Buck, the two men used to amuse themselves 'by interpreting the popular [English] songs of the day into Maori and singing them over together'.[30] Songs listed by Buck as so translated include 'Just One Girl', 'Soldiers of the Queen' and 'Home Sweet Home', all later printed, with others, by Heke and Ngata in a joint publication.[31] Several of these songs were still in the Maori repertoire

Fanny Rose Howie (1868–1916). Tyree Studio Collection,
Nelson Provincial Museum

Hone Heke (1869-1909).
PHOTO: *Alexander Turnbull Library,*
F 18846½

over 30 years later when they were reprinted in a souvenir programme of the Pomare Memorial meeting held at Waitara in June 1936.[32] At least two translations by Ngata, 'In Happy Moments' and 'The Old Folks at Home', date back to 1900. They were published in the January 1901 issue of the Maori newspaper *Te Pipiwharauroa*, with a letter in Maori from Ngata, who was then 26 years old, in which he explained that many people had asked for the words of the songs to be published.[33] They were amongst several written for a group of young people at Putiki, Wanganui, as part of the welcome ceremony to members of the Te Aute Old Students' Association and other visitors to the association's conference there.[34] It would appear, however, that some, at least, of the songs in Heke and Ngata's 1908 publication were composed not by them but by a cousin of Ngata's, Edward Rangiuia (*c*.1860–1918), of Ngaati Porou. Rangiuia was an accomplished musician who sang and played the piano for the Duke and Duchess of Cornwall and York during their royal tour of 1901 and later, in 1903, toured as a tenor overseas with Princess Te Rangi Pai. He stayed on in England after the tour, making a name for himself in show business and the music halls.[35] Accordinging to an article in the *Gisborne Times*, he composed the Maori version of 'Home Sweet Home' which Fanny Howie sang, as well as Maori versions of 'Ye Banks and Braes', 'Juanita', 'Swanee River' and 'The Last Rose of Summer'.[36] Of these, 'Home Sweet Home' appears as Song No.1 in Heke and Ngata's publication and 'Juanita' as Song No. 12.

Edward Rangiuia (c. 1860–1918).
PHOTO: *Alexander Turnbull Library,*
PA Collection 4777–2

Two of New Zealand's most widely known Maori songs are 'E pari raa' and 'Pookarekare ana'. Both songs have been attributed to Paraire Tomoana, the author of 'Hoea ra te waka nei' and other enduring favourites such as 'Tahi nei taru kino'.[37] The tune of 'E pari raa' is reported to have been adapted by Tomoana from the 'Blue Eyes Waltz' as played by a group called the Moteo Maori Orchestra.[38] The words are said to have been inspired by the death of Whakatomo Ellison, son of Mr and Mrs R. Ellison, of Opapa, near Hastings, who was killed in France during the First World War;[39] much later the song was performed as a poi by Ngaati Kahungungu tribe at the opening of Mahinarangi meeting house, Ngaruawahia, in March 1929.[40] Tomoana is said to have composed 'Pookarekare ana' in 1912 as a love song to his wife Kuini;[41] according to Phyllis Williams, in a broadcast talk,[42] actions were later added by Sir Apirana Ngata at Waiomatatini in 1917. But it would appear that neither man was the originator of the song. They themselves state that it emanated from the North of Auckland, moving thence to the East Cape where 'appropriate action' was added.[43]

Arguably the best-known Maori song of all time is 'Poo ata rau' ('Now is the Hour'), which, like 'E pari raa', made use of a borrowed waltz-time tune: in this case the 'Swiss Cradle Song' by Clement Scott, published by Palings around 1913. Composed and first performed around 1918 or 1919, the song achieved immense popularity after being recorded in the 1940s by numer-

319

ous pop artists of the day, including Gracie Fields,[44] Bing Crosby and the Andrew sisters. There are a number of conflicting stories about the origins of both the words and music, ably summarised in a newspaper article by Harry Dansey.[45] There are at least four claims as to who wrote the words and there has been controversy as well about the composer of the tune.[46]

Many New Zealanders, including the present writer at the age of four, had their introduction to Maori music through the medium of 78 rpm gramophone recordings. The first recordings, of singers Ana Hato (soprano) (1906–53) and her cousin, Deane Waretini (baritone) (1905–67), were made by Parlophone at Rotorua during the visit of the Duke and Duchess of York in February 1927 and in Sydney, Australia, in September 1929. The pianist accompanying some of the songs was Millie Mason, organist of the native church at Ohinemutu.[47] In 1930, recordings were made in New Zealand by Columbia from singers recruited mostly from Ngaati Whakaue tribe, of the now famous Rotorua Maori Choir with pianist Gil Dech who also conducted and directed the group. The songs were rehearsed over a period of three months and recorded from 14 to 26 April in the historic Tinohopu meeting house at Ohinemutu with shawls and carpets hung from the roof and walls to deaden the echo.[48] More than 30 songs were recorded, all in European melodic idiom, including most of those already mentioned above. Amongst them were many of the same songs recorded earlier by Ana Hato and Deane Waretini, together with additional items including favourite hymns in Maori such as 'Au e Ihu' ('Jesu Lover of my Soul') and 'Karaunatia' ('Crown Him with Many Crowns'). Some items were by the full choir and others by soloists Rotohiko Haupapa (baritone), Mere Amohau (contralto), Tiawhi Ratete (tenor) and Mere Te Mauri Meihana (soprano). Te Mauri Meihana was recorded again later, on the Regal Zonophone label, in September 1938 during a broadcasting tour of Australia . But it is Ana Hato and Deane Waretini who

Ana Hato (c.1906–53). PHOTO: *Rotorua Museum of Art &*
History Te Whare Taonga o Te Arawa, Rotorua

Rotorua Maori Choir

are best remembered, and it is the songs first popularised by them which have remained the enduring favourites in the hearts of New Zealanders. Not surprisingly, they also feature again and again in the repertoires of Maori concert parties before and since.

DEVELOPMENT OF ACTION SONG
Early concert parties

Standard items in the repertoires of nearly all early Maori concert parties, as indeed at Maori welcomes to royalty (see later), were poi dances performed by the women and haka dances performed either by the men or by the whole company. Action songs were as yet far in the future.

Dr M'Gauran's Troupe of Maori Warrior Chiefs, Wives and Children appeared in Sydney and Melbourne in 1862 with a melodrama entitled *The Pakeha Chief*. It was a simple tale with plenty of scope for the introduction of a battle, a canoe launching and 'Games, Sports, Chaunts, Revelries, Songs, Dances and the Great War Dance'. The latter was a haka which one newspaper described as 'extremely exciting and most grimly quaint in character . . . accompanied with an obligato of outrageous gestures and postures, and slapping of knees, breasts and hands'. The same group of 'Warrior Chiefs', re-formed under the management of M.G. Hegartz[49] of Melbourne, later sailed to England where they opened on 6 July 1863 to a packed house in the Alhambra on London's Leicester Square.[50] There, according to a less than flattering newspaper review, 'so wild and noisy were [their] demonstrations that no one could tell what they meant'.[51] They have been confused by some with a different, Methodist-sponsored Maori party who were in London at the same time with a government interpreter named William Jenkins.[52]

> Both parties toured the English midlands; the Maori Warrior Chiefs performing 'wild, half-naked haka' for appreciative music hall audiences while 'the distinguished New Zealanders' gave 'illustrated lectures' in town and church halls, visiting numerous factories and institutions.[53]

Another visit to Australia by a Maori concert party took place in 1879 when a group of between 30 and 40 men and women from Ngaati Maru tribe of the Thames area were taken by a Mr Ferris to the Sydney Exhibition to perform 'war-dances and illustrations of Maori life and manners'. Before leaving New Zealand they gave what was reported as a 'curious performance' at the Theatre Royal in Auckland, where 'They went through war-dances, hakas, village ceremonials, songs, tangis and other illustrative performances with excellent effect.'[54]

Before the turn of the century, at least one further group of Maori entertainers visited England. In 1895 a Maori family from Waikouaiti, near Dunedin, appeared in London as an adjunct of a limelight slide show of New Zealand scenes entitled 'Maori Picture, Song and Story'. Their accompanying musical programme is reported to have included 'quaint Native ballads and several gems of Maori sacred song'.[55]

Maggie Papakura

Maggie Papakura (1872–1930), born Margaret Patterson Thom, began her career as a guide in the Whakarewarewa thermal reserve, Rotorua, reaching a reputed high point with the royal visit in 1901 when she charmed the duchess and the press with her beauty and 'dulcet voice'.[56]

Maggie Papakura (1872–1930) at about 23 years of age

She was a member of the Te Arawa group which performed at the Christchurch Exhibition (see next). In 1910 she took a touring concert party to Melbourne and Sydney where she met with 'phenomenal success'.[57] The following year, she and 38 other members of the same group went on to

Princess Iwa. PHOTO: *Alexander Turnbull Library, C10617*

London where they performed during the coronation celebrations of George V and formed part of an exhibition for the Festival of Empire at White City, where a replica Maori village which had been used in Sydney was reconstructed. As reported by the *New Zealand Times*,[58] the repertoire of the group included native haka, poi dances, Maori love songs, war cries and 'part-singing in English which they were taught at school'. A much appreciated and reported item was their rendition of the 'Canoe Poi' (referred to above). A feature of their other poi dances, different from later practice, was for the leader to call out the changes 'as in physical exercises'.[59] The lead singer of the group was a South Island contralto, Eva Skerrett (born in 1890 at Stewart Island and brought up at Bluff) who was given the stage name of Princess Iwa. Billed as 'the Maori Nightingale', the 'Queen of Maori Song' and 'the Maid with the Laughing Eyes', she stayed on in England after the tour, performing from time to time at variety concerts in London and the provinces with a small repertoire of songs. They included 'Hoki hoki tonu mai', Princess Te Rangi Pai's 'slumber song' 'Hine e hine' and Alfred Hill's 'Waiata Poi' and 'Home, Little Maori Home'. Maggie Papakura also took up residence in England, where she became well known for her activities on behalf of Anzacs during the First World War and later as the author of a book, published posthumously, called *The Old-Time Maori*.[60]

Maggie Papakura's concert party, 1910. Maggie is in the second to front row, third from the left, seated next to Chief Mita Taupopoki. PHOTO: *Rotorua Museum of Art & History Te Whare Taonga o Te Arawa, Rotorua*

The emergence of action song

It is difficult to pinpoint when action songs as such first began. A complication to be taken into account is that the term itself had different connotations when it was first used. On 5 March 1918, for example, the children of Mt Albert Orphanage raised money for their piano fund with a performance at the Auckland Town Hall which included 'Action Songs'; and on 1 June at the same venue, there appeared a Band of Hope Gathering with '600 Action-Song Performers'. Neither party, however, was Maori. The rest of the orphans' concert consisted of 'Recitations, Drills, Choruses . . . Tableaux etc.', and the Band of Hope comprised groups named The Blacksmiths, Bubbles, Temperance Boys and Girls and the Dainty Domestics performing variety items such as a 'Sneezing Song, the Awkward Squad, Maypole Dance and Dance of the Flowers'.[61] The earliest Maori 'action songs' may have been songs with actions in the same sense and not necessarily identifiable with action songs as the term is now understood. Even as late as 1943, the connotation of the term may still have been quite broad: in the Souvenir Programme of the Ngarimu Victoria Cross Investiture meeting at Ruatoria, the women's haka of welcome, 'Haukiwi, hauweka', as performed by girls of the Hikurangi section of Ngaati Porou, is called an 'action song in 3/4 time'.[62]

Even putting the above aside, it would seem likely that the modern action song was introduced much later than has often been supposed. Samplings

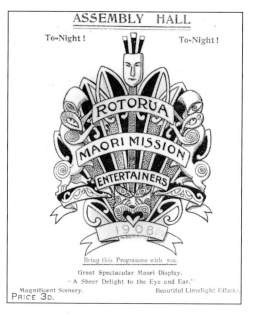

of early Maori concert programmes show a conspicuous absence of action songs in all tribal areas until the 1930s.

For example, a 1908 programme at Rotorua by a group called the Rotorua Maori Mission Entertainers — probably predecessors of the Rotorua Maori Choir — directed by the Rev. F.A. Bennett,[63] contains haka, poi and two American 'plantation' songs, but nothing resembling action songs.[64] An alternative programme by the same group similarly lacks action songs.[65] They are also absent from a 1914 programme of 'the original and famous Maori Choir of Rotorua' of Ngaati Whakaue under the direction of a Mr D. Smythe Papworth, which consisted rather of haka, poi, the matemate hand game, part songs, and songs such as 'The Old Folks at Home' in Maori and again 'Home, Little Maori Home' together with a set of orchestral waltzes especially composed by Mr Papworth.[66]

Another concert in 1914, on 4 December, was given at the Auckland Town Hall by 500 members of the Maori Contingent to raise money for the families of 12 sulphur miners who had been killed at White Island. According to a review of the concert: 'Much enthusiasm was aroused by the hakas performed by members of the Arawa and Ngati Porou tribes.' Aside from these, however, the only specifically Maori items reported were 'Hoki hoki tonu mai' and, once more, the ubiquitous 'Home, Little Maori Home'. The rest of the programme appears on the face of it to have been wholly European: a young Maori tenor, Noho, sang songs of which the best rendered were said to be 'Nellie Gray' and 'Where my Caravan has Rested'; and the soldiers sang wartime choruses such as 'Tipperary', the 'Red, White and Blue' and 'Tramp! Tramp! Tramp!'[67] It is possible that the last named, at least, was sung in Maori as it is amongst songs earlier translated into Maori and published by Heke and Ngata.[68]

Action songs were also absent from concert items presented in 1915 to the First Maori Battalion at Wellington.[69] Again they formed no part of a programme of Maori entertainment at the Wellington Town Hall in 1917 in aid of the Maori Soldiers' Fund: instead, entertainers from Te Ati Awa, Ngaati Raukawa and Tuuwharetoa tribes sang the usual haka, poi and other songs, supplemented with 'glees' such as 'Sweet and Low' and 'Come Where My Love Lies Dreaming'.[70] The programme of a 'Grand Maori Pageant' held at the Opera House, Wanganui, in aid of returned Maori soldiers in 1919 again has no mention of action songs.[71] The same is true of items by a group called the Hinemoa Maori Entertainers which performed at Rotorua under the management of twin guides known as Eileen and Georgina together with Guides Eva and Ruth in the mid 1920s. Their programme consisted of love ditties, poi songs including the canoe poi, men's and women's haka and songs such as Hill's 'Waiata Poi' and Tomoana's 'E pari raa', but again no action songs.[72]

A decade later in the same area, a group known as The Huia Maori Entertainers, under the management this time of Guides Susan, Mary, Eva and others, were presenting at Rotorua's Peerless and Lyric Theatres a programme of the by now standard items, with just one designated as an action song.

PEERLESS THEATRE
ROTORUA
To-night

The Huia Maori Entertainers
WILL GIVE THEIR
UNIQUE
ENTERTAINMENT

Even this was a tried and true favourite, now evidently enlivened with action: again 'E pari raa' to the tune of 'Blue Eyes', performed as a finale.[73] The use of 'E pari raa' as a farewell song may well have become a convention by the mid 1930s as it appears in the same role in other programmes of the period: e.g. in a 1930 programme of Maori entertainment at the Wellington Town Hall by a Wanganui Concert Party where it is described as an 'Action Chorus' and is again the sole such item.[74] Despite this use of the name, it is possible that the actions performed with 'E pari raa' on these occasions were poi. Another Wellington concert of the same year provides evidence that poi were sometimes described in such terms. In the second half was an item by Ngaati Porou women, 'Te Wiwi kia toa! Whaia ko te kaha', named in Maori as a 'Ngahau' and in English as an 'Action Song'.[75] The term 'ngahau' is glossed in Williams simply as a 'dance'.[76] In this case, however, it appears to have been a poi as six years later it was performed as such by the fledgling Ngati Poneke Club of Wellington.[77] Their concert is one of the first at which un-equivocal action songs were also performed. In the programme, there is con-siderable variation of nomenclature, including 'ruri with action', 'love ditties with action' and 'action songs'. The latter term, however, embraces at least one item known to be a true action song: namely, Ngata's 'He putiputi koe'. Another concert programme of the 1930s in which action songs are specifi-cally named was at the Auckland Town Hall on 1 March 1938, with Ana

Hato and Deane Waretini of recording fame as featured artists. In each half, besides the customary haka, poi and other items, was a bracket containing action songs.[78] By the 1940s, action songs were firmly established, though still not dominant in concert programmes. An example is a 1947 programme of the Taiporutu Club of Rotorua which includes four brackets of action songs amongst 22 items but still concludes with the by now traditional 'E pari raa'.[79] Te Awekotuku, in a study of the impact of tourism in Rotorua, concludes that it was not until well into the 1930s that action songs as such were included in the programmes of Rotorua concert parties, and another ten years elapsed before they became prominent.[80] The same appears to have been the case elsewhere though action songs must have become established informally before the mid 1930s, as shown by Apirana Ngata's report in a letter to Peter Buck of competition results at Waitangi in 1934. Action songs were distinguished from poi and other items, and Te Arawa was stated to have the best displays.[81]

Princess Te Puea

A Maori leader with a reputation second only to that of Sir Apirana Ngata (see later) as influential in the development of the Maori action song was Princess Te Puea Herangi (1884–1952) of Waikato. Her famous first concert party, which she called 'Te Pou o Mangatawhiri' (TPM), was a troupe of 44 performers whose initial concerts were given at Ngaruawahia and Tuakau in December 1922. In 1923 the group undertook its first tour, in the Waikato, Auckland, the Kaipara district and Northland. A report in the *Northern Advocate* of a concert at Whangarei is cited by Michael King as typical of press reaction throughout the tour:

> The concert . . . was really first-rate . . . It includes men's haka parties, women's pois and Hawaiian hula dances, and a dozen little Maori maids, whose charming dancing was one of popular features of the show. There was a fine string band consisting of steel guitars, mandolins, mandolas, banjos and the popular ukeleles. The stage was well set as a typical pa, and the use of pungas and nikau in the decorative effect gave the whole performance a pleasing harmony . . . Braves, wahines and piccaninnies, the whole party sing and with that naturalness that gives a good Maori display its unique charm . . . Born to be musical, they all keep perfect time in their movements and in their singing, while many a choir of Europeans might envy the skilful blending of their voices and instruments.[82]

The programme was presented in two halves. The first part, which was 'chiefly in Maori', consisted of 'hakas by the men [and] single and double poi dances by the women and little girls'. After the interval came 'less purely Maori' items such as 'song and instrumental items . . . laughable comedy . . . [and] Hawaiian dancing'.[83]

Other tours followed, including a marathon four-month tour in 1927–28, by a troupe of 25, which took them to Hawke's Bay, Palmerston North, Wanganui, Stratford, Gisborne, the East Coast and the Bay of Plenty. In June and July 1928 there followed a three-week season at Auckland's Majestic Theatre for which Te Puea's by now somewhat diminished party of 11 girls and six men was promoted as 'the most talented combination in all Maoriland'. Pre-concert publicity promised 'fine old Maori chants' and 'Tapu Karakias, never before sung in Public to European Ears'. The programme, which was shared with a romantic comedy movie featuring the film star Norma Shearer, was evidently quite short. The *Herald* review of the opening night mentioned only four items: a scene illustrating the arrival of the Tainui canoe at which chants were sung by the women and a 'paddling dance' was performed; another scene depicting the crowning of the first Maori King, Potatau; a series of women's long and short poi; and, as a final item, a 'stirring war chant [haka] by the whole company'.[84]

A similarly abbreviated programme was presented at the Deluxe Theatre, Wellington, during a two-week season beginning on 31 August 1928. Again the men performed 'hakas and war cries', the 'ten little Maori maids' contributed poi dances, and the programme ended with a 'combined haka' from the whole company. Te Puea's group was preceded by Scottish and Maori airs played by a Mr Aarons on the Wurlitzer organ and followed by a Metro–Goldwyn–Mayer film, *Annie Laurie*.[85]

Noteworthy in the reports of both 1923 and 1928 is a lack of any mention of action songs. Even in 1929, when Te Puea's group, amongst others,

Te Puea's Waikato songsters at Waitangi, 1934. Photo: *J.F. Louden*

entertained at the opening of Turongo meeting house, Ngaruawahia, the songs performed were not action songs but haka and poi.[86] It appears that if Te Puea was indeed one of the pioneers of action song, she did not begin to promote it until later. A photograph of her 'Waikato Songsters', poi-balls put aside and fastened at the waist, shows them performing what looks like an action song at Waitangi in 1934.

Rev. A.J. Seamer

A close associate of Te Puea in the 1930s was the Rev. A.J. Seamer who had begun to specialise in Maori work 30 years earlier and, when Te Puea knew him, was general superintendent of the Methodist Maori Mission.[87]

Rev. A.J. Seamer

Inspired possibly by Te Puea's TPM concert party, he formed and later toured overseas with his own choir, known as the Waiata Maori Choir. One of the members was the bass singer Inia Te Wiata who, according to his biographer, joined the choir in 1932 when he was 17 years old.[88] Again, there is no evidence that action songs were in the repertoire. In 1930 the choir toured New Zealand as the Maori Methodist Mission Party. An advertisement for one of its concerts held at the Papanui Methodist Church, Christchurch, on 9 June, invited local people to hear 'Weird Waiatas (seldom heard by Europeans), Sacred Poi Action Songs, Hymn Singing, Maori

Methodist Maori Choir 1932 and 1933

Greetings and Speeches etc.'[89] Significantly, the term 'action song' is here used not in its modern sense but to describe poi dances. An advertisement for a farewell performance of the same group, six weeks later, offered not action songs but 'Karanga, Poi Dances, Hakas, Instrumental Music, Haunting Melodies, Enchanting Harmonies, Ancient Games, [and again] Weird

Waiatas, Maori Songs, etc.'[90] A newspaper review of the performance again makes no mention of action songs. 'The rhythmic nature of the poi dances and hakas and the plaintive character of most of the musical items' is stated to have 'appealed greatly to the audience' as did an evidently wholly Pakeha solo from Airini Grennell (?1910–88) of a song by Sanderson entitled 'Nightingales of June'.[91] Grennell was still in the choir in 1937–38 when, as a group of 11 women and eight men, it toured Australia and England, performing amongst other places at Westminster Hall, and was presented to the recently crowned King George VI.[92]

Royal visits

Maori welcomes to royalty have been marked through the years by conspicuous displays of haka and poi but only recently as a venue for action songs.

The first royal visitor to New Zealand was Prince Alfred Ernest Albert (1844–1900), Duke of Edinburgh, the second son of Queen Victoria and Prince Albert, who came three times to New Zealand between 1869 and 1871 as captain of HMS *Galatea*. Few New Zealanders today have even heard of the duke, who is remembered mainly for having added his signature to graffiti on the Pink Terraces before the evidence of his vandalism was erased by the Tarawera eruption 16 years later.[93] Nevertheless, his visit made a considerable impact at the time. During his 1869 visit, he was treated to displays of haka in Wellington and Nelson,[94] and an official Maori welcome

Kirimatao Te Tautahi (1843–1913).
PHOTO: *Rotorua Museum of Art & History Te Whare Taonga o Te Arawa, Rotorua*

was held for him at Rotorua.[95] During his third visit in 1870, he bathed in the hot springs at Rotorua and viewed haka and poi dances led by Kirimatao;[96] additionally he spent a week in the Lake Country and Bay of Plenty with an Arawa escort when he expressed interest in the 'war songs' chanted around the watch-fires lit at night in front of the tents in the Maori encampment.[97]

Next was the visit in 1901 of the Duke and Duchess of Cornwall and York (later King George V and Queen Mary). The reception for them at Rotorua was a large-scale occasion with 5000 Maoris present,[98] and numerous haka and poi were performed in their honour (referred to extensively in the chapters above on these topics). Many of the poi dances, according to Scholefield, were given to the accompaniment of mouth-organs and accordions.[99]

In April 1920 Edward, Prince of Wales (later King Edward VIII) visited New Zealand. At Arawa Park, Rotorua, men's war dances and women's poi songs were performed by tribes from all parts of New Zealand. Amongst the highlights were a haka from Ngaati Porou tribe led by Apirana Ngata, a Te Arawa 'canoe poi' from the local Tuhourangi people led by Bella Papakura, and a poi from the Ngaati Raukawa tribe descriptive of the prince's trip to New Zealand. To the mouth-organs and accordions which accompanied the poi dances of 1901 were now added cornets and even, by one tribe, a full-sized piano. The tunes, according to Scholefield's official account of the prince's visit, were 'the favourite waltzes and two-steps of the *pakeha* ball-room'.[100]

The next royal visitors were the Duke and Duchess of York in 1927 (later King George VI and Queen Elizabeth). The Maori welcome to them at Rotorua was held at the racecourse adjacent to Arawa Park, as it had been for the duke's mother and father in 1901. This time the entertainment was wholly in the hands of the local Te Arawa people and their neighbours, the Ngaati Tuuwharetoa, with a small band from the Urewera. Again stirring displays of haka took place, as well as poi dances which were described as 'graceful and charming'.[101]

Prince Henry (1900–74), Duke of Gloucester and third son of George V and Queen Mary, visited New Zealand in 1934. At a Maori reception held at Arawa Park, Rotorua, he was welcomed with exhibitions of haka, poi and waiata from Bay of Plenty tribes, concluding with the famous 'Ka mate' haka. Amongst the items was a paatere performed by Ngaati Pikiao who had won a paatere competition at the inaugural Waitangi Day celebrations earlier in the year. Another unusual item was a haka waiata or 'action song' (referred to again later) depicting the coming of the Arawa canoe.[102]

Finally may be cited the visits of Queen Elizabeth II and the Duke of Edinburgh in 1953–54 and 1970. Maori receptions were held at Rotorua on the first occasion and at Gisborne in 1970. In both centres the usual haka and poi dances were presented. Additionally, at Rotorua, a single action song

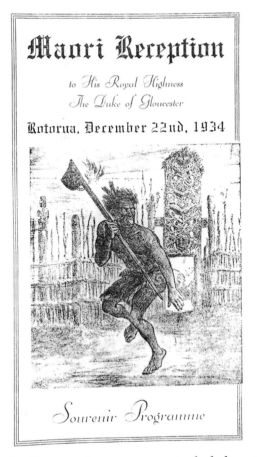

Maori Reception

to His Royal Highness
The Duke of Gloucester

Rotorua, December 22nd, 1934

Souvenir Programme

was performed. At Gisborne the programme included several action songs, by composers Kohine Ponika, Wi Huata, Mrs W. Pitama Riwai, Mrs D. Poipoi, W. Kerekere, and Kingi Ihaka.

With the 1970 royal tour, action songs may be regarded as coming of age. In number, in the prominence afforded them, in their themes and originality and in nomenclature, they represented a departure from earlier convention: for the first time in a royal tour they appeared in the official programme, together with the names of the composers, and were formally designated as 'waiata-a-ringa'.[103]

Christchurch exhibition

The world's earliest industrial exhibitions were held in France, with no fewer than 11 in Paris between 1797 and 1849. The first International Exhibition was the famous Crystal Palace Exhibition of 1851 in London, England. After this date, frequent such exhibitions were held throughout the world, beginning at New York in 1853. The Sydney Exhibition of 1879, where a Maori concert party performed, has already been mentioned.

The first New Zealand international exhibition took place in Dunedin in 1865. Next came the Christchurch International Exhibition of 1882, followed by the New Zealand and South Seas Exhibition of 1889–90 in Dunedin, the Christchurch Exhibition of 1906–07 and, again in Dunedin, the New Zealand and South Seas Exhibition of 1925–26.[104] There is no record of Maori entertainment at the earliest New Zealand exhibitions, or at the Dunedin exhibition of 1925–26, though musical events of other kinds took place. But the Christchurch Exhibition was an exception, possibly because of the precedent offered by the outstanding success of the Maori welcome to the Duke and Duchess of Cornwall and York a few years earlier. A Maori paa was erected in Hagley Park and haka and poi dances were performed daily by Arawa and Whanganui groups who were in residence throughout the exhibition.[105] In addition, late in 1906, Captain Gilbert Mair arrived from the North Island with a large party containing the best haka and poi dancers from Rotorua and surrounding districts. Amongst the items they performed were a canoe poi by Maggie Papakura's group[106] and a narrative dance depicting the building of a house, composed by Maggie Papakura's sister, the Rotorua guide Bella Reretupou. Though described as an 'action song' by the Christchurch *Weekly Press*, Bella's dance differed radically from action songs as they were later to develop.[107] The action song as it is now known had evidently not yet emerged.

While ruling out a direct connection with action song, Shennan has speculated that the Exhibition might have provided models for later Maori action songs in imitation of Cook Islands dances.[108] In the official record of the exhibition, Cowan states that some of Maori performers 'quickly learned one or two of the Rarotongan songs' from the Cook Islands contingent, and he refers specifically to an Aitutaki 'lifting song' 'Kii ana mai koia ko Rutaki-nuku', performed during a song-and-dance drama enacting the separation of Rangi (the sky) from Enua (the earth). This chant, he says:

> appealed with peculiar interest to the New Zealand Maoris, who quickly picked up the words and time actions, and greatly amused their fellows at night by imitating the capers, the drumming, and the singing of the Island men and women.[109]

The question nevertheless remains open. Although Cowan applies the term 'action-song' to the 'lifting' chant used in the Rangi/Enua enactment,[110] the latter appears to have been similar in nature to Bella's house-building dance and, in this event, neither performance would have been an 'action song' in the modern sense. Moreover, although there is unquestionably a striking resemblance between Maori and Cook Island action songs as currently performed, the origins of the latter have not yet been established and cannot be assumed to pre-date the Maori.

The haka waiata fallacy

A number of writers[111] have been concerned to demonstrate continuity between action song and traditional Maori music, maintaining that the action song developed from an early traditional form called the haka waiata. The first to make this claim appears to have been J. McEwen, who has since been copied directly or indirectly by the others. Mitcalfe obfuscates the issue completely by citing as a so-called '*haka waiata* (action song)' an early photograph, published on 20 May 1902 by the *Auckland Weekly News*, of dancers at a Kawhia regatta.[112] Examination of it shows it to be of four women performing an impromptu haka, captioned as such at the time. The first genuine mention of such a song type appears to be in 1924 and 1925, in lists published by Best[113] of types of Ngaati Porou haka where haka waiata are named as 'posture dances accompanied by a mild species of songs and fairly slow movements'.[114] In a review of Mitcalfe's book, Awatere refers to the name haka waiata as 'a contradiction in terms' because haka are recited whereas waiata are sung.[115] The name makes good sense, however, if it was an early coining for songs with actions such as those depicting canoe paddling. Another possibility is that it was a term for the newly emergent action song itself. It appears to have been used in the former sense at the Maori reception for the Duke of Gloucester at Rotorua in 1934, where the song 'Uia mai koia' (see Example 103), depicting the coming of the Arawa canoe, is named in Maori as a haka waiata and in English as an action song.[116] The same song is in the 1943 *Ngarimu Investiture Souvenir Programme*[117] and in the programme of the royal visit of 1954,[118] named on both occasions as an action song and again performed by Arawa women. If the above explanation is correct, and in view of the specifically modern connotation of the term 'action song', a better gloss for haka waiata would be 'song with actions'.

Maori gatherings and the role of Sir Apirana Ngata

Sir Apirana Ngata (1874–1950) has been called unequivocally by some the 'father of action song'.[119] Mitcalfe has argued to the contrary that Ngata's role has been overstressed,[120] but this judgement is based on his erroneous assumption that action songs originated with haka waiata and that the latter was an old traditional form. Shennan points out more credibly that Ngata could not have succeeded in popularising action song if the Maori people were not ready to respond to the innovation.[121] Nevertheless, Ngata's role in the development of action song was unquestionably a vital one and he could have been the originator. His early translations, with Hone Heke, of popular European songs into Maori have already been mentioned.[122] These were not action songs although they have been either represented or accepted as such by some writers.[123] However, as Shennan comments, it was no doubt a short haul from these to the idea of borrowing a Pakeha tune in order to set to it

Sir Apirana Ngata (1874–1950) aged about 36 years. Photo:
Alexander Turnbull Library, Smidt Collection G 1566¹/₁

an independently composed Maori text.[124] And with melody and text supplied, it would be a still shorter step to add actions.

During the First World War, Ngata is said to have popularised action songs by featuring them in concerts he organised all over New Zealand for the Maori Soldiers' Fund.[125] Concert groups prominent in the fund-raising came from Ngaati Kahungunu, Turanga (Gisborne) and Ngaati Porou.[126] The concerts and their fund-raising role are mentioned by Ngata and Tomoana in a pamphlet entitled 'A Noble Sacrifice . . . with Words and Actions'.[127] The work alluded to in the title was a poi drama by the two authors. In the pamphlet are the texts of Tomoana's canoe poi song 'Hoea ra te waka nei' together with Ngata's poetic description of the Maori haka, 'Scenes from the Past',[128] the Maori translation of 'Home Sweet Home' and 'E te ope tuatahi', composed jointly by the two men as a recruiting song and specifically named in the pamphlet as an action song. Certainly it is performed as such today,[129] and, if the same was true at the time of composition, it may well have been the first of the genre. Whether this was really the case, however, is uncertain because confirming information has not been found. In 1919 'A Noble Sacrifice' was performed at a Hui Aroha for returning Maori Battalion troops held at Gisborne, by a combined group consisting of Tomoana's Hawke's Bay Maori Entertainers and the Tairawhiti Maori Club.[130] One of the songs in it was 'Hoki hoki tonu mai'.[131] The performances at the Hui Aroha of songs with Pakeha tunes are referred to in a review by Wi Repa as 'he haka hou' 'a new haka',[132] again suggesting that, for some of these songs at least, a form of action was involved. It seems probable that the two groups which performed at the Hui Aroha did so also at Ngata's earlier fund-raising concerts, and the programmes they presented may have been the same. They appeared at the Auckland Town Hall for a ten-night season, from 20 to 30 December 1917, billed as 'The Maori Entertainers (Hawke's Bay and East Coast)'.[133] A review described two parts of the programme as showing the grief of the people '. . . when told that their sons are required to go to the war' and '. . . at losing their sons'. Ngata, in costume, gave 'a number of characteristic war dances, explaining to the audience the meaning of each attitude or gesticulation', and Olga Neketiri, described as 'the Maori Nightingale', sang several solos 'including a thrilling recruiting appeal'.[134] Ngata's use of haka demonstrations at the concerts suggests that his 'Scenes from the Past' was, in fact, part of the performance as, according to Buck, Ngata won an Olla Podrida competition with this work while at Te Aute, demonstrating the dances described in it himself 'with perfect grace of movement and gesture'.[135] The recruiting song referred to was doubtless Ngata and Tomoana's 'E te ope tuatahi', which seems amongst the most likely to have earned the 'haka hou' appellation later at Gisborne if it was performed there,[136] but, frustratingly, the review says nothing else about it. An unequivocal action song by Ngata, and possibly his most famous, is 'Karangatia ra', composed in 1919 for the return of the Maori Battalion from the war.

In the late 1890s, Ngata became a co-founder and secretary–organiser of the Young Maori Party, an association mostly of Old Boys of Te Aute Maori College, which aimed at improving the condition of the Maori people.[137] After entering Parliament in 1905, Ngata, in association with Maui Pomare (1876–1930), Peter Buck (1880–1951) and others, achieved enormous success and influence in promoting the aims of the party. One of the means employed was a revival in the construction of carved houses. For the openings, large-scale meetings were convened at which Ngata organised intertribal demonstrations of whaikoorero, haka, waiata and poi with the object of revitalising them. A precedent for the latter process had been set at Waitangi in 1934 when Ngata became involved in commemorative celebrations to acknowledge the gift to the nation of the Waitangi estate by Lord and Lady Bledisloe. Ngata sent Ngaati Porou instructors to teach chants and dances to the Ngaapuhi who had lost them.[138] Ngata himself was proud of the result, writing a month after the event to Peter Buck[139] that: 'As a demonstration of the renaissance in song, haka of all kinds and peruperu, the Waitangi celebrations eclipsed anything since 1901'.[140]

Ngata leading a haka at Waitangi, 1940. PHOTO: *B. Snowdon. Alexander Turnbull Library,*
F 29794¹/₂

Earlier (1919–23), he had facilitated a series of expeditions from the
Dominion Museum to record waiata and other oral tradition on dictaphone
cylinders. Later, during his tenure as Minister of Native Affairs, he installed
the cylinder machine in his parliamentary office and recorded more songs
(*c*.1931–35). When acetate-coated aluminium discs replaced phonograph
cylinders in the mid 1930s, Ngata seized the opportunity afforded by the
new technology and, from 1938 onwards, enlisted the aid of the New Zealand Broadcasting Service to record songs from the meetings he was in process of organising.[141] Between then and 1950, when Ngata died, ten events of
cultural and historical importance were recorded, beginning with the opening of Princess Te Puea's Turongo meeting house at Ngaruawahia in 1938
and ending with the Mataatua canoe celebrations of 1950. Ngata was present
at all of these events except the last, which took place two months after his
death. For the earliest meetings, Ngata recorded commentaries about the
various items; at subsequent ones he made use of the public address systems
which by then had come into use, commenting throughout, in English and
Maori, in his own inimitable way. All of the events were broadcast at the
time, recorded on acetate disc, have since been dubbed to tape, and both
these and the cylinder collection are now fully catalogued.[142] Amongst the
later recordings are numerous action songs, including the inaugural performance of Tuini Ngawai's tribute to Ngarimu at the Ngarimu Victoria Cross
investiture meeting at Ruatoria in 1943.

Sir Apirana Ngata at the microphone, Te Kaha,
1944. Photo: Alexander Turnbull Library,
Pascoe Collection F 1095¹/₄

In 1944, at Ruatoria, Ngata convened his Porourangi Maori Cultural
School where he delivered a series of lectures known as the Raurau-nui-a-
Toi lectures at which he offered advice on the fundamental movements of
posture dancing, including action song.[143] This appears to have been the
first attempt at codifying the movements. Ngata's rules are still respected
and adhered to, especially by his own tribe of Ngaati Porou, although variations between this tribe and others such as Te Arawa are now both acknowledged and allowable.[144]

Later concert parties

After the close of the Second World War, tourism increased in New Zealand,
coinciding, as it happened, with a resurgence of Maori culture. In her auto-
biography, Guide Rangi[145] of Rotorua (1896–1970) recalls that Maori people
all over New Zealand were opening new meeting houses and war memorial
halls; youth clubs were springing up to foster Maori arts; and Rotorua concert parties were in continual demand helping to raise funds, demonstrating
the arts, and performing at official openings. Amongst those doing so was
Guide Rangi's own concert party which travelled New Zealand without seeking payment, usually in return for travelling expenses, food and accommo-
dation.[146]

Guide Rangi (1896–1970) PHOTO: *Rotorua Museum of Art & History Te Whare Taonga o Te Arawa, Rotorua*

Clubs and culture groups

Since the mid 1930s, action songs have been promulgated most of all by clubs for young people which operate all over New Zealand, especially in the urban areas. Some of the better known are Ngati Poneke, Wellington, founded in 1936 with Kingi Tahiwi (1883–1948) as its first chairman; Te Hokowhitu-aa-Tuu at Tokomaru Bay, founded by Tuini Ngawai in 1939; Taiporutu, in Ohinemutu, founded in 1944 by Henry Taiporutu Mitchell (1877–1944) and led during its heyday by Hamuera Mitchell; Waihirere, Gisborne, founded in 1951 by Bill Kerekere; the Putiki Maori Club of Wanganui, founded in 1952; Ma Wai Hakona, Upper Hutt, founded in 1962 by Jock McEwen (1915–); the Auckland Anglican Maori Club, led for many years by Archdeacon Kingi Ihaka (1921–93); and Te Roopu Manutaki, Auckland, founded in 1969 by Peter Sharples (1941–).

An action song from the Waihirere group, 1968

Competitions

A major activity of Maori clubs and culture groups is preparing for and taking part in festivals and formal competitions. An early such competition was at the Waitangi Day celebrations of 1934, when a trophy called 'Te Rehia' was presented by Lady Bledisloe for competition in song, oratory and dance.[147] As late as 1940, Ngata was of the opinion that competitions or festivals to promote singing and dancing could not succeed if they were staged ad hoc because 'no Maori custom is appealed to and there is no enthusiasm'.[148] Competitions soon, nevertheless, became firmly established in their own right. Since the mid 1940s, church hui (meetings) have been venues for both competitions and new action songs: the best known are Catholic Easter gatherings called Hui Aranga, annual Anglican gatherings in May called Hui Topu, and annual events held by the Ratana Church. As well, the Waikato King Movement holds annual coronation anniversary celebrations at Ngaruawahia in May; and, since 1972, a biennial New Zealand Polynesian Festival (now renamed the Aotearoa Maori Performing Arts Festival) has been held at different centres where winning teams from district competitions compete for final places. Each team is given 20 minutes to present a poi, an action song, a haka, a traditional song and a choral item such as a hymn or anthem. Teams are judged on dress and appearance as well as performance criteria, and bonus points are given for originality. The overall winners go on to represent New Zealand at South Pacific festivals held first in Fiji in 1972 and subsequently each four years in a different Pacific host country.

The texts

Compared with waiata, the texts of action songs tend to be markedly simpler and to make use of stereotyped phrases to a greater degree. Some, according to Margaret Orbell, draw ideas and phrases from earlier pao and waiata.[149] But more so than traditional songs 'they have been adapted to themes from dairy farming to shearing to the exploits of soldiers in the two world wars. Their topicality both in words and melodies [see later] are probably their greatest appeal.'[150] Songs of greeting and farewell; laments and love songs; exhortatory, political, satirical and humorous songs are all in the repertoire.[151]

The actions

Some of the hand and other movements of action songs are non-mimetic and derived, according to Arapeta Awatere, from the impromptu movements employed in traditional paatere;[152] others are illustrative of the sentiments of the text.[153] The characteristic hand tremor, known as 'wiri', is a transfer from haka. The idea of uniform action must also have come from haka and may have been a fairly late development. Leo Fowler, in a 1972 newspaper article, states that a generation or more before this time, the actions were mostly non-uniform, with each individual interpreting the song in his or her own way. This happened both informally and on the marae and concert platform.[154] Ngoi Pewhairangi says the same of action songs performed in the 1940s by groups under the tutelage of Tuini Ngawai: in effect, 'each member could be a solo artist', in contrast with the 'almost military uniformity' which is now usual.[155] Such an earlier mode of performance is consistent with Awatere's view that the movements of action song were derived from paatere rather than the drilled movements of haka.

The music

Both in melodic idiom and in its use of harmony the music of action songs is European. As shown above, precedents for it include Maori hymnody, turn-of the-century poi songs, Ngata and Tomoana's adaptations of popular nineteenth-century songs, and early Maori songs, such as 'Hine e hine' and 'E pari raa', which were set to popular tunes. Until recently, most action songs have made similar use of borrowed tunes. A much-quoted example is Ngata's 'He putiputi koe' which was composed in 1925–26 to the tune of 'You're Just a Flower from an Old Bouquet'. In this case, however, the words as well as the tune appear to owe something to the donor song.[156]

A prolific borrower of tunes was Tuini Ngawai (1910–65) of Ngaati Porou whose first song, 'He nawe kei roto', is said to have been composed in 1930.[157] The melody of this song appears to have been original, but most of the many songs composed by Ngawai in the war years of 1939–45 and afterwards

The Patea Maori Club performing 'Poi e' in front of their meeting house.
PHOTO: *Rahena Broughton*

made use of pop tunes of the day. Her ever popular 'Arohaina mai',[158] composed in 1939 as a farewell for the C Company (Bay of Plenty and East Coast) of the Maori Battalion, has the tune of 'Love Walked In'; her 'Te Hokowhitu Toa', which became a favourite of the C Company, was to the tune of 'Lock my Heart and Throw Away the Key'; and her celebrated tribute to Victoria Cross winner Lt Te Moana-nui-a-Kiwa Ngarimu, 'E te hokowhitu a tu', was composed to the tune of 'In the Mood'.[159]

In recent years, original tunes, though still in European idiom, have become more common following a trend which began in the 1960s and 1970s when the New Zealand Broadcasting Corporation ran competitions offering trophies for the most original action song and poi tunes. Perhaps the most famous recent such song is 'Poi e', with words by Ngoi Pewhairangi (1922–85), tune by Delvanius Prime, and performed in 1983 by the Patea Maori Club. A 'triple platinum success', it reached the top of the New Zealand hit parade and stayed there for four consecutive weeks.[160]

In summary, the common elements between action song and traditional forms are seen to be either performance related, or extra musical. The words of action songs and the message or sentiments expressed in them are Maori; uniformity of movement, wiri hand movements and the use of regular metre are haka traits;[161] the core gestures appear to be based on those of traditional paatere; and the melody and harmony of the accompanying songs are European.

345

CHAPTER 21

CULTURAL RENAISSANCE AND NEO-WAIATA STYLE

In the early nineteenth century, older Maori people had difficulty accommo-
dating to European music. Today the middle-aged and younger generations
are having equal and opposite difficulties with the Maori system. As a result,
although waiata singing style was formerly resistant to change, European
elements are now being introduced into the music, accentuating trends first
seen in transitional waiata and pao dating from the turn of the century. How
and why these changes have taken place may now be examined.

In two earlier publications[1] the writer has documented Maori concepts
of accuracy in traditional singing and the extent to which change was allowable within the system.

In earlier chapters of this book it has already been emphasised that total
accuracy was and is the aim in esoteric songs such as karakia which were
hedged about with supernatural restrictions and penalties if mistakes were
made. It has also been shown that the same has become true of nominally
non-esoteric songs such as waiata. Applying to both is a vocabulary of mistakes and singing faults (see Chapter 6).

Concern for accuracy tends to focus on the texts of songs but is not
confined to them. Johannes Andersen states that he more than once saw
singers stop during a rehearsal to make a correction so small that he himself
was 'hardly if at all' able to notice the difference.[2] Andersen attributed this to
concern for melody as much as for words and, if a statement from A.S.
Thomson is correct, this was evidently true as early as 1859:

> Much care was taken to preserve uncontaminated the airs of ancient songs,
> for although ignorant of complicated music, many New Zealanders have
> correct ears for time and tunes.[3]

Captain Mair espoused similar views:

> . . . the Maori possessed a most critical ear and the slightest omission or
> misplacing of a note or intonation in (to us) their monotonous chaunts
> would be received with ridicule.[4]

On being asked about other singers, good singers in the 1960s commented adversely on anyone who was judged unable to carry the air of a waiata. A common complaint (in English) was that such a singer was 'flat' or had 'airs of his own' or had 'his own tunes'.[5] Often it was stated that 'no one can sing with him'. This may well be the crux of the matter because most songs are intended to be performed by groups; each song traditionally had its own air[6] and a text which was meant to be heard; and for this to be possible unanimity is essential.

This raises an apparent problem of how to reconcile Maori insistence on accuracy in waiata singing and the plentiful evidence of restraints upon change with the equally undoubted presence of song variants and the widespread Maori practice of reworking old songs to produce new ones. Reworking was discussed in Chapter 7 where it was shown that adapted songs were regarded no differently from others and that borrowing was, in effect, an accepted method of composition. The same was found, in principle, to apply to tunes. Tune variants occur usually when a song has been transported out of its area of origin and the normal process of group reinforcement of the original tune no longer applies. The same, however, can occur even within a tribal area when the singing tradition has become attenuated. The latter is a modern phenomenon, at odds with traditional practice, and very much a product of the process the writer has called song loss (Chapter 18). A case in point is the waiata 'Teeraa te marama hohoro te kake mai' which has been recorded in three different versions, all in the song's home area of Waikato. The singer of one of these versions[7] acknowledged that there was confusion in the district about the tune. One elder had his own tune, but he also had tunes of his own for other waiata and was universally known as a 'flat' singer; a second version, evidently the standard one, was sung throughout the Waikato; and the third was peculiar to the singer's own district around Morrinsville. This latter version almost certainly originated with a culture group which was formed in the 1960s in Morrinsville for the express purpose of enabling young people to learn waiata. Fifteen years later this group was often to be heard at meetings, and others of its songs also differed from the earlier and still extant approved versions. As a case study, the example is instructive. It demonstrates a common outcome if attempts are made by a group to learn waiata when most members of the group are unfamiliar with the style.

Since the 1950s, there have been significant social changes which have resulted in depopulation of rural Maori communities which hitherto had been the heartland of waiata and other traditional forms of song. While these areas retained a representative cross-section of their populations, and so long as there were large groups singing in marae context at frequent meetings, particular songs and, equally, waiata style itself, stayed intact. Young people could learn songs simply by joining in with the elders when they sang and no special effort was required of anyone. Over the past half century, however, Maoridom has undergone a prolonged exodus to the cities. This has contributed to a breakdown in the former method of transmission and has forced young people to learn songs, if at all, either as individuals or as members of urban culture groups. In an effort to revitalise waiata singing, a waiata section has been introduced into intertribal cultural competitions alongside the customary haka, poi and action songs; waiata schools using tape recordings have been held from time to time in a number of tribal areas; and the Archive of Maori and Pacific Music at the University of Auckland has offered a free dubbing service for over 20 years to provide recordings for groups and individuals who wish to learn songs. In so far as they have been successful, however, these measures have contributed less to the maintenance of the old style than to the emergence of a new one. As already indicated, in traditional marae context various constraints operated upon waiata singing to ensure that change was kept to a minimum. Accuracy was the aim: change was proscribed; experienced singers predominated; and there was universal disapproval of singers who did not conform. Thus, if an individual deviated, the rest of the group acted as a corrective, and variants of songs could, in the main, become established only outside their home areas.

In the case of the urban culture group, the above situation characteristically does not apply. Usually the group is taught by a single individual. The best that can happen is that the group will reproduce this individual's version of the song, complete with any variations — witting or unwitting — he or she may have introduced. This is true whether or not the individual concerned has presented the group with an adequate model. The problem is compounded when the members of the group are all or largely neophytes. Eventually, without the checks and balances of marae singing to act as a corrective, the new variant becomes the norm for the particular group. Nevertheless, at this point the new variant is peculiar to the group. It cannot enter general currency unless one further step takes place. If a group, having modified a song while learning it, subsequently splits up, its members will be able to perform the song only as individuals unless they further alter the song to agree with outside performers. If they fail to do so, other performers will be unable to sing with them and the variant will ultimately die. If, on the other hand, as at Morrinsville, the group remains intact and is large enough, it will be able to perform *as a group* in marae context, even in competition with other groups still performing the original version.

It is important to understand that whenever a neophyte group conscientiously attempts to learn a waiata and ends up with a product different from the original, any changes which have resulted from European influence will be of the kind designated in Chapter 17 as both compatible and non-central. Central elements are easily recognisable and will be faithfully reproduced by conscientious singers. Amongst them, in the Maori case, are such traits as narrow range, small melodic steps, few notes, centrically organised scales, two-phrase formal structure and the terminal glissando. Other traits such as scales and hetrometre, however characteristic they may be of the music system, are subject to change if they are non-central and as such are carried not consciously but subliminally by the practitioners.[8] Some changes to non-central elements of the Maori music system are of long standing. One is a move away from non-diatonic scales as documented by the analysis of Maori flute scales in Chapter 5. The flutes, which are known to have provided unison accompaniment of waiata tunes, are shown to have undergone a slow shift in preferred scales from the eighteenth century to the present. The latest change, coinciding with the beginning of European contact in the nineteenth century, is towards an increasing use of scales similar to the Western major and minor, and present-day practice by younger singers has accelerated this trend. Two mechanisms may be involved: one a simple dropping from the repertoire of non-diatonic songs, and the other an active transformation of older scales into segments of the major and minor.

Some elements of the neo-style now emerging from present-day urban culture groups appear to have entered by way of action song. Thus, when a paatere is performed by a culture group, the characteristic additive rhythms are now absent and the dancers move their bodies from side to side in time to a ubiquitous 'beat' not present in traditional paatere. Similar regularisation of traditional additive rhythms and imposition of metre occurs when such groups attempt to sing waiata. An evident import from hymn singing is a Europeanised manner of singing with use of vibrato and portamento. Other characteristics of neo-waiata style include melodic simplification and stereotyping, particularly in solo 'drag' figures; displacement of melodic emphases to different syllables of the text; and systematic changes in scales and placement of tonic. The latter, indeed, often utterly transforms the tonality, and it is in this respect that some of the more striking changes occur. Compare, for example, versions of a well-known Whaanau-a-Apanui song as sung (a) by a group of East Coast elders led by Herini Waititi in 1964 and (b) by the younger East Coast singer Rangi Te Kura Dewes (Example 104).[9]

Transformations of this kind are not aberrations. They are both inevitable and beyond the conscious control of the singers. In New Zealand, as everywhere in the Western world, on radio, television and in almost every

EXAMPLE 104 *Waiata: Line 3 of M&O 42 (a) as led by Herini Waititi (b) as sung by Rangi Te Kura Dewes*

public place, the music to which the whole population, including Maori, is exposed is not only inescapable but uncompromisingly European and over-whelmingly 'pop' in nature. Young Maori singers, whose main or even ex-clusive background and allegiance has been to European music, lack the experience of the Maori system which would enable them either to perceive changes when they occur or indeed even to recognise the melodic and other patterns required to learn a traditional song. Their first musical 'language' is European and it is the rules of the European system which they have intern-alised and which colour their perceptions of all music. As a result, they unknowingly transform the Maori patterns into the more familiar European ones. The problem becomes even more acute, and change correspondingly more likely, in the case of waiata learned for cultural competitions, because of an adjudication requirement that such waiata be original compositions.

Even if a culture group by dint of much practice, and with the aid of a skilled instructor, does succeed in learning a waiata without changing it, the group's hold on the song is likely to be tenuous.

WHAT OF THE FUTURE?

It is clear that efforts to salvage the older singing tradition by encouraging urban-based culture groups of young singers to learn or even compose waiata have created a potent source of unwitting change and mark a turning-point in the history of the style. Despite their own best efforts, such groups are transforming waiata style into a hybrid which is a blend of Maori and Euro-pean. It is a situation which upholders of tradition are bound to deplore: if 'authenticity' is the aim, efforts made over the past 20 years to revive the waiata-singing tradition must be said to have failed. In cultural terms, how-ever, it can be argued that this 'failure' is insignificant. Elsewhere, the writer has pointed out that, for its practitioners, waiata continues to be important because of its social relevance, particularly as an ingredient of the 'rituals of encounter' (see Chapter 1) which are played out at almost every Maori meet-ing.[10] Attempts in New Zealand to aid the revival of waiata singing have been a response to an expressed Maori need and it is this need and Maori acceptance of it that has fuelled the current renaissance. The product may not be fully 'authentic' but it is here, paradoxically, that the real hope lies. It is highly noticeable at Maori meetings that just one waiata, 'E paa too hau' (M&O 14), and one haka, 'Ka mate!' (Example 9), are performed over and over again. They are safe choices because they are known by almost everyone. But, if the demands of protocol are ever to move beyond such tokenism, the current barriers to composition in the style will need to fall. If and when waiata style comes fully to terms with the intrusive Western system, it is possible that a truly integrated blend of old and new will emerge, composition will again become commonplace, and the long process of attrition which has so diminished the traditional Maori repertoire will at last be at an end.

APPENDIX 1

PRONUNCIATION GUIDE TO MAORI

Maori has ten consonant sounds (written *h, k, m, n, ng, p, r, t, w, wh*) and five vowels (written *a, e, i, o, u*). Each vowel is either long or short. In the following list, adapted from Biggs's *Let's Learn Maori* (1969) and *English–Maori Maori–English Dictionary* (1990a), and throughout the present work, single vowels represent vowels which are pronounced short and double vowels those which are pronounced long.

Consonants are pronounced approximately as in English except for:

wh as in 'whale' (not 'wail'), or as *f*
ng as in 'singer', never as in 'finger'
r as in the Oxford pronunciation of 'very'

Vowels are pronounced:

short *a*, as in *manu*, like *u* in 'nut'
long *aa*, as in *maanu*, like *a* in 'Chicago'
short *i*, as in *pipi*, like *i* in 'pit'
long *ii*, as in *piipii*, like *ee* in 'peep'
short *e*, as in *peke*, like *e* in 'peck' or 'ferry'
long *ee*, as in *peeke*, like *ai* in 'pair' or in 'fairy'
short *o*, as in *hoko*, like *or* in 'report'
long *oo*, as in *kookoo*, like *ore* in 'pore'
short *u*, as in *putu*, like *u* in 'put'
long *uu*, as in *puutu*, like *oo* in 'moon'

Note, in particular, the correct pronunciation of *e* and *o*. A widespread misconception by speakers of New Zealand English is that the Maori *e* is pronounced like *ay* in 'day' (as in Latin or Italian). Another common error is to pronounce *o* as in the English word 'so'.

Diphthongs

When two vowels occur together, each retains its own sound, merging from one to the other. For a detailed pronunciation guide, see Biggs 1969:131-2.

In Maori it is the length of the vowel rather than its quality which carries meaning. Thus, *keke* means 'cake' but *kekee* means 'creak' and *keekee* is 'arm-pit'. Although, in pronouncing a Maori word, it is desirable to get both vowel quality and vowel length right, it is the latter which is the linguistically marked feature and, as such, of most importance if the pronunciation is to be understood.

APPENDIX 2

GLOSSARY OF PLANT, ANIMAL AND BIRD NAMES

Note: C&P = Cockayne & Phillips Turner (1950). Other references are to Fisher et al. (1975), McLintock (1966) and Williams (1975).

harakeke	*Phormium tenax*: flax (McLintock)
houhou	*Nothopanax arboreum*: five-finger, a tree (Williams)
huia	*Heteralocha acutirostris*: a bird with prized tail feathers (Williams)
kaaeaea	*Falco novaeseelandiae*: bush hawk (Williams)
kaakaa	*Nestor meridionalis*: native parrot (Williams)
kaakaapoo	*Strigops habroptilus*: ground parrot (Williams)
kaakaariki	*Cyanoramphus novaezelandiae*: small green parrot (Williams)
kaiwhiria	*Hedycarya aborea*: pigeonwood, a small tree or tall shrub (C&P)
kareao	*Rhipogonum scandens*: supplejack, a climbing plant (Williams)
kauri	*Agathis australis*: a lofty massive tree (C&P)
kawakawa	*Macropiper excelsum*: a low tree or shrub (C&P)
kereruu	*Hemiphaga novaeseelandiae*: wood pigeon (Williams)
kiekie	*Freycinetia banksii*: a climbing plant (Williams)
kiore	*Rattus exulans*: the native rat (McLintock)
kooauau	*Durvillea antarctica*: bull kelp (Williams)
koukou	*Nivox novaeseelandiae*: owl, morepork = *ruru* (Williams)
kurii	the Maori dog (Williams)
kuumara	*Ipomoea batatas*: sweet potato (Williams)
maahoe	*Melicytus ramiflorus*: whitey-wood, a small bushy tree (C&P)
maapara	wood saturated with resin (Williams)
maire	*Mida myrtifolia*: sandalwood, a slender tree or tall shrub (C&P)
mako	*Aristotelia serrata*: a tree (Williams)

mamaku   *Cyathea medullaris*: an edible tree-fern (Williams)
mataii   *Podocarpus spicatus*: black-pine, a tall tree (C&P)
moa   *Dinornis gigantea* and others: (extinct) flightless bird
         (Williams)

neinei   *Dracophyllum latifolium*: spiderwood, a tree (C&P)

paaua   *Haliotis iris*: a shellfish (McLintock)
porokaiwhiria   *see* kaiwhiria
poroporo   *Solanum aviculare*: a leafy shrub ((Fisher et al.)

raupoo   *Typha augustifolia*: bulrush, a swamp plant (McLintock)
ruru   *Nivox novaeseelandiae*: owl, morepork = *koukou* (Williams)

tanguru   *Oleria albida*: a shrub or small tree (Fisher et al.)
tarata   *Pittosporum eugenioides*: a small tree (C&P)
tiitoki   *Alectryon excelsum*: a medium sized tree (C&P)
toetoe   var. species: a native grass used for thatching (Williams)
tootara   *Podocarpus totara*: a tall massive tree (C&P)
tutu   *see* tuupaakihi
tuupaakihi   *Coriaria aborea*: a shrub (Williams)

whau   *Entelea arborescens*: a small tree or tall shrub (C&P)

APPENDIX 3

LIST OF SINGERS AND INFORMANTS

Note: The list gives only the names of the singers of the musical examples and the names of persons cited in the text. For a complete list of singers recorded, with dates of recording and vowel length indicated, see McLean & Curnow (1992a:319-37).

Name	Tribe
Ani, Onewhero Te (F)	Tuuhoe/Whakatoohea
Aperaniko, Rihipeti (F)	Ngaati Paamoana
Awahau (M)	[of Okaiawa]
Awatere, Arapeta (M)	Ngaapuhi/Ngaati Porou
Bailey, Tuku (F)	Te Ati Awa
Boyce, Kiri (F)	Ngaati Porou
Bubb, Ngatai (F)	Tuuhourangi, Te Arawa
Dewes, Rangi Te Kura (F)	Ngaati Porou
Haerewa, Tiripou (F)	Tuuhoe
Hanuera, Te Mamaeroa (F)	Ngaati Raukawa
Hawe, Kopeka (F)	Ngaaruahinerangi
Herewini, Paraire (M)	Waikato
Hikuroa, Poihi (M)	Ngaati Ruanui
Hoeta, Waina Te (F)	Ngaati Tuuwharetoa/Ngaati Awa
Hotene, Molly (F)	Ngaati Hauaa
Hughes, Kino (M)	Tuuhoe/Ngaati Maniapoto
Huia, Sam (M)	Ngaati Te Wehi of Waikato
Hurinui, Pei Te (M)	Ngaati Maniapoto
Iti, Henare (M)	Ngaati Ruaroa of Ngaati Maniapoto
Iwikau, Para (F)	Ngaati Whititama of Tuuwharetoa
Jacob, Lucy (F)	Ngaati Raukawa
Kahaki, Kiri (F)	Whaanau-a-Apanui
Kawhia, Pane (F)	[of Ruatoria]
Kawiti, Tawai (M)	Ngaati Hine
Kapa, Mutu (M)	Te Aupoouri/Waikato

Katene, Hamu (M)	Nga Rauru of Whanganui
Katene, Rangimotuhia (M)	Nga Rauru of Whanganui
Kati, Te Kehi (F)	Ngaati Tuuwharetoa
Kershaw, Ngakirikiri (F)	Ngaati Ruanui
Maha, Puarauehu (F)	Ngaaruahinerangi
Mahuta, Bob (M)	Waikato
Maipi, Joe Te (M)	Tuuhoe
Manihera, Ira (M)	Patu Heuheu/Ngaati Haka of Tuuhoe
Manuera, Eruera (M)	Ngaati Awa/Tuuhoe
Manuera, Hemi (M)	Te Aupoouri/Te Rarawa
Mariu, Makarena (F)	Ngaati Tuuwharetoa
Mauparaoa, Turanga (M)	Ngaati Manawa/Tuuhoe
Mitchell, Hamuera (M)	Ngaati Whakaue, Te Arawa
Mokena, Piri (M)	Ngaati Kahu/Ngaapuhi
Murray, Rawinia (F)	Whanganui
Natana, Ani Reweti (F)	Tuuhoe
Naera, Tame (M)	Ngaati Whakaue, Te Arawa
Ngata, Sir Apirana (M)	Ngaati Porou
Nicholas, Hannah (F)	Te Ati Awa
Nicholas, Jim (M)	[of Waitara]
Paul, Lizzy (F)	Te Ati Awa
Peita, Pakihi (M)	Waiariki of Te Rarawa
Penfold, Merimeri (F)	Ngaati Kurii/Te Aupoouri
Pirikahu, Pare (F)	Ngaati Mutunga/Ngaati Te Whiti of Te Ati Awa
Pohatu, Emere (F)	Ngaati Porou
Pokai, Miro (F)	Ngaaruahinerangi
Pokiha, Moa (M)	Ngaati Paamoana of Wainuiarua of Whanganui
Pokiha, Rangi (M)	Ngaati Paamoana of Wainuiarua of Whanganui
Pou, Eru (M)	[of Kaikohe]
Puata, Meri (F)	Te Ati Awa/Ngaati Maru
Rangi, Rev. W. (M)	
Rangihau, John (M)	Tuuhoe
Rangiihu, Hami (M)	Tuuhoe/Whakatoohea
Rangitauira, Te Hapai (F)	Whanganui
Ratahi, Moerangi (F)	Ngaati Awa
Rau, Marjorie (F)	Ngaati Mutunga/Ngaati Toa/Te Ati Awa
Raumati, Pare (F)	Ngaati Mutunga/Ngaati Tama of Te Ati Awa

Rawiri, Heremia (M)	Whanganui
Reweti, Moerewarewa (F)	Ngaati Ruanui
Ririkore, Mohi (M)	Taranaki
Stirling, Eruera (M)	Ngaati Porou
Tahuriorangi, Kurauia (F)	Ngaati Pikiao, Te Arawa
Tairakena, Uehoka (M)	Ngaati Maahanga of Waikato
Tamati, Whati (M)	Waikato
Toitupu, Ihaka (M)	Whanganui
Toka, Henare (M)	Ngaati Whaatua
Tomo, Marata Te (F)	Ngaati Tuuwharetoa/Maniapoto/ Raukawa
Tomo, Turau Te (M)	Ngaati Tuuwharetoa/Ngaati Kahungunu
Tuhua, Amohia Te Rei (F)	Waikato
Tuoro, Meha (F)	Ngaati Hau of Ngaapuhi
Waititi, Herini (M)	Whaanau-a-Apanui/Ngaati Porou
Watson, Ngati (F)	Puketapu of Te Ati Awa
Werahiko, Raupare (F)	Ngaati Toa/Ngaati Raukawa/ Tuuwharetoa
Wetere, Dick (M)	Ngaati Hikairo of Waikato
Wharemate, Matekino (M)	Ngaati Moerewa
Wharetapu, Toki (M)	Tuuhoe
White, Potete (M)	Ngaati Tama of Te Ati Awa
Wikiriwhi, Pirihira (F)	Ngaati Pikiao, Te Arawa
Wineera, Pairoa (F)	Ngaati Toa/Ngaati Huia of Raukawa

APPENDIX 4

ILLUSTRATION CREDITS

Institutions & Individuals

Alexander Turnbull Library: 38, 58, 61, 79, 187, 269, 282 lower, 285 upper, 313, 318, 319, 324, 338, 340, 341; Photo Archive, Anthropology Department, University of Auckland: 28, 29, 31, 77, 113, 149, 193; Auckland Art Gallery: 97, 295; Auckland Public Library: 290, 296; Canterbury Museum: 132; Hocken Library: 127, 133, 134, 292 R; M. Mclean: 178, 182 lower, 185 upper, 185 lower, 190. 321 lower (obtained from a collector), 332 (purchased from a bookseller); S.M. Mead: 98; Museum of New Zealand Te Papa Tongarewa: 19, 160, 188, 225; National Library of Australia: 13, 102; Nelson Provincial Museum: 317; Rotorua Museum of Art & History Te Whare Taonga o Te Arawa: 273, 321, 325, 333, 342; Taranaki Museum: 141; Wanganui Regional Museum: 288.

Publications

For full citations, see References. Photos from Hawksworth 1773, Parkinson 1773 and White 1891 copied by and reproduced by permission of Auckland Institute & Museum Te Papa Whakahiku. Photos from all other sources copied by Hamish MacDonald, Anthropology Department, University of Auckland. Photos from Best 1976 reproduced by permission of Museum of New Zealand Te Papa Tongarewa, from Simmons 1987 by permission of the author and from *Te Ao Hou* and *Tu Tangata* by permission of the Maori Purposes Fund Board.

Andersen 1934: 17 lower (after p.276, fig.61), 172 (p.209, fig.40), 174 (opp. p.300, fig.75), 177 (opp. p.291, fig.71), 182 upper (after p.290, fig.69 (right)); Angas 1847a: 32 (pl.LII), 55 (pl. LIII (lower)), 150 (pl. LIII (upper)), 167 lower (pl.58, figs 13, 14); Anonymous: 326 (Anon 1908a), 327 (Anon C.1935), 328 (Anon 1947), 335 (Anon 1934); Best 1976: 128 (p.102, fig.22), 154 (p.171, fig.48), 161 (p.155, fig.40), 167 upper (p.298, fig. 103), 169 (p.301, fig.105), 175 (p.295, fig.102a); Buick 1934: 54 lower (opp. p.56), 88 (p.32), 315 (opp. p.57), 330 (opp. p.48); Cowan 1910b: 106 (p.330), 314 (p.377), 316 (p.342); Cowan 1930: 136 upper (p.200); Davies 1855: 246 (p.329); Earle 1832: 62 (p.70), 112 upper (p.160); Elder 1932: 294 (opp. p.424); Gudgeon 1887: 292 L (p.422); Hawksworth 1773: 13 (v3, pl.14); Hochstetter 1867: 211 (p.314), 298 (p.306); McLean 1982: 196 (fig. 3), 197 (fig.4); Meade 1870: 81 (p.39); Morley 1900: 284 upper L (p.19), 284 upper R (P.69), 285 lower L (P.38); Papakura 1905: 323 (p.3); Parkinson 1773: 16 (pl.XV), 23 (pl.XVIII), 26 upper (pl.XXIV), 52 (pl.VII (R)), 53 (pl.XVII); Porter 1974: 285 lower R (frontispiece); Ramsden 1936: 282 upper (opp. p.76), 284 lower (opp. p.56); G.A. Selwyn 1847: 279 (frontispiece); Sherrin & Wallace 1890: 271 (p.394), 301 (p.400), 303 (p.586); Simmons 1987: 26 lower (p.48); *Te Ao Hou*: 112 lower (v.57, p.33), 136 lower (v.22, p.25), 343 (v.64, p.31); A. Thomson 1859: 51 (frontispiece); Trotter & McCullough 1981: 17 upper (p.12, fig.5); *Tu Tangata*: 151 (v.19, p.20), 158 (v.19, p.21), 345 (v.16, p.9); White 1891: 54 (p.[65]); W.J. Williams [c.1922]: 272 (opp. p.76), 331 (opp. p.225).

NOTES

Introduction

1 Salmond 1983:316.
2 Salmond 1991:317-19.
3 Henceforth abbreviated to Williams.
4 The pronunciation of singers' and informants' names can be ascertained from McLean & Curnow 1992a where they are double-vowelled.
5 While the present book was in press, a book was published by the Maori Language Commission (1996) containing 5500 such words. Amongst them are many musical terms including names for instruments of the orchestra (clarinet, horn, violin etc.); other musical instruments (bagpipes, banjo, harmonica etc.); voice registers (bass, tenor, soprano, etc.); time values (crotchet, quaver, semiquaver etc.); and other terms relating to music structure (harmony, key, key signature, note, rhythm, pitch, time signature, etc.).
6 Ngata & Ngata 1993.
7 McLean and Orbell 1975; Orbell 1978; Orbell 1991; Wedde & McQueen 1985.
8 Part 4 (Ngata 1990) is monolingual.
9 In 1958, when field work began, the distance travelled averaged 30 miles (48 km) per song; by the 1970s it had stretched to 200 miles (320 km) per song.
10 Accession numbers 91/001-92.
11 McLean 1983; McLean 1991; McLean & Curnow 1992a; McLean & Curnow 1992b.
12 See especially McLean & Curnow 1992a:5-6 for acknowledgements relating to field work.

Chapter 1

1 Except for the section on 'rituals of encounter', the account which follows refers principally to traditional Maori society.
2 Formerly known as Malayo-Polynesian.
3 Green 1977:22-23.
4 Bellwood 1978b:399, 400-4.
5 Houghton 1980:122; J. Davidson 1984:49, 50.
6 Available in full as Song 9 in McLean & Orbell.

7 Buck 1950:35.
8 ibid.:102.
9 In a long article, Barber (1992) seeks to discredit accounts of Maori cannibalism before 1815 but, in the main, does so unconvincingly. It would seem likely that the custom developed relatively late in New Zealand but was well established by the time of Cook's visit and escalated thereafter as the scale of tribal warfare increased.
10 Houghton 1980:95.
11 ibid.:97.
12 Davidson 1984:49.
13 Beaglehole 1962 (II):17-18.
14 Davidson 1984:157.
15 ibid:74.
16 Buck 1950:194. Buck says the general tool used for making holes in wood was the stone chisel, but the drill would also have been used for making the fingerholes of wooden flutes.
17 ibid.:271-2.
18 ibid.:274.
19 ibid.:277.
20 ibid.:110.
21 Best 1952:102.
22 Best loc.cit.
23 McLintock 1966:443.
24 Beaglehole 1962 (II):14.
25 Buck 1950:284-5.
26 Bellwood 1978b:403.
27 Bellwood 1978a:140; Davidson 1984:214.
28 Davidson ibid.:214-55.
29 Bellwood 1978b:405; McEwen 1966:409.
30 Buck 1950:314; McEwen loc.cit.
31 Teone Taare Tikao of Ngaai Tahu said to Herries Beattie (1939:156) that he was told the whorls and scrolls were first copied from the lines on the thumb.
32 Best 1976a:206.
33 Buddle 1851:45; Colenso 1880:59.
34 *Auckland Star*, 5.9.74, 'Camera captures a bit of history'.
35 Buck 1950:300.
36 Bellwood 1978b:406.
37 Robley 1896:167.

38   More detailed information on social organisation can be obtained from Book III, Ch.1 of Buck 1950, Ch.3 of Firth 1959 and Chs 1 & 2 of Metge 1967.

39   The Wesleyan John Warren (1814-83), who began as a missionary at Kaipara Heads in 1840, estimated that at this time 6–8 per cent of the Maori population was held in slavery at the mercy of chiefs who kept them as property and could kill them on a whim or at will (Warren 1863:10).

40   Firth 1959:106-7.

41   Orbell 1978:8.

42   D. Oliver 1961:71.

43   Quoted Firth 1959:135.

44   ibid.:136-7.

45   Salmond 1975:13.

46   D. Oliver 1961:72-73.

47   Firth 1959:246.

48   There is an extensive literature on traditional Maori religion including Best 1976b and Best 1982, Book IV of Buck 1950 and Johansen 1954.

49   Metge 1967:30.

50   Buck 1950:476.

51   The missionary William Williams claimed congregations in 1840 of 30,000 for the Church of England alone (O. Wilson 1965:473).

52   For a comprehensive discussion of Maori prophet movements, see Elsmore 1989.

53   Raureti 1978. For an account of the Ratana Church, see Elsmore ibid., Ch.47.

54   Firth 1959:412-13.

55   ibid.:413.

56   Buck 1950:387-8.

57   Firth 1959:413.

58   ibid.:400.

59   ibid.:401.

60   For information about Maori warfare see Ballara 1976 and Vayda 1960. An account from a Maori perspective is in Buck 1950:Ch.5.

61   Biggs 1990b:17.

62   Probably a shell trumpet.

63   Sharp 1968:41-42, 121.

64   Cook (quoted Salmond 1991:286).

65   A reference to the war dance.

66   Banks (quoted Salmond 1991:271).

67   Salmond 1975:19.

68   Later to be killed in Hawaii when he relaxed his vigilance.

69   Best 1982:27; Salmond 1991:395.

70   Dumont d'Urville was given a different explanation by the Maori. M. Quoy, who was a member of d'Urville's expedition to New Zealand in 1826-27, attributed the death of Marion to revenge for de Surville's act some time before

in carrying off a chief, stating: 'The inhabitants of the Bay of Islands, who seem well aware of what happened, assured M. d'Urville that it was members of the tribe from where Surville had stayed, who had suddenly appeared and fallen on Marion without anyone being able to stop them (Wright 1950:225). For other interpretations and for a detailed analysis, see Kelly 1951.

71   Fox 1976:29.

72   Roth 1891:29-35.

73   Fox 1976:7.

74   ibid.:5, 7.

75   Searle & Davidson 1975:3. Estimates of the number of volcanoes in Auckland range from 48 to more than 60, depending on which landforms are counted as separate. The currently most generally accepted figure is 48 (Hayward & Kermode 1994).

76   Cited by Bellwood 1978a:150.

77   Davidson 1984:58. Cook's own estimate in 1773 was 100,000, a figure dismissed by Davidson (loc.cit.) as no more than a guess. However, as Davidson observes, modern estimates also involve guesswork and some have been arrived at by working backwards from the number of paa sites.

78   Salmond 1975:127.

79   Walker 1975:24.

80   Salmond 1975:131.

81   ibid.:133.

82   ibid.:134.

83   Salmond ibid.:135-7; Shennan 1984:50; Tauroa 1986:31-34.

84   Tauroa ibid.:36.

85   Salmond 1975:140.

86   ibid.:142.

87   Salmond 1975:142, 145; Tauroa 1986:40-41.

88   Salmond 1975:143.

89   Best (1976a:205) calls it 'tangi tiikapa' or 'tangi whakakurepe', describing it as 'a wordless wailing accompanied by peculiar swayings of the body, quivering hands etc.'. Tiikapa means 'mournful' and whakakurepe refers to hand quivering (Williams).

90   Salmond 1975:145.

91   Salmond loc.cit.; Tauroa 1986:42.

92   A term used by John Logan Campbell (1881:172) who writes of old women of a funeral party breaking into 'a well sustained hum-m-m'.

93   Salmond 1975:146.

94   ibid.:147.

95   'Tangi aatahu' is given by Williams as a 'love spell' and Arapeta Awatere (interview 17.7.74) disputed this use of the term 'tangi koorero', saying it referred instead to a man giving a fare-

well speech while weeping.

96   Interviews Arapeta Awatere 6.3.73 &
17.7.74; Kino Hughes 18.4.72.

97   Awatere interview 17.7.74.

98   Polack 1838 (I):85.

99   Potts 1882:27.

100   Kerry-Nicholls 1884:309.

101   Salmond 1975:147.

102   ibid.:176-7.

103   Walker 1975:24-25.

104   Tauroa 1986:69.

Chapter 2

1   Williams 1975. Similarly, the habit of singing while near the house out of doors (koonewa)
was regarded as a bad omen (ibid.), doubtless
for the same reason.

2   Nicholas 1817 (I):71.

3   Burney MS 1772-73:[26].

4   Orbell 1985:57.

5   Orbell loc.cit.

6   Best 1976a:206-7; Buck 1950:491-4.

7   Williams 1975.

8   Buck 1950:490. Long vowels have been
added from Williams 1975.

9   Best 1972 (I):1123-7.

10   Best 1982:102-91.

11   Best 1976b:310-18; Buck 1950:494-507.

12   Best, too, is explicit elsewhere (1982:110),
that: 'Should any error be made in the repetition, the omission of a word for example, then
the charm was powerless to effect the desired
purpose; not only so but the error recoiled as it
were with the probable result of the death of
the reciter.'

13   Firth 1959:270.

14   Best 1976a:207; 1976b:308; Buck 1950:
490.

15   Shirres 1986:Ch.2.

16   ibid.:19.

17   ibid.:20, 23.

18   ibid.:25.

19   ibid.:22. Wiremu Maihi Te Rangikaheke (?–
1896) was a noted leader and scholar of Ngaati
Rangiwewehi tribe of Te Arawa. Under the pa-
tronage of Governor Grey he produced a large
body of written work now mostly in the Grey
Collection at the Auckland Public Library. Besides writing manuscripts of his own, he contributed to Grey's books and manuscripts on
Maori songs, proverbs and mythology (Oliver
et al.:1990).

20   Shirres uses the term 'rods' as a general term
for objects such as sticks, fern stalks or posts
used in ritual. Called toko, pou, raakau and

other names, these objects had multiple meanings depending upon the particular ritual. Commonly, however, they represented pathways or
conduits and served also as abiding places for
atua and the ancestors (Shirres ibid.:Ch.5).

21   Shirres 1986:47-49.

22   Firth 1959:270.

23   Buck 1950:499.

24   Pai Marire, also known as Hauhauism, began in Taranaki in the 1860s under the leadership of Te Ua Haumene (?–1866). For a modern
account see Clark 1975. For accounts of Pai
Marire beliefs and history see McLintock 1966
(II):458 and Elsmore 1989, Ch.25. Pai Marire
karakia are not recited like traditional ones but
are sung in distinctive style. Examples have been
recorded as McL 211-13, 442 and 613. Translations and commentary on portions of the liturgy can be found in Winks 1953.

25   The Ringatu religion was begun by Te Kooti
Rikirangi Te Turuki (?–1893) at about the same
time as Pai Marire. The services include long
passages of scripture sung from memory in
waiata style. The standard authority on Ringatu
is Greenwood 1942. See also McLintock (1966
(II):458-9) for a summary, Misur 1975 and
Elsmore 1987 (Ch.29) for a history of the development of the Ringatu Church, Tarei 1978
for an insider account and Salmond 1975:200-
2 for a description of Ringatu gatherings. The
most recent work on Te Kooti is Judith Binney's
definitive biography, *Redemption Songs* (Binney
1995). See Appendix D in Binney for an index
of waiata composed or adapted by Te Kooti.
Songs from her list in the McLean collection of
recordings are McL 663, 864, 865, 979, 980,
1058, and 1091. Others attributed to Te Kooti
but not in Binney's list are McL 35, 638, 669,
786, 866, 1266 and 1276. Examples of inoi
(prayers), hiimene (hymns), paanui (scripture
passsages) and waiata (psalms) from the Ringatu
liturgy have been recorded as McL 1179.

26   Mahuta 1974:29.

27   ibid.:66-67.

28   Alternative names for the watch song are
whakaoho (interview Arapeta Awatere 8.11.71)
and, especially in Northland, mataara. Most
Northland singers explained the latter term as a
'call to arms'. One item (McL 1086A), also called
mataara by its singer, was glossed instead as a
'taunting chant' performed without clothes by
the third challenger during the wero.

29   Interview Arapeta Awatere 8.11.71.

30   Mahuta 1974:29.

31   Another well-known watch song, again frequently performed as a tauparapara, is Song 26

in McLean & Orbell as sung in 1963 by Sam Huia of Waikato tribe.

32 Biggs 1964:46.
33 Ngata & Te Hurinui 1961:109.
34 Ngata & Te Hurinui 1970:91.
35 Hurinui [1960]:138-9.
36 Ngata & Te Hurinui 1970:91.
37 Pomare & Cowan 1930:276-7.
38 Best 1976a:204.
39 Interviews Awatere 1958 and 5.9.71.
40 Karetu 1993:47.
41 Interview Awatere 1958.
42 Best 1972:159-61.
43 From information provided by McLintock (1966 (I):897-8), it appears that the first All Blacks' haka was performed by a 'Native' team who delighted British crowds with it while on tour in 1888–89. It is not known what this haka was but the All Blacks of 1905 performed 'Ka mate' and this has remained the haka usually performed. Additionally, the 'Invincibles' of 1924–25 had their own haka beginning 'Kia whakangaawari au i ahau'.
44 Best 1976a:92.
45 ibid.:85
46 Angas 1847a:[4].
47 Thomson 1859 (I):193.
48 Best 1976a:85.
49 Andersen 1934:311-13.
50 Buck 1950:250.
51 Maning 1863:45.
52 Polack 1840 (I):86.
53 Earle 1832:89-90.
54 Awatere (1975:513, 514). In an interview (4.7.73), Awatere equated puha with the term 'pepeha'. He said it is a short form of ngeri to incite men to action, a virtual 'on parade' command. Baker (1861:58) confirms that the puha is 'short, spirited, and pronounced with a vehement tone and gesture'. He adds that it was used at public meetings to express a general feeling of unity and decision as, for instance, after two contending parties have made peace and join in singing a puha in token of amity. However, Best (1976a:204) and other writers agree in calling the puha a war song. Shortland (1854:153) equates it with 'hari' and 'peruperu', attributing the former term to Ngaapuhi tribe and the latter to Waikato.
55 Best 1903:74.
56 Awatere 1975:514.
57 Armstrong 1964:163.
58 Best 1903:78.
59 Buck 1950:392.
60 Shortland 1854:150-1.
61 Polack 1840 (II):2-4.

62 Beaglehole 1955:566.
63 Beaglehole 1962 (II):29.
64 J. Forster 1778:476.
65 Polack 1840 (I):86-87.
66 Rogers 1961:217.
67 Thomson 1859, vol.1.
68 Bidwill 1841:81.
69 Reed 1935:127.
70 Scherzer 1861-63:(III):101.
71 Thomson 1867:66.
72 Buller 1878:246-7.
73 Thomson 1859 (I):126.
74 Alexander 1863:40.
75 Buller 1878:246-7.
76 R. Taylor MS 1833-73 (IV):114.
77 Beaglehole 1967:996-7.
78 Beaglehole 1955:569.
79 Cook 1775 (II):268.
80 Beaglehole 1962 (II):29-30. According to Best (1982:285), the origin of the glaring eyes seen in posture dancing is said to be traced to the koukou or owl: 'The owl had been disturbed and irritated by the restless fantail, a small forest bird that is ever flitting about, and so glared wildly at the harmless creature.'
81 Angas 1847b:329; Bellingshausen in Debenham 1945:203; Bidwill 1841:81-82; Kerry-Nicholls 1884:339-41; Potts 1882:14; Shortland 1854:15; H. Williams in Rogers 1961; de Sainson in Wright 1950:208.
82 Maning 1863:45, 51.
83 Coote 1882:42; Dix & Oliver 1846:19-20; Donne 1927:125; Scherzer 1861-63: (III):102; S.R.G. in Andersen 1934:315.
84 Polack 1838 (I):83; Polack 1840 (I):88.
85 Cruise 1823:113-14.
86 Polack 1838 (I):82-83; 1840 (I):88.
87 Shortland 1854:151.
88 Beechey 1831:303-4.
89 Buller 1878:246.
90 Thomson 1859 (I):127.
91 Polack 1838 (I):162.
92 Dix & Oliver 1846:19-20.
93 Beaglehole 1962 (II):29.
94 Beaglehole 1967:996.
95 Cook 1775 (II):268.
96 Nicholas 1817 (I):364.
97 Debenham 1945:204.
98 St John 1873:172; Buller 1878:246; Thomson 1859 (I):126; Holloway MS n.d.:142; Taylor MS 1833-73 (IV):71.
99 Power 1849:29.
100 Kerry-Nicholls 1884:340.
101 Polack 1838 (I):83.
102 Cruise 1823:113.
103 Polack 1838 (I):82.

104 Bambridge MS 1843:31-32.

105 Beaglehole 1955:169, 566.

106 Taylor MS 1833-73 (IV):72; Kerry-Nicholls 1884:340.

107 Buller 1878:246-7.

108 Cruise 1823:113-14.

109 Morgan MS 1833-65:400, 447.

110 Buller 1878:246-7.

111 Wilkes 1845 (II):402-3.

112 De Sainson in Wright 1950:207; Polack 1840 (I):86-8; Bambridge MS 1843:31-32; Canon Stack in Reed 1935:126; Thomson 1859 (I):126.

113 Earle 1832:11.

114 Angas 1847a:[4].

115 Angas 1847b:329.

116 Vayda 1960:9.

117 Thomson 1859 (I):128.

118 Buck 1950:510.

119 Vayda 1960:58. Best (1982:615) states that during a fierce fight, the member of a tino toa, a really courageous man, was said to be remarkably prominent and that of a timid, nervous man the very reverse. He also says that ceremonial copulation was sometimes engaged in as a divinatory rite during the progress of a fight.

120 Cody 1953:122.

121 A term for this action is whakapohane 'to expose the person'; another, more specific, is whakaene 'present the posteriors in derision' (Williams). Arapeta Awatere (interview 2.7.73) described the latter as a 'taunt' and said genitalia could be presented in the same way. He himself had seen it three times on the marae. All the clothes were taken off 'right in the middle of hundreds of people looking on' and abusive words went with the actions.

122 Earle 1832:70; Polack 1838 (I):83; Morgan MS 1833-65:447; Buller 1878:247; Wakefield 1845 (I):98; Bidwill 1841:81; Bambridge MS 1843:31; Angas 1847a:[4]; Angas 1847 b:329; Thomson 1859 (I):126.

123 Beaglehole 1967:996.

124 Polack 1838 (I):81.

125 Nicholas 1817 (I):129.

126 Cruise 1823:113; H. Williams et al. n.d.:234; Dix & Oliver 1846:19.

127 Chapman MS 1830-69:(II):344; Hodgskin 1841:13.

128 Bidwill 1841:81.

129 Coote 1882:43.

130 Beechey 1831:303-4.

131 Best 1903:77.

132 Not every term is available in Williams. Best (1901:40) additionally gives 'piikari' for 'exhibiting the whites of the eyes'. Also, while broadly correct, Williams's definitions may at times lack alternative meanings as well as finer shades of meaning implicit in the terms. When interviewed about some of the above terms, Arapeta Awatere (interview 2.7.73) said 'mooteko' was a term used when grimacing was meant to be humorous. Ngangahu referred to 'pushing out the eyeballs so they are staring or glaring'. Best (1901:loc.cit.) refers to 'whaakapi' as grunting in the course of a derisive song and dance, but elsewhere (1903:77) he equates it with 'piikari'.

133 Awatere 1975:513.

134 Awatere (loc.cit.) is explicit about the nature of the jump in the tuutuungaarahu. He states that whereas left to right jumping belongs to the puha or peruperu, in the tuutuungaarahu it is straight up and down: 'At the highest point in the jump . . . the knees are bent, the ankles hit the rumps, then on the way down to the ground the legs straighten to hit the ground with terrific force, in unison, at the end of the jump.' In a recent book on haka, Karetu (1993:39) inexplicably reverses the two, stating that the jumping is up and down in the peruperu but side to side in the tuutuungaarahu. However, it would seem that Awatere is correct as a side to side jump would be inconsistent with the purpose of the tuutuungaarahu. Karetu (1993: loc.cit) is also at odds with Awatere concerning the whakatuuwaewae; he states that there is no jumping in this dance whereas Awatere equates it with the tuutuungaarahu.

135 Buck 1950:391.

136 Best 1924:106; 1976a:91.

137 Interview Arapeta Awatere 5.1.70.

138 Roth 1891:65.

139 Earle 1832:70.

140 McCormick 1963:30.

141 Maning 1863:52.

142 Beaglehole 1955:574.

143 Olivier 1985:331.

144 Thomson 1859 (I):126.

145 Shortland 1854:151.

146 Buller 1878:246.

147 Kerry-Nicholls 1884:31.

148 Polack 1840 (II):166-7.

149 Hodgskin 1841:13-14.

150 Interviews Awatere 26.7.70; 6.3.73; 2.7.73.

151 Kerry-Nicholls 1884:340.

152 Potts 1882:14.

153 Interview Awatere 15.1.70.

154 Best 1976a:93.

155 Interview Awatere 26.7.71.

156 Wakefield 1845 (I):98.

157 Beaglehole 1955:569.

158 Cruise 1823:31.

159 Beechey 1831:303-4; Stack in Reed 1935:126.
160 Earle 1832:70.
161 Maning 1863:52.
162 Holloway MS n.d.:142; Talbot 1882:16; Thomson 1859 (I):126.
163 Polack 1838 (I):82.
164 St John 1873:172.
165 Bidwill 1841:81-82.
166 Cook 1775 (II):268.
167 Beaglehole 1962 (II):29.
168 Wright 1950:208.
169 Nicholas 1817 (II):65.
170 Buller 1878:246.
171 Thomson 1859 (I):126.
172 Kerry-Nicholls 1884:341.
173 Talbot 1882:17.
174 Thomson 1859(I):194.
175 G. Forster 1777:220.
176 Coote 1882:42; S.R.G. in Andersen 1934:315; Talbot 1882:16.
177 Polack 1840 (I):86; 1838 (I):81).
178 Shortland 1854:151.
179 Hodgskin 1841:13.
180 Beaglehole 1962:420.
181 Nicholas 1817 (I):364.
182 Earle 1832:70.
183 Rogers 1961:290.
184 Wakefield 1845 (I):98.
185 Cruise 1823:30-1.
186 Polack 1840 (I):86-88.
187 In explanation of the out-thrust tongue, Karetu (1993:30-31) advances a view, heard recently by him at seminars held by Tuuhoe elders, that the tongue thrust out to full length in the haka is the symbol of the male penis and for this reason is not appropriate for women. It would appear, however, that, whatever its symbolism, women did make use of this gesture. Banks (Beaglehole 1962:420) refers to both men and women joining in a war song, distorting their faces, rolling their eyes and 'putting out their tongues'.
188 Buller 1878:246-7.
189 Thomson 1859 (I):126.
190 Potts 1882:14.
191 Best 1952:146.
192 G. Forster 1777:220.
193 Armstrong 1964:120.
194 Best 1976a:89-90.
195 Awatere 1975:514.
196 In his book, Armstrong acknowledges Awatere as one of his sources of information. When the present writer queried Awatere about Armstrong's dichotomy, Awatere said that Armstrong had attended a class of his for three weeks and had taken notes. In this course Awatere was talking mainly about haka taparahi and peruperu (interview Awatere 14.1.70).
197 Awatere loc.cit.
198 But he defines other terms in the same way. e.g. harakoa 'dancing and other amusements', motiha 'dance', ngahau 'dance', pekerangi 'a dance accompanied by song; used also as a verb'. All of these terms appear to be obsolete.
199 Best 1976a:86, 88.
200 Armstrong 1964:120.
201 Armstrong 1986:40.
202 Best 1976a:204.
203 Best 1908:742. Confirmed by Arapeta Awatere (interview 14.1.70) who stated it to be a Tuuhoe usage and Tuuhoe alone.
204 Interviews Hughes 18.4.72, Te Tomo 6.12.72.
205 Interview Awatere 1958.
206 Interview Awatere 14.1.70.
207 Armstrong 1964:120.
208 Karetu 1993:41.
209 Best loc.cit.
210 Interview Awatere 14.1.70.
211 Williams defines kootaratara as a dance of triumph.
212 Interview Awatere 14.1.70.
213 Best 1897:57-58.
214 Best 1976a:92-93.
215 Interview Awatere 14.1.70.
216 Best 1967:92.
217 Armstrong 1964:177.
218 Interview Hamuera Mitchell 16.4.85.
219 Armstrong 1964:177.
220 Best 1975:88.
221 Best 1976a:88.
222 ibid.
223 Interview Awatere 26.7.74.
224 Best 1976a:95.
225 R. Taylor MS 1833-73 (IV):71-72.
226 Best 1976a:204.
227 The term 'whakatea', which means 'show whites of eyes' (Williams), is also given by Best (1972:576) as an alternative name for the manawawera. Kino Hughes of Tuuhoe (interview 18.6.72) defined it as 'looking for a battle', 'asking for a fight', figuratively 'shaking a stick' at an advancing ope (group of persons).
228 Best 1901:40-41.
229 Interview Rangihau 26.11.71.
230 Interview Hughes 18.4.72.
231 Hughes loc.cit.
232 Oppenheim 1973:57-60 & Appendix 1.
233 Arapeta Awatere (interview 2.1.70) said that the pihe was used 'especially in the North' and was used also by tribes from Waikato,

Wanganui and Taranaki.

234 Kendall & Lee 1820:108-9.

235 W. Williams 1867:32.

236 Oppenheim op.cit.:57; Wright 1950:84, 120-1, 125, 160.

237 Sharp 1971:45-48.

238 Glasgow & Simmons 1973:28-29.

239 Dieffenbach 1843 (I):64.

240 Graham 1940.

241 ibid.:222.

242 Grey 1851.

243 This passage was paraphrased by Tregear from John White's semi-fictional novel, *Te Rou; or, the Maori at Home* (1874:266-9). The book purports to deal with real events of Ngaapuhi tribal history.

244 Tregear 1904:391.

245 Buck 1950:425.

246 Interview Awatere 2.1.70.

247 Interview H. Manuera 15.5.72.

248 Interview Kawiti 21.5.72.

249 The term 'tiitiiwai' is not in Williams. Possibly it refers to the use of sticks (tiitii) in the dance.

250 Loughnan 1902.

251 Andersen 1934:347.

252 Smith 1896-97:53.

253 Cowan 1983:44.

254 Kelly 1949:32.

255 Orbell 1985:57.

256 Interview Awatere 2.1.70.

257 Interview Marata Te Tomo 6.12.72.

258 Although widespread in Polynesia, handclapping as an accompaniment is unusual enough in New Zealand to mark this performance as a different dance form from the more widely reported haka. Two writers (St John 1873:172; Holloway MS n.d.:142) report handclapping as a frequent feature of haka they saw in *c.*1833 and in 1870 respectively. But in these cases the handclapping would have been an adjunct of body percussion and sporadic rather than continuous as implied in the de Surville account.

259 Ollivier & Hingley 1982:33, 83, 120, 168, 191.

260 Sharp 1971:48.

261 ibid.:95.

262 Thiercelin 1866 (II):142-4.

263 Best 1976a:101.

264 In an interview (5.9.71) Awatere explained that onioni denotes the action of copulation rather than copulation itself (which is ekeeke or mahimahi). It is also used for the movement of the hips in dancing if suggestive of the sexual act. If not suggestive of the sexual act, hip move-

ments are called kopikopi. When the legs 'break', i.e. the knees bend and the legs come apart, the movement becomes onioni rather than kopikopi. At other interviews (15.5.73 & 2.7.73), consistent with his earlier information, he said explicitly that kopikopi refers to rotating hip movement and onioni to the thrusting back and forth of copulation. If a woman does the latter on the marae, 'she is really asking someone to go and sleep with her'. It is never done by a man.

265 Salmond 1975:113.

266 Interview Awatere 15.5.73.

267 McCormick 1963:50-51.

268 Glasgow & Simmons 1973:22.

269 W. Williams MS 1825-55.

270 Shortland 1854:146.

271 Best 1976a:101, 118, 321.

272 Interview Mokena 17.5.72.

273 McGregor 1893:101-2.

274 Interview Arapeta Awatere 2.1.70.

275 Craik 1830:197.

276 McCormick 1963:52.

277 Tregear 1890:116. Perhaps Tregear gained the notion from the definition in Williams: '1. Rub backwards and forwards, saw. 2. Dance'. Alternatively, perhaps he was referring to onioni movements.

278 Burton [1885]:15.

279 Cowan 1910a:345-6.

280 Wright 1950:220.

281 Nicholas 1817 (I):182.

282 Walton 1839:62.

283 Polack 1838 (I):372.

284 Meade 1870:39.

285 Buchner 1878:143. Translation by Martin Sutton and Sally McLean.

286 Interview Awatere 15.1.70.

287 Scholes 1970:151.

288 Randel 1986:127.

289 Salmond 1975:100.

290 ibid.:140-1.

291 ibid.:137.

292 Interview Merimeri Penfold 16.9.77.

293 Salmond 1975:137

294 ibid.:137-8.

295 Interview Awatere 12.7.71.

296 Nicholas 1817 (I):127.

297 Tauroa 1986:37-38.

298 Interview Hughes 26.5.72.

299 Salmond 1975:144.

300 Armstrong 1964:136.

301 Anon 1943:8-9.

302 All three texts, with translations by Ngata, were published in 1943 in the *Ngarimu Investiture Souvenir Programme* (Anon 1943:14-15) as

items 6c, 6d and 6a respectively. 'Te urunga tuu' is reproduced from this source by Karetu (1993:45-47) who additionally provides a photograph of a 1990 performance. The text can also be found in Buick (1934:16-17). Ngata's text and translation of 'Ka panapana' is also available in Armstrong 1964:170. His text and translation of 'Haukiwi, hauweka' are reproduced in Armstrong 1964:171 and, together with diagrams of the movements, in Armstrong 1986:70-73.

303 Interview Awatere 16.10.73.

304 The recording is catalogue number RNZ 57.7 (McLean & Curnow 1991:153) in the collection of the AMPM at the University of Auckland.

305 The recording is catalogue number RNZ 57.8 (McLean & Curnow 1991:154) in the AMPM.

306 The recording is accessioned as tape number 0260.1 in the AMPM.

307 Maning 1863:55.

308 Kerry-Nicholls 1884:329-30.

309 Potts 1882:17.

310 Cowan 1910a:156-7.

311 Buck 1950:377.

312 Best 1976b:349.

313 Cyl 10.6, McLean & Curnow 1992b:93.

314 Interview Ani Natana 14.4.74.

315 Interview Rangihau 26.11.71.

316 Best (1977:237) explains that this procedure rendered the forest 'common' or clean of tapu, after which women were free to enter it and men could consume food within it.

317 Interview Awatere 5.1.70. Although itself now obsolete, it is possible that the huahua ceremonial described by Awatere and Rangihau is a relatively late development. In his *Forest Lore of the Maori*, Best (1977) makes no mention of it, although he gives information about a different form of bird ceremonial known as tau manu. No examples of the latter were recorded by the present writer but they are available amongst cylinder recordings made in the East Coast under Best's supervision in 1923 (see McLean & Curnow 1992b:142-3). Also recorded on cylinder is a 1921 performance of a tapatapa huahua which, from the cylinder recording documentation, appears to have been regarded by the recordists as a Wanganui equivalent of the tau manu (ibid.:127). Auditing these recordings reveals the singing style of tau manu and tapatapa huahua to be unrelated to that of the heriheri huahua. The tau manu are performed in waiata style and the Wanganui recording is also sung rather than recited.

318 Interview Jacob 29.11.73.

319 Interview Pohatu 27.11.76.

320 Jacob loc.cit.

321 Firth 1959:240.

322 Best 1924:146; 1976a:201, 206.

323 Best 1976a:206.

324 Best 1972:1124.

325 Interview Awatere 5.1.70.

326 Awatere loc.cit.

327 Makereti 1938:184.

328 Wilson 1894:31.

329 Best 1976d:157-8.

330 Colenso 1880:59-60.

331 Ironside 1890-92 (VII).

332 *NZ Herald*, 7.1.1974, p.4, 'Good Omen As Canoe Is Launched'.

333 Firth (1959:240), quoting Hare Hongi, gives 'kai whakahau' as another name for the leader.

334 Shortland 1854:140.

335 Thomson 1859 (I):136; Tregear 1904:72; Firth 1959:241.

336 Shortland 1854:140.

337 Best 1976c:105.

338 Quoted Best ibid.:107.

339 Best 1908:72.

340 Campbell 1881:79-82.

341 Firth 1959:235.

342 Armstrong 1964:156.

343 Best 1972:740-1.

344 Quoted Best 1976c:58.

345 Best 1976c:46.

346 Buck 1950:203-4.

347 Buck loc.cit.

348 Shortland 1854:143-6.

349 Potts 1882:11 and Pomare & Cowan 1930:288 name them specifically as ngeri.

350 Cruise 1823:299-300.

351 Polack 1838 (II):23.

352 Hochstetter 1867:438.

353 Potts 1882:11.

354 St John 1873:143.

355 Cowan 1910a:346-7.

356 Beaglehole 1962 (II):11, 29.

357 Beaglehole 1955:285.

358 A Tahitian term applied by Cook and his men to the Maori haka.

359 Beaglehole 1955:578.

360 Colenso 1880:57-58.

361 Cruise 1823:299; Polack 1838 (I):145.

362 Colenso 1880:57-58.

363 Wade 1842:64.

364 Campbell 1881:66-75.

365 The exhibition site was in north Hagley Park between Victoria Lake and the Avon River. The Maori paa site and canoe-launching area

bordered the lake (Anon [1906-07]:150).
366 Cowan 1910b:348.
367 Polack 1838 (I):146.
368 Hochstetter 1867:298.
369 St John 1873:143.
370 Potts 1882:11.
371 Best 1972:723; Grace 1959:93-94. Besides calling the song a hautuu, Awatere was fully aware also of Best's attestation as he preannounces the song as 'he kawa no Maataatua waka', a description which he could have obtained from Best's book.
372 Interview Awatere 3.4.73.

Chapter 3

1 Orbell 1985:57-58.
2 Ngata 1959, 1990; Ngata & Te Hurinui 1961, 1970.
3 Arapeta Awatere (interview 24.4.73) said this kind of singing was done mainly by the immediate family of a dead person before the bones were taken away to a cave or to be hung on a tree after which, in due time, they would be scraped and reburied. These days there is a verbal disputation instead.
4 Best 1924:302.
5 Best 1976a:203.
6 Interview Awatere 1958. A waiata puuremu was recorded in 1921 at Koriniti from Heremia Raawiri (McLean & Curnow 1992b:94, Cyl 11.1 (b)).
7 Best 1976a:203.
8 Best loc.cit.
9 Using a walking stick has considerable symbolic significance. Mead (1986:175-81), in the course of a detailed discussion, points out that the use of a stick by an orator does not imply old age or rheumatism. Possession of a tokotoko signals first that the owner of the stick is an orator and second that he has both authority to speak and the approval of the group he represents to do so.
10 Salmond 1975:172.
11 Tauroa 1986:51.
12 Grey 1928:xiii.
13 Shortland 1854:170.
14 Thomson 1859 (I):39-40.
15 Best 1976a:196. For a fuller account of this event see Orbell 1985:53-54.
16 Philips 1929:3.
17 Hurinui [1960]:159.
18 Ngata & Te Hurinui 1961.
19 Best 1975a:194.
20 Best loc.cit.
21 Orbell 1985:58.

22 Orbell 1990:190-1.
23 Orbell 1991:2.
24 ibid.:2, 19.
25 ibid.:111-12.
26 In a spoken announcement on a cylinder recording (Series 5 no. 94), Sir Apirana Ngata gives 'too' as the Ngaati Porou dialect equivalent of pao and ruri (McLean & Curnow 1992:195).
27 Orbell 1978:51.
28 Interview Hughes 18.6.72.
29 Interview Murray 20.2.64.
30 Orbell 1978:51.
31 McL 98, 693A, 830, 874 & 1089.
32 Best 1901:42.
33 Loughnan 1902.
34 Voluminous extracts from the Rotorua section of Loughnan's book (pp.61-133) were later published also in Andersen's *Maori Music* (1934:318-63) and some were also republished in Ngata 1908 & 1911 and Ngata & Tomoana 1919.
35 Loughnan 1902:94.
36 ibid.:97-98.
37 Interview Naatana 14.4.74.
38 Mitcalfe 1974:179.
39 Nicholas 1817 (I):317-18.
40 Dieffenbach 1843 (II):56-57.
41 Colenso 1880:59.
42 Best provides no reference for Halswell.
43 Best 1976a:103.
44 Shortland 1856:160.
45 Joseph Jenner Merrett (1816?-54) was a professional artist who came to Auckland and the Waikato in the 1840s, and found employment there as an interpreter.
46 Locke & Paul 1989:121.
47 ibid.:10.
48 Thomson 1859 (I):196.
49 Best 1976a:103.
50 ibid.:105.
51 ibid.:101.
52 Best 1976a:103, 106-7; Buck 1950:243-4.
53 Loughnan 1902:96.
54 Ngata's view that the long poi was the older form and short poi modern resurfaces also in other contexts. Arapeta Awatere (interview 26.7.71) told the writer that Ngata claimed the short poi, and some of the figures used for it, derived from the early use in Maori schools of 'Indian clubs', apparently used for physical education. Armstrong (1986:74) recounts two further notions about the origin of the short poi, the first that it was devised by commoner women because of pre-emption of the long poi by women of noble birth, and the other that it be-

gan in imitation of English soldiers twirling their drum sticks. Armstrong regards the latter two theories as doubtful and there is reason to reject Ngata's as well in view of the report by Marshall from the 1830s (above) that the string was short, and Shortland's report of 1856 (also above) that in 1842-45, when Shortland made his observations, the string was 3 or 4 feet long.

55 Best 1924:110.
56 St John 1873:172.
57 Burton [1885]:22.
58 Best 1901:42.
59 Interview Awatere 26.7.71.
60 Interview Awatere 2.1.70.
61 Beattie 1994:80-81.
62 ibid.:260.
63 ibid.:384.
64 Information abstracted from Houston 1965:170-1, McLintock 1966 (I):262-3, (III):655-6) and Sinclair 1959:144.
65 Scott 1975:123.
66 The exact number of people occupying the village is uncertain. Estimates of different authorities range from 1000 to 2500.
67 Gadd 1966:451.
68 Lyons 1975:69.
69 Scott ibid.:183.
70 Gadd 1966:451.
71 Orange et al. 1993:531. Scott (1975:211) records Te Whiti's Bible as a well-thumbed but un-annotated leatherbound 1868 edition, in the possession of a great-grand-daughter in 1975.
72 Gadd 1966:453.
73 ibid.:455; Lyons 1975:65.
74 Scott 1975:192.
75 Cowan 1930:200-1.
76 Cowan 1910a:150.
77 Orange et al.:542.
78 This geographical division is a result essentially of the tribal affiliations of the two leaders. Although both men had connections with the Taranaki tribe, Te Whiti was primarily of Te Atiawa descent and Tohu of Ngaati Ruanui (Elsmore 1989:238).
79 Interview Murray 20.2.64.
80 McLean & Curnow 1992b:109.
81 Interview Hawe 27.11.63.
82 At this later recording session no restrictions were placed upon the songs except that adaptations may not be made.
83 Interview Pirikahu 4.12.63.
84 Interviews Raumati 26-27.2.64.
85 Interview Marjorie Rau 10.11.63.
86 Interview Raumati 27.2.64.
87 Interview Hannah Nicholas 16.11.63.
88 Interview Paul 10.11.63. If this informa-

tion is correct, all but one of the Te Ati Awa poi have been recorded (as McL 486, 487, 488, 489, 497 & 626).

89 Interview Marjorie Rau 10.11.63.
90 Interview Pare Raumati 27.2.64.
91 Interview Pirikahu 4.12.63.
92 Interview Jim Nicholas 17.11.63.
93 J. Thomson 1991:198.
94 Buck 1898:9.
95 Interviews Mohi Ririkore 18.11.63; Puarauehu Maha 29.11.63.
96 Buck 1950:269.
97 Interview Awahou 1.12.63.
98 Interviews Awahou loc.cit. and Raumati 27.2.64.
99 Interview Pirikahu 4.12.63.
100 Hannah Nicholas at recording session 17.11.63.
101 Scott 1975:205.
102 Interview Marjorie Rau 10.11.63.
103 Best 1976a:161, 170.
104 Ngata 1959:xvii.
105 Best 1976a:209-10.
106 ibid.:49-50.
107 Ngata 1959:xvii.
108 Ngata & Te Hurinui 1961:xiii-xiv.
109 Best 1975:50-56.
110 Orbell 1978:61.
111 A view accepted also until recently by the present writer.
112 Dieffenbach 1843 (II):26-27.
113 Orbell 1978:61.
114 Interview Hughes 18.4.72.
115 NM 12, 93, 95, 211, 341. The only song of the five not from Ngaati Porou is NM 341 from Mohaka, but even this is nearby.

Chapter 4

1 Best 1925, 1976a.
2 Buck 1950:Ch.9.
3 Armstrong 1986.
4 Best 1976a:23.
5 Best (ibid.:165) also gives 'taatai whetuu', but the only meaning assigned to this by Williams is 'cluster of stars, constellation'; according to Best it was used not only as a breath-holding song but also as a charm to dispel a frost. Some of the other terms also had more than one meaning. Arapeta Awatere (interview 1.5.73) said that taki manawa refers both to an invocation that must be recited on one breath and the technique for doing so (hence the application to the game); pepe taki manawa, according to Awatere, is a form of invocation asking the god to bless one with sufficient power to perform

the taki manawa. Williams makes a different distinction between the two, evidently regarding taki manawa as the act of performing pepe taki manawa. The term 'whakataetae manawa' means literally 'to try the strength of the breath'.

6   Dieffenbach 1843 (II):32.
7   AMPM RNZM 161 (Dub of D10867 Tk 2). Also referred to by Ngata in Ramsden [1948]:109 where there is a text of the song.
8   Best 1976a:166.
9   Interview Arapeta Awatere 8.5.73.
10   Best 1976a:61-69.
11   Buck 1950:241.
12   Best 1976a:50, 52.
13   Buck 1950:239.
14   Best 1976a:69.
15   Anon 1966:29-33; Armstrong 1986:Ch.6.
16   Armstrong 1986:13-16.
17   Quoted Best 1976a:56.
18   ibid.:71.
19   Best 1976a:170-2; Buck 1950:248-9.
20   AMPM RNZM 101 (Dub of P416).
21   Buck 1950:249.
22   Bennett 1958:53.
23   Thomson 1859 (I):196.
24   Best 1976a:30-34.
25   Buck 1950:239.
26   McLean & Curnow 1992b:105.
27   Best 1976a:79.
28   Best loc.cit.
29   Andersen 1927:16.
30   Item 4 on Cyl 13 (1921) in McLean & Curnow 1992b:99.
31   Andersen 1927:136.
32   Armstrong 1986:11; Bennett 1958:52; Best 1976a:153-63; Williams 1976.
33   Best 1976a:159.
34   Item 3 on Cyl 12 (1920) in McLean & Curnow 1992b:70.
35   Item 3 on Cyl 8 (1920) in McLean & Curnow 1992b:67.
36   Best 1976a:160-1.
37   Bennett 1958:52.
38   Best 1976a:153, 166, 175-6, 178.

Chapter 5

1   Best 1924:170.
2   ibid.:166; Best 1976a:297. It is not unlikely that the maker of this pahuu had either seen slit-gongs from elsewhere in the Pacific or had been told of them by others. As early as 1805, Maori crew members were being taken on by whaling ships and some of them travelled widely.
3   Tregear 1904:65.
4   Potts 1882:16.

5   Angas 1847b (II):150.
6   Andersen 1934:201; Mair MS n.d.
7   Dieffenbach 1843 (II):132.
8   Thomson 1859 (I):132.
9   Mair MS n.d. In another manuscript, written most likely some ten years later, Mair (MS 1900:6) offers slightly different, though not inconsistent, information. The width of pahuu is there set at two to four feet (60 cm–1.2 m) and the length as 8–20 feet (2.4–6m).
10   Hamilton 1901:384.
11   Potts 1882:16. The Auckland pahu referred to is reputed to have been a greenstone slab which Best (1924:167; 1925:166) says was used, according to tradition, at the fortified place on One Tree Hill. Hamilton (1901:99) says this slab was called 'Whakaarewhataahuna'. It was owned by Kiwi, a chief at One Tree Hill. It was supposed to carry the mana of the Taamaki district, and possession of it was evidence of the ownership of the land. An article in the Auckland Star (2.2.1977) gives a different name for the slab, 'Kahotea', stating that it was buried for safekeeping somewhere on One Tree Hill before the battle at which Ngaiwi Waiohua tribe lost their lands to the invading Ngaati Whaatua.
12   Best 1925:165.
13   Best 1924; 1925; Andersen 1934; Buck 1950.
14   Morgan MS 1833-65:403.
15   Best 1925:165.
16   White 1885:175.
17   Buck 1950:254.
18   Potts 1882:16.
19   Angus 1847(II):150.
20   Buck 1950:388.
21   Vayda 1960:54.
22   Best 1927:86.
23   Chapman MS 1830-69:148.
24   Potts 1882:16.
25   Angas 1847 (II):151.
26   Best 1924:167; 1925:166-7; Andersen 1934:202-3.
27   Best 1925:167; Mair MS n.d.
28   Buck 1950:254.
29   Fox 1976:29.
30   McLean 1982a.
31   Bellwood 1978b:391.
32   Beattie 1994:78-79, 258-9, 483-4.
33   Best 1925:170, 173.
34   Buck 1950:256.
35   Hamilton 1901; Andersen 1934; Mair MS n.d.; MS 1900.
36   Best 1925:173. Best goes on to describe two forms of flax clapper from the East Coast as described to him by Tuta Nihoniho of Ngaati

Porou. In one, a short piece of the thick leaf base from the flax plant (*Phormium*) was split into two halves which were clapped together, one in each hand. These simple clappers were termed paakeekee. In another form (pakoko), the two halves were split only to within a few inches of the butt end and one was bent outwards to form a hinge, allowing the two halves to flap together when the instrument was shaken from the butt end.

37   Illustrated in Moyle 1989:20, item 140.

38   Roger Neich, pers.comm.

39   In Williams the word is given a long *a*, making it 'paakuru' in double vowel orthography. But in a letter to Johannes Andersen, Williams (MS 1932) states that the vowel is short and not long as he has it in his dictionary.

40   Information on the pakuru has been abstracted from Andersen 1929:91-92; Andersen 1934:207-11; Best 1925:171-3; Buck 1950:256; Hamilton 1901:385-6, 398; Tregear 1904:66; Williams 1957.

41   An aberrant description is that of White (1887-90 (II):130-1) who says it was suspended on the thumb of the left hand by a string tied to each end.

42   Captain Mair (quoted Andersen 1934:208) says the end was held near the mouth.

43   Mair MS n.d.

44   Colenso 1880:79.

45   Quoted Best 1925:172.

46   ibid:173 and White 1887-90 (II):131.

47   Mair MS n.d.

48   Hamilton 1901:385.

49   Hughes states that the tanguru tree grows among the rocks in the mountains above the snow line. It has very sweet-smelling flowers and grows about 5 feet (1.5 m) high.

50   Interview Hughes 29.11.71.

51   According to White (Best 1925:174), an alternative was a shaved down piece of mataii, tiitoki or maire wood.

52   W. Williams MS 1932.

53   Buck 1950:256.

54   Andersen 1929:91; 1934:298-9.

55   As attested by Colenso (1880:82), even old dessert knives were preferred to supplejack.

56   Colenso: ibid. As early as 1831, Polack (1838 (I):153-4) comments that the presentation of a jew's harp 'was received as an inestimable gift'.

57   Best 1925:164.

58   A Tuuhoe example has been recorded by Kino Hughes as McL 1012.

59   Best 1925:164; Williams 1975.

60   Best 1925:163-4.

61   Elsewhere, Best (1924:164) gives the dimensions as 16–20 inches (40–50 cm).

62   Hamilton 1901:374.

63   Best 1924:163; Williams 1975.

64   Buck 1950:267-8.

65   Fischer 1961:292-3.

66   Best 1925:175.

67   The same term is used throughout Polynesia. Specifically, it is reported for Aniwa, Niue, Ontong Java, Samoa, Tikopia, Tokelau and Tuvalu in Western Polynesia and Aitutaki, Austral Islands, Easter Island, Gambier Islands, Manihiki, Mangaia, Marquesas Islands, Pukapuka, Rarotonga and the Society Islands in Eastern Polynesia. Almost always it applies to the conch trumpet and the use when reported is invariably for signalling. As used by the Maori, the word entered into the names of many wind instruments, including trumpets not made from shells. By extension it also applied to other pipes or tubes, including the European gun.

68   Best 1925:158.

69   Moser 1888:51.

70   Andersen 1934:296.

71   Andersen ibid.:Fig.71, opp.291.

72   Cowan (1983(II):41) reports that it was also made from hollowed out tutu branches with mouthpieces.

73   Buck 1950:257; Best 1925:155-6.

74   St John 1873:59.

75   Cowan 1983(II):41, 52 fn.

76   Beattie 1994:78-9, 258-9, 484.

77   Williams 1975.

78   Andersen 1934:292.

79   Different authorities, including Williams, give a variety of names for the species of shell used, most of which the present writer has been unable to verify. However, a determination is possible from Moyle's catalogue (Moyle 1989) of the musical instrument collection of the Auckland Institute and Museum, assuming the collection to be representative. Seven of 30 specimens are identified as made from the large Pacific Triton, *Charonia tritonis* and 23 from the smaller New Zealand native Triton, *Charonia lampas capax*. Moyle (ibid.:18) states that use of the larger tropical triton dates only from the arrival of Europeans who brought them to New Zealand as trade items.

80   Fisher (1934-36:116-17) believes this feature to be unusual. Only one of six specimens excavated at Oruarangi near Thames had such holes but an x-ray examination of three *Charonia capax* shell trumpets at the Auckland Institute and Museum revealed holes for attaching the mouthpiece in two of them. The instruments

concerned were Nos. 81 and 16389 in the Auckland Museum collection, both illustrated by Andersen (1934:fig.64, opp. p.285). One of these instruments, called 'Te Awa a te atua', is putatively old. It is said to date back to the ancestral Te Arawa canoe.

81 According to Mair (MS n.d.) the gum was made from *Pittosporum* seeds.

82 Buck 1950:257; Polack 1840 (II):173.

83 Andersen 1934:285.

84 Polack 1840 (II):173.

85 Beaglehole 1962 (II):30.

86 G. Forster 1777:227. Monneron and L'Horme, who came to New Zealand with de Surville in 1769, both say the sound was similar to that of the *cornemuse*, translated by McNab (1914:283, 335) as 'bagpipe'. There was a type of eighteenth-century French bagpipe which was mouth- rather than bellows-blown (Sadie 1984 (I):105) and possibly this was the instrument referred to.

87 Best 1924:162; Buck 1950:258, 345.

88 According to Andersen (1934:287) the puupakapaka was a variety of puutaatara with a long mouthpiece. Williams confirms the long mouthpiece.

89 Best 1925:160; Williams 1975.

90 Maning 1906:40. In one of his manuscripts, Mair (MS n.d.) equates puutaatara with puuteetere (yet another variant), contrasting them with puukaaea. But he reverses the normal usage by assigning the former terms to the long wooden trumpet and the latter to the shell trumpet. In his other manuscript about musical instruments (Mair MS 1900), he uses the terms potipoti and puu moana for the shell trumpet and the more usual puukaaea and taatara for the wooden war trumpet. His inconsistent use of the term puukaaea in the two manuscripts, and the agreement of other writers on the meaning of puukaaea, suggests that the reversal in MS n.d. was an error.

91 Gathercole 1977.

92 Colenso 1880:79.

93 Oldman 1943:21, Pl.58.

94 Gathercole 1977:188, 190.

95 ibid.:188.

96 ibid.:190.

97 Oldman 1943:21.

98 Gathercole 1977:194.

99 ibid.:195.

100 ibid.:197.

101 Information on this instrument abstracted mainly from Andersen 1934:287; Best 1924:157-60; Best 1925:153-8; Buck 1950:258-9.

102 Mair MS n.d.

103 Wood 1868-70 (II):138.

104 Angas 1847b (II):152. Elsewhere, Angus (1847a:Pl.LVII 15.) calls the instrument a war-horn or pah trumpet, saying 'it is blown over the gateway of the pah for the same purpose as the war-bell [pahu]'.

105 Colenso 1880:80, fn.1.

106 Marshall 1836:24-25.

107 R. Taylor MS 1833-73 (10):89.

108 Roth 1891:44.

109 Angas 1847b (II):152.

110 Maning 1863:42.

111 G. Forster 1777:227.

112 Newman 1905:134-5.

112 Burney (MS 1772-73:[26]), although of the opinion that the Maori trumpet might be capable of more than one note, likewise states 'they constantly sound the same note'.

114 Best 1925:153.

115 Information mostly from Andersen 1934:273-5; Best 1925:128; Buck 1950:259-60.

116 Andersen 1929:94.

117 Andersen (1934:274) comments on the grim humour of the stylised mouths. He points out that the contraction of the lips in the middle of most such mouths resembles that seen in the lips of dried heads. A perusal of the many heads illustrated in Robley's *Moko; or Maori Tattooing* (1896) indeed reveals a startling similarity. The lips are invariably apart and, although not all display a contraction in the middle, most have shapes which can be seen in puutoorino. Robley (ibid.:87-91) remarks on the 'close imitation' of tattooing seen in carved images of ancestors on paa gates and elsewhere. This raises the possibility that the carvings around the mouths of puutoorino might be representative of real persons.

118 The bindings were not continuous like those of the puukaaea, but were characteristically spaced at intervals above and below the central sounding hole as well as two or more additional places, including the ends.

119 Andersen 1934:276-7; Buck 1950:260-1; Best 1925:128-34.

120 Andersen 1934: fig.60, between pp.276-7.

121 Buck 1950:261.

122 Parkinson 1773:131; Anon 1771:108.

123 Hamilton 1901:418; Tregear 1904:66.

124 G. Forster 1777:227.

125 Savage 1807:84.

126 Newman 1905:136.

127 Buck 1950:261. Elsewhere, Buck (1927:38) gives the name of his informant for this statement as Te Tahi-o-piripi of Ngaati Maniapoto tribe who claimed to have heard his grand-un-

cle playing the puutoorino in this way.

128 Andersen 1934:275, 278; Best 1925:130.

129 Colenso 1880:79.

130 Buck 1927:38.

131 Andersen 1934:275.

132 Hamilton 1901:388; Mair MS n.d.; Savage 1807:84;Tregear 1904:66.

133 Mair MS n.d.

134 *The Sketch*, 17.12.1919. Clipping in Skerrett MS 1911 et seq. p.103.

135 Another instrument which responds in a similar way is a fine 1807 puutoorino (no. 7107 A11) at the Peabody Museum at Salem, Massachusetts, the acoustics of which are discussed by Dodge & Brewster (1945:43-49). Using a lip fipple method of blowing, these authors were able to produce a 'flute-like and agreeable' f#" rising to g" with the end hole open. Partly closing the mid-vent lowered the note to f" (ibid:46). The present writer had no pitch pipe or tuning fork available and was therefore unable to test the absolute pitch. However, when portamento was applied using the traditional Maori oblique kooauau blowing technique, it was found that the instrument spoke naturally on three flute notes, breaking on to discrete pitches rather than varying continuously as would happen with a kooauau. With the instrument's trumpet sound notated as a nominal C, the flute notes were E, F#, G.

136 Other unusual instruments were two small puutoorino examined by the writer at the British Museum and two others at the Otago Museum (Oldman Coll. 25) and Museum of New Zealand (Web Coll. 1768). These had an extra hole, possibly intended for fingering with the thumb as ascribed to the whio (see later), on the back opposite the central sounding hole. The purpose of this hole could not, however, be tested on the instruments available. The British Museum specimens were unplayable. The Otago Museum specimen had loose and missing bindings. It could not be sounded as a flute and could be blown only with difficulty as a trumpet. The remaining instrument could be blown as a flute but not as a trumpet, perhaps because of the mouthpiece which was chipped. In flute mode, fingering either of the central holes succeeded only in blocking the sound.

137 Andersen 1934:273.

138 Newman may have gained his notion of the puutoorino as a 'nasal flute' from an illustration in Angas's *The New Zealanders* (1847:202) which shows a man blowing the puutoorino with his nose. Andersen (1934:275) points out that the man is blowing the instrument from the wrong

end and that this illustration is evidently an adaptation of a drawing by Sydney Parkinson of a Tahitian nose flute.

139 Quoted Best 1925:130.

140 Buck 1950:261.

141 Species of wood used for the kooauau are cited as houhou, kaiwhiria, mataii, neinei, poroporo, tuupaakihi (tutu) and whau (Andersen 1934:237; Best 1925:135; Buck 1950:264). Several of these had soft pith, easily hollowed out (Best loc.cit.). The writer's informant, Heenare Toka, said maahoe was often used because it was naturally hollow. The instrument was soaked in water to close the pores and improve the tone.

142 Andersen (1934:230-54) and Best (1925:134-46) both contain extensive reviews of the earlier literature on the kooauau and many illustrations. Recent work can be found in McLean 1968, McLean 1974 & McLean 1982a.

143 Beattie 1994:79, 258, 483.

144 Beattie reported everything told to him with scrupulous honesty, but not all of the information he obtained can be trusted. He was told, for example, by a Rapaki informant (Beattie 1994:259), that he had seen a kooauau flute with three holes being played by a tame kaakaa!

145 Both Andersen (1934:236) and Best (1925:135-6) provide details of two such methods given to Best by Iehu Nukunuku of Ngaati Porou, and Andersen (1934:232) gives yet another method obtained from Kiwi Amohau of Ngaati Whakaue tribe. In both, the kooauau was the length of the forefinger. In Amohau's method the three fingerholes were set opposite the first, second and third joints of the forefinger. Nukunuku's method used a combination of thumb width and finger joints to measure the spacings.

146 Vayda (1960:94) suggests that the making of artefacts from the bones of the enemy dead was undertaken when revenge was not fully satisfied by eating the flesh of an enemy. The bones were saved for uses which the Maori thought degrading and were made not only into flutes but also into such common and tapu-defiling objects as 'the heads of bird spears, the barbs of fish-hooks . . . and needles for sewing dog-skin mats'.

147 For a full discussion of the evidence for and against the nose-blowing of Maori flutes see Mclean 1974. The sole kooauau known to have been blown with the nose was collected by Bishop Herbert Williams from an old man who blew it in this way. It was played as a nose flute by blocking one of the open ends with the up-

per lip and blowing into the nearest fingerhole with a nostril. In a letter to Andersen, Williams (MS 1932) names the player as Tuteranginootii who played the instrument with his right nostril. The instrument concerned is in the Hawke's Bay Art Gallery and Museum (no. Napier 38/292) where the present writer was able to play it. It has one end cut square, facilitating blocking with the lip, but is otherwise a normal mouth flute. Blown with the mouth, it produced the second most common kooauau scale (semitone-tone–semitone). As a nose flute, because one of the fingerholes was in use by the nose, it of necessity produced only three notes (semitone-tone ascending) instead of the usual four (McLean 1974:82, 84). Elsdon Best elicited two East Coast terms for 'nose flute' but both may have been responses to leading questions. Nukunuku gave Best (1925:136) a method for making a 'kooauau whakatangi ihu' which translates as 'kooauau sounded by the nose'. Best (ibid:147) also states he was 'told that small gourds were occasionally converted into nose flutes (koaauau pongaihu)' Elsewhere, Best (MS 1923:21) credits this information to 'Ngati Porou natives' stating: 'My informants did not seem to know a specific word for the nose flute, but called it koauau pongaihu' [lit. 'nostril kooauau'].

148 Andersen 1934:231.

149 Best 1925:134.

150 Kennedy 1931:14. The location is uncertain. Dollimore (1962) lists two rivers of this name; one flows into Lake Waikaremoana; the other is in Taranaki.

151 Photographs of Nukunuku playing his gaspipe kooauau are in McLean & Curnow 1992b, Plate 2 & Plates 12-14.

152 McLean 1968:225.

153 Philips 1929:27.

154 Andersen 1929:99-100; 1934:249-50; 1946:vii-viii.

155 Andersen 1946:loc.cit.

156 Andersen 1934:250.

157 Song 215 in Ngata & Te Hurinui 1970 and Song 50 in McLean & Orbell.

158 McLean & Curnow 1992b:153, Cyl [34].

159 Andersen 1934:233, 237.

160 Andersen ibid.:233, 433; Best 1925:139.

161 Andersen ibid.:233.

162 Of the writer's two players of the kooauau, Pairoa Wineera used only the simple finger positions. Henare Toka, on the other hand, claimed to use seven of the eight possible finger positions, indicating that covering the bottom hole alone was never used and covering the two bottom holes was used less often than the remaining positions.

163 Beaglehole 1962 (II): Plate 9, 30. This instrument is now at the British Museum (no.5369).

164 The instrument, which unfortunately is unplayable, is Otago Museum flute D33.1379. D.R. Simmons (pers.comm.) says it was excavated at Oruarangi by Teviotdale.

165 Colenso 1880:81.

166 Parkinson 1773:opp. 128 Plate 26, fig.24 & 130.

167 Beaglehole 1962:(II): Plate 9, 30.

168 Cook 1775 (II):268-9.

169 Colenso 1880:81.

170 Hamilton 1901:225, 388; Tregear 1905:66. The only eye-witness account of a possible nguru is provided by L'Horme who saw in 1769 an instrument with the shape of an olive, but bigger and about 2 inches (5 cm) long, from which five or six sounds were produced 'as sweet as the notes of the flute' (McNab 1914:335). An abbreviated description of the same instrument is given by Monneron (ibid:283). The only barrier to accepting this instrument as a nguru is L'Horme's description of it as 'hollow all its length with a hole in the middle'. If the hole referred to was a fingerhole, then the instrument was aberrant. If it was a nguru it should have had three fingerholes. But if it was anything else it would not have been olive shaped. The problem evaporates if it is assumed that the entire statement refers to the bore of the instrument.

171 Marcuse 1964:364; 1975:581.

172 Andersen 1934:fig.53.

173 Heyerdahl 1952:671-2.

174 Bellwood 1978:311.

175 Buck 1950:267.

176 Fisher 1934-36:112 et seq.

177 Fischer 1961:294.

178 Izikowitz 1935:321.

179 Interview Groube 13.9.67; Simmons pers.comm.

180 Beaglehole 1966:149.

181 Simmons 1967:55-56.

182 Green & Green 1963:31-32.

183 ibid.:33.

184 Rotorua Maori are reported by Wade (1842:150) to have been making their own clay pipes in 1835 and by Colenso (1959) to be doing so in 1841–42, another indication that the Oruarangi tobacco pipe flute may have been of late manufacture.

185 They were flutes nos. 6, 7, 12, 19, 20 & 23 in McLean 1982a:155-6.

186 Edge-Partington 1890:386.

187 Andersen 1934:295, Fig.72C; Best

1925:158, Fig.96; Hamilton 1901:391; Buck 1950:261, Fig.72. Buck points out that no such specimens from New Zealand have either been reported by other writers or are in museums, and the rectilinear ornamentation on the instrument has no parallels in New Zealand. He might also have noted that Edge-Partington's identification becomes the more dubious by the appearance on the same page as the gourd instrument of a panpipe which is even less credibly attributed to New Zealand.

188 Andersen 1934:294.

189 ibid.:296.

190 Maingay 1984:79-81.

191 ibid.:81. Furthermore, the nguru fragments were found at a depth which places them close to the beginning of the sequence, making them early indeed. In a letter to Joan Maingay, the excavator of the site, Wilfred Shawcross (MS 1984), reports that on checking his field notebook he was able to find the very item, namely: '241 Gourd neck with holes, b:6 A/B=19 6/7=8 d=38'. He states: 'I am entirely confident about the provenance of this piece, and the depth record shows that it is early in the depositional sequence.' An enclosed plan shows the location of the find deep down at 38 inches on a scale of 50 inches. Puutoorino fragments were found at the same depth in adjacent squares.

192 Andersen 1934:264; Buck 1950:267.

193 Parkinson 1773:130.

194 Hamilton 1901:418.

195 Mair MS 1900:2.

196 Best 1925:147.

197 Andersen 1934:263; Buck 1950:267.

198 All nguru flutes seen by the writer have their widest space between the middle fingerhole and the lower (snout) hole. Some kooauau, by contrast, have equidistant fingerholes. It may be that the nguru spacing results not from makers' choice but is integral to the structure of the instrument. If so, the conventional spacing of fingerholes in the kooauau may be in imitation of the nguru, and the latter would necessarily be the older instrument of the two.

199 McLean 1982a.

200 NZ Herald, 3.5.94, p.1.

201 Two nguru flutes examined by the writer (nos. 37 & 42 in McLean 1982a) evidently had their under-snout holes added as an unsuccessful experiment after the instruments were completed, as these flutes cannot be played until the holes are blocked.

202 Andersen 1934:232.

203 Andersen 1929: 98; Andersen 1934:247.

204 Andersen 1934:249.

205 ibid.:243.

206 McLean 1968.

207 McLean 1982a.

208 Williams (1975) has the o long which would suggest that he did not think of the word as a transliteration. Best (1925:131), however, says that as far as he is aware the word is not native but a Maori rendering of 'flute', noting that Williams does not agree with him.

209 Beattie 1994:79, 258, 259, 483.

210 Mair MS n.d.

211 Mair MS 1900.

212 Illustrated in Moyle 1989:19, item 138 and Best 1925:140b, fig.74 (lower).

213 Illustrated in Best 1925:140b, fig.74 (middle).

214 ibid.:142.

215 White also gives a confused description of a second type of rehu made of mataii wood which was end-blown and appears to have lacked fingerholes (Best 1925:142; Williams MS 1932). According to White, the non-blowing end was beaten with the forefinger of the right hand.

216 Best 1925:133.

217 Moser 1888:51.

218 Tregear 1904:66. Tregear gives no authority for his statement and it may have been a notion of his own.

219 Illustrated in Best 1925:132g, fig.63 (upper).

220 Illustrated in Moyle 1989:20, item 139 and Best 1925:140b, fig.74 (upper).

221 Best 1925:142; Williams MS 1932.

222 Dieffenbach 1843:57.

223 McNab 1914:479.

224 White 1891:58, fig.10.

225 Bauke 1924. Paraphrased by Buck (1950:263) and quoted in full by Andersen (1934:255-6).

226 An obviously derivative embellishment of Bauke's description, in which the foot becomes the big toe, appears in a book called Legends and Mysteries of the Maori by Charles Wilson. It is repeated here not because it deserves to be taken seriously but only for the sake of completeness. Wilson (1932:41) writes of the practice of making a flute from an enemy's arm-bone from which 'the Maori musician, sitting on his haunches and using the upper surface of his big toe to stop the lower end while he blew across the aperture at the top . . . wove his melodies of love and war . . .'.

227 White 1891:58.

228 J. Thomson (1991:56-57) records that during the period of the Land Wars, from 1860–

1870, 11 of the 14 British regiments in New Zealand had their own bands. Additionally there were settlers' bands associated with the militia and, in various parts of the country, flute and drum bands. By the 1890s, the Maori themselves had established at least one drum and fife band using European instruments, by the followers of Te Whiti in Taranaki (Buck 1950:269).

Chapter 6

1   Interviews Awatere 1958 and 10.7.69. Elders who, in Awatere's recollection, used the term in this sense were Ahipene Mika, Sir Apirana Ngata and Aperahama Te Whainga, all of Ngaati Porou, as well as Puke Tari (Tuuhoe) and Rotu Rangi of Ruatoki. The common use of the term 'whakaeke' is for the 'entry' of a haka team to the stage in cultural competitions when, according to Awatere (interview 20.3.73) it implies unison and precision of movement. As a verb, one of the meanings of the word is 'to attack' (Williams). Other terms relating to mistakes and singing faults are listed in McLean 1965 (I):102.
2   Confirmed by Kino Hughes of Tuuhoe (interview 18.4.72) who said it is 'when people sing different tunes instead of all the same'. Marata Te Tomo of Ngaati Tuuwharetoa (interview 6.12.72) applied the term not to pitch but to time, saying it was used when singers are not together: 'one a bit faster, the other a bit slow'.
3   Interviews Awatere 1958.
4   Andersen 1934:421-2.
5   An evident synonym is pekerangi, given in Williams as: 'A voice pitched above the rest in singing: regarded as an *aituaa* [evil omen]'.
6   Interview Awatere 24.6.58.
7   Interview Awatere 28.8.73.
8   Interview Hughes 18.4.72.
9   Ngata & Te Hurinui 1961: 88, 89.
10   Best 1976a:186-7; Buck 1950:500.
11   Best 1959:18.
12   Best 1975a:166.
13   Interview Awatere 8.5.73.
14   Barratt 1979:93.
15   Thiercelin 1866 (II):142.
16   Thomson 1859 (I):164.
17   Interview Hughes 18.4.72.
18   Interviews Awatere 26.6.73 & 2.7.73.
19   Philips 1929:3.
20   Andersen 1934:431.
21   Interview Te Tomo 6.12.72.
22   Arapeta Awatere (interview 26.6.73) said that kaikaakaariki was a name not for the leader of paddlers in a canoe but for the fugleman when

a canoe was being dragged. It was also an old term in the Ngaati Porou and Ngaati Kahungunu tribal areas for the leader in a haka.
23   Armstrong 1964:178.
24   Interview Awatere 2.7.73. A cognate term (pootete) is used in the Tuuhoe and Ngaati Porou tribal areas not for a haka leader, but for the male tekoteko clown who taunts the enemy by spitting, sticking out his tongue, showing them his posterior and so on. The two terms pootete and tekoteko are interchangeable amongst these people (Awatere loc.cit.).
25   Andersen 1934:431.
26   Interviews Awatere 15.11.71; Hughes 18.6.72.
27   Interview Awatere 2.7.73.
28   Awatere loc.cit.
29   According to Arapeta Awatere (interviews 26.6.73 & 2.7.73), hautuu, kaihautuu, kai haapai and kai whakahau are all terms in general use; tribes north of Tauranga evidently do not have the usage 'kaitaki' or 'kaitaataki'; 'pooteketeke' is restricted to Tokomaru, Aotea and Kurahaupo canoe areas; 'kaituki' is a Tuuhoe term and 'tiitiitai' Tuuhoe and Ngaati Awa.
30   In 1963 and 1964 it was noted at Taranaki, Waikato, Ngaaiterangi, Tuuhoe and Ngaati Whakaue recording sessions during the recording of items McL 543, 565, 646, 654 & 724.
31   Interview Mahuta 3.1.69.
32   Interview Awatere 5.9.71.
33   Awatere loc.cit.
34   Interview Hughes 18.4.74.
35   Interviews Awatere 1958.
36   Interview Awatere 20.3.73.
37   Interview Hurinui 7.9.62.
38   Interview Awatere 5.9.71.
39   Interviews Kino Hughes 18.4.72; Arapeta Awatere 27.3.73.
40   Flatting of this kind is far from uniquely Maori and may, indeed, be universal. Anyone who has conducted an unaccompanied choir, particularly of untrained voices, will have noticed similar drooping of pitch.
41   Turau Te Tomo of Ngaati Tuuwharetoa, who recorded many songs with his wife Marata.
42   Beattie 1994:259. 'Reo' means 'voice', 'maru' means 'low', and 'takiri' could possibly refer to the high-pitched sound made by a humming top.
43   Awatere interview 27.9.71. The terminal glissando is a descending glide of the voice which typically takes place at the end of a song. There is more information about it in Ch. 14.
44   Interview Awatere 29.7.71.
45   Interview Hughes 18.4.72.
46   Interview Awatere 29.7.71.

47   The same tendency has been observed in other, unrelated, areas of the world. List (1963:7) attributes its appearance in Anglo-American folk song to error on the part of the singer who, during the first stanza, 'must set his tonality and adjust his vocal processes to the dictates of his ear. Not infrequently the singer finds that he has begun by singing a pitch pattern divergent from the one intended'.

48   Interview Kino Hughes 11.12.71. The same was stated independently by Kiri Boyce of Ngaati Porou (interview 11.12.71).

49   *NZ Herald*, 11.4.1991.

50   Firth 1959:210, 206.

51   ibid.:208.

52   ibid.:207.

53   ibid:208. This is not to say that women were helpless in the face of male magic when they perceived its tapu to be a threat to them. To judge from early missionary experience, it would appear that the Christian prayers of the missionaries were at first regarded by women as a form of male karakia against which they were obliged to direct their own countermagic. The missionary Hamlin noted in 1835 that women had to be persuaded to attend a missionary prayer as they thought 'it was the same as the Karakia and therefore they must not attend.' And Stack in 1834 noted that after a missionary had prayed for some Maori girls 'they performed a ceremony . . . to make common what . . . [his] . . . "Karakia" had made sacred' (Howe 1970:27).

54   The left-hand side is also associated with death and the setting sun and the right with life and the rising sun (Salmond 1975:47).

55   Vayda 1960:41.

56   ibid.:42.

57   Best 1976a:101.

58   Interview Awatere 11.10.71.

59   Interview Awatere 11.9.73. To 'kill an enemy' is a figurative expression. Joe Te Maipi (interview 10.3.64), when outlining to the writer the four main skills required of a man on the marae, said they were how to stand, how to hold a patu or taiaha (weapon), how to paatere, and how to 'kill' a man (reduce his mana). In the same context, a person who excels on the marae is known as a 'gun'.

Chapter 7

1   Merriam 1964:77.

2   Interview Awatere 18.9.73.

3   Anon 1956:46.

4   Williams 1975.

5   Best 1976a:194, 201-2.

6   Grey 1853:14.

7   Formulaic language in waiata is discussed in McLean & Orbell 1975:25-27.

8   McLean & Orbell 1975:29. As another example of textual adaptation, Margaret Orbell (pers.comm.) cites a number of speeches given in Davis (1855) in which are quoted songs adapted to include references to New Zealand's then Kawana (Governor), Sir George Grey.

9   Interview Awatere 6.11.73.

10   Interview Awatere 10.7.74.

11   Interview Awatere 16.10.73.

12   Song 14 in McLean & Orbell.

13   Mead 1969:399.

14   Song 50 in McLean & Orbell.

15   Interviews Awatere 6.3.73 & 18.9.73.

16   Andersen 1934:375.

17   Ngata 1990:ix.

18   Interview Awatere 31.7.74.

19   Interview 18.9.73.

20   Interview Potete White 6.10.62.

Chapter 8

1   Merriam 1964:82.

2   Interview Awatere 6.11.73.

3   Song 14 in McLean & Orbell.

4   McLintock 1966 (II):435-6.

5   Interview Murray 22.8.62.

6   Interview R. Pokiha 28.11.73.

7   Interview Lucy Jacob 29.11.73.

8   Family songs are another special case and attitudes to them varied. Ngati Watson of Te Atiawa was unwilling to sing family songs but happily recorded songs belonging to the community at large. Others, however, recorded family songs but not tribal ones.

9   Dieffenbach 1843 (II):57.

10   Gudgeon 1907:64.

11   Interview Wetere 23.2.63.

Chapter 9

1   Merriam 1964:146, 150.

2   Buck 1950:360.

3   King 1975:8.

4   Interview Awatere 2.7.73.

5   Interview Awatere 2.7.73 & 17.9.74.

6   Awatere 17.9.74.

7   Interview Iwikau 18.11.72.

8   Firth 1959:271.

9   As a case history, Salmond (1975:123-4) summarises the life story of Eruera Stirling of Ngaati Porou who was 'tohi'd' at a young age and became a tribal expert in genealogy, waiata

and marae ritual. Another such was Kino Hughes of Tuuhoe. He told the writer (interview 18.4.72) that he learned his first 24 waiata over a period of just three months in 1942 from an uncle who had performed a tohi on him which involved reciting a karakia and then biting his pupil's head.

10   In the Waikato and by Tuuhoe and Ngaati Porou tribes according to Arapeta Awatere (interview 31.7.74).

11   In the Te Arawa and Taranaki tribal areas (Awatere loc.cit.).

12   Barrère et al. 1980:59-60.

13   Elbert 1941:54.

14   Oliver 1974 (I):54.

15   Métraux 1957:186.

16   Best 1959. Earlier accounts are available by White (1887-90 (I):Ch.1) and Stack (1891). Beattie (1994: 365-74) includes information about schools of learning in the Canterbury area, South Island.

17   Hoani Te Whatahoro Jury (1841-1923) of Ngaati Kahungunu tribe.

18   Smith 1913 & 1915.

19   A meticulous appraisal of Smith's sources for this work and its relation to nearly 60 manuscripts generated from the original ones has been carried out by Simmons and Biggs (1970). Numerous additions and interpolations are isolated and volume 2 of Smith's book, in particular, is shown to be a late compilation from many sources. Another 95 MSS. are identified in a later reexamination by Simmons (1994). But Te Matorohanga's utterances themselves have long been shown to have been too uncritically accepted by Smith and Best as genuine Maori tradition: especially, their acceptance of Te Matorohanga's teaching of Io as a supreme Maori god, despite the evidence of the name itself as a far more likely transmutation of the Christian Jehovah (see Sorrenson 1979:77-78).

20   Buck 1950:449.

21   Best 1959:11.

22   Arapeta Awatere (interview 31.7.74) explained the tohi ritual as a dedication to the gods which put a 'stamp' on a child until he died. From his account, it must have been performed during thundery weather. If during the ceremony thunder came from the east, the direction of the rising sun, the child was dedicated to Rongo (god of peace) and was eligible to enter the whare waananga. If thunder came from the west, the direction of the setting sun, he was dedicated to Tuu or Whiro or one of the other gods. Such a child could not enter the whare waananga but was educated in the whare maire

where the arts of fighting, killing and black magic were taught.

23   Best (1959:9-10) says several ceremonies were performed before entry into the whare waananga including ceremonial cutting of the hair of the scholars.

24   As explained by Arapeta Awatere (interview 25.7.74), the sun was the symbol of Taane-nui-aa -rangi, the procurer of knowledge. Until midday, when it was increasing in light and strength, good things were taught. After midday the sun was declining in strength and Whiro, the god of evil and the patron of black magic, took over, especially at night which was the time the whare maire met for learning black magic.

25   Best 1959:18.

26   Stack 1891:367.

27   Best ibid.:6.

28   ibid.:15-6, 18, 22.

29   ibid.:23.

30   ibid.:24.

31   Locke 1881:433.

32   Interview Reweti 2.12.63. Food, especially cooked food, was regarded as destructive of tapu in Maoridom and, by extension, smoking was regarded as a form of food.

33   Interview Awatere 12.7.71.

34   Interview Penfold 16.9.77.

35   Best 1976a:20.

36   Interviews Awatere 6.11.73 and 31.7.74.

37   Best ibid.:312

38   Interview Awatere 31.7.74.

39   Interview Hughes 18.6.72.

40   Interviews Awatere 25.7.74 - 1.10.74.

41   'Behold the moon has risen over the horizon': a common song beginning, in this case probably referring to McL 861.

42   Interview Hughes 18.4.72.

43   Best 1959:18.

44   Interview Awatere 8.8.73.

Chapter 10

1   Polack 1838 (I):144.

2   Polack 1840 (II):168.

3   Cook 1775:268.

4   Interview Hughes 15.4.72. Nodding the head forward during singing he called 'he tungoutungou'. Moving the whole body sideways or forwards while singing was called turaturaki. This information was obtained from Kino Hughes in December 1974 by Margaret Orbell (interview 17.5.77).

5   Interview Awatere 1958.

6   Interview Hughes 22.1.72.

7   Interview Awatere 15.11.71.
8   Andersen 1934:430.
9   Awatere loc.cit.
10   Sparrman 1953:38.
11   Wright 1950:207-8.

Chapter 11

1   Andersen 1934:430.
2   Philips 1929:5. The latter term is not in Williams. The former term, as paaorooro, is given as an adjective meaning 'resounding'.
3   Again not in Williams. Awatere (loc.cit.) said it is a term used by Ngaati Kahungunu, Ngaati Porou, Tuuhoe, Whaanau-aa-Apanui and Ngaati Raahiri (Northland).
4   Interview Awatere 27.3.73.
5   Interview Te Tomo 6.12.72.
6   Interview Hughes 18.4.72.
7   In a PhD study of the first 800 songs recorded by the writer, slightly more than four-fifths of all sung items were found to have finals on the tonic. The remainder mostly had finals which fell below the tonic. Of these 48% had their finals on the m2 below the tonic, 31% on the M2 below the tonic and 14% on the m3 below the tonic (McLean 1965a:278).
8   McLean 1965a:207.
9   Chapman MS 1830-69(I):33-4.
10   R. Taylor MS 1833-73 (II):117.
11   S. Selwyn MS 1809-67:59.
12   Interview Beattie 5.2.64.
13   McLean 1969.
14   McL 876-903 and 1264-5, recorded in 1971 and 1976, and tapes MPF 3, 9-12 and 25 from a selection of Maori Purposes Fund Board recordings by W.T. Ngata, recorded in 1953–54.
15   Waardenberg 1983.
16   Criteria used were melodic departures involving each note, numbers of intervals involving the note, association with initial and final, and position within the range. The note with the highest count on most criteria was ranked as the tonic and notes of the next highest count were ranked as next most important.
17   In each and every flute scale given in Chapter 5, the tonic may be regarded as occurring on the second lowest note. Thus, for example, the type 1 scale of group 1, designated as S T T, would identify with the notes B C D E (ascending) in Fig.1, scale I.
18   McLean 1969.
19   Waardenberg 1983:309.

Chapter 12

1   The exact percentages of each melodic interval in the Mclean corpus of recorded songs were calculated as M2 (44%), m2 (43%), m3 (10%), M3 (2%), 4 (1%) (McLean 1965a:251).
2   Beaglehole 1962 (I):403-4.
3   Parkinson 1773:102.
4   McLean 1966.
5   Kendall & Lee 1820.
6   Davies 1855.
7   ibid.:326.
8   Apel 1956:303.
9   They are: Davies No.1: NM 229 'Teeraa te puukohu', AMPM 82/117.7 (MPFB 117.7); Davies No.2: NM 60 'Ra te haeata', McL139 and Davies No.4 NM83 'E pa koia', AMPM 82/040.4 (MPFB 40.4) & AMPM Museum of New Zealand Cyl. Coll. Series 5, Cyl.28.
10   Andersen 1934:277.
11   Interview Hami Rangiihu, 2.12.76.
12   Burrows MS 1933.
13   AMPM 82/029.2 (MPFB 29.2).
14   McLean 1968.
15   Most of the few cases found concerned the interval immediately above the intoning note, either by raising or lowering it, or by substituting for it. Two of seven possible resulting scales required irregular fingering. Additionally microtones could be produced from any finger position by means of blowing portamento (McLean 1965a:208).

Chapter 13

1   Davies 1855:327.
2   See 'Breathing' in Chapter 6.
3   Interview Arapeta Awatere 2.7.73.
4   Dieffenbach 1843 (II):57.

Chapter 14

1   Andersen 1934:430.
2   In Williams a general term meaning 'line, rank or row'.
3   Interview Awatere 27.9.71.
4   In the Waikato area, the end of line 'drag' is often non-melismatic, instead taking the form of an alternation of meaningless syllables (usually u-e). The device is a kind of throat tremolo which, according to Henare Toka (interview 12.8.63), is also used when playing the kooauau where it is evidence of good playing. The jaw is moved to modify the vowel sound and can be seen to move. The term for the device is 'oriori'. Arapeta Awatere (interview 6.3.73) confirmed 'quivering or tremolo of the voice' as one of the

meanings of oriori in the East Coast where he had heard it applied only to pao. The word may be cognatic with the Hawaiian 'olioli' which likewise refers to vocal tremolo at line endings in songs. If so, the corresponding Waikato device of throat tremolo must be very old and may well antedate the now more usual melisma at line endings.

5 Andersen 1934:430 confirmed by Arapeta Awatere, interview 15.11.71. Doubtless from 'taa' (breathe) and 'whakataa' (to allow time for breathing) (Williams).

6 For an example, see McLean & Orbell, Song 32.

7 G. Forster 1777 (II):478.

8 McLean 1968b:4.

9 Andersen 1934.

10 Best 1924:136, 137; 1976:186, 195, 196.

11 The word in this sense is evidently used figuratively. Williams defines it as 'to bring to land' a canoe.

12 Awatere interview 5.9.71.

13 Eruera Stirling interview 9.3.72.

14 Williams 1975.

15 Awatere interview 5.9.71.

Chapter 15

1 McLean & Orbell 1975:23.

2 Biggs 1980:48.

3 Salisbury 1983:148.

4 S. Fischer 1994:424.

5 McLean 1982b.

6 McLean 1981.

7 This process was evidently explicitly recognised, as there is terminology for it. According to Arapeta Awatere (interview 8.11.71), modifying a word in this and other ways to make it fit the music is known as the 'whatiiinga' of the 'kupu' (word) [perhaps from whati (to break)]. It applies where a diphthong is sung to two syllables instead of one, where a short vowel is sung long and where stresses appear in the wrong places producing odd groupings of words. Andersen (1934:430) erroneously glosses whatiinga as meaning drops of 'fractions of a tone'. Awatere (loc.cit) surmises the mistake may have been made because whatiinga is most likely to occur in leader drags.

8 In the present work, an under-dash is used to indicate ligatures in musical examples.

Chapter 17

1 Stonehouse 1966:202, 205.

2 Dawbin 1966:639-40.

3 Morrell & Hall 1957:13.

4 In their collection *Shanties by the Way*, Bailey & Roth (1967:12-7) provide both words and music of just four whalers' songs relating to New Zealand, all but one collected in the United States.

5 Sharp 1971:94.

6 Falkner 1966:573.

7 Religious professions of the New Zealand Maori population from 1926 to 1981 are tabulated by Davidson & Lineham (1987:178). Percentages of adherents for the main denominations 1926 / 1981 (in brackets) were Anglican 34 (20)%, Catholic 13 (15)%, Ratana 18 (11)%, Mormon 5 (7)%, Methodist 6 (5)%, Presbyterian 1 (3)% and Ringatu 6 (2)%. As can be seen, all but Catholics, Mormons and Presbyterians have declined as a proportion of the total since 1926. Over the same time span, 'All Others' have risen from 9% to 12% and 'No Religion or Object to State' from 6% to 24%. In the 1981 population at large, including Maoris (Department of Statistics 1985:89), there were proportionally more Anglicans (26%) and Presbyterians (16%) and fewer Catholics (14%) and Mormons (1%) with Methodists about the same (5%). It would appear, therefore, that although Anglican adherents still predominate in the Maori population, modest gains this century by the Catholics, Presbyterians and Mormons and the large increase in numbers professing no religion have been made at the expense of the Anglicans.

8 Elder 1934:147, 149.

9 Thomson 1859 (I):162.

10 Burdon 1941:25.

11 H. Williams et al. MS n.d.:271.

12 Ryburn 1979:68.

13 Creed MS 1844-54:2.

14 ibid.:1.8.1851.

15 McLintock 1966 (II):130-1.

16 Department of Statistics 1969:59.

17 J. Thomson 1991.

18 ibid:197. Discussed in the present book in the section on poi.

19 Thomson 1991:197-8

20 Buchner 1878:145; Stafford 1986:139.

21 For a full discussion see McLean 1986.

22 One of the few exceptions is an attractive recording made *c.*1936 by the New Zealand Broadcasting Service of the Hiruharama Native School Choir singing the traditional oriori 'Poo! poo!' (NM 145) in parallel harmony.

23 Martin 1884:71.

24 J. Thomson 1991:183.

25 Born in Gisborne, Mr Halbert studied the violin in Sydney under M. Henri Staehl, later

playing first desk with Staehl in the Sydney Philharmonic and Symphony orchestras under the baton of Henri Verbrugghen [first Director of the NSW Conservatorium of Music]. After moving to Invercargill, he took charge of the Majestic Theatre orchestra in the days of silent movies and continued there until the introduction of talkies (Obituary, *Southland Daily Times*, 6 Sept. 1958).

26   Some are listed by Katene 1991:5-6.

Chapter 18

1   McLean 1964 & 1965b.
2   For example, Eru Pou (interview 14.12.73) was willing to record only if the recordings were made at a meeting with a body present. As all of his songs, including pao, referred to death, he would not sing outside of this context, firmly believing that to do so would cause a death. He said he had once refused to teach a waiata school for this reason, stating as justification that another singer who agreed to do so died soon afterwards.
3   Grace 1959:170-2.
4   The story of Maui's attempt to conquer death has been told many times. For one version see Buck 1950:414-5. The original Maori version referring to the mistake in Maui's naming karakia and its consequences is in the Grey collection of New Zealand Maori manuscripts at the Auckland Public Library (GNZMM43, pp.908-9).
5   Interview, Pane Kawhia, 27.11.1976.
6   Interview Tawai Kawiti, 21.5.1972.
7   Smith 1899:257.

Chapter 19

1   Elder 1932:93.
2   W. Williams 1867:13.
3   Elder ibid.:272.
4   ibid.:93.
5   Yate 1835:199.
6   Thomson 1859 (I):316; W.J. Williams c.1922:104-5.
7   Carleton 1874 (I):150.
8   W. Williams 1867:171.
9   McCormick 1963:70-1.
10   Brown 1851:82-3.
11   W. Williams MS 1825-55. Journal entries for 3 & 5 Feb. 1840.
12   Wakefield 1845 (II):12.
13   Puckey MS 1831-68:188.
14   W. Williams MS 1825-55.:930.
15   Rough 1852:5.
16   Pratt 1932:126-7.

17   Heaphy 1959:229.
18   An indication of the quantities involved can be seen from a letter by William Williams to the CMS in 1846 (Porter 1974:393) in which he referred to the number of copies required of printings of the Prayer Book complete (10,000), the Psalters including Morning and Evening Service and the Psalms (10,000) and Morning and Evening Service without the Psalms (20,000) to which he added a request for 40,000 copies of the 40 or so hymns to this date to be struck off separately.
19   McLintock 1966 (II):867-8.
20   This and following W references are to entries in Herbert Williams, *A Bibliography of Printed Maori to 1900* (1924).
21   [Church of England]:1905. There is confusion in Williams 1924 and elsewhere concerning the numbering of the several editions and reprints of this work. The complete publishing history, so far as is known, appears to be 1883 (Napier: Harding [W649]); 1885 (ditto [W695]); 1887 (ditto [W735]; 1888 (ditto [W750]); 1890 (ditto [W783]); 1896 (Wellington: Coupland [W911]); 1900 (Auckland: Upton [NZNB sC854a]); 1905 (London: Society for Promoting Christian Knowledge). If reprints are regarded as editions, then the 1905 volume would be the eighth edition. However, judging by the number of hymns printed in each issue, and on this basis distinguishing reprints from editions, the correct nomenclature for editions would become 1883 (1st), 1887 (2nd), 1896 (3rd). The 1900 issue, identified by the NZNB as the 6th edition, has not been seen but on the above basis would rank as the 4th edition with the 1905 issue as the 5th.
22   Woon MS 1830-59.
23   [Methodist Church] 1927, 1938.
24   [Wesleyan Methodist Church] 1894:183.
25   Edward Marsh Williams (1818–1909) came to New Zealand with his father, the missionary Henry Williams, in 1823. He had a brief career after 1840 as an interpreter, clerk to the bench and postmaster before taking up farming in 1842. In 1861 he was appointed Resident Magistrate, Bay of Islands, and in 1887 as a judge of the Native Land Court (Startup [1981]:96).
26   Hobbs MS 1823-60 (II):167.
27   ibid:207-8.
28   Williment 1985:126.
29   Woon MS 1830-59.
30   Barrett 1852:356-7.
31   Marshall 1836:77, 338.
32   Pratt 1932:113-4.
33   Tucker 1879 (I):132-3; Hocken 1909:186.

34 S. Selwyn MS 1842-55.

35 H. Baker 1861.

36 Parry and Routley 1953:2-3.

37 Often an abbreviation was used, such as CM, SM and LM for Common Metre (86.86), Short Metre (66.86) and Long Metre (88.88) respectively.

38 A technical report on the Williams instrument (Stiller MS 1981:3) is specific that each of the barrels played five tunes rather than the ten usual for such instruments.

39 An organ to which the Paihia people had subscribed arrived on a later ship from the gift organ and was still in use at the Paihia church in 1955 (Smart MS 1955:1).

40 Williams Papers MS 1822-64:[Part 2]:137.

41 ibid.:203-4.

42 ibid.:210.

43 ibid.:215.

44 Stiller MS 1981:4.

45 Smart MS 1955:2.

46 Marshall 1836:247.

47 Rutherford 1940:97.

48 Smart MS 1955:1. In 1850 Henry Williams moved the organ to Pakaraka, where he had built his own church. In 1867 it passed to his son Edward and in 1897 to his grandson the Rev. A.O. Williams who took it to Wanganui (Smart loc.cit.).

49 The books owned by Hobbs are a copy, autographed in 1827, of a collection of metrical hymns and psalms entitled *The Boston Handel and Haydn Society Collection of Church Music* (first published *c*.1821); an undated publication entitled *A Selection of Hymn Tunes for the Use of the Sunday School in Elm Street, Manchester* obtained by Hobbs in 1837; and a copy of Gauntlet and Kearns two volume *The Comprehensive Tune Book* . . . published in London in 1846 and 1851.

50 Woon MS 1830-59.

51 Rippon was widely used in non-conformist chapels (Leaver 1981:10) and continued to appear in new editions until well after the mid-nineteenth century. The *Comprehensive Rippon* of 1844 contained over 1100 hymns (Scholes 1970:83).

52 Mason of London published at least ten editions of the Wesley *Collection* between 1837 and 1857. Without examining them for pagination, it is not possible to come closer than this in dating the Kinder Library copy.

53 The Garland who played the flute would have been Woon's eldest son of this name who, from an earlier Journal entry, was 10 years old on 5 July 1841, and therefore almost 13 years

old on 23 June 1845. From other Journal entries, there was also another James Garland who appears to have been a kitchen hand. Possibly Garland Woon was named after him.

54 If, as Woon states, this book celebrated the 100th year of Methodism, the probable date of first publication would have been about 1827. A later edition (Rogerson 1897) is in the Kinder Library at St John's, Auckland.

55 First published 1837. A later edition (Clark and Cobbin 1854) is in the Kinder Library at St John's, Auckland. Woon's memory failed him on two counts. The tune referred to is not in the *Centenary Tune Book* but is, as stated, in the *Union Tune Book* (1854) where it appears as tune 368 under the title not 'Holy Mount' but 'Holywell Mount'. It is an elaborate tune quite unsuitable for congregational singing but with two descant parts well adapted to playing on the flute.

56 Wesleyan Conference Office 1847.

57 The hymn 'Prostrate with eyes . . . ' is confirmed as Hymn 754 6-8's in the edition of Wesley's hymnal used by Woon and St Paul's by Arnold is the designated tune for Hymn 754 in the *Companion to the Wesleyan Hymn-Book*.

58 Hiles 1871.

59 Wesley 1877:ix.

60 Wesleyan Conference Office 1904 (cited in Methodist Conference Office 1933:xi).

61 [Church of England] 1862.

62 H. Purchas 1914:231.

63 W. Williams MS 1825-55:64.

64 The tune is no. 30 in *The Centenary Tune Book* (Rogerson 1897).

65 Glen 1992:196.

66 Orton 1755.

67 Leaver 1981:13.

68 Dearmer et al. 1932:v.

69 loc.cit.

70 Julian 1892.

71 McLintock 1966 (III):220.

72 Pybus 1954:60-1.

73 G. Selwyn et al. MS 1842-67:6.

74 Mary Anne Martin, wife of William Martin who had been appointed chief justice of New Zealand; articles later written by her were published posthumously as the New Zealand classic *Our Maoris by Lady Martin* (1884) (*DNZB* (I):275-6).

75 Wife of William Cotton (1813-79).

76 The spelling of 'bass' until the nineteenth century.

77 S. Selwyn MS 1842-55: 14 April 1842.

78 Davidson 1993:35.

79 Sarah Selwyn ibid.: 15 Aug. – 9 Sept. 1843.

80 Wife of William Dudley (b. *c.*1814)

81 Glen 1992:142.

82 McLintock 1966 (III):220; *DNZB* (I):388.

83 G. Selwyn et al. MS 1842-67:72.

84 He was ordained as a deacon of St John's College in September 1847 (Hocken 1909:514) and as priest in 1853. In 1847 he became first vicar of St Peter's, Onehunga, continuing there until 1875 when he resigned to resume medical practice (McLintock 1966 (II):890).

85 S. Selwyn MS 1809-67:66.

86 S. Selwyn MS 1842-55.

87 S. Selwyn MS 1809-67:85.

88 J. Davis 1911:28, 30, 31.

89 Purchas [1848].

90 *DNZB* (I):275-6.

91 Martin 1884:70-1.

92 McLintock 1966 (I):101.

93 Ashwell MS 1834-69 (I):231.

94 Swabey MS 1955-56:7-8.

95 R. Taylor MS 1833-73 (VII):166, 272.

96 Reed 1938:156.

97 Pleasing results were evidently also obtained at the Wesleyan Native Institution for Maori youths in Three Kings, Auckland, which began at Grafton in 1845 and moved to Three Kings in 1849 (Faulkner 1966:573). William Woon (MS 1830-59:4 Dec. 1850) visited Three Kings in 1850 and was impressed with the progress of the students: 'The singing was to me particularly attractive, and I wept for joy.' Singing was also a subject of instruction at a Native Boarding School at Turanga (Gisborne) run by the CMS missionary Thomas Grace. The results were, however, no more than 'satisfactory'; after six months' instruction in 1853, using 'Hullah's system of singing', Grace was able to report that the young people could take their respective parts in a number of songs and could also sing 'God Save the Queen' (Brittan et al. [1928]:280). John Pyke Hullah (1812-1884) was the originator of an acclaimed system of teaching vocal music. He published a book on the method in 1841 entitled *Wilem's Method of Teaching Singing Adapted to English Use* (Colles 1948 (II)678-9).

98 Seymour Spencer (*c.*1812-1898) who arrived with Selwyn in 1842 and was deaconed by him in 1843 (Glen 1992:207).

99 Bambridge MS 1842:23.

100 It was evidently, however, used in at least some urban Anglican churches with English congregations at about this time. William Cotton (MS 1845-46:40), one of the clergymen who came to New Zealand with Selwyn in 1842, in a diary entry of 1846, refers to chanting the psalms

in church for the first time at St Thomas' Tamaki, in the following terms: 'A miserable mess in the morning. Dale actually tried three different chants to one Psalm before he decided on the one he wished to have. In the afternoon it was very good.'

101 'Puseyite' was a derogatory term applied by Evangelicals to practitioners of the Tractarian or Oxford Movement which began in England in 1833 with the publication of a series of *Tracts for the Times* which advocated a revival of Catholic practice within the Church of England. Dr Edward Pusey (1800–1882) was one of the leaders of the movement.

102 Porter 1974:454.

103 ibid.:459.

104 Not the present St Paul's but a now demolished old St Paul's, first headquarters of the Anglican Church in the city .

105 Porter 1974.:506, 606.

106 Campbell 1881:257-8.

107 Chambers 1982:108.

108 Lyon MS 1873:35

109 R. Taylor MS 1833-73 (II):117.

110 H. Williams MS 1826-40 (IV):141.

111 Rogers 1961:456.

112 S. Selwyn MS 1809-67:59-60.

113 Clarke 1903:32-3.

114 A. Brown MS 1835-50 (I): 30-31 Mar., 1838.

115 ibid. (III): 8 Mar., 1845.

116 ibid.: 16 June 1846.

117 Hobbs MS 1823-60 (VII):708.

118 Swabey MS [1955-56]:84.

119 Morley 1900:181.

120 Whiteley MS 1832-63:141.

121 Methodist Church 1938.

122 About one-fifth of the Maori scales examined by the writer did not have their finals on the tonic. Of these about half had their final on the lower M2, as in the transcribed example.

123 Hymn 80 in the CMS Maori Hymnal (Church of England 1905) and Hymn 42 in the Wesleyan Maori Hymnal (Methodist Church 1938).

124 Thanks to Kevin Salisbury for pointing out that, except for a change of harmony involving the second to last note, this tune is a variant of the well known redemption song 'Pass Me Not, O Gentle Saviour'.

125 It occurred there because the missions in the area had lapsed and had been re-established only two years previously by the Rev. T.G. Hammond (Morley 1900:180-1).

126 Archive of Maori and Pacific Music tape 023.9, recorded by Bruce Biggs.

127 Church of England 1905.

128 A&M 240, Second Tune.

129 The 1562 volume was the first complete edition of Sternhold and Hopkins. It was preceded by others, without music and with fewer psalms, from 1549 onwards. The earliest edition to include melodies was published in 1556 (Leaver 1981:3-5).

130 Thomson 1859 (I):314.

131 Godley 1951:113; Ramsden 1951:164. On this account, a certain Mr Lloyd, said to be a 'great authority on music', was sure they must have been taught by Jesuits (Ramsden loc.cit).

132 Scholes 1970:34, 499.

133 e.g. in 1839, Kaitaia (Matthews [1940];114); in 1846 and 1854, East Coast (Baker MS 1827-67: 31 May 1846, 27 Dec. 1854); in 1848, Wanganui area (Hobbs MS 1823-60:3, Dec. 1848).

134 According to the present Maori Bishop, Ben Te Hara (interview 11.2.94), nothing has since changed.

135 Carleton 1874:150.

136 S. Selwyn MS 1809-67:60.

137 Anon [1841-42]:18; Fitzroy et al.:1839-45 (II):589; Lyon MS 1873:35; Ryburn 1979:68; S. Selwyn et al. MS 1842-67 (II):495; S. Selwyn MS 1842-55:6 Sept. 1842; Williams Papers MS 1822-64:22 Sept. 1828; W. Williams 1867:341.

138 Thomson 1859 (I):313.

139 The latest printing of it, entitled simply *Himene*, is an unpaginated volume published at Rotorua by Te Pihopatanga o Aotearoa [the Bishopric of New Zealand] in 1983. It is unchanged from the 1905 edition except for the abandonment of tune and metre indications and the addition of further hymns to a total of 209, including some by the late Archdeacon Kingi Ihaka of Auckland.

140 [Methodist Church] 1927 / 1938.

141 [Presbyterian Church] 1933.

142 Wesleyan Conference Office 1904.

143 [Presbyterian Church] 1907.

144 Stone [1876].

145 Cooper [1877].

146 Hymn 17 in the 1848 collection.

147 Hymn 71 in the 1848 collection.

148 Another tune for it, in the Presbyterian Maori hymnal (1933), is 'Stella'.

149 'Sliding' from note to note has been represented by some writers (e.g. Mitcalfe 1974:188; Katene 1991:3) as a carry-over from traditional waiata. In fact, it is absent from most waiata.

Chapter 20

1 Freedman & Siers 1974:86-7.

2 Recorded in 1958 from Te Mamaeroa Hanuera and others of Ngaati Raukawa.

3 The complete song appears as Song 5 in McLean & Orbell 1975.

4 Raven-Hart 1955; Thomas 1981.

5 Recorded in 1958 from the same group as in footnote 2.

6 St John 1873:59.

7 N. Taylor 1959:513.

8 Davis 1885: Nos 11 and 14. These songs were evidently taught to Maori students by Davis as Max Buchner (1878:157) mentions visiting Mr Davis's 'singing school' in 1876 where he heard 'several English songs translated into Maori.'

9 Located at Lake Rotomahana, 30 km from Rotorua, and destroyed utterly by the Mt Tarawera eruption of June 1886.

10 Waaka 1983:photo caption.

11 Hill 1917, [1926].

12 On the latter account, Hill's biographer John Thomson (1980:82) believes the probable musical origin of 'Waiata Poi' to have been a poi song popular in the days of Maggie and Bella Papakura. There is no reason, however, to doubt that Hill composed it himself. Early programmes confirm that it was in the repertoire of Maggie and Bella, but they were active after Hill composed the song and were careful to credit it to him in their programmes.

13 Other recorded poi with European or transitional tunes are McL 1079 & 1212.

14 It became well known after 1930 when a recording of it was made in Sydney by the Tahiwis under the title 'Waikato' (Parlophone A2995). The text, together with a translation and commentary by Margaret Orbell, is in *The Penguin Book of New Zealand Verse* (Wedde & McQueen 1985:133-5, 537-8).

15 As in classical poi songs, the subject of the song is sent on an imaginary journey. The text, with translation and commentary by Margaret Orbell are in Wedde & McQueen 1985:133-5 & 537-8.

16 Paraire Tomoana was a son of Captain Henare Tomoana [Member of Parliament for Eastern Maori]. He was born at Waipatu, near Hastings, and educated at Te Aute College. In addition to his accomplishments as a composer, he was an authority on Maori weather lore, a lay reader of the Church of England, editor of the Maori newspaper *Toa Takatini* and, in his youth, a prominent athlete (Obituary: *Daily Tele-*

graph, 15 April 1946).
17   According to Dansey (1975b:187-8).
18   Ngata & Tomoana 1919:3-5.
19   Andersen 1930:390.
20   McLean & Curnow 1992b:47. For words and music, see Armstrong & Ngata 1966:96, 98.
21   Del Mar 1924:73-4.
22   Anon 1914.
23   A transcription of the complete song, arranged as an action song, with actions and a translation, together with an equally well-known Ngaati Porou version of the song called 'Paikea', is available in Armstrong & Ngata 1966:63-9. According to these authors (ibid.:66), the actions and the waltz-time tune were adopted during the First World War.
24   Papakura 1905:24.
25   Bella (née Thom) Reretupou (d. 1950).
26   Cowan 1910b:333, 374.
27   *Yorkshire Gazette*, 28.10.1911. Clipping in Skerrett MS 1911 et seq. p.47.
28   The song, which accompanied visuals of a cartoon kiwi and cat, was used to close transmission every night for 15 years from 1979 until TV2 began 24-hour transmission on 20 Oct. 1994 (*NZ Herald*, 19 Oct. 1994, p.23) . For the music, see Freedman & Siers 1974:66-7.
29   MacDonald et al. 1991:314-6.
30   Buck 1951:25.
31   Heke and Ngata 1908.
32   Anon 1936b.
33   *Te Pipiwharauroa* 35:9.
34   Thanks to Sir Henare Ngata (pers.comm. 31.7.94) for this reference.
35   Dennan & Annabell 1968:54.
36   *Gisborne Times*, 28 Feb. 1901.
37   For words and music of 'Tahi nei taru kino', with actions, see Armstrong 1986:65-7. See also Freedman & Siers 1974:70-1.
38   Anon 1936b:81.
39   Anon 1930b: Item10.
40   Hurinui [1945]:38. For words and music see Freedman & Siers 1974:72-3.
41   Darby 1990. For texts of 'Pookarekare ana' and 'E pari raa', with translations and commentary by Margaret Orbell, see Wedde & McQueen 1985:105-6, 536-7.
42   RNZ recording, Programme 5: p.2 of transcript in Leo Fowler Papers, Alexander Turnbull Library.
43   Ngata & Tomoana 1919:10. For words and music see Freedman & Siers 1974:61-3.
44   According to Guide Rangi (Dennan & Annabell 1968:89), Gracie Fields heard this song for the first time at an informal concert in Guide Rangi's carved house at Whakarewarewa and

liked it so much she added it to her repertoire.
45   Dansey 1975a.
46   The composer is claimed in reality to have been an Australian, A.B. Saunders, who wrote the song under the pseudonym of Clement Scott and sold the full copyright to Palings for two guineas.
47   Anon 1927a. The information in this article is reproduced from an illustrated brochure issued by the Parlophone Company in the same year (Parlophone Co. 1927 (NZNB P197)).
48   Armstrong 1961; Mike Sutcliffe (pers.comm.).
49   The name of the entrepreneur is different in other accounts. A letter to the editor of the *NZ Herald* (2 March 1976) gives it not as Hegartz but as Haggerty, as does Thomson (1991:201) who refers to 'Haggerty's ragbag touring 'concert party' '.
50   Mackrell 1978:70-2.
51   *The Era*, 12 July 1863. Xerox in Don Stafford collection, Rotorua Public Library.
52   The tour of Jenkins's group of native chiefs is fully documented in Mackrell 1985.
53   Mackrell 1978:73.
54   *NZ Herald*, 6 Oct. 1879, p.5.
55   *New Zealand Mail*, 5 April 1895, p.15.
56   MacDonald et al. 1991:491.
57   *Weekly Graphic and New Zealand Mail*, 28 Dec. 1910, p.30. One of the members of the Sydney group was the future Guide Rangi, much later to lead a touring concert party of her own, but then only 13 years old.
58   *New Zealand Times*, 19 June 1911.
59   Press cutting in Skerrett MS 1911 et seq., p.25.
60   Dennan & Annabel 1968:53; MacDonald et al. 1991:492; Makereti 1938:22; Skerrett MS 1911 et seq.; Thomson 1991:201.
61   Advertisements in *NZ Herald*, 5 March 1918 and 1 June 1918.
62   Anon 1943:11. The writer is indebted to Sir Henare Ngata (pers.comm., 31.7.94) for pointing out that this and other women's haka poowhiri of Ngaati Porou, with their strong beat and use of action, come closest of the traditional forms to modern action song. It could be, on this account, that haka poowhiri should be numbered amongst the predecessors of action song. The association of both with Ngaati Porou strengthens the case as does the coincidence that both are performed by women. On the other hand, the programme note about the particular song (loc.cit.) as 'an adaptation of a very old women's *haka*' may indicate that it was, in fact, an action song with a borrowed haka text.

63   Rev. Frederick Bennett (1871-1950), later, in 1928, to become first Bishop of Aotearoa.

64   Anon 1908a. The same choir performed at the opening ceremony of the Maori Congress at the Wellington Town Hall on 14 July 1908, when, according to the *Dominion* newspaper (15 July 1908, pp.7-8), between the speeches, 'several ancient Maori songs were very sweetly sung' and, as an encore, the choir sang 'On the Banks of Afton Water.'

65   Anon 1908b.

66   *Bay of Plenty Times*, 3 June 1914. Transcript in Don Stafford Collection, Rotorua Public Library.

67   *NZ Herald*, 5 Dec. 1914, p.7.

68   Heke & Ngata 1908:Song 4.

69   Armstrong & Ngata 1966:6.

70   Anon 1917.

71   Anon 1919.

72   Anon c.1925. Date estimated by Te Awekotuku 1981:179.

73   Anon c.1935. Date estimated by Te Awekotuku 1981:App H.

74   Anon 1930d.

75   Anon 1930b.

76   Biggs (1990a) lists it as 'cheerful, hearty' or 'entertainment'.

77   Anon 1936a.

78   Anon 1938.

79   Anon 1947.

80   Te Awekotuku 1981:179.

81   Sorrenson 1986-88 (III):135.

82   King 1977:118.

83   Clipping in Michael King MS Papers 2096, Box 5, Folder 9, Alexander Turnbull Library, Wellington.

84   King 1977:134-7; *NZ Herald* 9 June, p.8; 15 June, Amusements Section; and 16 June, p.16.

85   Review in the *Dominion*, 1 Sept. 1928, p.6.

86   Hurinui 1945:36, 37, 38; King 1977:143.

87   King 1977:175.

88   Wiata 1976:13. This date could be too early as Te Wiata does not appear in the accompanying photographs of the choir taken in 1932 and 1933. He is, however, in a photograph of the choir taken in 1934 where a very young-looking Te Wiata appears second from the right in the back row (Downes 1979:91).

89   Anon 1930a.

90   Anon 1930c.

91   *The Press*, 24 July 1930, p.9.

92   MacDonald et al., 1991:256; Leaflets and cutting from *The Methodist Times*, 7 Oct. 1937 in Alexander Turnbull Library Ephemera Collection, A. Maori Concerts.

93   Conly 1985:7.

94   Loughnan 1902:377-80.

95   Anon 1970:33.

96   Kirimatao was still active nearly 30 years after the prince's visit. A note in the *Bay of Plenty Times* (15 Feb. 1899) announces a two-night season at the Theatre Royal, Tauranga, of a haka troupe just returned from the City Hall, Auckland, and an Exhibition North Shore Regatta. The troupe was 'under the management of two of the ladies of the highest rank in the Ngatiwhakaue tribe, Mesdames Kirimatao and Paea te Riri.' Extract filed under Concert Parties 1899 in Don Stafford Collection, Rotorua Public Library.

97   Loughnan 1902:390.

98   Stafford 1988:13.

99   Scholefield 1926:51.

100   Anon 1920; Scholefield ibid.:37, 47-51.

101   Anon 1927b.

102   Anon 1934; Stafford 1988:181.

103   Anon 1954; Anon 1970.

104   G. Thompson 1926:1-3.

105   Cowan 1910b:332; Shennan 1984:23.

106   Cowan ibid.:332-3.

107   Shennan 1984:24-5.

108   Shennan ibid. :24. Armstrong (1964:104; 1986:54-5) and Armstrong & Ngata (1966:6), claim a definite such connection, but their information must be wrong. They state that 'even before 1908' Princess Te Puea had been visited at her marae at Ngaruawahia by a group of 'Pacific Islanders' from whom she obtained the idea of action songs. This cannot be correct as construction of Te Puea's Ngaruawahia marae did not even begin until 1921 (King 1977:Ch.6).

109   Cowan 1910b:358-60.

110   Cowan ibid.:359.

111   Armstrong 1964:103; 1986:54, Armstrong & Ngata 1966:6, Barrow 1965:14-5, McEwen 1947:186, Mitcalfe 1974:172 and Youngerman 1974:93.

112   Mitcalfe 1974:192.

113   Best 1924:106; 1976a:88.

114   Best 1976a:loc.cit.

115   Awatere 1975:512.

116   Anon 1934:Item 9b. The same song was described as an action song at Waitangi in 1934 (Buick 1934:61).

117   Anon 1943:41.

118   Anon 1954:16.

119   Armstrong & Ngata 1966:2; Barrow 1965:15; Dennan & Annabel 1968:66; Pewhairangi 1985:xxv.

120   Mitcalfe 1974:194.

121   Shennan 1977:57.

122 Heke & Ngata 1908.

123 Armstrong & Ngata 1966:6; Barrow 1965:15; Mitcalfe 1974:192; Youngerman 1974:93.

124 Shennan 1984:43.

125 Armstrong & Ngata 1966:6.

126 Sir Henare Ngata, pers.comm., 31.7.94.

127 Ngata & Tomoana 1919:2.

128 Written for the Dialectic Society of Canterbury College in 1892 (Heke & Ngata 1908:[3]) while Ngata was a student there and first published in Heke & Ngata 1908.

129 Words, actions and music are in Armstrong & Ngata 1966:72-5.

130 McLean & Curnow 1992b:8-9.

131 Cylinder recordings of this song and of Tomoana's canoe song were recorded at the Hui Aroha from the Hawke's Bay Maori Entertainers on 13 April 1919 (see McLean & Curnow 1992b:46-7).

132 Repa 1919:10.

133 NZ Herald, 20 Dec. 1917, p.10. The Maori name for Tomoana's Hawke's Bay Maori Entertainers appears to have been 'Te Ope Ngahau o Heretaunga' as they are referred to by this name in a notice about the forthcoming Auckland Town Hall concerts in the 12 Oct. 1917 issue of Te Kopara (48:11).

134 NZ Herald, 22 Dec. 1917, p.9.

135 Buck 1951:30.

136 Shennan (1977:67;1984:41) telescopes the two references in Te Kopara about the Gisborne Hui Aroha and the Auckland Town Hall concerts respectively, giving the impression that they are one and the same. Although probably relevant to both, the haka hou term, however, refers specifically to the 1919 Gisborne performances rather than the 1917 Auckland ones.

137 Sinclair 1959:190.

138 Buick 1934:25.

139 Sorrenson 1986-88 (III):133.

140 Referring to the welcome at Rotorua of the Duke and Duchess of Cornwall and York.

141 Earlier this might not have been possible, but in 1936, after the election of the first Labour government in 1935, broadcasting in New Zealand was placed under the control of a Minister of the Crown (McLintock 1966 (I):249), opening the way to political influence.

142 McLean 1991; McLean & Curnow 1992b.

143 Ngata 1972.

144 Shennan 1984:61-2.

145 Rangitiaria Dennan.

146 Dennan & Annabel 1968:125.

147 Ngata 1940:333.

148 loc.cit.

149 Orbell 1975:60-1.

150 Sir Henare Ngata, pers.comm., 31.7.94.

151 Texts and translations by Margaret Orbell and others of representative action songs are in Wedde & McQueen 1985.

152 Interviews Awatere 12.7.71 and 26.7.71. Awatere demonstrated six such movements; all related to the position of the arms.

153 For a detailed analysis of action song ringa or movements see Shennan 1984 Ch.4; for a more technical analysis see Shennan 1977. For practical guides to teaching and performing action song see Armstrong & Ngata 1966 and publications of the New Zealand Department of Education such as Kururangi 1966. For the most recent guide, with photographs and diagrams of ringa, see Pewhairangi 1985:114 et seq.

154 Fowler 1972.

155 Pewhairangi 1985:xxv.

156 Anon 1936a:13.

157 Pewhairangi 1985:xiv.

158 For the text, with translation and commentary by Margaret Orbell, see Wedde & McQueen 1985:188-9, 538.

159 A mimeographed list identifying the tunes of nearly 180 of Tuini's songs was distributed with the book Tuini: Her Life and Her Songs (Pewhairangi et al. 1985).

160 MacDonald et al. 1991:516-7; Jennifer Coleman (pers.comm.).

161 Another such feature, which is becoming increasingly common, is the interpolation into action song performances of shouted interjections from the men.

Chapter 21

1   McLean 1961 & 1977a.

2   Andersen 1934:191.

3   Thomson 1859 (I):195.

4   Mair 1900:8.

5   Arapeta Awatere (interviews 12.7.71 & 27.9.71) said there is no Maori word for flat singing as such, as did Marata Te Tomo of Ngaati Tuuwharetoa (interview 6.12.72). Terms which might be used for it, according to Awatere, are kua hee ('wrong') and kua kawa ('sour' or 'bitter'). The meaning 'out-of-tune singing' for the latter term was also given by Kiri Boyce of Ngaati Porou (interview 11.12.71).

6   Numerous sources attest this; one of them is Colenso 1880:83.

7   McL 1240 recorded from Molly Hotene, 20.11.76.

8   There is no method short of extensive

analysis and interviews with knowledgeable informants to determine which elements of a music system are central and which non-central. Music terminology provides some clues as central elements may or may not be named by the practitioners but non-central elements never are. Thus, in the Maori case, there is a term, oro, for the intoning note and another, hiianga, for leader solos, but none for scale or most other elements of music structure.

9   McLean 1977b:34.
10   McLean1990:34.

REFERENCES

ABBREVIATIONS

AI&M Auckland Institute & Museum
AMPM Archive of Maori & Pacific Music
ATL Alexander Turnbull Library
AUP Auckland University Press
JPS Journal of the Polynesian Society
OUP Oxford University Press

BOOKS, ARTICLES & MANUSCRIPTS

Alexander, Charles M., n.d. *Alexander's Hymns No. 3*. London & Edinburgh: Marshall, Morgan & Scott.

Alexander, Col. Sir James, 1863. *Incidents of the Maori War: New Zealand in 1860–61*. London: Bentley.

Andersen, Johannes C., 1927. *Maori String Figures*. Memoirs of the Board of Maori Ethnological Research vol. 2. Wellington: Board of Maori Ethnological Research.

Andersen, Johannes C., 1929. 'Maori Musical Instruments'. *Art in New Zealand*, 2:91–101.

Andersen, Johannes C., 1934. *Maori Music with Its Polynesian Background*. Memoirs of the Polynesian Society, 10. New Plymouth: Avery.

Andersen, Johannes C., 1946. *Polynesian Literature*. New Plymouth: Avery.

Angas, George French, 1847a. *The New Zealanders Illustrated*. London: McLean.

Angas, George French, 1847b. *Savage Life and Scenes in Australia and New Zealand*. 2 vols. London: Smith, Elder.

Anon, 1771. *A Journal of a Voyage Round the World in . . . Endeavour in the Years 1768, 1769, 1770 and 1771*. London: Becket & Hondt.

Anon, [1841–42]. 'Journal Kept by One of the Passengers on Board the "Tomatin" with Extracts from Bishop Selwyn's Letters, Dec. 26, 1841 to Nov. 11, 1842'. Unpubl. typescript, AI&M Library, MS 273, vol.5.

Anon, [1906–07]. *Official Catalogue and Souvenir of the New Zealand International Exhibition 1906–1907*. Christchurch: Christchurch Press.

Anon, 1908a. [Concert Programme] *Assembly Hall . . . Rotorua Maori Mission Entertainers 1908*. [Auckland]: Brett. [AI&M Library Ephemera Collection, GN 672 (4).]

Anon, 1908b. [Concert Programme] *King's Theatre . . . Souvenir Programme Rotorua Maori Mission Entertainers 1908*. [ATL Ephemera Collection, A. Maori Concerts.]

Anon, 1914. [Concert Programme] *New Zealand Natives' Association: Grand Entertainment (Maori and Pakeha) in Grand Opera House Friday, 3rd July, 1914*. [ATL

REFERENCES

Ephemera Collection, B. Variety 1914.]

Anon, 1917. [Concert Programme] *Programme of Maori Entertainment in Aid of Lady Liverpool's and Mrs. Pomare's Maori Soldiers' Fund: Town Hall, Wellington Thursday, 7th November, 1917 . . .* in *Lady Liverpool Scrapbook*, ATL, Wellington, f 920/p/LIV.

Anon, 1919. [Concert Programme] *Souvenir Programme: Grand Maori Pageant in Aid of the Maori Returned Soldiers Union . . .* Wanganui: Wanganui Chronicle Print. [ATL Ephemera Collection, A. Maori Concerts 1919.]

Anon, 1920. *Souvenir of H.R.H. the Prince of Wales Visit to New Zealand: Reception in Auckland April 1920*. Auckland: Brett. [AI&M NZ Pamphlet Collection GT 5090.]

Anon, c.1925. [Concert Programme] *The Famous Hinemoa Maori Entertainers*. Rotorua: Chronicle Print.

Anon, 1927a. 'Parlophone Records Maori Songs'. *Australian Phonograph Monthly*, 20 May 1927, p.40.

Anon, 1927b. *Souvenir of the Visit of the Duke and Duchess of York February 1927*. [AI&M NZ Pamphlet Collection GT 5090.]

Anon, 1930a. [Advertisement for] *Home Mission Anniversary Rally / Papanui Methodist Church . . . June 9 . . .* Christchurch: Bascands (Printer). [ATL Ephemera Collection, B. Maori Concerts.]

Anon, 1930b. [Concert Programme] *Town Hall, Wellington. Wednesday, July 9th, 1930 at 8 p.m. Maori Entertainment to the British Rugby Team*. [ATL Ephemera Collection, A. Maori Concerts 1930.]

Anon, 1930c. [Advertisement for] *Farewell Programme by the Popular Methodist Maori Singers, Orators and Musicians . . . Civic Theatre . . . 23 July . . .* [Christchurch]. [ATL Ephemera Collection, A. Maori Concerts.]

Anon, 1930d. [Concert Programme] *Programme of Maori Entertainment Town Hall, Wellington / Thursday & Friday 9th and 10th October., 1930 at 8 p.m. Wanganui Maori Concert Party . . .* [ATL Ephemera Collection, A. Maori Concerts 1930.]

Anon, 1934. *Maori Reception to His Royal Highness the Duke of Gloucester Rotorua, December 22nd, 1934: Souvenir Programme*. [Rotorua]: Morning Post.

Anon, c.1935. [Concert Programme] *Peerless Theatre Rotorua . . . The Huia Maori Entertainers*. Rotorua. [Another copy, the same except *Lyric Theatre, Rotorua*, in ATL Ephemera Collection, A. Maori Concerts n.d.]

Anon, 1936a. [Concert Programme] *Programme of Maori Entertainment Town Hall, Wellington Wednesday & Thursday, 27th and 28th May, 1936, at 8 p.m.: Ngati-Poneke, Ngati Raukawa, Whanganui and Nga-Rauru Tribes*. Wellington: Blundel (Printer). [AI&M Pamphlet Collection GN 672.2.]

Anon, 1936b. *Waitara 1859–1936: Souvenir of Pomare Memorial Meeting Manukorihi Pa, Waitara, June 27th, 1936*. New Plymouth: McLeod & Slade (Printers).

Anon, 1938. [Concert Programme] *Catholic Maori Concert: Town Hall Auckland . . .* [AI&M Ephemera Collection.]

Anon, 1943. *Souvenir of the Ngarimu Victoria Cross Investiture Meeting . . . Whakarua Park Ruatoria East Coast 6 October 1943*.

Anon, 1947. [Concert programme] *Maori Entertainment by the Taiporutu Club Rotorua . . . Town Hall — Auckland Friday November 28th and Saturday, November 29th at 8 p.m.: Souvenir Programme*. Auckland: Business Printing Works.

Anon, 1954. *Reception to Her Majesty Queen Elizabeth II and His Royal Highness The*

Duke of Edinburgh by the Maori People at Rotorua on the 2nd Day of January 1954. Rotorua: Rotorua Newspapers Ltd.

Anon, 1956. 'Tuini Ngawai'. *Te Ao Hou* (Wellington): no.14 (vol. 4 no. 2):46–50.

Anon, 1966. *Games and Dances of the Maori: A Guide Book for Teachers*. Wellington: Curriculum Development Division, Department of Education. Revised edn.

Anon, 1970. *Reception to Her Majesty Queen Elizabeth / His Royal Highness The Duke of Edinburgh / His Royal Highness the Prince of Wales / and / Her Royal Highness the Princess Anne by the Maori People / Gisborne, 22 March 1970*.

Apel, Willi (ed.), 1956. *Harvard Dictionary of Music*. Cambridge, Mass.: Harvard University Press.

Armstrong, Alan, 1961. 'Still Popular After Thirty Years'. *Te Ao Hou* (Wellington), 36:63–65.

Armstrong, Alan, 1964. *Maori Games and Hakas: Instructions, Words and Actions*. Wellington: Reed.

Armstrong, Alan, 1986. *Games and Dances of the Maori People*. Wellington: Viking Seven Seas.

Armstrong, Alan & Reupena Ngata, 1966. *Maori Action Songs*. Revised & enlarged edn. Wellington: Reed.

Ashwell, Benjamin, MS 1834–69. Letters and Journals of the Rev. Benjamin Y. Ashwell . . . 1834–69. 2 vols. Unpubl. typescript, AI&M Library, MS 9.

Awatere, Arapeta, 1975. Review of Mitcalfe 1974. *JPS*, 84(4):510–19.

Awekotuku, Ngahuia Te, 1981. The Sociocultural Impact of Tourism on the Arawa People of Rotorua, New Zealand. PhD thesis, University of Waikato.

Bagnall, A.G. (ed.), 1969–85. *New Zealand National Bibliography to the Year 1960*. 6 vols. Wellington: Government Printer.

Bailey, Rona & Herbert Roth, 1967. *Shanties by the Way: A Selection of New Zealand Popular Songs and Ballads*. Christchurch: Whitcombe & Tombs.

Baker, Charles, MS 1827–67. Journal of Charles Baker 1827–1867. 6 vols. Unpubl. typescript, AI&M Library, MS 22.

Baker, Henry Williams (ed.), 1861. *Hymns Ancient and Modern with Introits and Anthems*. London: Novello.

Baker, William, 1861. 'On Popular Maori Poetry'. *Transactions of the Ethnological Society of London*, 1:44–59.

Ballara, Angela, 1976. 'The Role of Warfare in Maori Society in the Early Contact Period'. *JPS*, 85(4):487–506.

Bambridge, William, MS 1842. Diary Nov. 6, 1842 –Dec.2, 1842. Unpubl. typescript, AI&M Library, MS 483.

Bambridge, William, MS 1843. Journal 1843. Unpubl. typescript, AI&M Library, MS 463.

Barber, Ian, 1992. 'Archaeology, Ethnography, and the Record of Maori Cannibalism Before 1815: A Critical Review'. *JPS*, 101(3): 241–92.

Barratt, Glynn, 1979. *Bellingshausen: A Visit to New Zealand: 1820*. Palmerston North: Dunmore Press.

Barrère, Dorothy B., Mary Kawena Pukui & Marion Kelly, 1980. *Hula: Historical Perspectives*. Anthropological Records No. 30. Honolulu: B.P. Bishop Museum.

Barrett, Alfred, 1852. *The Life of the Rev. John Hewgill Bumby* . . . London: Mason.

Barrow, Tui Terence, 1965. *Traditional and Modern Music of the Maori*. Wellington:

REFERENCES

Seven Seas.

B[auke], W[illiam], 1924. 'Maori Music: Flutes and Flautists'. *New Zealand Herald Supplement*, 15 November.

Beaglehole, J.C. (ed.), 1955. *The Journals of Captain Cook on his Voyages of Discovery. Volume 1, The Voyage of the Endeavour 1768–1771*. Cambridge University Press for the Hakluyt Society.

Beaglehole, J.C. (ed.), 1962. *The Endeavour Journal of Joseph Banks 1768–1771*. 2 vols. Sydney: The Trustees of the Public Library of New South Wales in Association with Angus & Robertson.

Beaglehole, J.C., 1966. *The Exploration of the Pacific*. London: Adam & Black. 3rd edn.

Beaglehole, J.C. (ed.), 1967. *The Journals of Captain Cook on his Voyages of Discovery. Volume 3, The Voyage of the Resolution and Discovery 1776–1780*. Cambridge University Press for the Hakluyt Society.

Beattie, James Herries, 1939. *Tikao Talks*. Wellington: Reed.

Beattie, James Herries, 1994. *Traditional Lifeways of the Southern Maori*. Edited by Atholl Anderson. Dunedin: University of Otago Press in association with Otago Museum.

Beechey, Frederick W., 1831. *Narrative of a Voyage to the Pacific and Beering's Strait . . . in . . . 1825, 26, 27, 28*. 2 vols. London: Colburn & Bentley.

Bellwood, Peter, 1978a. *The Polynesians: Prehistory of an Island People*. London: Thames & Hudson.

Bellwood, Peter, 1978b. *Man's Conquest of the Pacific: The Prehistory of Southeast Asia and Oceania*. Auckland: Collins.

Bennett, Hemi, 1958. 'Games of the Old Time Maori'. *Te Ao Hou* (Wellington), 22:45–46; 24:52–53.

Best, Elsdon, 1897. 'Te Rehu-o-Tainui: The Evolution of a Maori *Atua*'. *JPS*, 6:42–66.

Best, Elsdon, 1901. 'On Maori Games'. *Transactions of the New Zealand Institute*, 34:34–69.

Best, Elsdon, 1903. 'Notes on the Art of War, Part V'. *JPS*, 12(2):65–84.

Best, Elsdon, 1908. 'Maori Songs,' in *New Zealand Official Yearbook 1908*, pp.739–46.

Best, Elsdon, MS 1923. Notes on Maori Musical Instruments. ATL, Wellington, Best Papers B, 13.

Best, Elsdon, 1924. *The Maori*, vol. 2. Wellington: Polynesian Society.

Best, Elsdon, 1925. *Games and Pastimes of the Maori*. Dominion Museum Bulletin, 8. Wellington: Government Printer. Reprinted 1976.

Best, Elsdon, 1927. *The Pa Maori*. Dominion Museum Bulletin, 6. Wellington: Government Printer.

Best, Elsdon, 1952. *The Maori As He Was*. Wellington: Government Printer. 2nd edn. First published 1924.

Best, Elsdon, 1959. *The Maori School of Learning: Its Objects, Methods and Ceremonial*. Dominion Museum Monograph No. 6. Wellington: Government Printer. First published 1923.

Best, Elsdon, 1972. *Tuhoe the Children of the Mist*. Vol. 1. Memoirs of the Polynesian Society, 6. Wellington: Reed. First published 1925.

Best, Elsdon, 1975. *The Whare Kohanga ('The Nest House') and Its Lore*. Dominion Museum Bulletin, 13. Wellington: Government Printer. First published 1929.

Best, Elsdon, 1976a. *Games and Pastimes of the Maori*. Dominion Museum Bulletin, 8. Wellington: Government Printer. First published 1925.

Best, Elsdon, 1976b. *Maori Religion and Mythology Part 1*. Dominion Museum Bulletin, 10. Wellington: Government Printer. First published 1924.

Best, Elsdon, 1976c. *The Maori Canoe*. Dominion Museum Bulletin, 7. Wellington: Government Printer. First published 1925.

Best, Elsdon, 1976d. *Maori Agriculture*. Dominion Museum Bulletin, 9. Wellington: Government Printer. First published 1925.

Best, Elsdon, 1977. *Forest Lore of the Maori*. Wellington: Government Printer. First published 1942.

Best, Elsdon, 1982. *Maori Religion and Mythology Part 2*. Dominion Museum Bulletin, 11. Wellington: Government Printer.

Bidwill, John C., 1841. *Rambles in New Zealand*. London: Orr.

Biggs, Bruce, 1964. 'The Oral Literature of the Polynesians'. *Te Ao Hou* (Wellington), 49:23–5, 45–7.

Biggs, Bruce, 1969. *Let's Learn Maori: A Guide to the Study of the Maori Language*. Wellington: Reed.

Biggs, Bruce, 1980. 'Traditional Maori Song Texts and the "Rule of Eight"'. *Paanui* (Anthropology Department, University of Auckland), 3:48–50.

Biggs, Bruce, 1990a. *English–Maori Maori–English Dictionary*. Auckland: AUP.

Biggs, Bruce, 1990b. 'In the Beginning,' in Keith Sinclair (ed.), *The Oxford Illustrated History of New Zealand*. Auckland: OUP.

Binney, Judith, 1995. *Redemption Songs*. Auckland: AUP/Bridget Williams Books.

Brittan, S.J, G.F.C.W. Grace & A.V. Grace, [1928]. *A Pioneer Missionary Among the Maoris 1850–1879 Being Letters and Journals of Thomas Samuel Grace*. Palmerston North: Bennett.

Brown, Rev. Alfred Nesbitt. MS 1835–50. Journal of the Rev. A.N. Brown. 4 vols. Unpubl. typescript, AI&M Library, MS 40.

Brown, William, 1851. *New Zealand and Its Aborigines*. London: Darling. 2nd edn.

Buchner, Max, 1878. *Reiser durch den Stillen Ozean . . .* Breslau: Kern's Verlag.

Buck, Peter, 1898. 'The Taranaki Maoris: Te Whiti and Parihaka,' in *Papers and Addresses Read before the Second Conference of the Te Aute College Students' Association, December 1997*. Napier, pp.7–12.

Buck, Peter, 1927. 'Historical Maori Artifacts'. *New Zealand Journal of Science and Technology*, 9:35–41.

Buck, Peter, 1950. *The Coming of the Maori*. Wellington: Maori Purposes Fund Board. 2nd edn.

Buck, Peter, 1951. 'He Poroporoaki — a Farewell Message: Personal Reminiscences on Sir Apirana Ngata'. *JPS*, 60 (1):22–31.

Buddle, Thomas, 1851. *The Aboriginals of New Zealand*. Auckland: Williamson & Wilson.

Buick, T. Lindsay, 1934. *Waitangi Ninety-four Years After*. New Plymouth: Avery.

Buller, Rev. James, 1878. *Forty Years in New Zealand*. London: Hodder & Stoughton.

Burdon, Randel M., 1941. *New Zealand Notables*. Christchurch: Caxton Press.

Burney, James, MS 1772–73. Journal on the Resolution and Adventure 1772–1773.

REFERENCES

MS in National Library of Australia, Canberra.

Burrows, Edwin G., MS 1933. Letter to J.C. Andersen. ATL MS Papers 148, 51b.

Burton, Alfred H., [1885]. *The Maori at Home*. Dunedin: Daily Times.

Butler, John Gare (ed.), 1828. *A Selection of Psalms and Hymns from the Best Authors*. Bridgnorth: Gitton (Printer).

Campbell, John Logan, 1881. *Poenamo: Sketches of the Early Days of New Zealand*. London: Williams & Norgate.

Carlton, Hugh, 1874. *The Life of Henry Williams*. 2 vols. Auckland: Upton.

Chambers, Wesley A., 1982. *Samuel Ironside in New Zealand 1839–1858*. Auckland: Richards.

Chapman, Thomas, MS 1830–69. Letters and Journals . . . 1830–1869. Unpubl. typescript, ATL, Wellington. Also at AI&M Library, MS 56.

[Church of England], 1862. *The New Zealand Hymnal*. Christchurch: Ward & Reeves (Printers).

[Church of England], 1905. *He Himene mo te Karakia ki te Atua. [Hymns in the Maori Language]*. London: Society for Promoting Christian Knowledge (First published 1883, Napier: Harding).

[Church of England], 1983. *Himene*. Rotorua: Te Pihopatanga o Aotearoa.

Clark, Paul, 1975. *'Hauhau': The Pai Marire Search for a Maori Identity*. Auckland: AUP/OUP.

Clark, T. & J.I. Cobbin, 1854. *The Union Tune Book: A Selection of Tunes and Chants* . . . London: Sunday School Union.

Clarke, George, 1903. *Notes on Early Life in New Zealand*. Hobart: Walch.

Cockayne, C.M.G. & E. Phillips Turner, 1950. *The Trees of New Zealand*. Wellington: Government Printer.

Cody, Joseph F., 1953. *Man of Two Worlds: Sir Maui Pomare*. Wellington: Reed.

Colenso, William, 1959. 'Excursion in the Northern Island of New Zealand, in the Summer of 1841–2 . . . ,' in Nancy M. Taylor (ed.), *Early Travellers in New Zealand*. Oxford: Clarendon Press, pp.3–57.

Colenso, William, 1880. 'Contributions Towards a Better Knowledge of the Maori Race'. Pt.3, 'On Their Poetical Genius'. *Transactions of the New Zealand Institute*, 13:57–84.

Colles, Henry C. (ed.), 1948. *Grove's Dictionary of Music and Musicians*. 4th edn. London: Macmillan.

Conly, Geoff, 1985. *Tarawera: The Destruction of the Pink and White Terraces*. Wellington: Grantham House.

Cook, James, 1775. 'An Account of a Voyage Round the World in the Years 1768, 1769, 1770 and 1771,' in John Hawkesworth (ed.), *An Account of the Voyages Undertaken by the Order of His Present Majesty for Making Discoveries in the Southern Hemisphere*. 2 vols. Dublin: Potts. 2nd edn.

Cooper, Joseph Thomas, [1877]. *The Hymnal Companion to the Book of Common Prayer*. London: Sampson, Low, Marston, Searle & Rivington. [2nd edn.]

Coote, Walter, 1882. *Wanderings South and East*. London: Sampson, Low, Marston & Rivington.

Cotton, William, MS 1845–46. Journal. Unpubl. typescript, Hocken Library, Dunedin, MS 171.

Cowan, James, 1910a. *The Maoris of New Zealand*. Christchurch, Wellington &

Dunedin: Whitcombe & Tombs.

Cowan, James, 1910b. *Official Record of the New Zealand International Exhibition of Arts and Industries Held at Christchurch, 1906–7: A Descriptive and Historical Account.* Wellington: Government Printer.

Cowan, James, 1930. *The Maori Yesterday and Today.* Wellington: Whitcombe & Tombs.

Cowan, James, 1983. *The New Zealand Wars.* 2 vols. Wellington: Government Printer. (Reprint of 1955 edn. First published 1922.)

Craik, George L., 1830. *The New Zealanders.* London: Knight.

Creed, Charles, MS 1844–54. Letters Waikouaiti, 1844–54, to the Wesleyan Mission Secretaries, London. Typescript. Hocken Library MS 440/17.

Cruise, Richard, 1823. *Journal of Ten Months' Residence in New Zealand.* London: Longman, Hurst, Rees, Orme & Brown.

Dansey, Harry, 1975a. 'Yes, But When Exactly Was "The Hour"?' *Auckland Star*, 29 March 1975.

Dansey, Harry, 1975b. 'A View of Death,' in Michael King (ed.), *Te Ao Hurihuri: The World Moves On.* Wellington: Hicks Smith, pp.173–89.

Darby, Bernie, 1990. 'Pokarekare ana'. *APRA*, 8(1):34.

Davidson, Allan K., 1993. *Selwyn's Legacy: The College of St. John the Evangelist Te Waimate and Auckland 1843–1992: A History.* Auckland: The College of St John the Evangelist.

Davidson, Allan K. & Peter J. Lineham, 1987. *Transplanted Christianity: Documents Illustrating Aspects of New Zealand Church History.* Auckland: College Communications.

Davidson, Janet, 1984. *The Prehistory of New Zealand.* Auckland: Longman Paul.

Davies, James A., 1855. 'On the Native Songs of New Zealand'. Appendix in Sir George Grey, *Polynesian Mythology.* London: Murray, pp.313–33.

Davis, Charles O., 1855. *Maori Mementos.* Auckland: Williamson & Wilson.

Davis, Charles O., 1873. *Temperance Songs etc. in the Maori Language.* Auckland: Field.

Davis, Charles O., 1885. *Te Honae: Being a Small Collection of Temperance and Sacred Melodies in Maori.* 2nd enlarged edn. Akarana: Brett.

Davis, John King, 1911. *History of St. John's College, Tamaki, Auckland.* Auckland: Abel, Dykes.

Dawbin, William H., 1966. 'Whaling in New Zealand Waters 1791–1963', in A.H. McLintock (ed.), *An Encyclopaedia of New Zealand.* Wellington: Government Printer, vol. 3, pp.638–42.

Dearmer, Percy, Ralph Vaughan Williams & Martin Shaw (eds), 1932. *Songs of Praise Enlarged Edition with Music.* London: OUP.

Debenham, Frank (ed.), 1945. *The Voyage of Captain Bellingshausen to the Antarctic Seas, 1819–1821.* London: Hakluyt Society. 2 vols.

Del Mar, Frances, 1924. *A Year Among the Maoris.* London: Benn.

Dennan, Rangitiaria with Ross Annabell, 1968. *Guide Rangi of Rotorua.* Christchurch: Whitcombe & Tombs.

Department of Statistics, 1969. *New Zealand Official Yearbook 1969.* 74th issue. Wellington: Department of Statistics.

Department of Statistics, 1985. *New Zealand Official Yearbook 1985.* 90th annual edn. Wellington: Department of Statistics.

Dieffenbach, Ernest, 1843. *Travels in New Zealand*. 2 vols. London: Murray.

[Dix, William G. & James Oliver], 1846. *Wreck of the 'Glide' with an Account of Life and Manners at the Fiji Islands*. Boston: Ticknor.

Dodge, Ernest & Edwin Brewster, 1945. 'The Acoustics of Three Maori Flutes'. *JPS*, 54(1):39–61.

Dollimore, E.S., 1962. *The New Zealand Guide*. Dunedin: Wise.

Donne, Thomas E., 1927. *The Maori Past and Present*. London: Seeley, Service.

Downes, Peter, 1979. *Top of the Bill: Entertainers Through the Years*. Wellington: Reed.

Earle, Augustus, 1832. *A Narrative of a Nine Months' Residence in New Zealand in 1827*. London: Longman, Rees et.al. [See also Earle 1966 below.]

Earle, Augustus, 1966. *Narrative of a Residence in New Zealand* and *Journal of a Residence in Tristan da Cunha*. Edited by E.H. McCormick. Oxford Clarendon Press. [This edition of Earle's *Narrative* includes illustrations by Earle not published in the 1832 edition.]

Edge-Partington, James, 1890. *An Album of the Weapons, Tools, Ornaments, Articles of Dress etc. of the Natives of the Pacific Islands*. Vol. 1. Manchester.

Elbert, Samuel, 1941. 'Chants and Love Songs of the Marquesas Islands, French Polynesia'. *JPS*, 50:53–91.

Elder, John R. (ed.), 1932. *The Letters and Journals of Samuel Marsden*. Dunedin: Coulls Somerville Wilkie & A.H. Reed.

Elder, John R. (ed.), 1934. *Marsden's Lieutenants*. Dunedin: Coulls Somerville Wilkie & A.H. Reed.

Ellis, E.M. & D.G. Ellis, 1978. *Early Prints of New Zealand*. Christchurch: Avon Fine Prints.

Elsmore, Bronwyn, 1989. *Mana from Heaven: A Century of Maori Prophets in New Zealand*. Tauranga: Moana Press.

Est, Thomas, 1592. *The Whole Booke of Psalmes: with Their Wonted Tunes . . .* London: Est.

Falkner, Nancy, 1966. 'Missions,' in A.H. McLintock (ed.), *An Encyclopaedia of New Zealand*. Wellington: Government Printer, vol. 3, pp.569–74.

Firth, Raymond, 1959. *Economics of the New Zealand Maori*. Wellington: Government Printer. 2nd edn. First published 1929.

Fischer, Hans, 1961. 'Polynesische Musikinstrumente: Innerpolynesische Gliederung — ausserpolynesische Parallelen'. *Zeitschrift für Ethnologie*, 86(2):282-302.

Fischer, Steven R., 1994. 'Rapanui's "Great Old Words": *E Timo Te Akoako*'. *JPS*, 103(4):413–43.

Fisher, Muriel E., E. Satchell & Janet M. Watkins, 1975. *Gardening with New Zealand Plants, Shrubs and Trees*. Auckland: Collins.

Fisher, Victor F., 1934–36. 'The Material Culture of Oruarangi, Matatoki, Thames: Pt. 1. Bone Ornaments and Implements; Pt. 4. Musical Instruments'. *Auckland Institute & Museum, Records*, 1(5):275–86; 2(2):111–18.

Fitzroy, Robert, P.P. King & Charles Darwin, 1839–45. *Narrative of the Surveying Voyages of HMS 'Adventure' and 'Beagle', 1826–1836*. 4 vols. London: Colburn.

Forster, George, 1777. *A Voyage Round the World in . . . Resolution . . . 1772, 3, 4 and 5*. 2 vols. London, White, Robson, Elmsley & Robinson.

Forster, John, R., 1778. *Observations Made During a Voyage Round the World*. London: Robinson.

Fowler, Leo, 1972. 'Maori Action Songs Are Finding Their Own Tunes'. *New Zealand Herald*, 4 February 1972.

Fox, Aileen, 1976. *Prehistoric Maori Fortifications in the North Island of New Zealand*. Monograph No. 6 of the New Zealand Archaeological Association. Auckland: Longman Paul.

Freedman, Sam & James Siers, 1974. *Maori Songs of New Zealand*. Wellington: Seven Seas.

Gadd, Bernard, 1966. 'The Teachings of Te Whiti o Rongomai'. *JPS*, 75(4):445–57.

Gathercole, Peter, 1977. 'A Maori Shell Trumpet at Cambridge,' in G. de G. Sieveking et.al. (eds), *Problems in Economic and Social Archaeology*. London: Duckworth, pp.187–99.

Gauntlet, Henry John & William Henry Kearns, 1846 & 1851. *The Comprehensive Tune Book . . .* London. 2 vols. (1st & 2nd series)

Glasgow, J. (transl.) & D.R. Simmons (ed.), 1973. *Customs and Habits of the New Zealanders 1838–42 by Father C. Servant Marist Missionary in the Hokianga*. Wellington: Reed.

Glen, Robert (ed.), 1992. *Mission and Moko: Aspects of the Work of the Church Missionary Society of New Zealand 1814–1882*. Christchurch: Latimer Fellowship of New Zealand.

Godley, John R. (ed.), 1951. *Letters from Early New Zealand by Charlotte Godley 1850–1853*. Christchurch: Whitcombe & Tombs.

Grace, John Te H., 1959. *Tuwharetoa: The History of the Maori People of the Taupo District*. Wellington: Reed.

Graham, George, 1940. 'Nukutawhiti: The Pihe (Lament) for Nukutawhiti . . .' *JPS*, 49(2):221–34.

Green, R.C., 1977. *Adaptation and Change in Maori Culture*. Albany: Stockton House.

Green, R.C. & K., 1963. 'Classic and Early Maori Sites on the Hauraki Plains'. *NZAA Newsletter*, 6:27–34.

Greenwood, William, 1942. *The Upraised Hand, or the Spiritual Significance of the Ringatu Faith*. Wellington: Polynesian Society Memoir, 21.

Grey, Sir George, 1851. *Ko nga Moteatea, me nga Hakirara o nga Maori*. Wellington: Stokes.

Grey, Sir George, 1853. *Ko nga Moteatea, me nga Hakirara o nga Maori*. Wellington: Stokes. [Same as 1851 printing with addition of 25 more songs.]

Grey, Sir George, 1928. *Nga Mahi a Nga Tupuna*. New Plymouth: Avery. 3rd edn. First published 1854.

Gudgeon, Thomas, 1887. *The Defenders of New Zealand*. Auckland: Brett.

Gudgeon, Walter E., 1907. 'The Tohunga Maori'. *JPS*, 16:63–91.

Hamilton, Augustus, 1901. *Maori Art*. Wellington: The New Zealand Institute.

Hayward, Bruce W. & Les O. Kermode, 1994. 'How Many Volcanoes in Auckland and How Old is Rangitoto?'. *Geological Society of New Zealand Newsletter*, 104:36–39.

Heaphy, Charles, 1959. 'Notes of an Expedition to Kawatiri and Araura, on the Western Coast of the Middle Island [1846],' in Nancy M. Taylor (ed.), *Early Travellers in New Zealand*. Oxford: Clarendon Press, pp.203–49.

REFERENCES

Heke, Hone & A.T. Ngata, 1908. *Souvenir of Maori Congress July 1908: Scenes from the Past with Maori Versions of Popular English Songs*. Christchurch: Whitcombe & Tombs.

Heyerdahl, Thor, 1952. *American Indians in the Pacific: The Theory Behind the Kon-Tiki Expedition*. London: Allen & Unwin.

Hiles, Henry, [1871]. *The Wesley Tune Book*. London: Novello, Ewer.

Hill, Alfred, 1917. *Waiata Maori (Maori Songs)*. Collected & arranged by Alfred Hill. Dunedin: McIndoe.

Hill, Alfred, [1926]. *Songs of the Maori*. Collected & arranged by Alfred Hill. Dunedin: McIndoe.

Hobbs, John, MS 1823–60. Diaries of John Hobbs. 7 vols. Unpubl. typescript, AI&M Library, MS 144.

Hochstetter, Ferdinand von, 1867. *New Zealand*. Stuttgart: Cotta.

Hocken, Thomas M., 1909. *A Bibliography of the Literature Relating to New Zealand*. Wellington: Government Printer.

Hodgskin, Richard, 1841. *A Narrative of Eight Months' Sojourn in New Zealand. . .* Coleraine: Printed for the author by S. Hart.

Holloway, Christopher, MS, n.d. Journal. In 'Book for Jottings on New Zealand'. MS in Auckland Public Library, NZ 995.4bH7.

Houghton, Philip, 1980. *The First New Zealanders*. Auckland: Hodder & Stoughton.

Houston, John, 1965. *Maori Life in Old Taranaki*. Wellington: Reed.

Howe, Kerry R., 1970. 'Missionaries, Maoris and "Civilisation" in the Upper Waikato 1833–63'. MA thesis, University of Auckland.

Hurinui, Pei Te, [1945]. *Mahinarangi (The Moonglow of the Heavens): A Tainui Saga*. Hawera: Ekdahl (Printer).

Hurinui, Pei Te, [1960]. *King Potatau: An Account of the Life of Potatau Te Wherowhero the First Maori King*. [Wellington]: The Polynesian Society.

Ironside, Samuel, 1890–92. 'Missionary Reminiscences in New Zealand'. *New Zealand Methodist* (1890–92), in Hocken Library, Bound in Pam 144/2.

Izikowitz, Karl G., 1935. *Musical and Other Sound Instruments of the South American Indians*. Göteborg: Elanders Boktryckeri Aktiebolag.

Johansen, Jørgen Prytz, 1954. *The Maori and His Religion in Its Non-ritualistic Aspects . . .* København: Munksgaard.

Julian, John, 1892. *A Dictionary of Hymnology*. London: Murray.

Karetu, Timoti, 1993. *Haka!: Te Tohu o Te Whenua Rangatira: The Dance of a Noble People*. Auckland: Reed.

Katene, Te Puhoho, 1991. 'The Maori World of Music,' in J. Thomson 1991:1–6.

Keesing, Felix, 1928. *The Changing Maori*. New Plymouth: Avery.

Kelly, Leslie G., 1949. *Tainui: The Story of Hoturoa and his Descendants*. Wellington: Polynesian Society.

Kelly, Leslie G., 1951. *Marion Dufresne at the Bay of Islands*. Wellington: Reed.

Kendall, Thomas & Samuel Lee, 1820. *A Grammar and Vocabulary of the Language of New Zealand*. London: Church Missionary Society.

Kennedy, Keith, 1931c. 'The Ancient Four-Note Musical Scale of the Maoris'. *Mankind*, 1:11–14.

Kerry-Nicholls, James H., 1884. *The King Country or Explorations in New Zealand: A Narrative of 600 Miles of Travel Through Maoriland*. London: Sampson, Low,

Marston, Searle & Rivington.

King, Michael (ed.), 1975. *Te Ao Hurihuri: The World Moves On*. Wellington: Hicks Smith.

King, Michael, 1977. *Te Puea: A Biography*. Auckland: Hodder & Stoughton.

Kururangi, Mere, 1964. *Action Songs*. Wellington: Government Printer.

Leach, James, 1789. *A New Sett of Hymn and Psalm Tunes, etc.* London: Preston.

Leaver, Robin, 1981. *English Hymns & Hymn Books: Catalogue of an Exhibition held in the Bodleian Library Oxford*. Oxford: Bodleian Library.

Ledger, James, 1881. *Pen and Ink Sketches of Parihaka and Neighbourhood with Scenes of Maori Life*. Dunedin: Fergusson & Mitchell.

List, George, 1963. 'An Approach to the Indexing of Ballad Tunes'. *The Folklore and Folk Music Archivist*, 6 (1):7–16.

Locke, Elsie & Janet Paul, 1989. *Mrs Hobson's Album* . . . Auckland: AUP.

Locke, Samuel, 1881. 'Historical Traditions of the Taupo and East Coast Tribes, Pt. 1'. *Transactions of the New Zealand Institute*, 15:433–59.

Loughnan, Robert A., 1902. *Royalty in New Zealand: The Visit of Their Royal Highnesses the Duke and Duchess of Cornwall and York to New Zealand, 10th to 27th June 1901*. Wellington: Government Printer.

Lyon, W.H., MS 1873. Holiday Notes 1873. Unpubl. typescript, AI&M Library.

Lyons, Daniel P., 1975. 'An Analysis of Three Maori Prophet Movements,' in I.H. Kawharu (ed.), *Conflict and Compromise: Essays on the Maori Since Colonisation*. Wellington: Reed, 55–79.

Macdonald, Charlotte, Merimeri Penfold & Bridget Williams, 1991. *The Book of New Zealand Women: Ko Kui ma te Kaupapa*. Wellington: Bridget Williams Books.

Mackrell, Brian, 1978. 'The Chief Attraction'. *New Zealand Listener*, 90(2026):70–3.

Mackrell, Brian, 1985. *Hariru Wikitoria: An Illustrated History of the Maori Tour of England, 1863*. Auckland: OUP.

McCormick, Eric H. (ed.), 1963. *New Zealand or Recollections of It by Edward Markham*. Wellington: Government Printer.

McEwen, J.M., 1947. 'The Development of Maori Culture Since the Advent of the Pakeha'. *JPS*, 56(2):173–87.

McEwen, J.M., 1966. 'Maori Art,' in A.H. McLintock (ed.), *An Encyclopaedia of New Zealand*. Wellington: Government Printer, vol. 2, pp.408–29.

McGregor, John, 1893. *Popular Maori Songs*. Supplements published 1898 (no.1), 1903 (no.2), 1905 (no.3), 1909 (no.4). Auckland: Champtaloup & Cooper.

McLean, Mervyn, 1961. 'Oral Transmission in Maori Music'. *Journal of the International Folk Music Council*, 13:59–62.

McLean, Mervyn, 1964. 'Can Maori Chant Survive?' *Te Ao Hou* (Wellington), 47:34–36.

Mclean, Mervyn, 1965a. 'Maori Chant'. 2 vols. PhD thesis, Otago University.

McLean, Mervyn, 1965b. 'Song Loss and Social Context Among the New Zealand Maori'. *Ethnomusicology*, 9(3):296–304.

McLean, Mervyn, 1966. 'A New Method of Melodic Interval Analysis as Applied to Maori Chant'. *Ethnomusicology*, 10(2):174–90.

McLean, Mervyn, 1968a. 'An Investigation of the Open Tube Maori Flute or Kooauau'. *JPS*, 77(3):213–41.

McLean, Mervyn, 1968b. 'Cueing as a Formal Device in Maori Chant'.

Ethnomusicology, 12(1):1–10.

McLean, Mervyn, 1969. 'An Analysis of 651 Maori Scales'. *Yearbook of the International Folk Music Council*, 1:123–64.

McLean, Mervyn, 1974. 'The New Zealand Nose Flute: Fact or Fallacy?' *Galpin Society Journal*, 27:79–94.

McLean, Mervyn, 1977a. 'Innovations in *Waiata* Style'. *Yearbook of the International Folk Music Council*, 9:27–37.

McLean, Mervyn, 1977b. Review of *Nga Moteatea Sung by Rangi Te Kura Dewes*. 12" 33$^1/_3$ rpm disc. Kiwi SLD–33. *JPS*, 86(1):142–3.

McLean, Mervyn, 1981. 'Text and Music in "Rule of Eight" Waiata,' in Jim Hollyman & Andrew Pawley (eds), *Studies in Pacific Languages and Cultures in Honour of Bruce Biggs*. Auckland: Linguistic Society of New Zealand, pp 53–63.

McLean, Mervyn, 1982a. 'A Chronological and Geographical Sequence of Maori Flute Scales'. *Man*, n.s.17:123–57.

McLean, Mervyn, 1982b. 'The "Rule of Eight" and Text/Music Relationships in Traditional Maori *Waiata*'. *Anthropological Linguistics*, 24(3):280–300.

McLean, Mervyn (ed.), 1983. *Catalogue of Maori Purposes Fund Board Recordings Recorded by W.T. Ngata 1953–58 MPFB 1–120*. Auckland: AMPM.

McLean, Mervyn, 1986. 'Towards a Typology of Musical Change: Missionaries and Adjustive Response in Oceania'. *World of Music* (Berlin), 28(1):29–43.

McLean, Mervyn, 1990. 'Preserving World Musics: Perspectives from New Zealand and Oceania,' in Kay Shelemay (ed.), *The Garland Library of Readings in Ethnomusicology: Volume 1, History, Definitions, and Scope of Ethnomusicology*. New York & London: Garland, pp.359–73. First published in *Studies in Music* (University of Western Australia), 17:23–37 (1983).

McLean, Mervyn (ed.), 1991. *Catalogue of Radio New Zealand Recordings of Maori Events 1938–1950 RNZ 1–60*. Auckland: AMPM.

McLean, Mervyn & Jeny Curnow (eds), 1992a. *Catalogue of McLean Collection Recordings of Traditional Maori Songs 1958–1979 McL 1–1283*. Auckland: AMPM.

McLean, Mervyn & Jeny Curnow (eds), 1992b. *Catalogue of Museum of New Zealand Recordings of Traditional Maori Songs 1919–c.1935*. Auckland: AMPM.

McLean, Mervyn & Margaret Orbell, 1975. *Traditional Songs of the Maori*. Wellington: Reed (2nd rev. edn, Auckland: AUP, 1990).

McLintock, A.H., 1966. *An Encyclopaedia of New Zealand*. 3 vols. Wellington: Government Printer.

McNab, Robert, 1914. *Historical Records of New Zealand*. 2 vols. Wellington: Government Printer.

Madan, Martin, 1760. *A Collection of Psalms and Hymns, Extracted from Various Authors*. London.

Mahuta, Robert, 1974. 'Whaikoorero: A Study of Formal Maori Speech.' MA thesis, University of Auckland.

Maingay, Joan, 1984. 'Notes on a Nguru from Kauri Point Swamp'. *NZ Archaeological Association Newsletter*, 27(2):79–82.

Mair, Gilbert, MS n.d. Notes on Musical Instruments of the New Zealanders. ATL, Wellington. MS papers 92, item 24 ('Miscellaneous data re Maori matters').

Mair, Gilbert, MS 1900. Letter to Mr Hamilton about musical instruments of the Maori. ATL, Wellington. Best Papers, B, 4 1/4.

Makereti [pseud. Maggie Papakura], 1938. *The Old-Time Maori*. London: Gollancz.

Maning, Frederick Edward, 1863. *Old New Zealand*. Auckland: Creighton & Scales.

Maori Language Commission, 1996. *Te Matatiki: Contemporary Maori Words*. Auckland: OUP.

Marcuse, Sibyl, 1964. *Musical Instruments: A Comprehensive Dictionary*. New York: Doubleday.

Marcuse, Sibyl, 1975. *A Survey of Musical Instruments*. London: David & Charles.

Marshall, William Barrett, 1836. *A Personal Narrative of Two Visits to New Zealand in His Majesty's Ship Alligator A.D. 1834*. London: Nisbet.

Martin, [Mary Ann], Lady, 1884. *Our Maoris by Lady Martin*. London: Society for Promoting Christian Knowledge.

Matthews, Sophia C. & L.J. Matthews, [1940]. *Matthews of Kaitaia: The Story of Joseph Matthews and the Kaitaia Mission*. Dunedin & Wellington: Reed.

Mead, Sidney Moko, 1969. 'Imagery, Symbolism and Social Values in Maori Chants'. *JPS*, 78(3):378–404.

Mead, Sidney Moko, 1986. *Te Toi Whakairo: The Art of Maori Carving*. Auckland: Reed Methuen.

Meade, Herbert, 1870. *A Ride Through the Disturbed Districts of New Zealand*. London: Murray

Merriam, Alan P., 1964. *The Anthropology of Music*. Northwestern University Press.

Metge, Joan, 1967. *The Maoris of New Zealand*. London: Routledge & Kegan Paul.

[Methodist Church], 1927. *Ko te Pukapuka o nga Inoi me era atu Tikanga a te Hahi Metoriti (Weteriana) nga Himene me nga Hakamareta me era atu Ritenga Hoki o te Hahi*. Ranana.

[Methodist Church], 1938. *Ko te Pukapuka o nga Inoi me era atu Tikanga a te Hahi Weteriana (Methodist) nga Himene me nga Hakamareta me era atu Ritenga Hoki o te Hahi*. Ranana: Epworth Press.

Methodist Conference Office, 1933. *The Methodist Hymn-Book for Use in Australia and New Zealand: Tunes*. London: Methodist Conference Office.

Métraux, Alfred, 1957. *Easter Island*. Translated from the French by Michael Bullock. New York: OUP.

Misur, Gilda Z., 1975. 'From Prophet Cult to Established Church: The Case of the Ringatu Movement,' in I.H. Kawharu (ed.), *Conflict and Compromise: Essays on the Maori Since Colonisation*. Wellington: Reed, pp. 97–115.

Mitcalfe, Barry, 1974. *Maori Poetry: The Singing Word*. Wellington: Price Milburn.

Mitchell, J.H., 1944. *Takitimu*. Wellington: Reed.

Morgan, John, MS 1833–65. Letters and Journals of the Rev. John Morgan, Missionary at Otawhao, 1833–1865. 3 vols. Unpubl. typescript, AI&M Library, MS 213.

Morley, William, 1900. *The History of Methodism in New Zealand*. Wellington: McKee.

Morrell, W.P. & D.O.W. Hall, 1957. *A History of New Zealand Life*. Christchurch: Whitcombe & Tombs.

Moser, Thomas, 1888. *Mahoe Leaves*. Wanganui: Jones. 2nd edn.

Moyle, Richard M., 1989. *The Sounds of Oceania: An Illustrated Catalogue of the Sound Producing Instruments of Oceania in the Auckland Institute and Museum*. Auckland: AI&M.

Newman, Alfred K., 1905. 'On the Musical Notes and Other Features of the Long Maori Trumpet'. *Transactions of the New Zealand Institute*, 38:134–9.

REFERENCES

Newton, John & William Cowper, 1779. *Olney Hymns in Three Books*. London: Oliver.

Ngata, Apirana T., 1908. 'The Poi Dance,' in Hone Heke & A.T. Ngata, *Souvenir of Maori Congress July 1908: Scenes from the Past with Maori Versions of Popular Songs*. Wellington: Whitcombe & Tombs, pp.11–15.

Ngata, Apirana T., 1911. 'The Poi-dance,' in Hoani Parata, *The Maori of New Zealand, Past, Present and Future*. London: Hughes, pp.31–42.

Ngata, Apirana T., 1940. 'Maori Arts and Crafts,' in I.L.G. Sutherland (ed.), *The Maori People Today*. London: OUP, pp.307–35.

Ngata, Apirana T., 1959. *Nga Moteatea*, Part 1 . Wellington: Polynesian Society.

Ngata, Apirana T., 1972. *Rauru-nui-a-Toi Lectures and Ngati-Kahungunu Origins*. Wellington: Department of Anthropology, Victoria University of Wellington. Multilith.

Ngata, Apirana T., 1990. *Nga Moteatea*, Part 4. Edited by Tamati Maturangi Reedy. Auckland: Polynesian Society.

Ngata, Apirana T. & Pei Te Hurinui, 1961. *Nga Moteatea*, Part 2. Wellington: Polynesian Society.

Ngata, Apirana T. & Pei Te Hurinui, 1970. *Nga Moteatea*, Part 3. Wellington: Polynesian Society.

Ngata, Apirana T. & P.H. Tomoana, 1919. *'A Noble Sacrifice' and 'Hoea Ra Te Waka Nei' (Come Where Duty Calls)* . Wellington: NZ Free Lance.

Nicholas, John L., 1817. *Narrative of a Voyage to New Zealand*. 2 vols. London: Black.

Oliver, Douglas, 1961. *The Pacific Islands*. Revised edn. New York: Doubleday.

Oliver, Douglas, 1974. *Ancient Tahitian Society*. 3 vols. Honolulu: University Press of Hawaii.

Oliver, W.H. et al. (eds), 1990. *The Dictionary of New Zealand Biography, Volume 1, 1769–1869*. Wellington: Bridget Williams Books/Department of Internal Affairs.

Ollivier, Isabel (transl.), 1985. *Extracts from Journals Relating to the Visit to New Zealand in May–July 1772 of the French Ships* Mascarin *and* Marquis de Castries *Under the Command of M.-J. Marion du Fresne. Early Eyewitness Accounts of Maori Life: 2*. Wellington: ATL Endowment Trust.

Ollivier, Isabel & Cheryl Hingley (transls.), 1982. *Extracts from Early Eyewitness Accounts of Maori Life I: Journals Relating to the Visit to New Zealand of the French Ship* St. Jean Baptiste *in December 1769 under the Command of J.F.M. de Surville*. Wellington: ATL Endowment Trust.

Oppenheim, Roger S., 1973. *Maori Death Customs*. Wellington: Reed.

Orange, Claudia et al. (eds), 1993. *The Dictionary of New Zealand Biography, Volume 2, 1870–1900*. Wellington: Department of Internal Affairs.

Orbell, Margaret, 1978. *Maori Poetry: An Introductory Anthology*. Auckland: Heinemann.

Orbell, Margaret, 1985. 'The Maori Tradition,' in Ian Wedde & Harvey McQueen (eds), *The Penguin Book of New Zealand Verse*. Auckland: Penguin Books, pp. 53–61.

Orbell, Margaret, 1990. '"My Summit Where I Sit": Form and Content in Maori Women's Love Songs', in Ruth Finnegan & Margaret Orbell (eds), *Oral Tradition* (Columbus, Ohio) [Special Issue on South Pacific Oral Traditions], 5(2–3):185–204.

Orbell, Margaret, 1991. *Waiata: Maori Songs in History*. Auckland: Reed.

Orton, Job (ed.), 1755. *Hymns Founded on Various Texts*. Eddows & Cotton.

Papakura, Maggie, 1905. *Guide to the Hot Lakes District and Some Maori Legends*. Auckland: Brett.

Parkinson, Sydney, 1773. *A Journal of a Voyage to the South Seas in His Majesty's Ship, the Endeavour*. London: Stanfield Parkinson.

Parlophone Co., [1927]. *Maori Recordings Made at Rotorua During the Visit of the Duke and Duchess of York by the Parlophone Co*. Sydney: Mortons.

Parry, K.L. & Erik Routley, 1953. *Companion to Congregational Praise*. London: Independent Press.

Pewhairangi, Ngoi et al., 1985. *Tuini: Her Life and Songs*. Gisborne: Te Rau Press.

Philips, Irene Margaret Constance, 1929. 'Maori Music: An Historical Survey'. MA thesis, University of Auckland.

Polack, Joel Samuel, 1838. *New Zealand: Being a Narrative of Travels and Adventures During a Residence in That Country Between the Years 1831 and 1837*. 2 vols. London: Bentley.

Polack, Joel Samuel, 1840. *Manners and Customs of the New Zealanders*. London: Madden.

Pomare, Maui & James Cowan, 1930. *Legends of the Maori* [vol. 1]. Wellington: Fine Arts (NZ) Ltd.

Porter, Frances (ed.), 1974. *The Turanga Journals 1840–1850: Letters and Journals of William and Jane Williams Missionaries to Poverty Bay*. Wellington: Price Milburn for Victoria University Press.

Potts, Thomas H., 1882. *Out in the Open: A Budget of Scraps of Natural History Gathered in New Zealand*. Christchurch: Lyttelton Times.

Power, W. Tyrone, 1849. *Sketches in New Zealand*. London: Longman, Brown, Green & Longmans.

Pratt, Albert Rugby, 1932. *The Pioneering Days of Southern Maoriland*. London: Epworth.

[Presbyterian Church], 1907. *Church Praise*. Revised edn. London: Nisbet.

[Presbyterian Church], 1933. *Nga Waiata me Nga Himene a Te Hahi Perehipitiriana mo Te Karakia ki te Atua: Presbyterian Maori Hymnal for the Use of Maori Members and Adherents*. Christchurch: Presbyterian Bookroom. Puckey, William, MS 1831–68. Journals and Letters of the Rev. William Puckey . . . 1831–1868. 2 vols. Unpubl. typescript, AI&M Library, MS 250.

Purchas, Arthur, 1848. *Tunes for Different Metres* . . . Auckland: St John's College Press.

Purchas, Arthur, 1866. *The Tune Book for the New Zealand Hymnal*. Auckland: Waite & Batcher.

Purchas, Arthur (ed.), 1871. *The New Zealand Hymnal with Tunes*. London: Collins.

Purchas, Henry T., 1914. *A History of the English Church in New Zealand*. Simpson & Williams.

Pybus, Thomas A., 1954. *Maori and Missionary: Early Christian Missions in the South Island of New Zealand*. Wellington: Reed.

Ramsden, [George] Eric, 1936. *Marsden and the Missions*. Dunedin & Wellington: Reed.

Ramsden, George Eric, [1948]. *Sir Apirana Ngata and Maori Culture*. Wellington:

Reed.

Ramsden, George Eric, 1949. 'Modern Maoris and Their Music'. *New Zealand Magazine*, 28(2):17–19.

Ramsden, George Eric, 1951. *Rangiatea: The Story of the Otaki Church* . . . Wellington: Reed.

Randel, Don (ed.), 1986. *The New Harvard Dictionary of Music*. Cambridge, Mass.: Belknap Press.

Raureti, Moana, 1978. 'The Origins of the Ratana Movement,' in Michael King (ed.), *Tihe Mauriora: Aspects of Maoritanga*. Methuen, pp.42–66.

Raven-hart, Major R., 1955. 'Musical Acculturation in Tonga'. *Oceania*, 26:110–17.

Ravenscroft, Thomas, 1621. *The Whole Booke of Psalmes with the Hymnes Evangelicall and Songs Spirituall* . . . London: Company of Stationers.

Reed, A.H. (ed.), 1935. *Early Maoriland Adventures of J.W. Stack*. Dunedin & Wellington: Reed.

Reed, A.H. (ed.), 1938. *Further Maoriland Adventures of J.W. and E. Stack*. Dunedin & Wellington: Reed.

Repa, Wi, 1919. 'Te Hui Aroha'. *Te Kopara*, 64:7–10.

Rippon, John, *c*.1791. *A Selection of Psalm and Hymn Tunes* . . . *Adapted Principally to Dr. Watt's Hymns and Psalms* . . . [London: The Author.]

Robley, Major-General Horatio G., 1896. *Moko: or Maori Tattooing*. London: Chapman & Hall.

Rogers, Lawrence M., (ed.), 1961. *The Early Journals of Henry Williams* . . . *1826–40*. Christchurch: Pegasus Press.

Rogerson, Alfred, 1897. *The Centenary Tune Book: A Selection of Old Methodist Tunes*. London: Kelly.

Roth, Henry Ling (transl.), 1891. *Crozet's Voyage to Tasmania, New Zealand, the Ladrone Islands, and the Philippines in the Years 1771–1772*. London: Truslove & Shirley.

Rough, David, 1852. *Narrative of a Journey Through Part of the North Island of New Zealand*. London: Society for Promoting Christian Knowledge.

Rutherford, James (ed.), 1940. *The Founding of New Zealand: Journals of Felton Mathew, First Surveyor-General of New Zealand, and his Wife 1840–1847*. Dunedin & Wellington: Reed.

Ryburn, H.J., 1979. *Te Hemara: James Hamlin 1803–1865 Friend of the Maoris*. Dunedin: McIndoe (Printer).

Sadie, Stanley (ed.), 1980. *The New Grove Dictionary of Musical Instruments*. 3 vols. London: Macmillan.

St John, Lt Col. John Henry, 1873. *Pakeha Rambles Through Maori Lands*. Wellington: Burrett.

Salisbury, Kevin, 1983. 'Pukapukan People and Their Music'. MA thesis (Music), University of Auckland.

Salmond, Anne, 1975. *Hui: A Study of Maori Ceremonial Gatherings*. Wellington: Reed.

Salmond, Anne, 1983. 'The Study of Traditional Maori Society: The State of the Art'. *JPS*, 92(3):309:31.

Salmond, Anne, 1991. *Two Worlds: First Meetings Between Maori and Europeans 1642–1772*. Auckland: Viking. Issued in paperback 1993.

Sankey, Ira D., n.d. *Sacred Songs and Solos: Revised and Enlarged, with Standard Hymns . . . 1200 pieces.* London: Morgan & Scott.

Savage, John, 1807. *Some Account of New Zealand.* London: Murray.

Scherzer, Karl, 1861–63. *Narrative of the Circumnavigation of the Globe by the Austrian Frigate Novarra . . . in the Years 1857, 1858 and 1859.* 3 vols. London: Saunders.

Scholefield, Guy H., 1926. *Visit of His Royal Highness The Prince of Wales to the Dominion of New Zealand April to May 1920.* Wellington: Government Printer.

Scholes, Percy A., 1970. *The Oxford Companion to Music.* 10th edn. London: OUP.

Scott, Dick, 1975. *Ask That Mountain: The Story of Parihaka.* Auckland: Heinemann/Southern Cross.

Searle, E.J., & Janet Davidson, 1975. *A Picture Guide to the Volcanic Cones of Auckland.* Auckland: AI&M. First published 1973.

Selwyn, George Augustus, 1838. *Are Cathedral Institutions Useless? A Practical Answer to This Question.* London: Parker.

Selwyn, George Augustus, 1847. *Annals of the Diocese of New Zealand.* London, Society for the Promotion of Christian Knowledge.

Selwyn, George Augustus et al., MS 1842–67. Letters from Bishop Selwyn and Others. 2 vols. Typescript.

Selwyn, Sarah H., MS 1809–67. Reminiscences 1809–67. Typescript, AI&M Library, MS 273, vol.4.

Selwyn, Sarah, MS 1842–55. Letters and Extracts from Letters Written Mostly by Mrs. S.H. Selwyn . . . 1842–55. Typescript, unpaginated. Auckland Public Library.

Sharp, Andrew, 1968. *The Voyages of Janszoon Tasman.* Oxford: Clarendon Press.

Sharp, Andrew (ed.), 1971. *Duperrey's Visit to New Zealand in 1824.* Wellington: ATL.

Shawcross, Wilfred, MS 1984. Letter to J. Maingay, 1 May 1984.

Shennan, Jennifer, 1977. 'Waiata-A-Ringa: A Movement Study of Action Songs, the Dance Genre Developed in the Twentieth Century by the Maori People of New Zealand'. MA thesis, University of Auckland.

Shennan, Jennifer, 1984. *The Maori Action Song: Waiata a ringa, waiata kori, no whea tenei ahua hou.* Studies in Education No. 36. Wellington: New Zealand Council for Educational Research.

Sherrin, Richard A. & J.H. Wallace, 1890. *Early History of New Zealand.* Auckland: Brett.

Shirres, Michael, 1986. 'An Introduction to Karakia.' PhD thesis (Anthropology), University of Auckland.

Shortland, Edward, 1854. *Traditions and Superstitions of the New Zealanders.* London: Longman, Brown, Green & Longmans.

Shortland, Edward, 1856. *Traditions and Superstitions of the New Zealanders.* London: Longman, Brown, Green & Longmans. 2nd edn.

Simmons, David, 1967. 'Little Papanui and Otago Prehistory'. *Records of the Otago Museum, Anthropology Number 4.* 63pp.

Simmons, David, 1987. *Maori Auckland.* Auckland: Bush Press.

Simmons, David, 1994. 'The Words of Te Matorohanga'. *JPS,* 103(2):115–70.

Simmons, David & Bruce Biggs, 1970. 'The Sources of "The Lore of the Whare

REFERENCES

Wananga"'. *JPS*, 79(1):22–42.

Sinclair, Keith, 1959. *A History of New Zealand*. London: Penguin Books.

Skerrett, Eva, MS 1911 et seq. Scrapbook Containing Newspaper Clippings from Maggie Papakura's Concert Party Tour of Britain in 1911. Rotorua Museum of Art & History.

Smart, M.J., MS 1955. Letter dated 6.7.55 to R. Castle concerning a barrel-organ made for the missionaries F. & W. Williams. Typescript, Wanganui Regional Museum. 2pp.

Smith, S. Percy, 1896–97. *The Peopling of the North*. Supplement, *JPS*, vols. 5–6.

Smith, S. Percy, 1899. 'On the Tohunga-Maori'. *Transactions of the New Zealand Institute*, 32:253–70.

Smith, S. Percy, 1913. *The Lore of the Whare-Wananga, Part 1*. New Plymouth: Avery.

Smith, S. Percy, 1915. *The Lore of the Whare-Wananga, Part 2*. New Plymouth: Avery.

Sorrenson, M.P.K., 1979. *Maori Origins and Migrations: The Genesis of Some Pakeha Myths and Legends*. Auckland: AUP.

Sorrenson, M.P.K. (ed.), 1986–88. *Na To Hoa Aroha From Your Dear Friend: The Correspondence Between Sir Apirana Ngata and Sir Peter Buck 1925–50*. 3 vols. Auckland: AUP.

Sparrman, Anders, 1953. *A Voyage Round the World with Captain James Cook in H.M.S. Resolution*. London: Hale.

S.R.G., n.d. [A Waikato War Dance], in Andersen 1934:314–15.

Stack, James W., 1891. 'Notes on 'Maori Literature''. *Reports of the Australasian Association for the Advancement of Science*, 3:366–94.

Stafford, Don M., 1986. *The Founding Years in Rotorua: A History of Events to 1900*. Auckland: Richards.

Stafford, Don M., 1988. *The New Century in Rotorua: A History of Events from 1900*. Auckland: Richards.

Startup, R.M., [1981]. *Quill & Wax: Men and Women of the New Zealand Post Office to 1860*. The author.

Sternhold, Thomas & John Hopkins, 1562. *The Whole Booke of Psalmes Collected into Englysh Metre . . .* London: Day.

Stiller, John, MS 1981. Documentation of Barrel Organ Built by A. Buckingham 1829. Typescript. 14pp. including 13 plates. Wanganui Regional Museum.

Stone, Alfred (ed.), [1876]. *The Bristol Tune Book: A Manual of Tunes and Chants*. London: Novello, Ewer.

Stonehouse, Bernard, 1966. 'Seals and Sealing,' in A.H. McLintock (ed.), *An Encyclopaedia of New Zealand*. Wellington: Government Printer, vol. 3, pp.202–5.

Swabey, Frances, MS 1955–56. The Biography of Elizabeth Colenso. Unpubl. typescript, AI&M Library, MS 75.

Talbot, Thorpe, 1882. *The New Guide to the Lakes and Hot Springs and a Month in Hot Water*. Auckland: Wilson & Horton.

Tarei, Wi, 1978. 'A Church Called Ringatu,' in Michael King (ed.), *Tihe Mauriora: Aspects of Maoritanga*. Methuen, pp.60–6.

Tate, Nahum & Nicholas Brady, 1696. *A New Version of the Psalms of David, Fitted to the Tunes Used in Churches*. London: The Company of Stationers.

Tauroa, Hiwi & Pat, 1986. *Te Marae: A Guide to Customs and Protocol*. Auckland: Reed Methuen.

Taylor, Nancy M. (ed.), 1959. *Early Travellers in New Zealand*. Oxford: Clarendon Press.

Taylor, Richard, MS 1833–73. Journal of the Rev. Richard Taylor. 15 vols. Unpubl. typescript, AI&M Library. MS 302.

Thiercelin, Le, 1866. *Journal d'un Baleinier: voyages en Océanie*. 2 vols. Paris: Librairie de L. Hachette.

Thomas, Allan, 1981. 'The Study of Acculturated Music in Oceania: "Cheap and Tawdry Borrowed Tunes"?' *JPS*, 90(2):183–91.

Thompson, George E., 1926. *Official Record of the New Zealand and South Seas International Exhibition Dunedin — 1925–1926*. Dunedin: Coulls Somerville Wilkie.

Thomson, Arthur S., 1859. *The Story of New Zealand*. 2 vols. London: Murray.

Thomson, John Mansfield, 1980. *A Distant Music: The Life and Times of Alfred Hill 1870–1960*. Auckland: OUP.

Thomson, John Mansfield, 1991. *The Oxford History of New Zealand Music*. Auckland: OUP.

Thomson, John Turnbull, 1867. *Rambles with a Philosopher*. Dunedin: Mills, Dick.

Tregear, Edward, 1890. 'The Maoris of New Zealand'. *Journal of the Royal Anthropological Institute of Great Britain and Ireland*, 19:97–123.

Tregear, Edward, 1904. *The Maori Race*. Wanganui: Willis.

Trotter, Michael & Beverley McCullough, 1971. *Prehistoric Rock Art of New Zealand*. Wellington: Reed.

Tucker, Henry W., 1879. *Memoir of the Life and Episcopate of George Augustus Selwyn D.D.* 2 vols. London: Wells Gardner.

Vayda, Andrew P., 1960. *Maori Warfare*. Wellington: Polynesian Society Maori Monographs, 2.

Waardenberg, Gerald E. van, 1983. 'Songs of Tai Tokerau: An Analysis of 135 Northland Songs'. M.Mus. thesis, University of Auckland.

Wade, William R., 1842. *A Journey in the Northern Island of New Zealand*. Hobart Town: Rolwegan.

Wakefield, Edward Jerningham, 1845. *Adventure in New Zealand from 1838 to 1844*. 2 vols. London: Murray.

Walker, Ranginui, 1975. 'Marae: A Place to Stand,' in Michael King (ed.), *Te Ao Hurihuri: The World Moves On*. Wellington: Hicks Smith, pp.21–34.

Walton, John, 1839. *Twelve Months' Residence in New Zealand*. Glasgow: McPhun.

Warren, John, 1863. *The Christian Mission to the Aborigines of New Zealand . . .* Auckland: Creighton & Scales.

Wedde, Ian & Harvey McQueen (eds), 1985. *The Penguin Book of New Zealand Verse*. Auckland: Penguin Books.

Wesley, John, 1780. *Collection of Hymns for the Use of the People Called Methodists . . . with a Supplement*. London: Paramore.

Wesley, John, 1877. *Collection of Hymns for the Use of the People Called Methodists . . . Edition with Tunes*. London: Wesleyan Conference Office.

Wesleyan Conference Office, 1847. *A Companion to the Wesleyan Hymn-Book*. London: Wesleyan Conference Office .

Wesleyan Conference Office, [1904]. *The Methodist Hymn-Book with Tunes*. Edited by Sir Frederick Bridge. London: Wesleyan Conference Office.

[Wesleyan Methodist Church], 1845. *Ko te Pukapuka o nga Inoinga o te Hahi o Ingarani*

REFERENCES

me nga Himene Weteriana . . . Mangungu.

[Wesleyan Methodist Church], 1894. *Ko te Pukapuka o nga Inoinga* . . . Akarana: Wilson.

White, John, 1874. *Te Rou; or The Maori at Home*. London: Sampson Low Marston & Searle.

White, John, 1885. 'Maori Customs and Superstitions, Being the Subject of Two Lectures Delivered at the Mechanics' Institute in Auckland, During the Year 1861,' in Thomas W. Gudgeon (ed.), *The History and Doings (Traditions) of the Maori*. Auckland: Brett.

White, John, 1887–90. *The Ancient History of the Maori*. 6 vols. Wellington: Government Printer.

White, John, 1891. *Illustrations Prepared for White's Ancient History of the Maori*. Wellington: Government Printer. Unpaginated.

Whiteley, John, MS 1832–63. Journal of the Rev. John Whiteley Missionary to New Zealand 1832–1863. Unpubl. typescript, AI&M Library, MS 331.

Wiata, Beryl Te, 1976. *Most Happy Fella: A Biography of Inia Te Wiata*. Wellington: Reed.

Wilkes, Charles, 1845. *Narrative of the United States Exploring Expedition During the Years 1838, 1839, 1840, 1841, 1842*. 5 vols. & atlas. Philadelphia: Lea & Blanchard.

Williams Papers MS 1822–64. Letters and Journals Written by the Rev. Henry and Mrs. Marianne Williams . . . 1822–1864. Typescript, Auckland Public Library.

Williams, Henry et.al. MS n.d. Letters and Papers of Henry and Marianne Williams also William and Jane Williams, Paihia. Unpubl. typescript, AI&M Library, MS335, Vol.F.

Williams, Henry, MS 1826–40. Journal of Henry Williams. 4 vols. Unpubl. typescript, AI&M Library, W72c.

Williams, Herbert, 1924. *A Bibliography of Printed Maori to 1900*. Dominion Museum Monograph, 7. Wellington: Government Printer.

Williams, Herbert, MS 1932. Letter to Johannes Andersen dated 16.6.32. [Contains Williams's translation of parts of a Maori MS by John White dealing with musical instruments. Interleaved with Andersen's copy of Best's *Games and Pastimes of the Maori* (1925) at AI&M Library NZ Collection GN 672.6 G1 Copy 2.]

Williams, Herbert, 1975. *A Dictionary of the Maori Language*. Wellington: Government Printer. 7th edn. First published 1844.

Williams, William, MS 1825–55. Journal of William Williams August 21st, 1825 to December 18th, 1855. 9 vols. Unpubl. typescript. AI&M Library, W72c.

Williams, William, 1867. *Christianity among the New Zealanders*. London: Seeley, Jackson & Halliday.

Williams, William James, c.1922. *Centenary Sketches of New Zealand Methodism*. Christchurch: Lyttelton Times.

Williment, T.M.I., 1985. *John Hobbs 1800–1883: Wesleyan Missionary to the Ngapuhi Tribe of Northern New Zealand*. Wellington: Government Printer.

Wilson, Charles A., 1932. *Legends and Mysteries of the Maori*. London: Harrap.

Wilson, John Alexander, 1894. *Sketches of Ancient Maori Life and History*. Auckland: Champtaloup & Cooper.

Wilson, Ormond, 1965. 'Papahurihia, First Maori Prophet'. *JPS*, 74(4): 473–83.

Winks, Robin W., 1953. 'The Doctrine of Hau-Hauism'. *JPS*, 62(3):199–236.

Wood, John G., 1868–70. *The Natural History of Man*. 2 vols. New York: Routledge.

Woon, William, MS 1830–59. Journal Kept as a Wesleyan Missionary in Tonga and New Zealand, 1830–1859. Hocken Library, Dunedin, MS 969.

Wright, Olive (ed.), 1950. *New Zealand 1826–1827 from the French of Dumont D'Urville: An English Translation of* The Voyage of the *Astrolabe* in New Zealand, 1840. Wellington: Wingfield Press.

Yate, William, 1835. *An Account of New Zealand*. London: Seeley & Burnside.

Youngerman, Suzanne, 1974. 'Maori Dancing Since the Eighteenth Century'. *Ethnomusicology*, 18(1):75–100.

NEWSPAPERS

Auckland Star

Auckland Weekly News

Bay of Plenty Times

Daily Telegraph

Dominion

The Era

Evening Post

Gisborne Times

Te Kopara

The Methodist Times

New Zealand Herald

New Zealand Mail

New Zealand Times

Northern Advocate

Te Pipiwharauroa

The Press

The Sketch

Southland Times

Weekly Graphic & New Zealand Mail

Yorkshire Gazette

INDEX